Effectively Representing Clients in Family Mediation

Forrest S. Mosten
Hon. Elizabeth Potter Scully
Lara Traum

AMERICAN BAR ASSOCIATION
Family Law Section

Cover design by Mary Anne Kulchawik/ABA Design

Printed in the United States of America.

27 26 25 24 23 5 4 3 2 1

A catalog record for this book is available from the Library of Congress.

Contents

Acknowledgments

An essential underpinning of mediation is the creative use of collaboration. Throughout our career and in writing this book, we have been blessed and helped by so many people who have given generously of their talent, time, and caring.

FORREST ("WOODY") S. MOSTEN

In 1995, just when I was drowning in the drafting stage of my first ABA book, Jeff Jacobson appeared deus ex machina and volunteered to help. A promising law student at UCLA with a proven passion and commitment to peace, Jeff sacrificed countless hours researching, writing, and editing the ever-moving manuscript. Jeff is now a leading family lawyer in Los Angeles recognized for his peacemaking. Andrea Kushner, then a law student from cross-town rival University of Southern California (by way of Birmingham, Alabama), devoted countless hours in competently researching the newest developments and providing source material for the notes and bibliography. Andrea has become an accomplished estate planner.

My professional associations in family law, mediation, collaborative law, and legal access have provided inspiration and friendship, which have contributed to this book. I am indebted to the members of my Family Law and Mediation Study Groups with whom I have developed ideas over the years. The countless professionals who contribute to many mediation and collaborative practice organizations have provided comments and sources that have found their way into the book. My friends at Los Angeles County Bar, San Diego Bar, Association of Family and Conciliation Courts, the Beverly Hills Bar Academy of Professional Family Law Mediators, International Academy of Collaborative Professionals, Collaborative Practice San Diego, Los Angeles Collaborative Family Law Association, Divorce Solutions of Orange County (Honorary Member) Resolution UK, and the American Bar Association have supported and contributed to my work. Will Hornsby of the ABA deserves special mention as the walking sourcebook on legal access policy and research.

My thanks to Barbara Kahn Stark, Lynne Ustach, and other members of the ABA Family Law Publications Development Board for making sure that my books reflect the needs of the ABA Section of Family Law. I will always appreciate Jeffrey Salyards, editor of my last four ABA books, who is always available, candid, and helpful.

I am fortunate to have learned from some of the world's authorities in client counseling and mediation. The late Professor David Binder of UCLA, Professor

The late Thomas Shaffer of Notre Dame, the late David Binder and the late psychologist/lawyer Dr. Robert Redmount all taught me client-centered counseling as a law student and throughout my career. The late Dr. Constance Ahrons and Dr. Mary Lund have given me expanded views of family systems and therapeutic interventions through our joint teaching and co-mediation. I also wish to thank all my faculty colleagues at UCLA School of Law for their constant flow of ideas and personal support. My students in both Mediation Clinic and Lawyer as Peacemaker update my thinking, and the students whom I supervise in their independent research papers stimulate an evolving agenda of scholarship.

My colleagues throughout the country and internationally provide me with ideas and projects. David Hoffman, from Boston, and I speak at least weekly, sharing approaches to practice and teaching, and he always provides a peacemaking and creative perspective. John Lande from the University of Missouri is the consummate collegial presenter and co-author, and I marvel how we are always able to reconcile different perspectives. Ron Ousky, former IACP President from Minneapolis, is always sharing cutting-edge ideas that shape my thinking. Professor Andrew Schepard, longtime editor of the Family Court Review, has provided me inspiration with his contributions to both mediation and collaborative law as well as has afforded me the opportunity to test out my own scholarship and "not yet ready for prime time ideas" by publishing my articles and special issues. Finally, my 40-year friendship with Sir Geoffrey Bindman of London, England, provides me with a never-ending stream of approaches from his lifelong commitment to human rights and legal access.

My career and my life have been inspired by the late Louis M. Brown, to whom the first edition of this book was dedicated. Until his death at age 87 on September 19, 1996, Louis was my teacher, role model, and friend for more than 25 years—and with whom I enjoyed discussing and debating most of the issues and trends featured in this book. Louis's legendary body of work and ambitious agenda for the 21st century offer a challenge that will take our profession several decades to even partially fulfill. One of the great fortunes of my professional life is my teaching and writing partnership with Judge Elizabeth Potter Scully. Liz's brilliance and hard work are demonstrated on the pages of this book. I wish to thank Lara Traum for her brilliant mind and incomparable work ethic—both of which have shaped this book. Since we met when she was a precocious law student scholar, Lara has inspired and revitalized my own work through our writing partnership and she has carried the heaviest load in the writing or this book.

Finally, I wish to thank my in-home editor and consultant, Jody Mosten, for her tireless patience and unfailing support and encouragement during both editions. Jody, a far better writer and certainly more organized, agrees that our personal collaboration on this project has taken over our lives—fortunately, we continue to have so much fun together in the process.

As I am now past Medicare age, I feel comfortable that many future editions of this book will be in Liz and Lara's most capable stewardship. Until then, we will continue laughing together about our writing, training, and the joys and marvels of life.

HON. ELIZABETH POTTER SCULLY

Like Woody, I have been fortunate enough to enjoy a career marked by warm and sustaining relationships with talented teachers and colleagues. Professor Melissa L. Nelken at U.C. Hastings College of the Law introduced me to mediation. Our stellar family law team at Luce Forward Hamilton & Scripps LLP in San Diego, California, taught me about teamwork, pursuit of excellence, and a client-focused practice. I am forever indebted to my brilliant former law partners, Jeffery S. Jacobson and David P. Shebby. My colleagues in FLAMES (Family Law Attorney Mediators Engaged in Study) and collaborative practice group A Better Divorce were unfailingly gracious, both personally and professionally, and I treasured their support and insight in my law and mediation practice. In 2022, as this book was nearing completion, the California collaborative family law community unexpectedly and tragically lost a leader in financial specialist Warren Sacks. Through the sheer force of his own abiding commitment and effort, Warren pushed collaborative family law forward, cultivating warm and supportive relationships with colleagues along the way and reminding us in his life and in his legacy the tremendous amount of good each one of us can bring about when we devote ourselves to things that truly matter.

My new role as a judicial officer has been a joy and an education, and I am thrilled to have started out in my dream assignment, a family law home court. I am grateful to my generous and talented colleagues and to the leadership of our division, whose forward-looking and passionate commitment to service—particularly in promoting mediation/consensual dispute resolution and meeting the needs of self-represented litigants—is an inspiration.

I am beyond lucky in the love and support of family and friends. Oz Pathare, who is as generously prodigious with Oxford commas as he is with support and encouragement, deserves special mention. I also appreciate Tom Scully for his flexibility, reliability, and devotion to our beloved and brilliant child, who has managed to grow several inches taller than both parents since the last edition of this book.

Last but not least, I acknowledge my co-authors. Lara's insight is a breath of fresh air, and her energy, clarity, and passion shine through these pages. Woody is a gifted teacher, mediation visionary, and tireless advocate for sanity and innovation in our field. The teaching, writing, and speaking opportunities our collaboration has opened for me have been among the most transformative and satisfying of my career, and I am so grateful to count him and Jody among my most valued friends.

LARA TRAUM

Mediators start in the home and radiate outward, and I have been blessed with just that. My mother (and law partner) Alla Roytberg became a practicing mediator when I was a young child, and the topics of family harmony, family disharmony, and proactive approaches to honoring different models were part of the air that I breathed growing up. She remains my model for most things, and opened the door to this world of constructive thought leaders, where I have been blessed to build incredible professional relationships of my own.

From initial trainings with Adam Berner to a monumental clinic with Robert K. Collins at Cardozo and a peacemaking life led by Lela Love's example, I learned that there was no singular identity to hold as a person seeking to help people through challenging times. Since then, I have been blessed with colleagues throughout New York that have become trusted and respected friends, especially those in the New York State Council on Divorce Mediation and Long Island Collaborative Practice Group.

Of course the mentor, colleague, friend, and kindred soul that exceeds all with his brilliance, his patience, his guidance, and his advocacy for next generation practitioners is our beloved and esteemed co-author, Woody Mosten. His exceptional contributions to the field are numerous, but it is his peacemaking soul and generous spirit that truly astound—it is entirely due to his tireless belief in me that I have been granted numerous opportunities to write, teach, and engage with a broader audience interested in providing peace to families in flux. I am endlessly grateful to him for the industry that he has built, the collaborative energy that he fosters among community colleagues, and his truly authentic innovations, all in pursuit of making peace.

SUSAN GUTHRIE

I have been extremely fortunate to have been blessed with many mentors and supportive colleagues through the many years of my career, and, to this very day, their wisdom and encouragement have been invaluable in helping me to achieve my goals and to advance the field of dispute resolution. There is no individual more deserving of my gratitude and thanks than my training partner, Woody Mosten, who has encouraged me and helped me to grow as a professional and as a person. The opportunity to work, train with, and call him my friend has inspired me to do better and to be better in all ways. We would all be better off in this world if, before speaking or acting, we asked ourselves, "what would Woody do?" and act accordingly. I send him my eternal thanks and love.

Foreword

By David A. Hoffman[1]

I appreciate the invitation to welcome readers to this important and immensely useful book. Before describing some of its major contributions to the theory and practice of mediation advocacy, I think it's worth reflecting on how far we have come since Woody's first book was published by the American Bar Association in 1997—a time when mediation was often viewed askance by lawyers.

I recall a bar association meeting in the mid-1990s in which I was on a panel giving a presentation about mediation. I felt a bit out of my depth because my fellow panelist was one of the major figures of the mediation field, Prof. Frank Sander (my former law school advisor), and I was a mediation newbie. After we had completed our remarks, a young lawyer, looking genuinely puzzled, posed the following question. "Why," he asked, "would I ever want to refer a new client to mediation?" He went on: "I just finished law school. I just passed the bar. I am struggling to make a living. If I send a new client to mediation, I will be losing money. I don't get it!"

Frank and I just looked at each other for a moment, a bit stunned by the candor and cluelessness of what we had just heard. Then each of us tried to explain, as gently as we could, that (a) lawyers have a fiduciary duty to recommend mediation if that's what would best serve the *client's* interests, and (b) there is an important role for lawyers to play in mediation, either in the mediation itself or "coaching from the sidelines."[2] We also pointed out that whatever revenues might be lost by recommending mediation in appropriate cases might be more than made up in additional referrals from clients who were more satisfied with mediated outcomes than the outcomes that could be obtained in court.

Fortunately, times have changed, in part because of the efforts of the authors of this book—Woody Mosten, Elizabeth Scully, and Lara Traum—who deserve our appreciation for their leadership and sound advice.

---

1. David A. Hoffman is the John H. Watson, Jr. Lecturer on Law at Harvard Law School, where he teaches courses on Mediation; Legal Profession: Collaborative Law; and Diversity and Dispute Resolution. He is also the founding member of Boston Law Collaborative, LLC, where he serves as a mediator, arbitrator, and Collaborative Law attorney.

2. *See generally* David Hoffman & Karen Tosh, *Coaching from the Sidelines: Effective Advocacy in Divorce Mediation*, 17 Mass. Fam. L.J. 85 (1999), https://tinyurl.com/hoffman-coaching.

So, fast forward to 2022, and the questions from lawyers are different. The main question is no longer *whether* lawyers should discuss mediation as an option for their clients, but instead *how.* Today, lawyers are looking for advice about selecting a mediator, preparing clients for mediation, and coaching the clients through the negotiation to a settlement. And this book is where lawyers will find answers to those questions—in abundance, with wise perspectives, examples from cases, and bullet-point practice tips.

One of the important contributions that the authors make in this book is to situate the lawyer's role in mediation as part of the broader movement of "unbundled services"—a movement that Woody launched in the 1990s with pioneering lectures and articles on that subject[3] and the first book on unbundling, published by the American Bar Association.[4]

Building on this critical insight, the authors have added a section on the role of Collaborative Law, which is a form of unbundling—and more generally, commitments by lawyers in connection with the mediation process that they will not litigate the case. By means of this simple commitment, whether formalized in a Collaborative Law participation agreement or simply an engagement letter, lawyers can create more robust support for the mediation process and enhance the parties' confidence that they are each fully committed to the mediation process.

In addition, the authors have included a timely "bonus chapter" by Susan Guthrie on "Representing Clients in Online Mediation," which by itself is worth the price of admission. This topic is vitally important to lawyers in all settings, but especially in mediation, where videoconferencing runs the risk—if not well managed—of preventing the participants from experiencing the emotional nuances of in-person negotiation and discussion.

Finally, the authors make an important contribution to our field by highlighting the way in which our work is part of a broader mission of peacemaking that is so urgently needed in our world today. Readers of this book will find that the theoretical insights and skills described here are applicable in many other settings. And, in my opinion, it is a particularly wise insight (to be found in Chapter 12) that even litigators—indeed, lawyers of all kinds—can be peacemakers if they bring that orientation to their work: "Peacemaking is not a process, but a set of values, personal attributes, goals, and behaviors that guide and illuminate your work."

Lawyers have a unique opportunity to contribute to making the world a better place. Learning how to represent and advise clients effectively in mediation can be one of the most powerful contributions of that kind, supporting the efforts of mediators to "bring peace into the room"—a mission that lawyers can share.

---

3. *See, e.g.*, Forrest Mosten, *Unbundling of Legal Services and the Family Lawyer*, 28 Fam. L.Q. 421 (1994).

4. Forrest Mosten, Unbundling Legal Services: A Guide to Delivering Legal Services a la Carte (2000); Forrest Mosten & Hon. Elizabeth Potter Scully, Unbundled Legal Services: a Family Lawyer's Guide (2017).

About the Authors

Forrest "Woody" Mosten has been in private mediation practice since 1979, is an international master trainer in mediation and collaborative practice, and is recognized as "The Father of Unbundling."

Woody is certified as a Specialist in Family Law by the California State Bar Board of Legal Specialization and handles family law matters involving substantial assets and high-conflict parenting matters both as a lawyer representing clients and as a neutral mediator—and he never goes to court. Woody is the cofounder of the Mosten Guthrie Online Training Academy for Mediation and Collaborative Practice and is the author of six other books, *Collaborative Divorce Handbook* (2009), *Building a Successful Collaborative Practice* (2018 with Adam Cordover), *Mediation Career Guide* (2001), *Complete Guide to Mediation*, 2nd edition (2015 with Elizabeth Potter Scully) *Unbundled Legal Services* (with Elizabeth Potter Scully), and *Unbundling Legal Services* (2000) and numerous articles. Since 1989, he has been chair of the International Client Consultation Competition that bears his name (www.brownmosten.com).

Woody is the recipient of the ABA Lawyer as Problem Solver Award, the ABA Lifetime Award for Legal Access, the New York State Council on Divorce Mediation Lifetime Service Award, Academy of Professional Family Mediators Lifetime Career Award, the Los Angeles County Bar Conflict Prevention Award, and he was named Peacemaker of the Year and received the President's Award by the Southern California Mediation Association, which has also established the Forrest S. Mosten Star Award for Innovation in Mediation. In 2022, Woody was inagurated by the ADR Times into the Whose Who of ADR. Since 2002, Woody has been an adjunct professor at UCLA School of Law where he teaches Mediation, Lawyer as Peacemaker, and Family Law Practice: A Non-Litigation Approach. Woody can be reached at www.MostenMediation.com or www.MostenGuthrie.com.

Hon. Elizabeth Scully sits in a family law assignment on the Los Angeles Superior Court. She received her AB in Classics (Latin) magna cum laude from Harvard in 1993 and her JD from the University of California Hastings College of the Law in 1996. Prior to taking the bench in December 2020, she was a certified Family Law Specialist (California State Bar Board of Legal Specialization) in private practice and a founding partner of Jacobson Scully LLP, providing mediation, collaborative and minor's counsel services, in addition to traditional litigation representation. As an attorney, she was also vice president of the Board of Directors of Levitt Quinn, a nonprofit law firm serving the working poor, and a member of A Better Divorce, a collaborative practice group in Los Angeles's South Bay. She has taught experiential courses in mediation and in negotiation theory and practice at UCLA School of Law and has co-authored numerous books and articles (with Woody and others) on topics relating to consensual dispute resolution in the family law context. She was co-recipient of the Association of Family and Conciliation Court's 2016 Meyer Elkin Essay Award, honoring the best article in *Family Court Review*.

Lara Traum is a partner at Roytberg Traum Law and Mediation, P.C. She practices matrimonial and family law in New York, New Jersey, and Connecticut, and practices as a family and matrimonial mediator throughout the United States and internationally, in English and in Russian. Lara received her BA from NYU in music, literature, and Judaic studies in 2010 and her JD from the Benjamin N. Cardozo School of Law in 2016, where she graduated cum laude with a concentration in family and matrimonial law and a Jacob Burns Medal for Scholastic Achievement after serving as editor in chief of the *Cardozo Journal of Conflict Resolution*. Lara serves on the Board of Directors of the New York State Council on Divorce Mediation and is an active member of Long Island Collaborative Divorce Professionals. Outside her practice, Lara lectures on matrimonial and conflict resolution matters, publishes academic works on mediation and family law, and performs as a musician in various venues throughout New York City. Lara has been a co-trainer with Woody and co-author for numerous articles.

Susan Guthrie has been a family law attorney and mediator in private practice for more than 32 years. She specializes in high net worth and complex matrimonial matters and has worked exclusively online with clients around the world since 2016. Susan created the Learn to Mediate Online® Training Program in 2018 and since then has helped more than 24,000 attorneys and dispute resolution professionals to transition smoothly to a virtual practice. Her role in supporting the massive shift to online practice during the pandemic earned her the devotion of many colleagues around the world and the moniker, "The Diva of Online Mediation." In 2020, the Southern California Mediation Association (SCMA) awarded Susan the L. Randolph Lowry Award, which is awarded annually to an individual who has inspired the field through their passion and dedication to education in the field of dispute resolution.

In 2020, Susan partnered with Woody Mosten to found the Mosten Guthrie Online Training Academy for Mediation and Collaborative Practice, which provides gold standard training and support for the peacemakers of the world. In addition to her training programs through the Mosten Guthrie Academy, Susan frequently provides programs and presentations at professionals events and conferences around the world.

Susan is the current vice chair of the American Bar Association's Section of Dispute Resolution and is looking forward to her year as chair commencing in 2024.

CHAPTER 1

Expanding Your Practice by Representing Clients in Mediation

At 6:00 a.m. on August 5, 2021, Charles Zolot, a tireless and introverted Queens lawyer committed to assisting New York families through their divorce processes and bankruptcy proceedings since 1982, was found lying on the ground of his law office by the building janitor—he had been stabbed to death by a former client. According to authorities, he was "found on his back and showed signs of having been beaten on his face and chest and was declared dead at the scene." He had been due in Queens Supreme Court for a preliminary conference that morning.[1]

Emotional tension, intense conflict, tight deadlines, high overhead, unpaid bills, and fear of malpractice—these are only *some* of the pressures that family lawyers encounter every day. It is no wonder that we often become burned out, cynical, or testy. The lawyer "locker room" banter is filled with malaise, cynicism, and dissatisfaction. Instead of waking up eager to get to the office and meet clients, many family lawyers live for their vacations—then for their retirement. Fallout from this career dissatisfaction impacts colleagues, office staff, and family members—and most importantly, the families we serve.

Instead of feeling that our efforts contribute meaningfully to our clients' lives and to society, we often feel like hired-guns hired to play out family pathology, ultimately trying to protect ourselves from the very clients who hired us. We may begin to view our careers as one more set of written pleadings, one more court hearing, one more hostile interaction with opposing counsel, one more haggle over the bedroom set or an alternating Wednesday overnight visit. Instead of maintaining an energetic, positive commitment to our life's work, many of us see our offices as prison cells and clients and courts as our perpetual jailers.

Yet, most of us are not ready to take down our shingles and opt for a life of selling insurance or tending our gardens. How did we get here? And where are we going?

We enter family law practice for a variety of reasons. For some, a job with a family lawyer may be our first (or only) job offer. Others are drawn to the human

1. https://www.nydailynews.com/new-york/nyc-crime/ny-bruised-man-found-dead-queens-law-office-20210805-5tiv3syfbvadjpaz7mnemgizia-story.html.

interest aspect of this work (we are interested in people and want to help them), the emotional intensity, or the ability to gain courtroom experience.

Some of us enjoy the breadth of the substantive issues family law cases pose (we are known, after all, as the last true generalists of the legal world) and the challenge of cutting-edge legal issues such as interstate and federal rights of same sex and chosen families. Others are attracted by the varied and complex procedural issues, ranging from jurisdictional disputes to the interplay between criminal law and domestic violence to the possibility of a child having more than two legal parents. Many of us are interested in the family as a system and our role in promoting the healthy development of children and the emotional recovery of their parents. Others find meaning in helping people in crisis. Still others are drawn to the public policy and political issues, such as family violence, cultural competence, gender power imbalances, and societal responses to evolving concepts of family.

Whatever our motivations were when we first embarked, at this moment in our careers, we are challenged by forces inside and outside the legal profession. Most family lawyers are influenced, albeit unconsciously, by the English solicitor-barrister model of law practice. In that model, solicitors handle client concerns, collect the fees, and pay the barristers to provide the quality courtroom advocacy for which they are recognized worldwide. In the American integrated system, most lawyers perform roles of both solicitor and barrister. We are "full service" providers: we file court documents, examine witnesses, present evidence, and make legal arguments in court—and are also charged with helping our clients make the best decisions possible for themselves and their children. American family lawyers are also responsible for interviewing and advising the client "up close and personal." In addition to client care responsibilities, we face practice development chores like office design, updating firm blogs and websites, fee collection, and paying suppliers of staples, exhibit tabs, and letterhead. In addition to operating a profitable business, we must make time to attend continuing legal education seminars and read new court opinions as well as practice development books (such as this one) to deliver a high-quality product to an ever more demanding client population.

Instead of yearning for the good old days (if they were even good, that may be fiction), we need to recognize that the days of just practicing traditional family law are gone for good (if they were ever here in the first place) and concentrate instead on embracing the current societal forces that are transforming family law practice in the 21st century.

CONSUMERISM

We are a nation of consumers. People clip coupons (or print Groupons) for groceries or concert tickets, click on promotional links, bargain with the car dealer in person or online, choose the credit cards that offer free airline miles and rewards, download apps for discounts and credits, and routinely access social media platforms to learn about products and services on provider pages. Many clients began their romantic journeys by utilizing dating apps and proceeded to create wedding websites, register for digital registries, and post their babies' photos on Instagram.

Potential clients remain consumers when they shop for legal services to solve their family problems; they seek competitive rates, lightning speed responsiveness, virtual consultation options, and continued customization of process options.

In the good old days (circa 1970), before there was such a glut of lawyers, before lawyer advertising and the rise (and fall) of legal clinics, it was harder for people to find lawyers. Clients rarely attempted to negotiate the price, terms, or extent of legal services. Most clients did not know they could negotiate the financial terms of their business relationships with their lawyers—they were so insecure and needy that discussing fees with their lawyers was the last thing on their minds. The truth is that lawyers typically rejected clients' attempts at fee negotiation. It was a seller's market. "If you want my talent, time, and stomach lining, you'll pay my fee" was the message we sent out. To be fair, in some ways it was a kinder, gentler world. Lawyers were more ready and able to work on a handshake, would often carry unpaid fees for months and years, and rarely sued clients (or each other).

Today, clients have access to all kinds of information about attorneys before they even pick up the phone or their computer calendars to book an initial consultation. The prevalence of social media makes it easy to confer at the touch of a button with a wide range of friends and acquaintances about attorney referrals. Websites such as LinkedIn and Google searches help clients instantly identify attorneys with whom they believe they will share a personal connection or who have been publicly endorsed by another professional whom the client knows and trusts. Online attorney evaluation websites such as Avvo, Martindale-Hubbell, Super Lawyers, and Best Lawyers put ratings, reviews, profiles, and disciplinary records at clients' fingertips, making the search for an attorney as easy as figuring out where to go for frozen yogurt. Even Yelp and Google Reviews have drastically altered how clients vet prospective attorneys and determine whom to retain.

Moreover, clients often comparison shop and "kick the tires" in various law offices before plunking down a retainer. Good faith comparison shopping is an accepted consumer practice (in contrast to the outrageous behavior of some people who contact every top lawyer in town for the sole purpose of creating a conflict of interest that will preclude a particular lawyer from representing their spouse).

Clients want a friendly, accessible office space or the ability to conduct their relationships with their lawyers entirely online. They want professional, complete websites that describe the backgrounds of the service providers, the range of services offered by the firm, and resources for clients to learn more and help themselves. They want clear explanations of the fees, payment options (e.g., credit cards, Zelle, Square, Pay Pal, and Venmo), and any available financing terms. Just as on a car lot, clients often expect to negotiate the terms of their contracts. Savvy clients want to know about lawyer availability for office or Zoom visits and for telephone conversations when it is convenient for the client, not just the lawyer. Many clients want to know when and how associates and staff members will participate and under what circumstances will the attorney delegate tasks. Clients are vitally interested in reducing their legal costs and retaining control.

Lawyers compete fiercely in the divorce marketplace with one another and with a burgeoning number of nonlawyer providers, including paralegals, website (e.g., Legal Zoom) document preparation services, and, most recently, licensed legal technicians, as in a Washington state statute governing Limited License Legal Technician (LLLT) Rule (APR 28) that now authorizes non-attorneys who meet certain educational requirements to advise and assist clients in approved practice areas of law.

Consumers have learned (and are continuing to learn) purchasing techniques and ways to improve their leverage in the lawyer-client relationship. Clients expect lawyers to understand, react positively, and accommodate these consumer-oriented trends. Consumers have expressed their unequivocal preference for user-friendly, price-sensitive products and services outside the legal services arena. Why should shopping for legal services be any different?

Family law mediation got its jump start from consumers who believed that the family lawyer's main service product (spouses each being represented by adversarial lawyers operating in or around the courthouse) was not meeting their financial or personal needs. Clients did not see resolution through imposed court decision (or coerced by the imminence of a court hearing) as meeting their consumer concerns, namely, cost, privacy, client control, speed, and self-generated creative solutions.

Since the birth of modern family law mediation, which is often credited to the 1978 publication of *Structured Mediation in Divorce Settlement* by O.J. Coogler, an Atlanta attorney, the prevailing view has been that mediation has grown and succeeded in spite of, not because of, family lawyers.[2]

The following quote from Nathan Davidovich from an article on www.mediate.com sums up this view:

> Unfortunately, the lawyer sometimes gets caught up in the client's insistence that the lawyer be his/her "mouthpiece," including mimicking the emotions of the client. There then develops a point in the litigation process in which the process becomes self-sustaining (a goal in and of itself), leaving little hope for early peaceful resolution.[3]

A premise of this book is that family lawyers who are mediation savvy, mediation-friendly in their representational work, or serve as neutral mediators themselves will find consumer reception both positive and profitable. Mediation is a growth industry for the neutrals as well as the auxiliary aligned professionals assisting clients during the mediation. Lawyers who embrace mediation are on the cutting edge and will be less vulnerable to the self-representation movement, growth of nonlawyer providers, malpractice, and other economic forces.

---

2. Some critiques of *mediation include Richard E. Crouch, The Dark Side of Mediation: Still Unexplored, in* ALTERNATIVE MEANS OF DISPUTE RESOLUTION 39 (Howard Davidson et al. eds., 1982); Penelope E. Bryan, Killing Us Softly: Divorce Mediation and the Politics of Power, 40 Buff. L. Rev. 441 (1992); Diana Richmond, Torture by ADR, Fam. L. Monthly 66 (Apr. 1994).

3. Nathan Davidovich, *Mediation: A Process to Regain Control of Your Life,* Mediate.com. (June 15, 2000).

Giving Up Litigation Was the Most Profitable Decision of My Career[4]

Over two decades ago, Woody decided to focus totally on peacemaking and to refuse any further litigation. He reflects:

"While I was afraid that my family would eat tuna casserole four times a week, with the support of my wife, I turned down large retainers and referred all potential court clients to competent litigators in my community. Much like Canadian peacemaker Nancy Cameron, I felt that I had been a rider of two horses:

> I have often thought of this dual role of conflict resolver and courtroom advocate as akin to being asked to ride two horses. At some point to remain riding it will be necessary to commit to one horse or the other. The difference between the skills I bring as a collaborative practitioner and those I used settling within a litigation template is the difference between riding one horse rather than two. NANCY CAMERON, COLLABORATIVE PRACTICE: DEEPENING THE DIALOGUE 66, 97 (2004).

"My practice is now divided roughly into two equal parts. I serve as a neutral mediator 50 percent of the time, and the other half is composed of four representative roles: client representative during mediations presided by other neutrals (often with a litigator co-counsel); collaborative lawyer; unbundled lawyer for self-represented parties; and transaction lawyer building relationship agreements such as premarital, post-marital, cohabitation, and other matters involving long-range relationships such as business partnerships, probate disputes, and adoption and surrogacy agreements. Rather than being a financial disaster, my decision to be a non-court family lawyer resulted in rapid growth of my practice beyond my most optimistic expectations. My gross receipts increased by over 33 percent during my first year of practice and uncollectible fees went down from 30 percent of gross billables to 2 percent."

GROWTH OF THE SELF-REPRESENTED MOVEMENT

The ultimate consumer reaction today is "No thanks, I will do it myself." The do-it-yourself self-help movement has impacted business for contractors, plumbers, and carpenters in the construction industry. Home Depot, YouTube tutorials, and other havens for the home do-it-yourselfers have flourished at the expense of licensed service providers. Instead of being looked down on or stigmatized, it has become almost glamorous to make things from scratch and rely on oneself instead of professional service providers. The same has been true across industries, including real estate (Zillow, Trulia, Realtor.com, Streeteasy), tax preparation (Turbo Tax), the securities industry (Schwab), trading (Robinhood), and medicine (Lemonaid, DocsApp, MDLive).[5]

---

4. The following is adapted from Forrest S. Mosten, *Lawyer as Peacemaker: Building a Successful Law Practice without Ever Going to Court*, *43(3)* FAM. L.Q. 489–518 (FALL 2009).

5. By the time you read this book, many of these companies that are thriving in 2022 may have changed names or gone out of business. This realm is expanding, evolving, and changing on a daily basis.

The legal profession has already experienced this phenomenon in the field of real estate closings. Not too many years ago, the transfer of title and negotiation of contract terms were seen as so complex and important that the common practice was to go to a lawyer for a home sale. Consumers saw the lawyer's fees (a customary 1 percent of the sales price) for these services as necessary, non-negotiable, and appropriate. Today, primarily in the western United States, the title insurance and escrow industries have virtually replaced lawyers in residential home closings with great savings to the consumer and with virtually no diminution in quality service (actually, service of escrow companies is generally better, much more affordable than offered by lawyers). (In New York, lawyers are still the gatekeepers of real estate transactions.)

The same trend is influencing traditional adversarial representation in divorce cases, and the transition has been rough. Litigants are voting with their feet and demonstrating their consumer preference by using paralegal document services or online services at a fraction of the cost or self-representing with the assistance of court-connected and commercial self-help books and materials. (Legal Zoom[6] and Nolo Press are major self-help providers.) The rate of litigants without lawyers in divorce matters is striking. According to the National Center on Court Statistics, of New York state's 299,619 incoming domestic relations cases in 2020, 244,082 featured self-represented litigants, and of New York's outgoing cases, more than 88 percent were self-represented. Overall, among states reporting to the National Center on Court Statistics in 2020, more than 54 percent of outgoing domestic relations cases featured self-represented cases.[7] (As we discussed these trends, with outrage and concern for underserved families, one of the authors found herself particularly embarrassed by the fact that her home state of New York featured the highest rate of self-represented litigants among all surveyed states in the United States, especially as family court cases for nearly all self-represented litigants stalled for 6 to 12 months at a time during the COVID-19 pandemic.) While training of new judicial officers increasingly addresses best practices for handling cases involving self-represented litigants, and while many judicial officers are deeply committed to improving access to justice, the interactions between some judges and some self-represented litigants remain frustrating and unproductive.

Because self-represented litigants are not familiar faces, do not wear the right court uniforms, and generally do not know what to do or how to do it correctly, they may get the impression that they are unwelcome intruders in the courthouse.

---

6. Some lawyers in Texas were so threatened by Nolo Press that: Claiming that only lawyers could provide legal information and that Nolo's publications were guilty of practicing law without a license, the Supreme Court of Texas' Unauthorized Practice of Law subcommittee ordered Nolo to appear before a closed hearing at Austin on August 20, 1998, to explain why sale of its books and software should not be prohibited. The Texas legislature came to the rescue by exempting books from the unauthorized practice of law providing such books provided proper disclaimers that the books' information was not legal intended as legal advice. *See The Brief Story of Texas vs. Nolo*, Nolo (Apr. 11, 2011), https://blog.nolo.com/blog/2011/04/11/the-brief-story-of-texas-vs-nolo/.

7. American Bar Association, *Unbundling Resource Center* (updated 2020), https://www.americanbar.org/groups/delivery_legal_services/resources/; for an interstate statistical survey, see S. Gibson, B. Harris, N. Waters, K. Genthon, M. Hamilton & D. Robinson, eds., NCSC CSP STAT., www.courtstatistics.org (last revised Jan. 6, 2022).

Court clerks are generally forbidden by statute or court rules from providing help to the public in filling out court forms. (It is not atypical to encounter posted signs in courtrooms that read "Clerk Cannot Give Legal Advice" or words to that effect.)[8] Judges sometimes caution struggling self-represented litigants by telling them that they will be held to the same standards as lawyers appearing in the courtroom. Other than referring self-representers to the court's self-help center, the court's website, or a general suggestion to seek out nonprofit or low-cost legal assistance, however, there may be no practical mechanism for connecting litigants to resources that might help them. Time constraints posed by crowded court calendars leave little time for extra explanations and little space for questions. Communication barriers, be they due to lack of English proficiency, literacy issues, narrative style, demeanor, or other causes, complicate matters even further. It is little wonder that self-represented litigants feel abused by the court system that is ironically supported by their tax dollars.[6]

Litigants without lawyers are, however, effecting change in the court system, especially as the number of self-represented litigants continues to increase in many jurisdictions. According to the National Center for State Courts in the United States, more than 88 percent of family law litigants in New York, 82 percent of family law litigants in Minnesota, and 81 percent of family law litigants in Hawaii appear pro se.[9] (Again, despite efforts and reforms in the New York Unified Court System, New York still leads in shameful access to legal resources.) A 2010 American Bar Association report, surveying judges from jurisdictions around the country concluded a decade ago that the number of pro se filings was increasing, and recent statistics only confirm the trend in many jurisdictions.[10] Reacting to consumer demand and going further due to bold and innovative court leadership supported by state and local government, Maricopa County. Arizona initiated consumer-oriented reforms that include less complex procedures, uniform support guidelines, model pleadings, and courthouse assistance, which includes paid facilitators to help people fill out forms. Unlike most jurisdictions, Maricopa offers night court, child care, client libraries in the courthouse and in community public libraries, and a large court referral list of lawyers trained in unbundled services (see Chapter 5) who are willing to help self-represented litigants.

Now, approximately 30 years later, many jurisdictions have picked up the gauntlet thrown by Maricopa County and have gone to great lengths to accommodate self-represented parties by providing a wide range of support and resources. In August 2014, the American Bar Association Standing Committee on the Delivery of Legal Services published "The Self-Help Center Census: A National Survey." The ABA identified approximately 500 self-help centers around the country, 222 of which responded to an online survey. The Census, based on the results of

---

8. https://nacmnet.org/sites/default/files/images/StaffCannotGiveLegalAdvice.pdf. *See, e.g.,* California Court Form MC800, which details what court clerks can and cannot do for litigants, http://www.courts.ca.gov/documents/mc800.pdf.

9. Gibson et al., *supra* note 7. For comparison, *see* Madelynn Herman, *Self-Representation: Pro Se Statistics*, Nat'l Ctr. for State Courts (Sept. 25, 2006).

10. Justice Linda Klein et al., *Report on the Survey of Judges on the Impact of the Economic Downturn on Representation in the Courts,* ABA Coalition for Justice (2010).

that survey, sheds light on the structure and operation of self-help centers around the country, including details on staffing, funding, consumers, and types of services provided. It illustrates the extent to which self-help centers are a vibrant and effective resource nationwide.[11]

NONLAWYER PROVIDERS

Despite the plethora of books, online information, YouTube and Instagram tutorials, and available forms, some litigants still want the help and advice of a dedicated human being. Many of them, however, are not going to lawyers. A major 2011 Access Across America Civil Justice Infrastructure Mapping Project conducted by the ABA[12] found that a significant number of identified legal needs were handled by nonlegal helpers. Combined with the many needs that were handled on a citizen's own initiative and those that were not remedied at all, it concluded that a majority of identified legal needs never reached a lawyer's office.

With the loosening of restrictions on unauthorized practice, the proliferation of independent paralegal and document preparation services is staggering. In 1995, the ABA Commission on Nonlawyer Practice recognized this consumer preference and recommended that the legal profession take an open-access approach—rather than punish paralegals through prosecution for unauthorized practice. This report, in addition to a long line of U.S. Supreme Court decisions opening up legal service access and competition was further reinforced by the 2011 ABA Civil Justice Infrastructure Mapping Project,[13] sending a strong message to us: develop new competitive service products or continue to lose a share of the divorce market.[14]

FEAR OF DISCONTENTED CLIENTS

Ironically, the growing protection for clients against lawyer professional negligence has caused an increase in legal fees. We are increasingly afraid of our own clients. The more we operate out of fear of clients, the less motivation we have to give our clients options for saving costs. Many lawyers believe it poses less risk to get an adverse judicial decision than to be blamed by the client for the compromises inherent in any settlement. Malpractice is harder to prove in second-guessing a lawyer's litigation strategy, especially when the case is over-lawyered, than to protect against later client claims that the lawyer did not do enough.

---

11. www.americanbar.org/content/dam/aba/administrative/delivery_legal_services/ls_del_self_help_center_census.authcheckdam.pdf.

12. ABA Consortium on Legal Needs and the Public, Comprehensive Legal Needs Study (1994).

13. Rebecca Sandefur, et al., First Report of the Civil Justice Infrastructure Mapping Project (2011).

14. The trend among U.S. Supreme Court cases is to support entrepreneurial and consumer-oriented marketing of professional services. *See* Bates v. State Bar of Arizona, 433 U.S. 350 (1977) (holding blanket bans on lawyer advertising unconstitutional); Edenfield v. Fane, 113 S. Ct. 1792 (1993) (permitting a Florida certified public accountant to personally solicit clients).

This type of defensive lawyering causes lawyer bills to go up—with a concurrent downward slide of the public's view of our profession. The buzz around the 2019 Netflix film exposé *Marriage Story* demonstrates just some of the discontent with the family law profession.

Instead of synergy and collaboration, clients and family lawyers seem to be in a no-win war against each other. Citizens' groups, the plaintiff bar, and state legislatures are engaged in efforts to increase the protections for clients by beefing up lawyer discipline, expanding rights to sue for malpractice, cutting back or eliminating malpractice immunity, and increasing client rights in the attorney-client relationship. We face requirements of written agreements, disclosure to clients of the existence of malpractice insurance, limitations on use of arbitration in malpractice claims, and "one-way"[15] mandatory use of arbitration by clients in fee disputes.

As availability of malpractice coverage is reduced and rates for coverage increase (as well as the ever-growing cost of deductibles), we feel unprotected from and fearful of our own clients. With increased flexibility of courts to extend statutes of limitations for client claims of professional negligence, in addition to an increasing anti-lawyer sentiment in civil juries, family lawyers are motivated to withdraw as counsel of record quickly to start the statute of limitations period running and to limit their advice and representation to the matter presented by the client.[16] Fearful of being sued for wrong advice or failure to investigate or engage experts properly, many family lawyers are increasingly recommending (or insisting) that their clients engage a growing stable of experts (e.g., CPAs, real estate and business appraisers, tax lawyers, financial planners), who may improve client information but whose primary function may be to protect and indemnify the lawyer who arranges for their services.

The result of this unfortunate trend is to increase the transaction costs of clients getting a divorce. Lawyers are charging higher initial deposits, and the overall bills after litigation claim a larger and larger percentage of the average marital estate. Even when the case is over, a second piece of litigation is often commenced against the client for the collection of unpaid fees or a third action might be initiated against the lawyer for client claims of professional negligence, ethical violations, or other transgressions. We become more selective in taking on clients, particularly those with difficult legal and financial issues or troublesome personal dynamics, when these are often the clients who need us the most. One basis for client selection is the ability or willingness of the client to pay higher fees than in other areas of the law, which is seen by many of us as a fair trade-off for taking on increased risk and client hassle. The result is that fewer potential clients can afford us to provide needed legal services. People who can't or won't

15. "One-Way": Clients have a right to choose between binding and nonbinding arbitration. Lawyers must accede to the client's choice.

16. *See* ABA Standing Committee on Professional Liability, Lawyer's Desk Guide to Malpractice (1992); Miller v. Metzinger, 154 Cal. Rptr. 22, 27 (Ct. App. 1979) ("When a party seeking legal advice consults an attorney at law and secures that advice, the relationship of attorney and client is established prima facie."); *see also* Forrest S. Mosten, *Unbundling Legal Services in 2014: Recommendations for the Courts*, 53 ABA Judge's J. 10 (Jan. 2014).

pay higher fees still have problems involving custody, support, or property division. They still want to adopt children or terminate parental rights. If lawyers are not economically available, consumers will be forced to make other choices in the marketplace to meet their needs.

LAWYER BASHING, STRESS OF LAW PRACTICE, RESULTANT LAWYER MALAISE

In a preemptive (and some would say overtly political) strike against a marked increase in lawyer jokes and client violence against lawyers, a former California State Bar president received national press by calling for lawyer jokes to be banned as hate speech. Following the despicable carnage, death, and destruction at the San Francisco law firm of Petit and Martin by a disgruntled client, that bar leader chose to appeal to the basest self-interested motives in lawyers to attack societal antipathy by self-protective (and perhaps constitutionally deficient) lawyer-sponsored legislation and an intensification of the us-versus-them mentality on the part of the nearly one million U.S. lawyers. To our profession's credit, the hate-speech trial balloon burst—but the underlying safety concerns about disgruntled clients remain.

We family lawyers fear the public's wrath at the highest level. With the rise in domestic violence being reported and handled in the courts, security has become a major concern. Office security is a frequent topic at family law conferences. Some police forces have developed special units for judges' protection against litigants. Such a unit was involved recently when a lawyer in our community, as well as the judge and the other family lawyer, was threatened by a former client. Unfortunately, such incidents are far too common.

Lawyer stress is also a major problem. Lawyers are 3.6 times more likely to suffer from the effects of stress and depression than are members of other professions.[17] According to the New York State Bar Association's 2017 National Task Force on Attorney Well-Being and the ABA/Hazelton Betty Ford Foundation's study on substance abuse and mental health issues among attorneys, 20.6 percent of lawyers screened positive for alcohol-dependent drinking, 28 percent of lawyers suffer from depression, 19 percent of lawyers struggle with anxiety; and 23 percent of lawyers experience significant stress. This stress is aggravated by conflict generated within families, between lawyers, and by an unwelcoming and underbudgeted court system. The most intense pressure comes from our clients; it also comes from the clients' parents, children, employees, accountants, and therapists. We may expect hassles from a client's estranged spouse, opposing counsel, court-appointed experts, creditors, or even from the clerks and judges at the courthouse. However, when pressure, threats, neediness, and emotion come at us from the client's new spouse, significant other, or parents, our stress can reach crisis levels.

17. Nancy Neal Yeend, *How ADR Benefits Law Firm Management*, *in* CALIFORNIA ADR PRACTICE GUIDE § 31.04 (1992).

It is amazing that, despite these pressures, virtually every Comprehensive Legal Needs Study reports high levels of client satisfaction with and trust in lawyers' problem resolution. This satisfaction drops off considerably when we steer our clients into the adversarial court system. In fact, much less satisfaction was experienced with the courts than with lawyers.[18]

Clients report high satisfaction with lawyers' honesty and explanation of the process, with their keeping clients informed of the progress of the case, and with their promptness in carrying out document work and returning phone calls. The lesson for us is that the public can maintain high confidence in and satisfaction with our professional services if we help them solve their problems by minimizing their contact with the court system.

ECONOMIC PRESSURES OF OPERATING A FAMILY LAW PRACTICE

Family law offices traditionally have been operated and managed like litigation firms. Most of us generally require a deposit or retainer to be applied against fees earned and make arrangements to have additional fees paid on a monthly basis, upon certain events (e.g., income tax refund or house sale), or at the end of the case. The deposit is calibrated to balance two competing goals: it should be high enough to cover anticipated costs of service but low enough not to scare away the client and to compete successfully with local family lawyers and other nonlawyer service providers bidding for the client's work. With remote work removing geographic obstacles and the advent of the Uniform Bar Exam, currently adopted by 36 states and expanding access to licensure, the pool of competing professionals becomes even more expansive. However, unlike large corporate or personal injury defense offices, which also bill by the hour (often at lower rates and generally with more secure sources of payment), we often represent clients with limited resources (even more limited at the time of divorce). The financial "hit" for our clients is even greater when they are supporting two households on one income. There are also other nonrecurring divorce-related expenses, such as child custody evaluators, vocational counselors, moving costs, and other start-up expenses for new residences.

Several other factors exacerbate the limited ability of family law clients to pay legal fees. First, it is difficult to estimate the amount of work needed in any litigation, particularly in family law matters. Assessments of the degree of conflict or complexity of the issues involved are often distorted. Clients invariably hope for a quick and simple resolution and often color their initial presentations with that hope. Even when both spouses start high in their desire to be amicable and

---

18. Comprehensive Legal Needs Study, *supra* note 12, at 32–35 (High satisfaction was generated with respect to the lawyer's honesty and explanation of the process and for keeping the client informed of the progress of the case and promptness in carrying out document work and returning phone calls. Much less satisfaction was experienced with courts than with lawyers.). In Australia, a longitudinal study of 723 divorcing people found high satisfaction with lawyer services until and unless the dispute was decided by a court. P. McDonald, Settling (1986).

conciliatory, the role, style, and chemistry of the lawyers affect the time, cost, and manner of resolution. Fees can escalate because of a personality conflict between lawyers or between a spouse and the other spouse's new significant other. These variables may not be anticipated at the outset, and fees often end up much higher than originally anticipated.

In addition to resource limitations and unexpected developments, the nature of divorce litigation makes fee payment problematic. Satisfied clients pay their bills faster and more fully.[19] Family law clients finishing litigation are rarely satisfied. In the rare instance when a client "wins" in court, the fees expended and/or problems with compliance or modification often nullify the initial victory in the client's mind. The result is that the client is faced with a large outstanding bill with little or no money to pay it. Monday morning quarterbacking, remorse, and general dissatisfaction further reduce otherwise low motivation for clients to pay for our services. Add in any lawyer mistake or poor communication and even a winning client may be resistant to the idea of full payment. We are considered the last in line for payment—long after rent, food, car maintenance, child and spousal support, credit card payments, and even an occasional vacation.

These problems intensify when a client has been on the short end of a court result or feels unfairly treated in a negotiated settlement. A look at the economics of a family law litigation practice might be helpful. Assuming that you currently have an uncollectible rate in the 30 percent range, it means that you are working 30 percent of the time for free. From another perspective, you must work about 130 percent of your normal schedule to be paid for every hour you are currently billing.

Therefore, if providing litigation services is not fulfilling some of your financial goals, you might consider offering other family law service products with higher rates of collection. Because you either write off unpaid bills with attendant loss of income or try collecting and risk being sued for malpractice, alternative income sources, such as representing clients in mediation and unbundled legal services, may be attractive.

Despite the pressures discussed in this chapter, think about why you choose to devote so much of your life dealing with family conflict. Also think about what it is like to be a client going through a family crisis. Many of these consumers are choosing a different way—the path of mediation.

LAWYER BENEFITS OF HAVING CLIENTS ATTEND MEDIATION

Higher consumer satisfaction with mediation over court litigation (or even lawyer-lawyer negotiation) has been found in study after study.[20] This doesn't mean that it is necessary to close your law office and open a mediation practice,

19. According to Hubspot, 68 percent of consumers say they are willing to pay more for products and services from a brand known to offer good customer service experiences. https://cdn2.hubspot.net/hubfs/2771217/Content/2018%20Customer%20Service%20Expectations%20Gladly.pdf.

20. Keri Szejda & Amy S. Ebesu Hubbard, *Neutrality and Satisfaction in the Mediation Session: Party and Mediator Perspectives*, 30(3) Int'l J. Conflict Mgmt. 329–48 (2019).

although that is an option to consider. Just as bypass surgery might motivate a person to follow a low-fat diet, we must accept the fact that many clients who face catastrophic family law conflict prefer mediation. With this acceptance, family lawyers have a few options:

1. Assess the current market and service offerings and continue to offer litigation representational services with the hope that demand for such current service offerings holds steady.
2. Modify existing service products (adversarial representation) to meet consumer demand.
3. Offer new service products (mediation, client coaching, Collaborative Law, preventive checkups) to supplement your current full-service product.

Attorney Benefits in a Mediator's Market

The first step in the market assessment process is to understand that clients prefer mediation for working out family problems and seek family lawyers who are mediation-friendly. Also, if we understand that embracing mediation is in our own best interest as a profession, acceptance of mediation will be accelerated. Benefits to attorneys include:

- Retaining or increasing our share of the divorce market.
- Increasing profits.
- Achieving higher rates of payment.
- Reducing malpractice exposure.
- Increasing control.
- Having a better quality of life.

Family Lawyers Retain or Increase Our Share of the Divorce Market

Just as they go to the dentist or pay 6 percent to a real estate broker to sell the family home, divorce clients have paid for lawyers because they believed that they had no other choice. Apparently, however, clients now believe that they do have other choices. Clients are doing the work themselves; turning to nonlawyer providers; or, when they do use lawyers, trying to unbundle and limit the lawyer's work and attendant costs. See Chapter 5 for discussion on unbundling, also called *limited scope representation.* Family law consumers are also demanding mediation, so lawyers should represent parties in mediation for no other reason than to stay in business. As Woody told a *Wall Street Journal* reporter long ago: "Lawyers may see the difference as being between a $10,000 fee for full-service representation and a $1,000 fee for serving as an unbundled lawyer consultant during a mediation. Actually, the true difference may be between the $1,000 fee as mediation consultant or receiving no fee at all."[21]

21. Junda Woo, *Entrepreneurial Lawyers Coach Clients to Represent Themselves*, Wall St. J., Oct. 13, 1993, at B1, B6.

In the areas of commercial and business litigation, corporate counsel are more closely monitoring the activities and billings of outside law firms conducting the litigation. More law firms are being selected on the strength of their alternative dispute resolution (ADR) orientation, their conduct, and the training of their lawyers to support their clients' preferred outcome in mediation. Companies are fed up with receiving high bills for legal work that doesn't solve problems, is protracted, and is costly to them in terms of their reputations in the industry. The same consumer revolution is taking place in family law. The continued high attendance of family lawyers in mediation and unbundling training courses indicates that we are truly hearing this message.

Mediation Increases Profits

While maintaining a steady flow of clients is the lifeblood of any professional practice, being paid for work performed does not hurt either.

Performing professional services and not getting paid causes defensive and self-destructive business practices that only worsen our standing in the marketplace. Due to experiences of client nonpayment, lawyer banter includes wisdom such as "If you don't get it up front, you'll never get it!" Yet, the practice of demanding retainers reduces consumer access to qualified family lawyers, and clients go elsewhere—or do without lawyers altogether.

A second consequence of client nonpayment is self-destructive retaliation toward family lawyers by lawyers in other fields who charge less. For example, insurance defense lawyers often charge less than 50 percent the rate of family lawyers due to the dependability of payment and the expectation of repeat business (also due to the economic bargaining leverage and sophistication of insurance companies). Commercial litigators also generally charge less than we do. Personal injury attorneys might take cases fully on contingency. We justify our rates in part by invoking uncollectibility realities and the increased emotional burdens that we face. It is also true that we have increased leverage in fee setting due to our clients' vulnerability. Our clients who have used lawyers in other fields of law may find our rates to be confusing and off-putting.

Higher retainers and hourly rates may also turn off referral sources, which have been traditional feeders for the family law bar. Hardworking estate planners and civil litigators may refer clients to family lawyers even if their hourly fees are higher than their own. But just as escrow companies and title companies became replacement referrals for real estate lawyers in residential home closings, lawyers in other fields have fiduciary duties to their clients to help them make informed decisions regarding cost.

Given a choice between a family lawyer who is limited to full-package adversarial representation and a second lawyer who supplements the adversarial model with a meditative limited scope approach, many nonlawyers such as therapists and accountants may recommend the less expensive alternative.

In sum, family lawyers who represent parties in mediation enjoy greater profitability in their practices in a few ways:

- Clients are increasingly selecting family lawyers who support mediation and are skilled in guiding them through the mediation process.

- Referral sources, lawyers, related professionals (e.g., accountants and therapists), and the general public are also preferring lawyers who supplement trial orientation with an emphasis on dispute resolution.
- Because overall fees incurred during a mediated divorce are lower, family lawyers using mediation can reduce the amount of upfront retainer, making their services more affordable and less of an economic barrier for prospective clients.[22]

Clients selecting mediation and unbundled use of lawyers' discrete services do not incur such runaway bills, pay in a timelier way and in full, and have lower uncollectible fees at the end of the attorney-client relationship.[23] Satisfied clients are the best marketing tool available to help us reduce future client acquisition costs, thereby increase our profits.

Higher Collection Rates and Lower Malpractice Exposure

Many malpractice claims are filed in the form of cross-complaints for malpractice in response to our lawsuits for nonpayment of fees. To protect ourselves, many family lawyers make a management practice never to sue clients for unpaid fees. We simply eat the loss. This approach does reduce malpractice actions, but it costs both us and future clients, who may pay higher fees, set as a response to uncollectibility.

If you represent clients in mediation, you can decrease your malpractice exposure in several ways. Satisfied clients more often pay their bills. Smaller bills are more often paid or are less costly to write off. Decreased motivation to sue for fees reduces malpractice exposure. Many clients are willing to "let sleeping dogs lie," provided they are not sued to pay up. When those dogs awake, malpractice cross-complaints are not far behind.

Control

Just like our clients, we want greater empowerment and predictability in our lives. Just as for Alice in her journey through Wonderland, our long-held beliefs about the levers of control may not hold true. Let's look at trial work. Many young lawyers fantasize about the ability to hold a courtroom spellbound with their silver-tongued eloquence. As a judicial officer in family court, Judge Scully observes that

> the truth is that regardless of how heady it might feel to deliver a well-planned cross-examination or final argument, lawyers lose total control when the matter is submitted; the decision-making rests entirely in someone else's hands. And in family law, where so much is left to the discretion of the court, my assessment of the case may be very different from the lawyer's.

---

22. In contrast to most lawyers who do court work, mediators and lawyers representing mediation clients often eliminate the requirement of a retainer, or other front-end deposit.

23. Brette Sember, *Eight Ways to Lower the Cost of a Divorce*, Forbes. Next Avenue (July 22, 2019, 11:36 AM), https://www.forbes.com/sites/nextavenue/2019/07/22/8-ways-to-lower-the-cost-of-a-divorce/?sh=9fe04c04a316.

True, there are appellate courts. However, if the cost, time, and odds against success are not daunting enough, the best result possible after an appeal is a decision to reverse that obliges the parties to pay for yet another trial. We know that although the appellate process is a safeguard against naked abuse, it is rarely used and even more rarely successful.

Seasoned litigators often opine that a bad settlement is generally better than a good court verdict. This wisdom is based on sad experience with how clients view the litigation process. If the case is won, it's because the client deserved the win. If the case is lost, it's the lawyer's fault. In addition to client retaliation of nonpayment, bad-mouthing to referral sources, or worse, losing often makes the lawyer feel empty and worthless. All the work, late nights, and emotional investment didn't pay off. In fact, the client may be hostile, vindictive, or even dangerous. In those situations, an estate-planning practice or even barista work may seem like a better career option.

Judicial decisions that are too one-sided (even in our client's favor) can intensify and perpetuate family conflict. When the losing client feels disenfranchised (and as though he or she has nothing further to lose), any incentive to modify behavior or comply with court edicts may drop away. All experienced litigators have encountered situations in which they won the battle triumphantly, only to watch their clients lose the war.

Clients choose mediation because it empowers them and restores their control. The same advantages inure to us when we advance the client's position through creative proposals and persuade the opposing party and counsel. This is quality lawyering at its best—not subject to being stymied by the start of a hearing or a judge's order. Lawyers who represent mediation parties report a high level of satisfaction by clients and control for lawyers in this process.

Following Your Heart Pays Off in the Long Run

A highly respected peacemaking lawyer learned the long and hard way to follow her heart. Betty was a university professor who yearned for more. She heard about mediation-centered lawyering and gave up her tenured position to attend a well-ranked law school. Her sole motivation was to be a family mediator and lawyer coach for mediation upon graduation.

Betty's talent and success got in her way. First, there was the invitation to law review and then to be a law review editor. Upon graduation, she was offered a highly paid job in a large corporate firm in a city where she did not want to live. While she was seduced by the money, she was even more drawn by the fact that such a prestigious firm had made her an offer.

Two horrible years passed and Betty landed in the hospital with a permanent disability due to the stress and competition of the firm. On the advice of her doctor, she quit the firm, took a year off from work, and moved to a small town in a bucolic setting. She opened a bakery and spent five years blissfully baking and hiking.

Throughout this hiatus in her active legal career, Betty maintained her law license by attending Continuing Legal Education programs. During a program on legal ethics, Betty learned that mediation was taking off. With her apron still on, Betty started attending local bar association meetings and met a renegade lawyer who was offering unbundled and mediation services to the unrepresented. Betty teamed up with her and quickly had so many clients that she sold her bakery (for a handsome profit).

Betty is now the happiest lawyer we know. She is doing fulfilling work, can support herself, and has control over her life such that her stress is reduced and her culinary creativity has expanded—but as an avocation for her friends and family!

Better Lives for Us

Representing clients in mediation also gives us flexibility in our careers and personal time. Litigators are subject to time pressures (many artificially self-created) imposed by opposing counsel, court rules, and the presiding judicial officer. While any job has time constraints, few can expose us to lockup or monetary sanctions for turning papers in late. It is true that bosses yell and there are hurtful political intrigues in academia and business, but few careers rival the abuse lawyers absorb. Hurtful, public ad hominem comments by opposing counsel and humiliation in court are not uncommon. We must develop thick hides, but even with that armor, it is difficult to accept the cancellation of a family vacation, or the inability to attend a child's piano recital dictated by a judge's unwillingness to continue a hearing, or the petty vindictiveness of opposing counsel. It is true that professional codes of courtesy and civility are emerging, as is the use of punitive sanctions for outrageously discourteous conduct. However, the notion that lawyers need leeway to be zealous advocates can work against the imposition of sanctions for litigation conduct. Adding mediation representation to our mix of professional activities may ameliorate some of this pressure. Mediation scheduling does require some personal compromise on the lawyer's part to meet the demands of the client, the opposing counsel and party, and the mediator. However, none of us can recall a lawyer ever canceling a vacation to attend a mediation session. Also, if lawyers have family responsibilities, medical appointments, car repairs, or personal exercise or enrichment, consensual appointments give more flexibility than does an 8:30 a.m. court calendar call.

Those of us who regularly represent mediation parties appreciate the reduced stress in our lives stemming from more control and less naked conflict. Client demands are every bit as rigorous when mediation is utilized; some would say demands even increase, because the responsibility for results remains with us rather than being relinquished to the judge. However, as client empowerment and informed decision-making become the shared values of both the lawyer and client, we become less a shaman and more a coach. It is true that coaches in professional sports get blamed and fired with steady regularity. Still, the player who misses the free throw rarely blames the coach. In contrast, family law litigators are often blamed by ungrateful clients for the disappointments of a judge's decision. The occasional thank-you card or even fully paid bill is often not enough to compensate for the frustrations and unhappiness of handling family conflict in the courtroom. Burnout is common, and even the most lauded litigators lament, "The practice of law would be great if it wasn't for the clients. They are a pain in the foot."[24]

24. Noted antitrust lawyer Maxwell Blecker in Katrina M. Dewey, *Meet Them in Court: What California Top Litigators Have in Common: Guts and Glory*, CAL. BUS. L. REV. 10 (JULY 10, 1995).

Part of lawyer stress is having to live up to the white knight image that we ourselves have cultivated. By surrendering this omniscient role and becoming more of a partner in the lawyer-client team, we get the monkey partly off our backs. Most lawyers know that it is the clients who created their own problems long before we were called to the rescue. Instead of taking on the mission of "making everything better," mediation helps us concentrate on giving the client the tools and resources for making the best decisions themselves. The distinction may not be apparent at first glance, but it is meaningful in the attempt to be a helper, not a principal, in the conflict.

Mediation is not a panacea. Still, mediation-friendly lawyers have increased career and life satisfaction. By sparing a family the ravages of court battle and ending strife more quickly, we can reduce that family's pain. Many mediations catalyze communication, awareness of parenting needs, and the transformation of the spouses from fiery foes to collaborative colleagues as described in *The Good Divorce* by the late Dr. Constance Ahrons.[25] Guiding a family into mediation and modeling effective problem solving can provide profound personal satisfaction. Clients frequently express their appreciation, and you can be a major contributor to positive systemic family transition. Increased awareness of how to solve problems without threats or tantrums and increased understanding of our own underlying interests improves our decision-making and personal relationships outside the office.

Such total turnabout in professional and personal orientation is not mandatory, of course. However, we believe you will find value if you are open to enjoying this new approach, whether it generates new career and personal directions or simply makes your current family law practice more satisfying.

25. Constance Ahrons, The Good Divorce 57–58 (1994). See https://constanceahrons.com/ (last visited Aug. 7, 2022).

CHAPTER 2

Family Lawyer as Dispute Resolution Manager

The courts of this country should not be the places where resolution of disputes begins. They should be the places where the disputes end after alternative methods of resolving disputes have been considered and tried.[1]

—Sandra Day O'Connor

Courts are often seen as the dispute resolution forum of first, rather than last, resort. Law schools focus on the study of appellate cases that, in every single instance, resulted from an appeal of an adversarial court proceeding. Continuing education and specialist training for judges and lawyers concentrate on substantive law and litigation strategy. Years ago, in courses on family law specialization, the subject of alternative dispute resolution (ADR) was barely even mentioned. When Woody Mosten became a family law specialist in 1987, the 50-hour course spent less than five minutes on mediation.

Clients are increasingly hiring lawyers who are committed and trained to effectuate early, low-cost settlements. Once clients have accepted the reality of settlement, client attention should be shifted to *when* the case will settle and *what process* will be utilized to effectuate settlement. For example, in recognition of this reality, the family court of Australia has established court rules that accept mediation as the norm and litigation as the exception in resolving family law matters. In this jurisdiction, mediation, Collaborative Law, and negotiation (bottom-up processes) are labeled primary dispute resolution (PDR), and litigation, evaluation, and arbitration (top-down processes) have been renamed alternative dispute resolution (ADR). Just as the change in custody language (e.g., "time-sharing" and "parental decision-making" as opposed to "custody") in Florida and other states has changed the mindset in handling parenting of divorced children, perhaps the Australian labeling change will be the start of a movement in this country to rethink the language of the process of dispute resolution. Language is powerful, and adjustments can affect social change.

1. Sandra Day O'Connor, quoted in CLARE, ROUNTREE, AND MANLEE, ALTERNATIVE DISPUTE RESOLUTION IN NORTH CAROLINA: A NEW CIVIL PROCEDURE (2003).

DISPUTE RESOLUTION MANAGER AS LAWYER OF RECORD

When a client engages a lawyer for full-service representation, the lawyer plays many roles. In addition to being a courtroom barrister, the lawyer can be a manager of dispute resolution. Dispute management includes educating the client about dispute resolution options both inside the courthouse and in the private sector, helping the client select the appropriate option(s), and effectively representing the client within the chosen process to obtain a settlement.

ETHICAL DUTY TO ADVISE ABOUT ADR

The role of the dispute resolution manager requires a different orientation and an evolved set of skills that go beyond courtroom advocacy. The modern lawyer continually stresses client education and client-centered decision-making to ensure informed consent of the client in the process of dispute resolution as well as informed consent about substantive rights and court procedures. This duty to advise clients on appropriate dispute resolution options has been the subject of regulation of professional responsibility, federal and state legislation, bar association policy and activity, judiciary policy, and extensive comment within the academic literature.

RULES OF PROFESSIONAL RESPONSIBILITY

The lawyer's obligation to discuss options to litigation is consistent with ABA Model Rule 1.1, which requires a lawyer to ensure that client's *best interests* are served. Model Rules 1.4 and 1.2a require competent lawyers to consult their clients about resolution options so that the client can make an informed decision about the terms and transactional costs of settlement.[2] "A study of large-firm lawyers found that although lawyers often initially express the 'standard take' of a duty to seek every possible advantage, most acknowledge that some hyper-aggressive tactics are inappropriate even if they are legal."[3]

Colorado was the first state to include an explicit ADR provision in its Rules of Professional Conduct. Rule 2.1 of the Colorado Rules of Professional Conduct, enacted on January 1, 1993, provides that "in a matter involving or expected to involve litigation, the lawyer should advise the client of alternative forms of

---

2. Paul Laurie & Sharon Press, *The Lawyer's Obligation to Advise Clients of Dispute Settlement Options*, ABA Disp. Resol. Mag., Summer 2014, at 34.

3. The Uniform Act Reporter also cites the following: *see also* Marshall J. Breger, *Should an Attorney Be Required to Advise a Client of ADR Options?*, 13 Geo. J. Legal Ethics 427, apps. I and II (2000) (providing a comprehensive list of court rules, state statutes, and ethics provisions). *See generally* Bobbi McAdoo, *A Report to the Minnesota Supreme Court: The Impact of Rule 114 on Civil Litigation Practice in Minnesota*, 25 Hamline L. Rev. 401 (2002) (discussing the Minnesota rule requiring ADR to be considered in civil cases); Bobbi McAdoo & Art Hinshaw, *The Challenge of Institutionalizing Alternative Dispute Resolution: Attorney Perspectives on the Effect of Rule 17 on Civil Litigation in Missouri*, 67 Mo. L. Rev. 473 (2002) (empirical studies analyzing the impact of rules requiring lawyers to discuss ADR with clients).

dispute resolution which might reasonably be pursued to attempt to resolve the legal dispute or to reach the legal objective sought."

While the rule says a great deal about the growing importance of ADR, the language is merely aspirational. The rule does not say that lawyers have a duty to *use* ADR in a case where it is appropriate; instead, lawyers should simply advise a client about the use of ADR—and leave the decision up to the client. To advise means "to offer judgment"—competently and in the best interests of the client. A duty to advise is not satisfied by merely casually mentioning ADR options. The new rules require lawyers to be adept and comfortable with ADR and to advise clients about it knowledgeably with sufficient detail to provide informed consent to the client.

This is not an easy task to perform. In Woody and Liz Potter Scully's course at UCLA School of Law, they devote a full class to this subject, and students struggle in their efforts to explain and compare options. Lara Traum provides workshops to law school graduates in New York about how to conduct process consultations. Many struggle with the concept.

In the prefatory comments to the Uniform Collaborative Act (2010), the reporter (Professor Andrew Schepard) provides a comprehensive overview of this duty to advise:

> In many states lawyers are required to present clients with alternative dispute resolution options—mediation, expert evaluation, arbitration—in addition to litigation. Professionalism creeds in Texas ("I will advise my client regarding the availability of mediation, arbitration, and other alternative methods of resolving and settling disputes.") and Ohio, for example, require such discussion between lawyers and clients. In other states, similar obligations are imposed on lawyers by statute or court rule. See, e.g., Ark. Code. Ann. § 16-7-204 (1999) ("All attorneys . . . are encouraged to advise their clients about the dispute resolution process options available to them and to assist them in the selection of the technique or procedure"); N.J. Ct. R. 1:40-1 (giving attorneys the responsibility to discuss alternative resolution procedures with their clients).

Some states, including Connecticut, Georgia, Massachusetts, Minnesota, Missouri, Texas, and Virginia, clearly outline that lawyers have a mandatory duty to counsel clients about ADR options.[4] For example, according to Georgia Ethical Consideration 7-5, enacted in 1993 and revised in 2001: "A lawyer as advisor has a duty

4. *See* Rules & Regs. of the State Bar of Ga. R. 3-107, Ethical Consideration 7-5 ("A lawyer as adviser has a duty to advise the client as to various forms of dispute resolution. When a matter is likely to involve litigation, a lawyer has a duty to inform the client of forms of dispute resolution that might constitute reasonable alternatives to litigation. . . ."). The Massachusetts Supreme Court mandates that attorneys discuss ADR with their clients, while the Massachusetts Rules of Professional Conduct only suggest that attorneys help clients make informed decisions by discussing trial or negotiation strategy. Mass. Sup. Jud. Ct. r. 1:18, Disp. Resol. r. 5 (2016); Mass. Sup. Jud. Ct. r. 3:07, Mass. R. Prof. Cond. r. 1.4 cmt. 5 (2016). *See also* Minn. r. 114.03(B) (2010); Mo. S. Ct. r. 17.02(b) ("Counsel shall advise their clients of the availability of alternative dispute resolution programs."). *See also* Gerald F. Phillips, *The Obligation of Attorneys to Inform Clients about ADR*, 31 W. St. U. L. Rev. 239, 246–47 (2004) (discussing Virginia's mandatory obligation for a lawyer to advise clients about appropriate ADR by adding comments to Model Rules 1.2, 1.4, and 2.1).

to advise the client as to various forms of dispute resolution. When a matter is likely to involve litigation, a lawyer has a duty to inform the client of forms of dispute resolution which might constitute reasonable alternatives to litigation." The Georgia rule has led to a requirement that lawyers, so that they have the requisite knowledge to inform clients about options to litigation, educate themselves about these options through a mandatory three hours of continuing legal education in ADR.

States such as Oregon and California place the onus to inform parties of ADR options on courts.[5] In Alaska, Arkansas, Colorado, Delaware, Hawaii, Louisiana, and New Jersey, lawyers are encouraged to inform their clients of ADR options, but there is no explicit mandate to do so.[6] While many scholars believe that lawyers have an ethical duty to advise clients of ADR options, formalities surrounding such requirements differ by jurisdiction. In states such as New York, where no codified duty exists, some attorneys are still learning about the existence of ADR options themselves. While New York courts describe ADR options in materials distributed to all litigants, the journey toward a mandate to educate clients accordingly will likely be a long one.

Despite the view of some family lawyers that Collaborative Law is "practice-lite," Collaborative lawyers face the most stringent requirements of informed consent in the field of family law. The most stringent requirement for informed consent of options is imposed on Collaborative Lawyers in Rule 14 of the Uniform Act due to the higher informed consent requirements of a limited-scope engagement required in Collaborative Law (the limited scope is not providing litigation services):

Before a prospective party signs a Collaborative Law Participation Agreement, a prospective Collaborative Lawyer shall:

1. Assess with the prospective party factors the lawyer reasonably believes relate to whether a Collaborative Law process is appropriate for the prospective party's matter;

---

5. *See* Or. Rev. Stat. § 36.185. Cal. St. Civil Rule 3.221.

6. *See* Alaska R. Prof. Cond. r. 2.1 cmt. 5 ("a lawyer should advise the client of alternative forms of dispute resolution which might reasonably be pursued); Ark. Code Ann. § 16-7-204 (2016) ("An attorney . . . is encouraged to advise his or her client about the dispute resolution process options available to him or her and to assist him or her in the selection of the technique or procedure . . . deemed appropriate. . . ."); Colo. R. Prof. Cond. r. 2.1 ("In representing a client, a lawyer shall exercise independent professional judgment and render candid advice. In rendering advice, a lawyer may refer not only to law but to other considerations such as moral, economic, social and political factors, that may be relevant to the client's situation. In a matter involving or expected to involve litigation, a lawyer should advise the client of alternative forms of dispute resolution that might reasonably be pursued to attempt to resolve the legal dispute or to reach the legal objective sought."); Del. R. S. Ct. 71(B) (Delaware State Bar Association Statement of Principles of Lawyer Conduct) ("Before choosing a forum, a lawyer should review with the client all alternatives, including alternate methods of dispute resolution."); Haw. R. Prof. Cond. r. 2.1 cmt. 5 (Similarly, when a matter is likely to involve litigation, it may be necessary under Rule 1.4 to inform the client of forms of dispute resolution that might constitute reasonable alternatives to litigation.); Louisiana Mediation Act, LA. R.S. § 9:4102 ("Counsel are encouraged to discuss with their clients the appropriateness of using mediation in any civil case pending in the courts."); N.J. Ct. r. 1.40-1 ("Attorneys have a responsibility to become familiar with available [court-provided dispute resolution] programs and inform their clients of them.").

2. Provide the prospective party with information that the lawyer reasonably believes is sufficient for the party to make an informed decision about the material benefits and risks of a Collaborative Law process as compared to the material benefits and risks of other reasonably available alternatives for resolving the proposed collaborative matter, such as litigation, mediation, arbitration, or expert evaluation; and
3. Advise the prospective party that:
   A. After signing an agreement if a party initiates a proceeding or seeks tribunal intervention in a pending proceeding related to the collaborative matter, the Collaborative Law process terminates;
   B. Participation in a Collaborative Law process is voluntary and any party has the right to terminate unilaterally a Collaborative Law process with or without cause; and
   C. The Collaborative Lawyer and any lawyer in a law firm with which the Collaborative Lawyer is associated may not appear before a tribunal to represent a party in a proceeding related to the collaborative matter, except as authorized by Rule 9(c), 10(b), or 11(b).

An interesting proposal that was never enacted was authored in California by Senator Newton Russell, a strong advocate of mediation, who introduced the following straightforward bill [Senate Bill 1427 (January 24, 1996), adding section 6068.7 to the Business and Professions Code], which would have impacted the way lawyers advise clients about mediation:

> In any county that has established court-approved mediation services . . . it is the duty of every attorney to advise a client in a matter involving or expected to involve litigation of alternative forms of dispute resolution which may reasonably be pursued to attempt to resolve a legal dispute or to reach the desired legal objective.
>
> a. When a complaint is filed in a civil action, a plaintiff shall serve on each defendant and counsel for a plaintiff shall provide to each plaintiff that he or she represents, a notice concerning California's policy to promote the use of mediation. The notice, which shall be prepared by the Judicial Council, shall educate parties and attorneys about mediation and encourage them to evaluate their cases earlier for possible use of mediation and to agree to a mediation process without court intervention.
>
> b. In the mediation process, the attorneys may use reference materials already developed including, but not limited to, materials prepared by the legal profession, the Judicial Council, and the State Bar.[7]

Several family law presiding judges have taken the informed consent discussion directly to litigants in two main ways. The first is posting large-print recommendations to use mediation directly on court forms (see San Mateo, California, forms in the Resources section).

Other presiding judges communicate directly to litigants about ADR is a letter sent to all family law parties. The Los Angeles Superior Court Letter printed in both English and Spanish is also set out in the Resources section.

7. Cal. S.B. 1427, 1993–94 Reg. Sess. (1994).

In New York State, Hon. Lawrence K. Marks spearheaded a presumptive mediation initiative wherein matrimonial judges throughout the state refer parties to 90 minutes of free mediation at the parties' preliminary court conference, presuming that all matrimonial matters should consider mediation as the first point of conflict resolution unless deemed ineligible due to domestic violence or other documented history of criminal activity. While still at its inception and well behind the mandated mediation provisions governing other states' processes, New York has started to embrace ADR, albeit with a wary hug.

A litigation midpoint scheme often requires that parties attend an ADR Status Conference or otherwise elect an alternative process somewhere along the litigation timeline. California Civil Procedure (section 1775-1775.16) requires an ADR Status Conference after both sides' initial pleadings have been filed and requires parties to engage in either court-mandated mediation or arbitration in all civil cases (no money was authorized by the courts or the state legislature to pay the neutrals to provide this statutory required process).

In addition to the varied focus of required court mediation and settlement conferences, the public policy of settlement is reflected in allocating lawyers' fees. For example, California Family Code section 271 permits the court to "base an award of attorneys' fees and costs on the extent to which the conduct of each party or attorney furthers or frustrates the policy of the law to promote settlement of litigation and, where possible, to reduce the cost of litigation by encouraging cooperation between the parties and attorneys."

In essence, the statute motivates lawyers and parties, through the distribution of fees and costs, to "out-nice" the other side. To do this and to engage in behavior that promotes settlement, the parties must be informed by their lawyers of various nonlitigation alternatives that promote settlement.

VOLUNTARY ADR PLEDGES

Voluntary ADR pledges provide the inspiration for many family lawyers to inform their clients about various alternatives to litigation. Although voluntary pledges lack the enforcement mechanisms of statutes or court rules, they do create a major incentive for us to inform clients about alternatives to litigation. By prominently displaying an ADR pledge in our office, we have a marketing tool that will attract clients who are searching for a lawyer who emphasizes client centered decision making. Of course, we must live up to this pledge and develop an earned reputation for informing clients about and exploring various alternatives to litigation.

Nearly thirty years ago, in 1993, the Beverly Hills Bar Association (3,000 members) adopted an association-wide ADR pledge designed to educate its members about the duty to inform clients about and to initiate ADR options and to have its members publicly declare their commitment to utilizing alternatives to litigation. A copy of the pledge is included in the Resources section. The California Association of Realtors has gone one step further by inserting a mediation clause in its standard home sale contract, requiring brokers to discuss this issue with both parties involved in the transaction. ADR pledges and ADR advice projects have been adopted by other lawyer groups, trade associations, individual businesses, and consumer groups. Such pledges have even crossed borders, as ADR pledges were undertaken by the UK, France, Poland, and in the Singapore Charter.[8]

In a broader way, the state of Maryland used bus benches, media ads, and other types of outreach to promote mediation as a method for citizens to resolve disputes.[9]

MALPRACTICE EXPOSURE

Family lawyers are now in a catch-22. A plethora of cases holds lawyers liable for professional negligence if a settlement is entered into without reasonable discovery. Lawyers who settle difficult cases—trading off legal rights for a complete package—are far more likely to be sued for legal malpractice than are lawyers who litigate fully to judicial resolution.[10] This causes defensive over-lawyering. However, many family lawyers would rather over-lawyer and risk nonpayment of their bills or escalation of conflict than be vulnerable to a malpractice claim from a remorseful client.

Paul Lurie and Sharon Press state:

> We could imagine clients bringing malpractice claims against their lawyers for
>
> 1. failing to properly consult with their clients about discovery and motion practice alternatives and their cost implications and
> 2. failing to properly use the mediation process to reduce the costs of settlements.
>
> Now, with the emerging duty to inform clients of ADR alternatives, you could be liable for litigating competently but having a client complain that the lawyer did not diligently and prudently explore settlement—even when the client clearly declares: "I am not open to compromise. I will not settle."[11]

In their courageous and brilliant article, Lurie and Press cite Federal District Judge Patrick Walsh who echoes this warning:

> The scorched-earth practice many lawyers employ, attempting to discover "everything" without regard to cost and aggressively litigating when production is not forthcoming, seems inconsistent with the goals of the civil rules—the just, speedy, and inexpensive resolution of the case—in what

8. Rafel Morek, *New ADR Pledge*, Wolters Kluwer (Mar. 9, 2013), http://mediationblog.kluwerarbitration.com/2013/03/09/new-adr-pledge/.

9. Maryland Mediation and Conflict Resolution Office. ADR Consumer's Guide: Services in Maryland (3d ed. 2007), https://msa.maryland.gov/megafile/msa/speccol/sc5300/sc5339/000113/012000/012580/unrestricted/20100456e.pdf.

10. Louie Castoria, *Settle and Sue: Settlements as Preludes to Malpractice Claims*, Thomson Reuters (May 2017).

11. Paul Lurie & Sharon Press, *From the Bench: Rethinking Civil Litigation in Federal District Court*, 40 ABA J. Sec. of Litig. 6 (2013).

one assumes is the client's goal: obtaining the best possible result for the least amount of money.[12]

If you think we are kidding, ask the partners of Finizio & Finizio. The Florida Court of Appeals concluded that neither a plaintiff's knowing and voluntary entry into the marital settlement agreement nor the fact that the marital settlement agreement was subject to modification in the family court barred plaintiff's legal malpractice action against her divorce attorney.[13]

In *Miller v. Finizio & Finizio, P.A.*,[14] the defendants represented a wife who entered into a settlement agreement with her husband, largely dealing with custody and child support. At the hearing, the parties additionally allocuted that the wife would pay $60,000 to the husband's attorney's trust account as and for a quitclaim deed to the marital home, that they both waived spousal support, and that all other terms were addressed by the settlement agreement. The wife attested, under oath, to entering the agreement voluntarily and agreed to be bound by its terms.

Immediately upon entry of the final judgment, incorporating the settlement agreement, the wife sued her matrimonial attorneys. She claimed that they failed to obtain sufficient financial disclosures from the husband, implying that equitable distribution would be addressed separately, after the agreement was signed. She asserted that the settlement agreement she had signed was significantly unfavorable as a result.

While the trial court agreed with the defendant attorneys, the Court of Appeals sided with the wife and reversed the trial court's grant of summary judgment. The court concluded that her voluntary acceptance of the settlement agreement did not bar her legal malpractice action, that attorneys are not insulated from liability for failing to exercise ordinary skill and care in resolving settlement disputes, and that her redressable harm warranted action. While the attorneys had strategically pursued settlement rather than a fully litigated discovery process to pursue financial disclosure in furtherance of the client's objectives, the court concluded that the decision to pursue financial disclosure differently was within the purview of client decision-making.

The outcome of *Miller* seems to undermine the historical distinction between overall client objectives which require client consent, and technical/tactical concerns traditionally reserved for lawyer discretion.

A clear distinction between objectives and means sometimes cannot be clearly drawn, and, in many cases, the client-lawyer relationship partakes of a joint undertaking. The lawyer should assume responsibility for technical and legal tactical issues but should defer to the client regarding such questions as the

---

12. *Id.* at 6, citing Patrick J. Walsh.

13. *See* Miller v. Finizio & Finizio, P.A., 2017 WL 3616392 (Fla. 4th DCA Aug. 23, 2017). *See also* Jensen v. Hillsboro L. Grp., PC, 2017 WL 4018897 (Or. App. Sept. 13, 2017); Cesso v. Todd, 92 Mass. App. Ct. 131 (Aug. 28, 2017) Hodges v. Carter, 239 N.C. 517, 80 S.E.2d 144 (1954).

14. *Miller*, 2017 WL 3616392.

expense to be incurred and the concern for third persons who might be affected adversely.

Although professional rules make a point of asserting that they do not apply in malpractice suits, courts have applied various mandatory requirements to measure an appropriate standard of reasonable care for lawyers, codifying the Best Judgment Rule first explored in *Hodges v. Carter.*[15]

Implicitly sanctioning the underlying purposes of statutes, court rules, and voluntary pledges incorporating the emerging duty to advise on ADR options, the comments of Rule 2.1 of the ABA Model Rules of Professional Responsibility state:

> Advice couched in narrowly legal terms may be of little value to a client, especially where practical considerations, such as cost or effects on other people, are predominant. Purely technical legal advice, therefore, can sometimes be inadequate.

A client may expressly or impliedly ask us for purely technical advice. When such request is made by a client experienced in legal matters, we may accept it at face value. When such a request is made by a client inexperienced in legal matters, however, our responsibility as advisor may include indicating that more may be involved than strictly legal considerations.

The *Garris* court[16] translated the duty of informed consent into a standard of reasonable care: It is a duty requiring attorneys to advise and counsel a client as to all facts, circumstances and consequences which are necessary to enable the client to make an informed decision on matters such as . . . desirability of attempting settlement.[17]

Shouldered with the duty to attempt to effectuate a reasonable settlement, we clearly have a duty to initiate conversations with our clients about the desirability of settlement and to counsel clients as to the best means to effectuate a settlement if it is determined that settlement is appropriate. Although *Garris* dealt with attorney-to-attorney negotiations within the framework of non-family law litigation in the court system, the principles of *Garris* go beyond this setting. We must inform our clients about the relevant facts and circumstances concerning the process of settlement. In today's sophisticated family law practice, those facts should include nonjudicial alternatives such as private mediation, private adjudication, mini-trial, and other appropriate alternatives to resolving disputes (ADR). These options may have a significant impact on cost, privacy, timing of adjudication, emotional turmoil, and family relationships.

---

15. Hodges v. Carter, 239 N.C. 517, 80 S.E.2d 144 (1954).
16. Garris v. Severson Merson Berke & Melchior, 205 Cal. App. 3d 301 (1988 Depublished).
17. *See Id.*

Monitor Your Negative Assumptions

Lawyers are trained to focus on the problem in our client's best interest. If you were a good student, you may have learned this lesson too well and may have developed a bit of cynicism and mistrust, not only toward the other side but also toward your client.

Just think about the following:

- Do most people tell the truth most of the time?
- Do most people honor most of the agreements that they make?
- Do most people want harmony in their divorced family rather than conflict?

If the answer to all three questions is no, is it possible that your lens of people has become unfairly jaded?

Because some people lie, do you focus on being vigilant against deception rather than working productively with the facts as related by your client and the other spouse?

Because some people breach or default on their agreements, should you focus on this problem rather than build agreements that will most likely be kept?

Because good people going through a divorce sometimes act their worst, can you focus on what they do well and use such positive behavior as a foundation?

We are neither naïve nor unrealistic when we suggest that you reflect on your assumptions about our clients and the families we serve. If you have learned the lesson of "letting it go" to prevent unnecessary posturing, perhaps you can take the next step to challenging negative assumptions that often prevent agreements from forming.

HOW TO ADVISE CLIENTS PROPERLY ABOUT ALTERNATIVES TO LITIGATION

In their mediation course at the UCLA School of Law and in conducting CLE programs for practicing lawyers, Woody and Liz have found that the teaching module that seems to gain the most traction is the step-by-step protocol of advising a client about options to litigation.

Veteran lawyers often resist such training with a dismissive "I have done this for years." However, even lawyers with many years of experience generally concede that performing the following protocol may go far beyond what they had been doing prior to this training.

1. Explain to Client the Purpose of This Portion of the Consultation (Learn Options to Litigation to Have Full Information before Making a Decision and Certainly before Filing a Lawsuit)

In their seminal book *Lawyers as Counselor*,[18] the late David Binder, Paul Bergman, Paul Trembly and Ian Weinstein discuss the importance of a "prefatory introduction" to each phase of the client counseling process. In this protocol, the prefatory introduction explains to your client that to have full information before making a decision about an effective course of action, and certainly before taking

18. David A. Binder, Paul Bergman, Paul R. Tremblay & Ian S. Weinstein, Lawyers as Counselors, A Client-Centered Approach (2019).

a major step such as filing a lawsuit, the client must have full information about what the options are, what the positives and negatives of each option are, and how they compare to each other given the client's situation.

The Louis M. Brown and Forrest S. Mosten International Client Consultation Competition (affiliated with the International Bar Association, www.brownmosten.com) adopts the work of Binder and accepted ABA Professional Rule 1.2(c) in assessing the counseling skills of international law students using two central criteria that may be of guidance to us in our daily work with clients:

Criterion 3: Learning the Client's Goals, Expectations, and Needs. The lawyer should learn the client's goals and initial expectations and, after input from the client, modify or restate them as necessary, giving attention to the emotional aspects of the problems.

Criterion 6: Developing Reasoned Courses of Action (Options). The lawyer, consistently with the analysis of the client's problem, should develop a set of potentially effective and feasible options, both legal and nonlegal. The lawyers may discuss appropriate use of creative peacemaking and alternative processes such as unbundled legal representation (in which the lawyer performs discrete tasks as part of representation that is limited in scope), Collaborative Law, mediation, arbitration, expert consultation and evaluation, and prevention of future disputes.

2. Explain Litigation—Benefits and Mythology

Although our clients may talk about going to court, very few people truly understand what litigation really entails and how their understanding of litigation from *Perry Mason* and *Boston Legal* may differ significantly from that of their local family court.

Your explanation about litigation should include the following topics:

- A description of the court that is involved and its location
- The judges who serve in that court, and their backgrounds and suitability
- The timeline for completion of a court-contested divorce
- The expectation of the client's personal involvement: witness in discovery and hearings, preparation of documents, attendance at meetings with lawyer, mandated and anticipated negotiation and mediation sessions, and time in the courthouse
- The range of costs for the client, and the entire family
- The other professionals that might participate in the process (attorneys for children, forensic evaluators, appraisers, et al.)
- The impact of litigation on key family relationships and risks to the children
- The emotional toll on the client

As part of our explanation, we should test what myths the client has about how courts work and the impact of the litigation process and help debunk any myths that exist, including the following beliefs:

- Every judge will be perfectly unbiased and impartial to both parties at all times.
- The judge will be a former family law practitioner and therefore a family law expert;

- The process will be speedy because "Justice Delayed Is Justice Denied."
- Your client will be able to fully tell his or her story to the judge;
- The law is clear and will be applied to the client's situation in easily predictable ways.
- Your ability to cross-examine the other spouse will ensure that the truth will come out in court;
- Once there is a judge's decision, the other side will quickly comply with the ruling.

3. Explain the Existence of Options (Within and Outside Courthouse)

The following chart lays out both court-based and private sector options:

Family Law Alternative Dispute Resolution Options

Inside the Courthouse	Private Sector
Court-staffed mediation for custody and visitation cases	Self-help
Custody evaluation	Informal third-party assistance
Mandatory (or presumptive) mediation for financial issues	Divorce counseling
Meet and confer requirements	Community mediation centers (public and private)
Special masters or referees	Mediators, licensed and unlicensed
Mandatory settlement conference	Binding arbitration
Negotiated settlement in the hall	Med-arb and arb-med

As demonstrated in this chart and discussed throughout this book, there are many options for dispute resolution. Just as mediators who may have been trial lawyers often lose their edge in witness examination and court argument, many litigators do not stay current with evolving options and techniques for settlement. More important, many litigators feel very comfortable in their roles as advocates within the courtroom setting, using the leverage of litigation pressure to obtain negotiated results. They often do not view conflict in a mediated way—relying on adversarial strategies that inherently disincentivize de-escalation and collaboration—although clients often expect their lawyers to operate differently. This fear of change is understandable. Few professionals want to pioneer untested new approaches that may not be accepted easily by their clients. The answer is not that we should force our clients to use mediation in every situation. Rather we should be diagnostic problem solvers who widen the universe of client choices to improve client process decision-making. By increasing the options, mediation will be utilized more frequently to the benefit of the individual client and to the family law system as a whole.

4. Explain Options—Benefits and Downsides

Clients have many options for dispute resolution, each of which has benefits and downsides. Some options don't even involve attorneys or third parties. One option is client self-resolution—when based on reflective self-interest, the client simply takes one of his or her claims off the table. Sometimes this kind of resolution prevents the client from giving in or taking an appeasement route and can constitute one of the best decisions of the client's life. Another option is party-party resolution. We are often surprised how often clients seek legal services without having explored the option of sitting down for a cup of coffee with the other party to try to work out a problem. Sometimes clients don't realize they have that choice. Sometimes they are afraid to try. Although such conversations can be challenging, with our support and coaching, clients often make more progress with the other party directly than they ever imagined.

As soon as attorneys are involved, there is an opportunity for lawyer-lawyer resolution. Even if our preference would be to have the parties more actively involved in decisions affecting their own lives, we can still support our client's desire to avoid conflict and honor our client's informed decision to use us as a buffer.

Another choice is a four-way settlement conference. With a peacemaking approach to this customary process option, we can maximize the possibility of reconciliation and healing. For example, we can encourage clients to speak directly to each other using their own words, choose not to use jargon or legalese, and make it okay for clients to choose to subordinate legal rights and financial gain in favor of a settlement with which they can live and that meets other kinds of needs.

Of course, there are formalized dispute resolution processes involving third-party neutrals and/or team members besides attorneys and clients. For a collaborative settlement conference—which may resemble a traditional four-way settlement conference but is functionally different—our mission is to explain the benefits and costs of signing an attorney disqualification clause, explain different models of collaborative practice, and explain how the other party might react in a collaborative setting compared with other process options.[19] If you are not trained in collaborative practice or offer only one model of collaborative practice that might not be the best fit for a particular client, part of your peacemaker approach will be to refer clients to other lawyers in your community who offer other models.

Finally, there is the option of mediation. Given the many models of mediation and choices of mediators with different orientations, backgrounds, and areas of substantive expertise, our peacemaker responsibility is to explain this menu of mediator possibilities. If we invest in mediation training, we can enhance our ability to encourage clients to consider mediation early and seriously.

5. Compare and Contrast Non-Court Options with Litigation and with Each Other Using the Following Factors

Speed: How quickly can each process get started, and how long will it take to conclusion?

19. Forrest S. Mosten & Adam Cordover, Building a Successful Collaborative Family Law Practice (2018).

Privacy: How will each process protect the privacy of the family members from unwanted publicity or oversight? Will problematic personal and financial behavior stay behind closed doors?

Control over process: How will each process give our client a say and control over what the ground rules are, who the decision-maker is, and how comfortable the process will be?

Control over result: How does each process permit our client to influence the result and to walk away if the result is not satisfactory?

Relationships: How will each process impact our client's relationship with the children, the other spouse, business associates, members of a religious or geographic community, and others in your client's life?

Impact on children: How will each process affect our client's children's functioning, happiness, and welfare?

Financial cost: What is the range of money will our client spend for each process option?

Family health: How will combat during divorce affect family health?

Logistics: How will our clients participate in the process based on their work and lifestyle schedules as well as their geographic locations, virtually or in person?

Figure 2.1 illustrates how the use of mediation can accelerate completion of the divorce process, which will facilitate healing of the parties. Leading researchers Mavis Hetherington and John Kelly have found that separation engenders crisis and psychological symptoms and that it takes approximately two years to return to normal baseline functioning. Prolonged conflict leads to polarization, development of self-protective believe systems, and exacerbation of personality disorders. Figure 2.1 developed by Dr. Wendy Hutchins-Cook of Seattle captures this research. You should make copies of it and provide it to your clients to explain why the speedier resolution of mediation may benefit them and their children.

This document can be framed and displayed prominently in a law office. It may be accompanied by an ADR pledge certificate from the bar recognizing the signatory as being committed to the use of mediation and related processes. A signed copy of an ADR pledge can be sent to clients or referred to in our promotional literature. It can also be sent to opposing counsel as an introduction or as part of an attempt to commence mediation or another alternative dispute resolution process. A copy of the ADR pledge is in the Resources section.

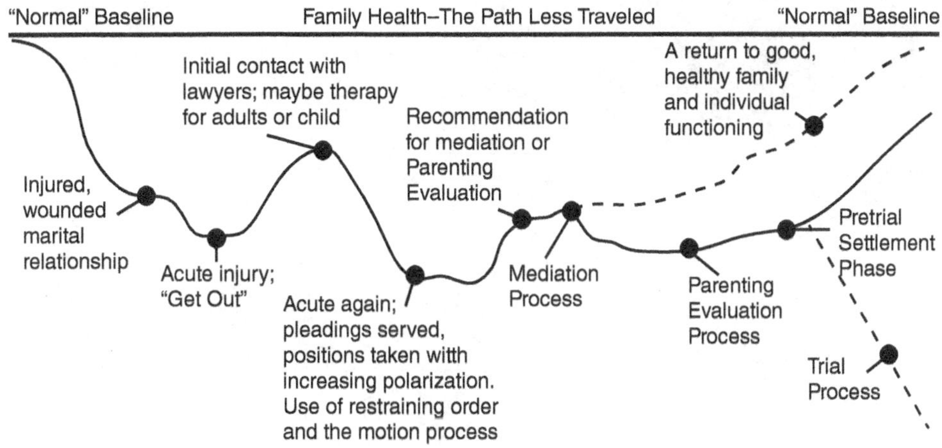

Family Health Baseline Criteria

- Individual members have the energy and attention for daily and longterm tasks and goals, and children move unimpeded through their development;
- Parents are present, not distracted from attending to children;
- Children are able to express "appropriate egocentrism"; they are not taking care of their parents.

Figure 2.1 ADR Pledge of the Beverly Hills Bar Association
Source: Wendy Hutchins-Cook, PhD, November 3, 1995, Presented at *AFCC Northwest Regional Conference*

PRACTICE TIPS

1. Prepare a summary of the dispute resolution options for your website so that a potential client can start thinking about these issues before the first appointment.
2. Provide the client with a brochure or other materials explaining your philosophy to promote settlement and providing an explanation and comparison of mediation and other nonlitigation options. The comparison of options authored by John Lande and Gregg Herman in the Resources section is a good start.
3. Offer the client an opportunity to view a video or read books in your office or on our website concerning the litigation process and alternatives.
4. Display an ADR pledge in our office or on your website and provide the client with a signed copy.
5. Include a provision in your attorney-client fee agreement in which the client acknowledges receipt and understanding of information about the benefits of mediation and other ADR options.
6. Before filing of the first contested court action or filing of a response, send your client a confirming letter concerning nonlitigation options.
7. Advise your client on selection of mediators and other professionals who will support client self-determination and informed consent.

CHAPTER 3

Mediation Confidentiality

A principal purpose [of mediation confidentiality] is to assure prospective participants that their interests will not be damaged, first, by attempting this alternative means of resolution, and then, once mediation is chosen, by making and communicating the candid disclosures and assessments that are most likely to produce a fair and reasonable mediation settlement.

—*Cassel v. Superior Court,* 51 Cal. 4th 113 (2011)

A CORE PRINCIPLE

Confidentiality is a core principle of mediation. Confidentiality, in fact, is expressly identified as the prime concern of the Uniform Mediation Act (UMA), which states, "The Uniform Mediation Act (UMA), created in 2001, is designed to address this core concern about the confidentiality of mediation proceedings." The underlying premise is that the effectiveness of mediation depends on the candor of the participants. As the drafters of the UMA put it, "Parties engaged in mediation, as well as non-party participants, must be able to speak with full candor for a mediation to be successful and for a settlement to be voluntary." This is in keeping with the common law principle that settlement discussions are precluded from discovery.

Parties engaged in mediation, as well as nonparty participants, must be able to speak with full candor for a mediation to be successful and for a settlement to be voluntary. For this reason, the central rule of the UMA is that a mediation communication is confidential and, if privileged, is not subject to discovery or admission into evidence in a formal proceeding.[1] In proceedings following a mediation, a party may refuse to disclose, and prevent any other person from disclosing, a mediation communication. Mediators and nonparty participants may refuse to disclose their own statements made during mediation and may prevent others from disclosing them, as well. Thus, for a person's own mediation communication to be disclosed in a subsequent hearing, that person must agree and

1. Uniform Mediation Act § 5(a).

so must the parties to the mediation. To be effective, waiver of these privileges must be in a record or made orally during a proceeding. There is no waiver by conduct.[2]

There are many reasons why protection of confidentiality is so important. Brainstorming of options is an essential component of mediation, and the willingness to share new ideas requires a sense of safety. If participants feel as though admissions, positions, and proposals made in mediation could be used against them later, this will chill the kind of free, honest communication that is necessary to feed the mediation process.

Interest-based negotiations require that participants identify their underlying needs and concerns honestly. Posturing, to the extent it masks interests, is contrary to the goals of mediation. In *Lake Utopia Paper Ltd. v. Connelly Containers, Inc.*,[3] the court noted,

> If participants cannot rely on the confidential treatment of everything that transpires during these sessions then counsel of necessity will feel constrained to conduct themselves in a cautious, tight-lipped, non-committal manner more suitable to poker players in a high-stakes game than to adversaries attempting to arrive at a just resolution of a civil dispute.[4]

CONFIDENTIALITY: A KEY BENEFIT

Parties benefit from mediation confidentiality. It stands in stark contrast to the public nature of traditional litigation. In many states, some or all of family law cases are matters of public record and the ability to seal them or restrict access to them is limited by First Amendment concerns and strong public policy favoring the transparency of the judicial system. Clients are increasingly vigilant about informational, as well as personal, privacy. Personal information in divorce files (financial, medical, etc.) can damage business relationships, render parties vulnerable to fraud or identify theft, and may be accessed directly by the children later on, causing irreparable psychological damage to the children and to the remaining family system.[5] In this internet age, privacy is a commodity whose value is on the rise.

Family court records may contain personally identifying information, including names and birthdates of minor children, address records, school information, financial records, and account information. The records may also contain especially sensitive information such as medical and mental health records and employment histories. It is easy to attach documents inadvertently to court filings that contain Social Security numbers, and it is expensive and cumbersome—if not

2. Per Mediation Act Summary, by National Conference of Commissioners on Uniform State Laws.

3. Lake Utopia Paper Ltd. v. Connelly Containers, Inc., 608 F.2d 928 (2d Cir. 1979), *cert. denied*, 444 U.S. 1076, 62 L. Ed. 2d 758, 100 S. Ct. 1093 (1980).

4. *Id.* at 930.

5. Uniform Law Commission summary of the Uniform Mediation Act; Uniform Mediation Act and Official Comments, J. Disp. Resol. (2003).

impossible—to redact or retract confidential information from a public court file once it has gone in. One has only to peruse the examples of identity theft schemes set out on the IRS website to see the myriad ways in which personal information available via public court records could be criminally appropriated and misused.[6] Disclosure of personal information in public records is of particular concern in cases involving stalking, harassment, and domestic violence. Even if the appropriation of personal information is not criminal, but commercial (direct marketers, potential employers), you should advise clients to be aware of the implications of personal information being available for strangers to access and disseminate.

In addition to identity theft and fraud, there are other profound reasons you should advise clients to keep the details of their family law cases out of public reach to the greatest possible extent. High-profile or high-net-worth clients, for example, may be sensitive to release of their personal data, given the heightened risk of harassment and/or interest in information "going viral." Just think of how former Dodgers owners Frank and Jamie McCourt and billionaires Ronald W. Burke and Kirk Kerkorian were portrayed in the media during their divorces.

For other clients, financial allegations in the public record (e.g., unreported cash income, employees paid off the books, excessive perquisites) could raise red flags with taxing authorities, exposing your clients to possible civil and criminal consequences. In some states, trial judges, as officers of the court, are obligated to report to the proper authorities evidence of any illegal activity.[7] In other states, even if they are not required to report the activity, judges may elect to alert tax authorities to issues of which they become aware during the litigation process.

Privacy can be of particular concern to parents of children with special physical, emotional, or educational needs. Clients should consider how public disclosures concerning a child's physical and/or mental health might impact access to health insurance, affect the child's ability to obtain accommodations or services from school districts, or subject the child to embarrassment, social stigma, or discrimination.

Finally, there may be cultural reasons that clients value confidentiality. If you have clients who are members of tight-knit religious, ethnic, or neighborhood communities, you may want to discuss mediation confidentiality with them and explain how it can limit public access to their private disputes. In this way, you can demonstrate your sensitivity to cultural attitudes toward divorce and/or preferences for private ordering of familial disputes. Some cultural communities seeking refuge in the United States from totalitarian and communist regimes alike have brought their distrust of government oversight with them and structured their family businesses and household finances accordingly. Others have felt that a system that bars state involvement in religion, bars bigamy, and creates other parameters that make it impossible for public environments to fully honor families built on religious tenets that differ from the socially endorsed norms would fear

6. There is a vigorous public policy debate in progress over whether public records, including family court files, should be freely available by anyone via the internet. The issue of online access to public records, with which court administrators are now struggling, will likely be an increasingly significant privacy concern in the coming years.

7. https://www.irs.gov/tax-professionals/2014-irsac-small-business-self-employed-report.

being outed as being from a particular religion or cultural group. Without trust in confidentiality as part of a process distanced from the public record, members of many such communities might be hesitant to seek formal family dispute resolution altogether, to the detriment of their futures and families.

Mediation confidentiality is not absolute (see discussion that follows), and mediation may not be the panacea for all privacy concerns. For example, there may be an ethical duty to terminate a mediation that is furthering criminal activity or an IRS audit may trump mediation confidentiality. But for most parties, you need to inform them that mediation does offer significantly more privacy and confidentiality than does traditional litigation.

SOURCES OF CONFIDENTIALITY RULES

There are various sources of rules governing mediation confidentiality in the family law context. It is crucial for you to be familiar with the specific rules at play in your jurisdiction in order to properly advise clients as to the parameters of their participation in a given mediation and the impact of that participation on concerns of privacy confidentiality.

The ABA Model Standards for Mediators addresses confidentiality. Specifically, per ABA Model Standard VII, "A family mediator shall maintain the confidentiality of all information acquired in the mediation process, unless the mediator is permitted or required to reveal the information by law or agreement of the participants." Application of these standards, of course, may be affected by laws, rules, or contractual agreements.[8]

The UMA contains detailed provisions regarding mediation confidentiality. On March 25, 2021, Georgia became the 11th state to adopt all or most of the terms of the UMA, joining Hawaii, Idaho, South Dakota, Vermont, Utah, Ohio, Washington, New Jersey, Iowa, Illinois, Nebraska, and the District of Columbia. However, even among the states that have adopted it, many have added, deleted, or altered confidentiality provisions, creating exceptions and limiting the scope of the confidentiality protections in the UMA.[9] Often the state variations involve confidentiality of mediation statements in child abuse and neglect proceedings. In Nebraska and Ohio, for example, there is an absolute exception to confidentiality (i.e., "no privilege") for a mediation communication that is a threat or statement of a plan to inflict bodily injury or commit a crime of violence; intentionally

8. *See*, *e.g.*, Sheridan v. Sheridan, 247 N.J. Super. 552 (Ch. Div. 1990).

9. ABA Model Standards of Conduct for Mediators, at i (1995): "Various aspects of a mediation, including some matters covered by these Standards, may also be affected by applicable law, court rules, regulations, other applicable professional rules, mediation rules to which the parties have agreed and other agreements of the parties. These sources may create conflicts with, and may take precedence over, these Standards. However, a mediator should make every effort to comply with the spirit and intent of these Standards in resolving such conflicts." *See also* Model Standards of Practice for Family and Divorce Mediation (2000), promulgated by The Association of Family and Conciliation Courts, The Family Law Section of the American Bar Association, National Council of Dispute Resolution Organizations (NCDRO) as well as many other organizations. https://www.afccnet.org/Resource-Center/Practice-Guidelines.

used to plan a crime, attempt to commit a crime, or conceal an ongoing crime or ongoing criminal activity; sought or offered to prove or disprove a claim or complaint of professional misconduct or malpractice filed against a mediator; sought or offered to prove or disprove a claim or complaint of professional misconduct or malpractice filed against a mediation party, nonparty participant, or representative of a party based on conduct occurring during a mediation; or sought or offered to prove or disprove abuse, neglect, abandonment, or exploitation in a proceeding in which a child or adult protective services agency is a party.[10] California's statutory scheme, which is arguably the most protective of mediation confidentiality in the world, does not exempt any such statements from mediation confidentiality. Most states currently have some statute that addresses mediation confidentiality, even if simply to distinguish state guidelines from the UMA. State laws and court rules on the subject vary widely in scope, approach, and application.[11]

There are a wide range of possible consequences (formal, informal, serious, and nominal) for disclosing information inside or outside court proceedings protected by mediation confidentiality. In states where confidentiality in mediation is protected by statute, such conduct may be sanctionable by the court. It could form the basis for a mistrial. It could anger the judicial officer or compromise your client's credibility or your own. It could undoubtedly impact the willingness of the opposing party or counsel to participate in settlement discussions or mediation with you in the future. If egregious enough, it can result in dismissal of the case with prejudice.[12] Of course, in states where mediation confidentiality is still not protected by statute, such as New York state, consequences are nominal, at best.

For state-by-state information about privacy policies vis-à-vis court records, see the National Center for State Courts website:
https://ncsc.contentdm.oclc.org/digital/collection/accessfair/id/203/.

CONFLICTING PUBLIC POLICIES

Though confidentiality can be a key benefit and a selling point of mediation, there are instances in which it conflicts directly with other compelling public policies such as transparency of process, full financial disclosure, attorney professional responsibility, and even the promotion of fairness of result and treatment of parties. Where mediation confidentiality conflicts with other important public policies, there are potential pitfalls as well as opportunities for sophisticated, client-centered lawyering. As a result, states such as New York have erred on the side of caution, stalling Senate Bill S1017 (that seeks to adopt the UMA) in committee review since 2017.

---

10. *See* California Law Revision Comm'n, Memorandum 2014-24, http://www.clrc.ca.gov/pub/2014/MM14-24.pdf.

11. Dorcas Quek Anderson, Piercing the Veil of Confidentiality in Mediation to Ensure Good Faith Participation—An Untenable Position?, 31 Sing. Acad. L.J. 713 (2019).

12. Ohio Rev. Code 2710.05; NE ST § 25-2935(a)(7). The numerous state statutes address mediation confidentiality and mediator protections and "are remarkable both for their variations in approach and the narrow subject matters to which they apply."

For example, in states with laws that are highly protective of mediation confidentiality, it may be virtually impossible for clients to set aside mediated agreements—even those that turn out, for example, to have been based on inaccurate or incomplete financial disclosures. This is because much of the evidence on which a set-aside claim would necessarily be based (e.g., what was disclosed and when) is protected by mediation confidentiality and therefore is inadmissible in court.[13] Buyer's remorse is frequent in family law settlements, and before entering mediation, you need to advise your clients in advance that it will not be easy for them to "undo" deals once they are done.

Similarly, even potentially incompetent advice rendered to a client by an attorney may be covered by mediation confidentiality and thus inadmissible to show attorney malpractice.[14] This means you should inform your client before starting a mediation that by participating they may essentially be relinquishing claims for malpractice against you. Most clients would not otherwise understand that their agreement to mediate their family law matter could operate as a legal malpractice waiver. As fiduciaries, with ethical obligations to bring to clients' attention areas in which your own interests conflict or may conflict with theirs, you should disclose this issue and obtain informed client consent before proceeding with mediation. A sample letter to your client setting out these risks before entering mediation is contained in the Resources section.

On the other hand, a 2014 federal bad faith insurance case in California not only admitted mediation communication when there was no objection during the trial, but also went further to say that any objection would have been overruled because the mediation statements were necessary to rule on whether the parties were acting in bad faith and for the court to understand why a settlement could not be reached.[15]

---

13. J. Michael Hand v. Walnut Valley Sailing Club, Case No. 11-3228 (10th Cir., Apr. 4, 2012). (No sanction short of dismissal "would adequately admonish [Mr. Hand] for his complete disregard for and willful violation of the confidentiality rule, deter similar conduct by others in the future, restore respect for [the] Court's authority, repair the damage caused by [Mr. Hand] to the integrity of the Court's ADR program, and minimize prejudice"); Paranzino v. Barnett Bank, 690 So. 2d 725 (1997).

14. A California case, *Lappe v. Super. Ct.*, 232 Cal. App. 4th 774 (2014), however, held that statutorily mandated financial disclosures are not "prepared for the purpose of mediation" within the meaning of the confidentiality provisions in the California Evidence Code and therefore those provisions do not apply. The trial court had determined that the California Supreme Court's rejection of judicially crafted exceptions to mediation confidentiality, coupled with the parties' stipulated agreement precluding discovery or admission of their mandated financial disclosure statements, meant that those disclosure statements were protected by mediation confidentiality. Presumably, any statement other than one reflected on a mandated financial disclosure would be protected.

15. Cassell v. Super. Ct. (Wasserman, Comden, Casselman & Pearson, LLP), 51 Cal. 4th 113 (2010) (California Supreme Court holds that mediation confidentiality protections extend to communications made outside mediation between a disputant and his or her attorney.).

EXCEPTIONS TO MEDIATION CONFIDENTIALITY

You must advise your clients that mediation confidentiality is not absolute. Even in states with broad confidentiality protections, confidentiality does not attach in every context and various exceptions exist. In most jurisdictions, for example, confidentiality can be overruled by duties imposed on mediators to report child abuse[16] or criminal acts, by constitutional rights of defendants in criminal cases, or by other requirements, regardless of the parties' agreements.

Evidence otherwise admissible or subject to discovery outside mediation or mediation consultation does not always become inadmissible or protected from disclosure solely by reason of its introduction or use in a mediation or mediation consultation.[17] Legislators are understandably loath to have mediation used as a pretext to shield materials from disclosure in other situations.

Many statutory schemes governing mediation confidentiality apply only to legal proceedings. This is an important limitation, for oftentimes no law prohibits your client or client's spouse from disclosing through mainstream or social media what took place during mediation. Your client must be informed that there is no legal bar stopping the client's spouse or another participant in the mediation from talking about such matters with business or professional colleagues, extended family members, or friends and others in the neighborhood or religious community. If parties want to bargain for confidentiality agreements to cover these nonlegal contexts, they are generally free to do so in a separate confidentiality or nondisclosure agreement that needs to be negotiated before the mediation begins or during the mediation itself. The use of Non-Disclosure Agreements to supplement confidentiality statutes is quite prevalent in mediations, especially those involving businesses with non-spouse owners.

Recently, the increased use of Zoom, Microsoft Teams, and other videoconferencing programs as part of the mediation process has given rise to new questions about confidentiality. Mediated sessions taking place virtually might be differently susceptible to third-party intrusion, recording, and other logistical breaches of confidentiality that have yet to be addressed in practice and ethics codes among mediators and professional institutions in various jurisdictions. While some practitioners have started addressing such technological loopholes in their retainer agreements, formal protocols surrounding confidentiality in the virtual arena are still in formation. You might wish to review the Bonus Chapter discussing Online mediations.

Given the complexities of mediation confidentiality and its exceptions, counseling a client simply that "mediation is confidential" and leaving it at that will not result in full informed consent by clients and arguably falls below the standard of care.

---

16. Milhouse v. Travelers Com. Ins. Co., F. Supp. 2d (C.D. Cal. 2013). As of the date of publication, this case is pending in the Federal Ninth Circuit Court of Appeals, case numbers 13-56959 and 13-57029.

17. *See* Art Hinshaw, *Mediators as Mandatory Reporters of Child Abuse: Preserving Mediation's Core Values*, 34(2) Fla. St. U. L. Rev. (2007), https://ir.law.fsu.edu/cgi/viewcontent.cgi?referer=&httpsredir=1&article=1177&context=lr.

SETTLEMENT AGREEMENTS

If a settlement is reached during mediation, can a party introduce the settlement agreement in a court proceeding for enforcement? It depends. With 50 state jurisdictions in addition to federal jurisdiction, there is no uniform or cohesive body of law governing the enforcement of settlement agreements achieved through a mediation process in the United States.[18]

Although there is strong policy protecting mediation confidentiality, an equally strong policy promotes the enforcement of settlement agreements. After all, as cases are diverted to alternative dispute resolution (ADR), including mediation, court efficiency improves. Reduced caseloads, in turn, increase the public's satisfaction with the judicial branch as other matters move through the system more efficiently.[19] Section 6 of the Uniform Mediation Act provides that a written agreement signed by all parties is an exception to mediation confidentiality. This kind of confidentiality exception enables litigants to rely on a written settlement agreement produced in mediation and to bring it to the court for enforcement even when the agreement is the result of a confidential mediation.

There is a general consensus that the UMA requirement of a written agreement, which makes evidence of oral agreements inadmissible, is correct and will eliminate many disputes and many situations in which mediation confidentiality would be breached.[20]

Whether you are acting as the mediator or representing a party in mediation, there are practical steps you can take to help maximize the likelihood that a mediated agreement will be admissible and enforceable in court. These include:

---

18. *See, e.g.*, Cal. Evid. Code § 1120; *see also* https://www.nysenate.gov/legislation/bills/2017/s1017.

19. www.arbitralwomen.org/files/publication/5809170924333.pdf, at 37. *See* Peter Robinson, *Centuries of Contract Common Law Can't Be All Wrong: Why the UMA's Exception to the Mediation Confidentiality in Enforcement Proceedings Should Be Embraced and Broadened*, J. Disp. Resol. 135 (2003); Peter Thompson, *Enforcing Rights Generated in Court Connected Mediation—Tension between the Aspirations of a Private Facilitative Process and the Reality of the Public Adversarial Justice*, 19 Ohio St. J. Disp. Resol. 509 (2004); Ellen Deason, *Enforcing Mediated Settlement Agreements: Contract Law Collides with Confidentiality*, 35 UC Davis L. Rev. 33 (2001); Alla Roytberg, *Mediating the Multicultural Fugue of Divorce Mediation*, 5 NYSBA 72 (2012).

20. *See In re* Tft-Lcd (Flat Panel) Antitrust Litigation, U.S. District Court (N.D. Cal.), Multi-District Litigation, Case No. M 07-1827 SI, C 12-02214 SI, relating to Sony Electronics Inc. et al. v. HannStar Display Corp. (Dec. 3, 2013). Sony had moved for summary judgment, alleging HannStar had reneged on a commitment to pay a confidential settlement sum proposed by a mediator and arguing that a series of emails between the parties and their mediator formed a binding contract that was admissible in evidence to prove breach. The court "reluctantly" denied summary judgment, holding that because the emails did not affirmatively provide that the agreement the parties reached was enforceable or binding, mediation confidentiality rendered the purported settlement agreement inadmissible. It stated, "although it may be inequitable to permit HannStar to avoid its agreement to settle, such inequity alone does not permit the Court to fashion a new exception to the mediation confidentiality statute. Rather, because the parties failed to include an affirmative statement to the effect that they intended their settlement to be enforceable or binding, the e-mails are inadmissible as evidence of settlement." The moral of this story is that failure to include the "magic words" can sometimes lead to catastrophic consequences.

1. Make sure all of the material terms of the parties' agreement are included and clearly stated.
2. Include a statement that the parties intend the agreement to be binding and enforceable by the court and/or that the court shall retain jurisdiction over the parties to enforce the settlement until it is fully performed.
3. Include provisions expressly addressing the admissibility of the agreement in evidence in any enforcement proceeding.[18]
4. Include provisions expressly addressing whether mediation confidentiality will be waived and, if so, to what extent in any enforcement proceeding.
5. Include representations by the parties as to capacity, access to legal counsel, voluntariness, authority to act, and lack of duress.
6. Have the parties individually, as well as counsel, sign the settlement agreement.

PRACTICE TIPS

1. Advise clients about the strict confidentiality protections in mediation.
2. Understand the specific laws/rules governing mediation confidentiality in your jurisdiction, including what constitutes a "mediation" for confidentiality purposes? When does it begin and when does it end? Who is covered? What communications are covered? Does the protection attach only in the context of civil litigation, or is it broader?
3. Ask clients whether they have any concerns about confidentiality. If they do, ascertain the specific nature of those concerns.
4. Contract specifically in the mediation agreement regarding mediation confidentiality. For example, when mediating on Zoom or another videoconference or teleconference platform, specific provisions in an agreement to mediate should recite whether parties agree that they shall (1) not record the mediation sessions, (2) not have other off-screen or off-phone participants listen to the mediation sessions; and so on.
5. Obtain and document informed consent from clients on mediation confidentiality issues.
6. Draft mediated settlement agreements carefully to anticipate and forestall conflicts between confidentiality and enforcement.
7. In addition to any law promoting mediation confidentiality, make sure all parties, counsel, mediator (and co-mediators), and other participants (experts, family members, business associates) sign a separate mediation confidentiality agreement.
8. Advise clients that the mediator's role is to facilitate settlement and that the mediator cannot later be a witness in court.
9. Advise clients that they cannot rely on deals made or later use communication between spouses outside the presence of the mediator if those deals or communication are not written up or if counsel of record do not sign off.
10. Make sure the mediator follows the confidentiality rules in the mediation contract and conduct and takes steps to ensure that all mediation communication and writings are marked as confidential. For example, ask the media-

tor to put the following header on all summary letters and draft agreement: "Confidential and Inadmissible: Prepared During the Course of Mediation."

11. Attempt to negotiate a mediated case management protocol regarding negotiations of ultimate settlement terms and resolution of discovery, law and motion, and other contested pretrial issues.
12. Advise clients that evidence existing before a mediation will not be immune from disclosure if used in a mediation, for better or for worse.
13. Be prepared to guide your client and even participate in sessions as a non-adversarial resource and coach to improve the quality of the agreements reached so that difficult challenges to confidentiality and mediation settlements will not be necessary.
14. Never ask the mediator to offer court testimony in any form (written or oral) about the mediation. If mediation terminates and the matter is litigated, be prepared with legal authority to object to any testimony offered by the mediator and put the mediator and other party/lawyer on notice of your position. Remember, written affidavits and declarations by a mediator are still testimony.
15. Be cognizant that lawyers or parties may still be permitted to testify about the conduct during a mediation as long as mediation communications are excluded.
16. Make sure parties understand that there is no binding deal unless both parties (and counsel of record) sign a written agreement. The written settlement agreement should unambiguously and directly express the parties' intent to be bound and to permit disclosure and enforcement of the signed mediated agreement in a court of law and to request the court to enforce the provisions of the settlement reached in mediation.
17. If there are essential issues to be worked out after a basic agreement in principle has been reached, take the time to resolve those issue on the day of the mediation or schedule a return session.
18. Never represent to court that a matter is resolved in mediation unless all essential drafting terms have been worked out.
19. Advise your client never to initial or sign any document unless it is first reviewed by you and make sure the client knows that such document may be admissible in court as a binding agreement.
20. Advise your client prior to starting mediation that attorney negligence during a mediation may be inadmissible in a subsequent malpractice or fee dispute with a client even if such conversations are not in the presence of a mediator.
21. In online mediations, pay special attention to confidentiality issues and request specific agreement and affirmation from participants that no one will be participating offscreen whose presence has not been disclosed.

CHAPTER 4

Representing Clients in Court-Ordered Mediation

". . . THE COURT on its own volition finds that reducing conflict through a process that promotes an amicable agreement on the issues is in the best interest of the parties, therefore both parties are required to attend mediation to resolve the contested issues."

—Order of Referral to Family Court Mediation,
First Judicial Circuit of Florida

"In an effort to provide an expeditious, expense-saving, fair and beneficial alternative to traditional litigation in the resolution of domestic relations controversies, these rules establish a program of court-annexed mediation which shall operate in cases pending in the Domestic Relations Division of the Circuit Court of Cook County. Parties and their representatives are required to attend mediation sessions, but are not compelled to reach an agreement. The program includes mediators employed by Cook County and private mediators. In addition, the parties may agree to utilize other forms of alternative dispute resolution ('ADR')."

—Cook County (IL) Circuit Court Rule 13.4(e)

"Most civil disputes are resolved without filing a lawsuit, and most civil lawsuits are resolved without a trial. The courts and others offer a variety of Alternative Dispute Resolution (ADR) processes to help people resolve disputes without a trial. ADR is usually less formal, less expensive, and less time-consuming than a trial."

— California Courts Website (www.courts.ca.gov/programs-adr.htm)

Many jurisdictions have court-mandated mediation requiring litigants to participate. In court programs, the mediation takes place in either the courthouse or the office of a court- referred or contract mediator. The mediation might be conducted by court staff mediators, private providers under contract with the court, or pro bono volunteer mediators. In the National Standards of Court Connected

Mediation Programs (called National Standards from now on),[1] the exclusive use of volunteer mediators is discouraged. Concerns abound about whether the exclusive use of volunteer mediators discourages expert mediators from participating in court-connected programs, relegating participants in court-connected mediation programs to the assistance of novice providers alone, regardless of the complexities of the issues at hand. While child custody and visitation are the issues most often mandated by court-annexed or court-referred mediation, some court systems provide for mediation of economic distributive issues as well (support, property, lawyer fees, and costs). With the deluge of court budget cuts in recent years, some jurisdictions' existing court mediation programs are in trouble or are being eliminated, regardless of format. Still other jurisdictions, such as the New York State Unified Court System, are reconsidering a long-standing culture of skepticism surrounding the role of court-referred mediation programs and are now implementing streamlined presumptive mediation programs for all matrimonial litigants, diverting cases from overloaded dockets to the desks of alternative conflict resolvers.

COURT-ANNEXED MEDIATION

Court-annexed mediation is authorized by either statute or local court rule. Sometimes individual judges impose the requirement in their own courtrooms. *Mandatory* generally means the parties are required to participate in mediation before a court hearing is permitted, except in rare emergencies or with a waiver by the court. *Mandatory* does not mean that the parties are required to reach agreement, only that they must participate meaningfully (yes, we struggle to define "meaningfully").

Are Mandatory Mediation Proceedings Confidential?

There are major differences in how confidentiality is handled throughout the U.S. In some jurisdictions, all mediation communication is protected by confidentiality. Any disclosure of mediation communication to the court may be subject to contempt, monetary sanctions, or other judicially discretionary remedies. Any issues that remain unsettled can be resolved by the court. However, even in jurisdictions that preserve confidentiality, statutorily mandated reporting of endangering subject matter such as allegations or mediator suspicion of child violence or sexual abuse, physical danger to a party or third person, or threats to commit crimes may be reported to law enforcement or the court by mediation participants (including the mediator). Therapists often have a duty to report child abuse or domestic violence whenever it is discovered (even when they are not acting as treating therapists). Lawyers have an opposite duty of confidentiality,

1. Press Release, Hon. Lawrence K. Marks, NYUCS, Court System to Implement Presumptive Early Alternative Dispute Resolution or Civil Cases (May 14, 2019), https://ww2.nycourts.gov/sites/default/files/document/files/2019-05/PR19_09_0.pdf.

and generally may not report past criminal acts or abuse if revealed by a client in professional conversation. Lawyer/mediators serving in a court mediation program may be required to report such harmful behavior; private lawyer/mediators, however, generally do not have a right or duty to report unless so authorized in advance by written agreement or unless there is reasonable suspicion of imminent harm to a mediation participant or to others. This area remains in flux and needs further study and standardization.

In nonconfidential jurisdictions, if agreement is not reached, the mediator may be asked by the judge to give a report, including observations, findings, and recommendations. Depending on the jurisdiction and the judicial officer involved, the mediator report may be given in writing, orally in open court subject to cross-examination, or on camera on or off the record. In California, neighboring counties may have very different rules regarding confidentiality. For example, Los Angeles County has confidential child-custody mediation, whereas Ventura (immediately north) is nonconfidential. Absent a statute authorizing nonconfidentiality, such jurisdictions operate contrary to the confidentiality proscriptions of 8.1(e) and to 12.1–3 of the National Standards, which limits communication by a mediator to the court, and contrary to 11.5, which warns against a court's adverse response to non-settlement by the parties.[2] In New York, no standardized approach has been codified to date.

When Does Court-Annexed Mediation Take Place?

Jurisdictions vary widely as to the required timing of the mediation. Mediation may take place as late as the date of the hearing. Progressive jurisdictions require mediation soon after an action is filed; a few courts require mediation before a hearing date is set. Rules may differ from courtroom to courtroom within the same jurisdiction or differ based on the type of issue involved.

Who Participates in Court-Annexed Mediation?

Absent extraordinary circumstances like the pandemic, in which many court mediation programs went online, litigants were generally required to be physically present at the mediation. (The acceptance of hybrid and virtual settings might, however, remain the norm long after memories of the culture-shifting pandemic have dimmed.) Lawyers may or may not be permitted to participate in the sessions, whether in person or online. In some jurisdictions, lawyers are present at the beginning to set out the issues and give their perspectives. Parties are always permitted to consult with their attorneys at any stage of the mediation as attorneys may wait in the hall or be available by telephone during the mediation.

2. National Standards of Court Connected Mediation Programs § B.4 [hereinafter Nat'l Standards].

Try Not to Second-Guess the Mediator or Micromanage the Process

With the best of motives, many lawyers have a difficult time letting go and trusting their clients and the mediator to get the job done without them. It's a bit of a control struggle. Most lawyers like control and struggle in the role of a non-playing coach; they want to peel off their warm-ups and join the huddle! Here is one example:

After successfully resolving approximately 100 issues and sub-issues, Mike and Karen were down to the last issue: would spousal support be subject to downward modification if Karen cohabited romantically with another person? Both parties knew that under the law, such cohabitation was a statutory basis for reduction of spousal support because there is a presumption of reduced need on the part of the payee spouse. Karen had already agreed to shave two years off her support period and was not willing to further compromise her financial health during a possible future cohabitation. Karen was adamant on this point.

Mike's lawyer, screaming from the sidelines, was coaching him to hold firm: "She can't have it both ways. Every judge in the courthouse would reduce spousal support—many would even terminate payments—if a payee spouse lives with a member of the opposite sex." The lawyer called the mediator, faxed her, even bent her ear when they ran into each other picking tomatoes at the local farmer's market.

The twist in the story is that Mike wanted to wrap up the mediation, and he could even understand Karen's concerns. However, he was nervous and afraid—afraid of his own financial future, afraid of letting down his lawyer, afraid of looking like an emasculated wimp (Karen was the moving party in the divorce). He needed to talk out his concern and think aloud about his future.

Mike then met with the mediator three times in private caucus—90 minutes each time. At the end, he was willing to concede the issue. He just wanted recognition from his wife that she appreciated his movement, that he was a good guy. Mike's lawyer was upset to the very end, but both Mike and Karen moved on with their lives.

In some court mediations involving financial issues, the parties themselves may not be permitted to be in the mediation room or to speak directly to the other party or to the mediator. The lawyers alone might mediate and involve the clients only if an impasse occurs on one or more issues. In such models, the lawyers shuffle in and out of the mediation room, meet with their clients, and then return to the mediation room.

New spouses or nonmarried partners of the parties may be allowed to participate in mediation sessions if the mediator deems them necessary and/or helpful. In such situations, there may be a conflict. Quite often a problem between a new romantic partner and a party is driving the litigation. In such cases, opening up participation can be instrumental in achieving resolution because the concerns of the new romantic partner could be surfaced—and resolved.

Do the Parties Meet Individually or Together with the Mediator?

Based on the needs and requests of the parties, the mediator determines the agenda of the session and whether the sessions are to be individual or conjoint. It is common for the mediator to use several configurations within a single mediation:

meet together, alone with each party shuttling in and out several times, jointly again, with or without counsel—the combinations are endless. Some considerations for joint and separate sessions are outlined in the following table.

	Joint	**Separate**
Party Selection	Some jurisdictions do not permit party opt-outs from an initial joint mediation session.	Some jurisdictions do not permit party opt-outs from an initial joint mediation session.
Court/ Jurisdictional Policy	Some jurisdictions, such as NY, mandate joint sessions for at least the first 90 minutes of a court-referred mediation session.	Some jurisdictions allow parties to select their preferred way of engaging in the mediation process, including selection of separate session work.
Domestic Violence	Most jurisdictions currently bar parties from participating in joint sessions. Some jurisdictions are now evaluating whether joint mediation sessions might become an option if sessions are entirely virtual.	Some jurisdictions still bar parties from participating in mediation, even in separate sessions.
Mediator Selection	Some jurisdictions mandate that parties participate in at least one joint mediation session, regardless of the mediator's preference.	Some jurisdictions defer to the mediator's preferences and have no bar against caucused or fully separate sessions utilizing shuttle diplomacy.

In cases of alleged physical or sexual abuse, statutory authority or local practice may require that the parties not meet in joint sessions and/or can only attend mediation in separate sessions when requested by the alleged victim for physical protection or to prevent coercion or duress. In California, for example, a statutory scheme expressly permits the victim to have a support person or advocate in the mediation session to increase security and emotional support, and confers a right to insist that the parties not meet together.[3]

In New York, a history of domestic violence or the existence of standing orders of protections typically disqualifies a case from being eligible for a court referral to mediation. However, some New York mediators receiving court-referred cases have reported receiving referrals featuring parties with full stay away orders of protection and have proceeded despite such standing orders due to the fact that meetings could be conducted in joint session, online, with parties safely logging in from different locations. While controversial, the bar has not been absolute.

3. Cal. Fam. Code § 6303 (amended by Stats. 2019, ch. 115, sec. 62. (AB 1817) effective Jan. 1, 2020).

How Are Mediated Agreements Finalized?

Many jurisdictions have the parties recite their agreement reached in mediation verbally to a judge, at which time the judge can turn the mediation agreement into a court order after allocution. Some court models include the mediator working with the parties to finalize the agreement in writing. In other situations, the lawyers will draft the court stipulation and the mediator will participate only in case of drafting trouble. Some jurisdictions, such as Los Angeles County, have a cooling-off period for court ordered custody and visitation mediations that permits either party to revoke an agreement reached in court-ordered mediation for any reason within a specified number of days; otherwise, such written agreement reached in mediation and signed by the parties automatically becomes an order of the court. Courts must determine whether a cooling-off period is waivable. A revoked agreement reached in mediation is generally inadmissible in any future court proceeding (check local practices to ascertain whether revoked agreements remain in the court file or otherwise accessible to the parties, the public or the judicial officer). New York has no such revocation period.

Some of the different ways of finalizing mediated agreements are outlined in the following table.

Oral	Written
Parties recite their agreements orally to a judge in court and the judge incorporates the recitation in the court order.	Mediators work with the parties to draft the final agreement, in writing, which is then signed and notarized.
	Mediators work with lawyers representing each party to draft the stipulations emanating from the mediated conclusions, which are then signed or allocuted.
Revocation Period:	Some jurisdictions permit parties to revoke an agreement reached in mediation within a specific period of time, after which the agreement is in full force and effect.

What Happens If a Party Refuses to Participate in a Mediation Required by the Court?

This is also an area of great variation. The general minimum requirement is for the parties to appear in person before the mediator, although this basic compliance is sometimes waived due to hardship (cross-country residence or illness), or the emergency nature of issues requiring an immediate hearing, or just because the judicial officer has an open courtroom in which to start a hearing or otherwise grants an exception. Waivers have become increasingly rare as parties with certain geographic and logistical limitations that previously warranted a waiver are now expected to appear virtually. Failure to appear at mediation may be sanctionable.[4] Even in 2005, John Lande noted that at least 22 states had statutes

4. Dude v. Cong. Plaza, LLC, 17-CV-80522, 2018 WL 4203886 (S.D. Fla. Aug. 29, 2018). *See also* Black v. Sakelios, No. CA2013-10-094 (C.A. Ohio, June 16, 2014) (A death in the family was

requiring good-faith participation in mediation, although a thorough understanding of what that entails has been inconsistent and hotly debated.[5]

Once the parties show up, jurisdictions vary in the extent to which they monitor what actually happens in the mediation. In nonconfidential jurisdictions where the mediator is permitted to make a recommendation, the mediator often informs the judge when a party refuses to participate (and may identify the culprit). In some confidential jurisdictions, as long as the parties physically appear, the mediation requirement is fulfilled even if they stay less than five minutes and sit silent like sphinxes. Other models leave it up to the mediator to release the parties after there has been "meaningful participation," an intentionally vague term. If a party merely articulates a position, no matter how unreasonable, does this constitute meaningful participation? What if a party literally shouts down the other so that neither side can be heard?

Commentary to section 5.1 of the National Standards takes the view that participants must show up but need not negotiate an agreement to avoid inappropriate pressure to settle:

> . . . the intention of the Standard is to clarify that by referring parties to mediation on a mandatory basis a court should require only that they attend an initial mediation session, discuss the case, and be educated about the process in order to make an informed choice about their continued participation.[6]

It is difficult to define meaningful participation in the mediation context. The National Standards provide for courts to establish deadlines that may be extended if continuation is found to assist resolution. Such vague requirements, however, do not provide the parties with sufficient guidance on what constitutes compliance and suggest the difficulty of defining meaningful participation.

Possible sanctions for failure to participate in good faith in mediation, depending on the jurisdiction, include attorney fee awards, payment of other reasonable expenses incurred due to failure to appear, civil or criminal contempt, revocation of counsel's pro hac vice status, a stay of proceedings pending compliance with court orders for mediation, entry of default judgment, preclusion of claims, or even dismissal with prejudice. At the very least, absent some compelling explanation, such conduct is likely to create a negative impression in the eyes of the bench officer, especially in the custody and visitation context.

Courts have not hesitated, sometimes sua sponte, to sanction a party that did not abide by certain fundamental courtesies that went beyond filing the required

---

a sufficient reason for a party to miss a court-ordered mediation, but failure to let the mediator or other side know was nonetheless grounds for imposing sanctions); Rommel v. Torpey, No. 68804-9-I (C.A. Wash., Apr. 28, 2014) (trial court did not err in dismissing ill plaintiff's case after she twice failed to participate in court-ordered mediation); U.S. Bank v. Sawyer, 2014 ME 81 (S.C. Me., June 24, 2014) (Supreme Court of Maine upheld the dismissal with prejudice of a complaint, following a warning, after multi-session mediation in which party exhibited lack of good faith).

5. John Lande, *Why a Good-Faith Requirement Is a Bad Idea for Mediation*, 23 Alternatives To High Cost Litig. 1 (2005).

6. Nat'l Standards § 5.1 cmt.

documents and showing up with the proper representatives, as in *Dude v. Congress Plaza, LLC.*[7]

According to James Coben's 2019 article "Evaluating the Singapore Convention through a US Centric Litigation Lens: Lessons Learned from Nearly Two Decades of Mediation Disputes in American Federal and State Courts, "In 1999–2003 . . . sanctions were a topic of disputing [mediation issues] 10% of the time" whereas between 2013 and 2017, disputes about sanctions only occurred 4 percent of the time, suggesting that the ordering of sanctions due to a failure to participate in court-ordered mediation became increasingly accepted.[8]

What Issues Are Covered by Court-Annexed Mediation?

In many states, the only issues subject to mandatory mediation are custody and visitation disputes. In some states, the court mediation service (often inaptly named *conciliation court*) can be utilized for marriage counseling, domestic violence, or other issues of personal conduct and communication. Many court systems have mandatory parental educational components ranging from the required viewing of a video to a required lecture, classes, or training in parenting or divorced-couple communication that could span several weeks.

In Los Angeles County, parents participating in required custody mediation must watch a brief mediation orientation video called *Our Children First* and file proof of completion with the court. Due to budget constraints, classes have been replaced with online mini-courses in many jurisdictions. Los Angeles County's "Between Two Parents" program, for example, is a six-week-long online course in the form of a simulated workshop in which common co-parenting disputes are illustrated and addressed. The course is primarily intended for high-conflict situations, and participation has to be court ordered. Parties must wait a week between sessions, as there are exercises and assignments to complete following each session. The PEACE Program developed by Professor Andrew Schepard of Hofstra University, Hempstead, New York, is probably the nation's most comprehensive parent education program. Some courts require court mediation for the financial distributive issues, such as child support, spousal support, allocation of assets and debts, and disputes over payment of costs and lawyer fees. In court programs limited to children's issues, parents generally may not bring up economic issues. In other courts, staff mediators will be limited to custody/visitation, but economic issues may be mediated by volunteer lawyers or others selected by a community bar association. In such court programs, qualifications and training of mediators vary widely, as do the techniques utilized.

---

7. Dude v. Cong. Plaza. LLC, 17-CV-80522, 2018 WL 4203886 (S.D. Fla. Aug. 29, 2018) (ordering sanctions of $41,712 after deeming a plaintiff's refusal to attend court-ordered mediation due to "little knowledge of the facts" and a cardiologist's advice that participation might "trigger potentially life threatening cardiac arrhythmias" a failure to attend and participate in good faith). The court referred to Fed. R. Civ. P. 16, as well as the court's "inherent power" to "achieve the orderly and expeditions disposition of cases" which allows sanctions for bad faith.

8. James Coben, *Evaluating the Singapore Convention through a U.S.-Centric Litigation Lens: Lessons Learned from Nearly Two Decades of Mediation Disputes in American Federal and State Courts*, 20 Cardozo J. Conflict Resol. 1063 (2019).

MEDIATION BY COURT REFERRAL

An approach used in many jurisdictions is the mandatory referral of the parties to a mediator outside the courthouse. In some schemes, court-referred mediation replaces hearing-day mediation; in others, it supplements the courthouse system. Some mediators are paid by the court system or by the parties themselves, and others volunteer their time through community mediation programs. The mediations may be time-limited (one or two hours) or left to the mediator's discretion and largesse. Some systems let parties select their mediator from a list, with the judicial officer assigning mediation only in case of impasse. In others, the assignment of the mediator is imposed and final, except for challenge due to legal grounds (i.e., bias or conflict of interest). Just as in courthouse programs, the issues, mediator skill, experience, and dispute resolution processes vary greatly. The National Standards recognize mandatory referral outside the court and underscore the court responsibility of such mediators to report information to the court to permit monitoring. The standards urge courts to set up a complaint mechanism. The standards also encourage the parties to have the right to substitute a private mediator unless a court specifically prohibits it. How the mediator gets paid varies throughout the country.

A successful model for outside mediation has been developed by New Jersey through its Complementary Dispute Resolution Program (CDR), codified under Rule 1:40 of the Rules Governing the Courts of the State of New Jersey.

The New Jersey program provides for not only referral to a mediator at no charge for CDR qualified mediators but also provides for party selection of a non-court-administered program in which the mediators are compensated. New Jersey family law specialist Cary Cheifetz of Skoloff, Wolfe, reports that the program is well accepted by the Family Law Bar and has evolved beyond the initial rules:

> If the referral is made to an early settlement panel, . . . there is no fee associated; however occasionally a complex matter is referred to what is known as a blue ribbon panel, . . . i.e., two highly respected and experienced lawyers. It is customary that the panelists be compensated if the proceeding takes more than one session. It is usually negotiated among the lawyers for the parties, the judge, and the panelists. I know it sounds very informal, but our judges generally feel that non-compensation can be a burden and that there are limits to pro bono work, especially if the parties have privately retained counsel and have assets.[9]

Another growing approach is referral to an outside mediator in which the parties initially bear the costs equally at market rates or a fee determined by the court. This type of referral calls for early mediation in all civil cases with the court having the discretion to determine on good cause not to order early mediation.

---

9. New Jersey Rules of General Application 1:40, Complementary Dispute Resolution Process (adopted Sept. 1992, subparagraphs (b)(1), (b)(3), (b)(4), (b)(5), (b)(6), (b)(8), paragraph (c), and subparagraph (c)(3) amended July 30, 2021, to be effective Sept. 1, 2021.).

If this model (facetiously called a mediation work bill) continues to gain acceptance, the current oversupply of trained mediators might be transformed to a demand for many more mediators in both the courts and the private sector.

Still other models, such as that in New York, feature court referrals to credentialed outside mediators, typically attorney-mediators, that have been vetted for inclusion in a court roster. These mediators provide 90 minutes of free mediation to parties and charge a capped rate thereafter, with rate caps determined by each court on a county-by-county basis.

MALPRACTICE PROTECTION FOR COURT MEDIATORS

Many family lawyers who want to participate in court mediation may fear being sued by hostile litigants. Lawyers who volunteer their time may be particularly reluctant to offer this public service if the risk for such public service is being named in a lawsuit.

In their seminal article on court mediation, Margaret Shaw, Linda Singer, and Linda Povich summarize statutory schemes for mediation immunity and indemnification.[10]

However, the National Standards takes an anti-immunity position, finding that "granting mediators immunity from liability inappropriately denies recourse to litigants injured by incompetent service, especially when litigants are required to pay for the service." This position is in conflict with the California case of *Howard v. Drapkin*,[11] which provides quasi-judicial immunity to protect mediators and to encourage them to provide mediation for the court system, as well as more extreme iterations of immunity such as extending judicial immunity to mediators "in the same manner and same extend as a judge."[12] These malpractice policies are still works in progress.

THE ROLE OF LAWYERS IN COURT MEDIATION

Although it is becoming much less frequent today, some lawyers (particularly those with little family law experience), do not trust the court-annexed mediation process or want to use it solely as an adversarial tool. These lawyers may script their clients fully or give detailed coaching on what to accept during the mediation negotiations. They may even instruct the clients to leave the mediation room prematurely to avoid the potential for compromise and to get into a court hearing (while maintaining plausible deniability for purposes of avoiding sanctions for not participating "meaningfully").

In attempting to avoid interfering with lawyer control (often alternatively labeled a litigant's confidence in the lawyer), some mediators will abort the mediation if one or both parties seem to be in an anti-mediation trance enabled by their lawyers. Having the lawyers participate in the sessions and become part of

---

10. https://ur.booksc.me/book/10036580/28fe09.
11. Howard v. Drapkin, 222 Cal. App. 3d 843 (1990).
12. Fla. Stat. ch. 44.107, codified in 2001.

the process may be a remedy for this problem. Participation of the lawyers in the sessions may have a downside in the form of causing interference with the mediator's efforts, increasing the adversarial tone, removing control and empowerment of the parties, and increasing the complexity of the negotiation.

The court-annexed system in New Zealand addressed this problem 30 years ago by requiring the lawyers to sit behind their clients and limiting the lawyers' participation unless the clients ask to consult with them. In that instance, the clients had to take the initiative to turn 180 degrees to make eye contact with their lawyers and initiate the lawyer-client conference outside. When the mediation resumes, it is the party (not the lawyer) who carries the dialogue with the other spouse and the mediator. This practice is less prevalent today and has not caught on in this country.[13]

The Role of Lawyers in Court Mediation

The National Standards for Court-Connected Mediation Programs set out the following role for lawyers in court mediation:

> 10.1 Courts should encourage attorneys to advise their clients on the advantages, disadvantages, and strategies for using mediation.
>
> COMMENTARY: Lawyers have several possible functions to perform in connection with their clients' participation in mediation:
>
> 1. Before their clients decide whether to mediate, lawyers may give initial advice concerning whether it is in the client's best interest to participate in mediation and what substantive rights will govern if the case goes to trial.
> 2. Lawyers may attend mediation sessions and participate directly in mediation. Alternatively, they may participate indirectly by advising clients before, during or after mediation sessions.
> 3. Lawyers may review draft agreements reached in mediation or, alternatively, they may draft the agreements themselves.
> 4. Following mediation, lawyers may complete the legal process, by filing a consent decree if agreement is reached, or by continuing the pretrial process if issues remain to be resolved by the court.
> 5. If necessary, lawyers may act to enforce any agreements reached in mediation.

MANDATORY SETTLEMENT CONFERENCES

Most court systems have a built-in procedure for the parties to come to court with their lawyers to try to settle the case prior to a trial. Generally, the process includes an opportunity for at least the lawyers, and often the parties, to have some time with a judicial officer. A mandatory settlement conference (MSC) is a "late stage" process: generally held within 30 to 60 days of trial. The parties are

13. Heyo Berg, Mediation in New Zealand: Widely Accepted and Successful in Mediation: Principles and Regulation in Comparative Perspective (Jan. 2013).

expected to have completed all discovery; exchanged witness lists and documents; and received court rulings on pretrial motions such as joinder of necessary parties, summary judgments, and necessary discovery compliance. In short, prior to an MSC, lawyers and parties are expected to have explored settlement, to have completed their preparations, and to be ready for trial. To ensure that the parties are truly ready, most courts require the parties to submit in advance some form of MSC brief setting forth the facts of the case, issues in contention, a proposal for settlement with supporting argument (including legal authorities), and support documentation. This can be a very expensive process.

In progressive jurisdictions, the MSC can be effective in stopping the litigation by adopting a number of rules to facilitate settlement, inducing rules and procedures affecting judicial attitude, which include:

1. Setting MSCs early to allow sufficient time prior to the trial for meaningful negotiations that won't be aborted in favor of preparing for trial.
2. Allocating judicial resources so that the judge assigned to preside at the MSC is skilled, energetic, patient, and devoted to quality settlements.
3. It is crucial that MSC judges be freed from competing trial or administrative duties so that they can have the time and focus to serve the parties and lawyers attending the MSC.
4. Setting a low number of cases so that the MSC judge can devote sufficient time and attention to each matter.
5. Many courts utilize experienced family lawyers to serve as MSC judge pro tem or to handle less-complex matters, warm up the parties while waiting for the judge, act as a co-settlement officer with the judge, or take over the process.
6. Making sure that all people necessary to accomplish settlement are present at the MSC. Quite often a spouse's parent (holding a promissory note or being ready to fund a buyout), a business partner, a real estate broker or mortgage lender, accountant(s) (personal, business, and/or forensic), a personal injury lawyer handling a spouse's personal injury or disability claim, a child-care provider, a therapist, a vocational counselor, or another relevant person might hold the key to settlement and should be present.
7. Devote sufficient court space, auxiliary resources, and amenities to the settlement process. Private, carpeted, air-conditioned rooms with round tables and sufficient comfortable chairs for all in attendance affirm settlement as a court priority.

IS THE MSC JUDGE ALSO THE TRIAL JUDGE?

There is a difference of opinion here. Many judges and lawyers contend that the all-purpose judge system as used in the federal district courts makes parties accountable in settlement discussions because an unreasonable negotiating position that propels the case to the court will be remembered by the trial judge. Also, aware of the jurist's read of the case, parties will adopt more realistic settlement positions. The other school of thought is that by utilizing a different settlement judge, parties will be encouraged to take more expansive, creative, and less positional settlement proposals without the trial judge's being aware of such positions—thereby easing the concerns of the more polarized and inflexible party.

It should come as no surprise that many courts do not have the resources or the will to meet these proposed standards. Unfortunately, many MSCs are held within days of trial (or simultaneously on the date of trial); many cases are set on the same day—each for its own MSC; the judge's other duties often limit the time available; only the lawyers, not the parties, may see the judge (then perhaps only in separate sessions); and the parties wait on wooden benches in public corridors. Lawyer discussions are conducted (if at all) in the hallways and on the courthouse steps, driven by fatigue, frustration, and fear of continually rising costs and the impending trial.

MEDIATION VERSUS MANDATORY SETTLEMENT CONFERENCES

Even in progressive jurisdictions, many family lawyers view MSCs as synonymous with mediation. If a lawyer's client or the opposing lawyer suggests early mediation (either inside or outside the courthouse), a common response is, "Why should my client spend money to pay a mediator or pay additional lawyer fees when we'll have to mediate at the MSC anyway?"

MSCs differ from mediation in many ways, including:

The black-robed jurist (even if the robe is temporarily on a hanger) represents the court's authority, which often has an arm-twisting effect on parties. Such authority often produces settlements—based in part on reliance on that authority. Although a mediator may provide neutral legal information, including predictions of outcome in court, the mediation is premised on the parties controlling the outcome through negotiation facilitated (not controlled) by the mediator.

While the MSC judge may consider emotions and values and how the family will function after the settlement, the main motivation of the court is to settle the case and remove it from the trial docket. Therefore, the MSC judge may focus the parties on the anticipated legal outcome and encourage, persuade, and sometimes threaten the parties to accept that outcome by settlement rather than have it imposed judicially after a costly trial. According to Leonard L. Riskin and Nancy Welsh, such court-led initiatives are structured "so that litigation issues predominate; other potential issues—personal, psychological, relational, communitarian—disappear."[14]

- In mediation, the parties are encouraged to reach agreement only if it is in their best short- and long-term interest. The mediator will explore underlying fears and concerns of the parties and work with them to fashion an agreement that addresses those concerns.

14. Leonard L. Riskin & Welsh, Nancy, *Is That All There Is? "The Problem" in Court-Oriented Mediation*, 15 GEO. MASON L. REV. (2008).

- The MSC is generally held in the courthouse, and the experience is colder, more formal, more legalistic, less flexible, and less client-focused than a private mediation. Given that the vast majority of family law cases settle prior to an MSC, the ones that have not settled tend to involve structural barriers to settlement, complex interpersonal dynamics, high-conflict litigants, unreasonable or unprepared attorneys, or other challenging characteristics that drain judicial resources disproportionately and—rightly or wrongly—engender frustration on the part of judicial officers or court staff. In private mediation, only one case is set, and the mediator has been booked to devote exclusive time to this matter. The mediation starts at the appointed time (usually!!) and continues, uninterrupted by other business, for the time that was blocked off in advance.
- Many MSC judges are the best settlement judicial officers in the courthouse, and those assigned to family law MSCs often have extensive family law experience, both in practice and on the bench. The extent to which even these judicial stars have received training in progressive negotiation theory or advanced mediation techniques varies widely. In other venues, the MSC judge may have little experience in family law and thus a reluctance to embrace a proactive settlement role. In deference to the autonomy of the lawyers, or perhaps out of habitual tendency to "stay in their lane" as a finder of fact, many MSC judges throw up their hands when the settlement gap appears insurmountable rather than proactively leaning on attorneys and parties to generate movement toward settlement. Due to a crowded calendar, a narrow view of the nature and causes of conflict, an inadequate inventory of impasse-breaking skills and techniques, some judges take a quick hard look and choose to use their limited time to resolve cases that they believe have the best chance of settling. Many times this triage approach is the correct call because the case might never have settled or might have settled only after many hours of direct judicial intervention. In other situations, failure to invest the time in a tough case results in a drain of judicial time not only in the shorter term but in future post-judgment litigation as well.
- In jurisdictions where the date on which the MSC is set is also the deadline to serve witness lists and exhibit lists for trial, the clients will have already paid for a substantial level of trial preparation and will not enjoy the full economic benefit of early settlement.
- MSCs may or may not, depending on local court rules, enjoy the protections of mediation confidentiality. In Los Angeles County, for example, MSCs are not covered. The lack of a bar on admissibility for statements made during an MSC necessarily impacts what people may be willing to say, thereby constraining discussions in a manner that may work against creative resolution.

In contrast, professional mediators are specially trained in proactive settlement and are paid to ply their craft in such difficult cases. Helping the parties work through an impasse by acknowledging those areas of agreement that may be preserved even if some issues need a decision imposed by a judge is a common auxiliary mediator skill.

The MSC judge is generally free to the parties, whereas paying for a private mediator is an additional out-of-pocket cost. However, the initial cost differential needs further exploration. The preparation for an MSC in both generating quality advocacy and complying with court requirements can be very expensive. Yet, competent preparation for a mediation is prob ably not much less expensive, if at all. The major costs of an MSC are the hours and hours of waiting for available judicial input and the price of lost opportunity by lack of time or settlement expertise of the MSC judge, resulting in a trial. Also, once they have reached an equitable and enforceable agreement through mediation, the parties may be better prepared to settle follow-up matters on their own or can return to mediation to build on their prior success at resolution, resulting in major cost savings from reduced re-litigation. A generic estimate of private mediation costs is included in the Resources section.

Mediation vs. Mandatory Settlement Conferencing

Mediation	Mandatory Settlement Conferencing
Mediator presents no aura of authority and parties are in control	Robed jurist representing court authority
Mediator Goal: guide parties towards best long- and short-term outcomes reflective of party interests	MSC Goal: settle and remove from court docket
Specifically trained in proactively guiding through negotiation	Led by family law experts who might lack advanced mediation or negotiation training; triage-like style as opposed to deep structural exploration
Variable cost	Generally free, though requiring expensive and extensive legal preparation

PRACTICE TIPS

1. At the beginning of client representation, learn about the court-annexed mediation requirements and options in your jurisdiction, including timing, staffing, settlement styles of staff mediators and MSC judges, courthouse facilities, virtual mediation options and protocols, and permitted roles of counsel. If your jurisdiction requires that court-referred mediations be scheduled within a specific time period, ensure that you contact the assigned or selected mediator to begin the scheduling process immediately upon receipt of the Order of Reference from the court.
2. At the earliest available opportunity, educate the client about the philosophy and procedures in court-annexed mediation. Compare and contrast court-annexed mediation with court hearings and with dispute resolution options in the private sector.
3. If there is any emergent need to reschedule a court-annexed mediation, promptly advise the other party and the mediator both orally and in writing and make efforts to reschedule as soon as possible.

4. Confirm in writing that the client is aware of the date, time, and location of the court-annexed mediation. Send a written reminder. Parties often miss court mediations because of technical issues signing in or confusion about how to access the mediation session, especially if it is online. Where mediation is mandatory, missing it can result in delays, which significantly prejudice your client's interests. Help the client contact the mediation office in advance to get questions answered and make sure the client has all phone numbers, access codes, and equipment he or she needs in order to access the mediation session.
5. Prepare written materials and a DVD or online visual presentation to teach clients about court-annexed mediation. Encourage clients to take a field trip to the court house to gain comfort and information to make informed process decisions. In the event that your clients will be participating in a virtual mediation, provide them with links to examples of mediation sessions specific to your jurisdiction, many of which are available on YouTube.
6. Prior to the date of court mediation or an MSC, schedule a client conference to explain every anticipated step of the day's activities, including the highlighting of unknown variables (how long the day will last, which decisions will be made, and where and with whom the various configurations of discussions will take place). Discuss the need to have emotional support at the courthouse and to bring reading material and/or work to pass the time. Also stress the importance of not booking any appointments for the afternoon and arranging child care so that time or child pressures will not add to the client's anxiety.
7. Find out whether the court-annexed mediation is confidential or nonconfidential. If it is nonconfidential, carefully educate your client about the use of mediation statements and the power of the mediator to make recommendations to the judge.
8. If your client is a victim of spousal violence, consider requesting separate sessions to reduce intimidation and fear. Also advise your client to think about arranging to have an emotional support person or victim advocate. If your jurisdiction bars victims of spousal violence from participating in court-annexed mediation, advise your client accordingly.
9. During the court mediation, if lawyers are not permitted to participate, be available for client consultation in the hallway or by telephone.
10. When an MSC is scheduled, suggest the possibility of private mediation first, giving the parties two chances (with different formats) to settle.

CHAPTER 4.5

Representing Clients in Online Mediations

Susan Guthrie

> *"Zoom was the gateway drug."*
>
> Colin Rule, 2021, ODR Pioneer and CEO Mediate.com

For lawyers and dispute resolution professionals, indeed the world at large, 2020 and the pandemic was a transformational event. The type of occurrence where practitioners will always see their world as what we did before COVID, and what we do now on the other side. Central to it all was the migration to online practice and the massive acceptance of the integration of technology into the day-to-day practice of law.

In the 21st century post-pandemic, working with, and representing, clients in family law matters necessarily involves proficiency in the use of online technologies. Practitioners not only must be able and capable advocates and advisors to their clients, but they must also be well-versed in videoconferencing, the use of assistive technology, and the additional challenges that the virtual world adds into the ethics of representation. Although, as my colleague, ODR Pioneer Colin Rule, has stated, "Zoom was the gateway drug" that eased many practitioners into working online, there is much more to representing your client in an online mediation room than skill in the basics of using a videoconferencing program.

Of utmost importance is that attorneys, charged with a duty of competence in the representation of clients[1] be thoughtful and intentional throughout each phase of the online mediation experience. *The duty of competence includes competence in relevant technology.* ABA Model Rule 1.1 reads:

> A lawyer shall provide competent representation to a client. Competent representation requires the legal knowledge, skill, thoroughness and preparation reasonably necessary for the representation.

1. Model Rules of Pro. Conduct r 1.1 Competence (Am. Bar Ass'n).

In 2012, the ABA amended Comment 8 to Rule 1.1 to read (emphasis added):

> To maintain the requisite knowledge and skill, a lawyer shall keep abreast of changes in the law and its practice, *including the benefits and risks associated with relevant technology.*

Therefore, for every practitioner, the first question must be, are you competent to represent a client in an online mediation in all ways, both practical and ethical? The information in this chapter is intended to give you the basics of essential information and skills needed to meet the standards of competency, but actual practice and mastery of the technology cannot be gained by reading alone and a competent practitioner will put in the time to familiarize themselves with any and all technology being used in an online mediation.

In addition to examining your readiness to represent your client in an online mediation, attorneys must also consider whether their client is also competent to participate in an online proceeding and whether it is in your client's best interests to mediate online.

DO YOU WANT TO MEDIATE ONLINE?

One of the first questions that an attorney must consider when entering mediation with their client, is whether it is best to mediate online or to select an in-person process. There is an additional choice of a hybrid process, where some participants meet in person and others, for various reasons, appear virtually, which will be addressed later in this chapter.

While there are several factors to be considered in making this decision, the following are those that most greatly impact attorneys and clients in the process:

Pros:

- Convenience in scheduling and attendance
- The ability to work with mediators and other professionals who best suit your case not limited by geography
- Ability to participate from a comfortable and supportive environment
- Physical safety for participants is especially important in high conflict and domestic violence cases
- Less travel expense and time savings for all participants
- Ability to have all stakeholders, experts, and support people more easily available

Cons:

- Expense of necessary equipment and technology
- Technological skill needed for all participants
- A perception that the process is less personal
- Possibility of greater distractions for participants
- Technology failures can cause major disruptions of the process
- Challenges to confidentiality and privacy due to remote location of participants

These factors should be considered and reviewed by the attorney and with the client in advance of selecting a mediator and process. For many, the pros will far outweigh the cons: the good news is that with proper preparation and forethought the cons can be eliminated or substantially reduced.

HOW TO SELECT YOUR MEDIATOR FOR AN ONLINE MEDIATION

Many mediators and dispute resolution professionals shifted to online practice during the pandemic and, for most, the transition was successful. Many neutrals who successfully made the online shift learned through training, practice, and experience how to translate the in-person mediation experience into the virtual setting, and many have actually learned to optimize the process with additional technology and skills designed to enhance the virtual process.

In selecting a mediator for your online mediation, in addition to the usual considerations, it is helpful to determine the following:

- How much experience does the mediator have with online mediations? As with any practice, the more experience the mediator has with working online, the better prepared they usually will be for your mediation process.
- Has the mediator received training in online mediation, including the ethical considerations of the virtual process? With the rapid shift online necessitated by the pandemic, some practitioners sought out training in online mediation while others took a self-help approach. Neither is dispositive of a good practitioner, but a mediator who has received training in the online process is much more likely to be prepared for the difficulties presented online as well as the ethical challenges.
- What videoconferencing platform and other technology does the mediator use/offer for your mediation sessions? By far, the most popular videoconferencing platform currently used by online mediators is Zoom, with it's ease of use and mediation-friendly functionality, but there are other platforms and additional technologies that may be needed when a process is fully remote. Document transmission, communication, notetaking, document execution, and payment portals all may be required when participants are in separate physical locations. A competent online mediator will have online resources for all needed functionalities.
- Does the mediator offer a technology walk-through in advance of any online mediation sessions commencing? Many experienced online mediators will offer a "test-run" of the videoconferencing platform and/or other technology for counsel in advance of the mediation sessions so that attorneys have full understanding of the technology and can transmit that knowledge to their clients and any other participants on their side such as experts and other support personnel. Remember, the attorney is in charge of preparing each member of their team to participate in the online mediation.

- Does the mediator offer pre-mediation virtual meetings with individual attorneys and their clients? A pre-mediation meeting, especially in an online setting, provides many advantages for attorneys and their clients in a virtual mediation. This will be more fully discussed later in this chapter.
- Does the mediator provide handouts or additional information regarding the online mediation process for participants? *As stated earlier, the attorney is responsible for onboarding all of the participants on their side of the matter, including their client, in advance of the online mediation. Materials provided by the mediator, that offer guidance on that mediator's process and establish protocols, are extremely helpful in accomplishing this task.*

Taking the time to find a mediator who is experienced in online mediation and who has taken the time and effort to establish a process that is geared toward providing a seamless and smooth experience for all participants will make the role of the attorneys in the matter that much easier.

PREPARATION IS EVERYTHING

There is likely not an attorney out there that does not live by the credo "Prepare, prepare and then prepare some more," but this is never truer than when it comes to online mediation. As will be outlined in this chapter, potential pitfalls and problems may arise that are particular to an online mediation, but the truth is, with the proper preparation of all participants, those problems and pitfalls can be eliminated or greatly reduced.

EQUIPMENT AND SETUP

Computer and setup: Although videoconferencing platforms such as Zoom are designed to function on desktop and laptop computers, tablets, and smartphones, it is far preferable to participate in an online mediation on a computer for a variety of reasons. Most importantly, the view of the participants on the screen can be maximized and is largest on a computer screen. When the only view of other participants each person has is a thumbnail on a screen, the larger the better to see the nuances of expression and more. In addition, most practitioners appreciate the ability to set up additional monitors so that they can display the videoconference on one screen and have documents, programs, or other functions open on the additional monitors. This reduces the need to switch between screens on one computer.

■ **ONLINE PRO TIP:** Include more than one monitor in your computer setup for online mediations so that you can have your documents, notes, and other helpful information at your fingertips without having to switch away from the mediation session on the main screen. Many experienced online practitioners work with three or more monitors when in a mediation session. For example:

- Screen 1: Zoom platform
- Screen 2: Pleadings and other relevant paperwork
- Screen 3: Jamboard, whiteboard, Word document, ADR Notable or other program for notetaking and brainstorming
- Screen 4: Financial software such as Dissomaster, Family Law Software, and/or dtour.life

Camera/microphone/lighting: One oft-cited concern with online mediation is the loss of body-language cues due to the limitations of the video thumbnails, which generally only feature each participant from the shoulders up. While it is true that the whole-body view is not available, the vast majority of human communication is through facial expressions and audible nuance, which are both quite available in an online medium. In fact, nonverbal communication, such as facial gestures and expressions, constitutes 55 percent of our overall communication. The eyes and the mouth are the two main organs that help in reading other's faces. Eye contact can be used to show empathy and concern for others, to manage feelings, to express interest, or to help with communication.[2] With that in mind, it is important that the video and audio for each participant be crisp and clear to enhance the visual and audible cues. If not, consider investing in an external camera and microphone. One last tip: Lighting is also important so that each participant is seen clearly. Ideally a light on either side of the computer screen facing toward you or a ring light in front of you will work best. A green screen can also be helpful if you are using a virtual background to stabilize any imagery.

■ **ONLINE PRO TIP:** Eye contact is extremely important and is a skill that must be mastered online. The placement of your camera at the center top side of your screen is key and looking into the camera will give the appearance of eye contact to the other participants.

■ **ONLINE PRO TIP:** If you, your client, or one of your participants prefers to turn their video off so that they will not be visible onscreen during the mediation, be sure to consider the wisdom of that choice in light of the importance of visual cues in online communication. It may be a better choice to leave that camera on! One example to close your camera is during the parties' opening statements so that they can speak directly with each other without the interference or control of professionals.

The all-important internet connection: There is no element of the online setup that is more important than having a secure and strong internet connection. For reasons of privacy and confidentiality, which will be discussed more in-depth later in this chapter, all online mediation sessions must take place with all participants

2. Nour Mheidly, Mohamad Y. Fares, Hussein Zalzale & Jawad Fares, *Effect of Face Masks on Interpersonal Communication during the COVID-19 Pandemic*, FRONT PUB. HEALTH. 8: 582191 (2020), doi: 10.3389/fpubh.2020.582191.

joining from a secure internet connection. Because the security of a publicly available Wi-Fi connection cannot be ensured, they should not be used. In addition, there is little that is more disruptive to an online mediation than when one or more participants have a poor internet connection. The distortion of the live video feed will create unintelligible audio and a frozen or unviewable video picture. If possible, each participant should have a private ethernet or strong Wi-Fi connection installed in advance of the mediation. If one must participate from a public, remote location, a personal hotspot can provide a more stable connection than shared, public Wi-Fi.

■ **ONLINE PRO TIP:** Do not underestimate the importance of a strong internet connection. The emotional reaction of other participants to technology issues on the part of another participant can lead to unconscious or conscious feelings of irritation and bias. Make sure that you have a test run. Invest necessary money in equipment and the proper consultant.

Appearance: Some consideration should be given to your appearance, at least from the shoulders up, as you will be onscreen and visible throughout the videoconferencing process. In addition, if you get up from your desk or seated position, be aware that you will be visible on screen unless you turn off your video feed before you do so. This has led to many an embarrassing moment as pajamas, shorts, bunny slippers, and more have been inadvertently displayed in business meetings online. Although somewhat funny perhaps, this is not conducive to a professional mediation. Further, as many participants will we connecting from their homes or office settings, additional effort should be put into creating a background that is pleasant, businesslike, and neutral so as not to distract from the process. Many professionals prefer to use a virtual background, which can be branded and customized.

If using a virtual background with an older computer, you may find that the virtual background does not work well and that it seems to shimmer, waver and disappear around your image. You may wish to invest in a green screen in that event. A green screen is a relatively inexpensive piece of equipment that you set up behind your desk so that there is a uniform background for the virtual background to be set against and can eliminate the visual issues. One other option offered by Zoom and some other platforms is to blur your background while you stay in focus. This blurring effect can also defuse an unprofessional or otherwise unsuitable background.

When selecting your background, whether it be virtual or real, it is important to remember that too much visual stimulation onscreen is one factor in Zoom fatigue.[3] A busy or crowded background for a participant may lead to overstimulation for the other participants as their brains work to process the details and elements in the background. This effect is multiplied when several participants have busy backgrounds.

3. Liz Fosslien & Mollie West Duffy, *How to Combat Zoom Fatigue*, HARV. BUS. REV. (Apr. 29, 2020), https://hbr.org/2020/04/how-to-combat-zoom-fatigue.

Therefore, it is best to select a neutral and simple background, and many professionals select either a plain color as a background or an image that is non-stimulating and neutral such as a beach, office environment, or living room-type space.

Here are some examples of neutral virtual backgrounds:

Practice, practice, practice: Spend time before the mediation practicing and becoming comfortable with all of the technology and programs used by your mediator. Do not assume that you will figure it out on the day of the mediation or that the mediator will walk you through it. This includes understanding the functionality of the videoconferencing platform used by your mediator, including screensharing, chat, document transmission, breakout rooms, waiting rooms, and more. Beyond the videoconferencing program, also practice on any assistive technology that the mediator may be using such as a document execution program (i.e., Docusign, HelloSign, etc.) Each of these programs generally allows for a document or documents to be uploaded, signature and other information prompts added for the signers, and then automates forwarding the documents for execution via secure email.

Review all information and protocols received from your mediator: As mentioned earlier in this chapter, most experienced online mediators will have established protocols and informational handouts for participants. All of this information is important to a smooth mediation and often includes critical information and directives concerning ethical issues such as privacy and confidentiality.

ONBOARDING YOUR CLIENT AND TEAM MEMBERS

■ **ONLINE PRO TIP:** It is an excellent idea to establish an onboarding protocol regarding online mediations for educating clients and team members. Many attorneys will designate this task to a trusted staff member. Onboarding protocol includes an established process for getting each participant properly set up, educated, and provided an opportunity to practice in advance of any online appearance in the matter. The onboarding protocol should include the elements outlined in this chapter to ensure that clients and participants are ready for the online process. In addition, see the sample client, participant, attorney, and mediator handouts provided.

With the preparation just outlined, attorneys should be prepared to participate in the online mediation process. However, it is just as important that clients and all other participants on your team also be just as prepared, which means that you as the attorney for your client have the responsibility of ensuring that each team member is educated concerning the information provided. Equipment, including peripherals, programs, technology, and protocols, all needs to be reviewed and understood by each person. This includes your client, your staff members, your experts and witnesses, and any support people who may be a part of the mediation.

When it comes to the communications from the mediator, remember that the mediator is often limited to communicating solely with the attorneys involved so that all pertinent information must be forwarded by you to your client and participants in advance of the mediation.

Important tips and issues for client and participant education: Often the following information will be included in the communications from your mediator, but, if it is not, these are the key points to make your client and team aware of:

- **Privacy issues:** All participants should be in a private location and in a place where they cannot be overheard. With increased online activity and work-from-home as a result of the pandemic, many people have become accustomed to other people working in close proximity to them. As privacy is a valued benefit of mediation, all participants must be cautioned not to intentionally, or unintentionally, violate the privacy of the proceeding.
- **Interruptions:** Advise clients and participants to take all reasonable precautions to ensure they will be able to participate free of interruptions during the time allotted for the mediation session. Because many remote participants are located in their offices or homes for the videoconference, there is a much greater opportunity for interruptions throughout the day, so planning ahead for child care, turning off phones, and warning others that you are unavailable is helpful.
- **Technology failure protocol:** Despite all the preparation in the world, tech failures will happen. The internet may go out in your area, a computer will randomly choose to update and reboot, or a batter will die. The best plan is to have a plan and to keep it simple. Often, a directive to try to sign back in to the meeting if possible is the first step, and if unsuccessful or not possible, to call you, the attorney, on your phone or cell phone.
- **Confidentiality:** Issues around confidentiality in an online mediation center on two main factors: (1) the improper sharing of confidential information due to a technology glitch or error or intentional act on the part of a participant and (2) participants may be physically located in other jurisdictions, which may have varying confidentiality rules or laws. It is suggested that all attorneys and practitioners in online mediations acquaint themselves with the issues. Attorney Jeff Kichaven has written extensively on the issue of the jurisdictional complications of mediation confidentiality. Kichaven posits that:

> In the COVID-19 era, the risk [of confidentiality clauses not being upheld in subsequent litigation] has increased. Mediation has gone online. More cases involve participants in multiple states. The choice of which state's confidentiality or privilege law should apply is less obvious. The result? A court adjudicating a confidentiality claim has more discretion to pick and choose the evidence law of a state that allows mediation-related evidence to be admitted—regardless of whether the mediator has promised or the participants have agreed to keep that evidence confidential.[4]

The issues of disclosure of confidential information, whether intentional or unintentional in an online mediation is something that must be reviewed and understood by all participants. This is another reason why competence with the technology, a secure internet connection, and privacy for all participants must be required and enforced.

---

4. Jeff Kichaven, *Mediator Confidentiality Promises Carry Serious Risks*, Law 360 (July 20, 2020, 4:35 PM), https://www.law360.com/articles/1293390/mediator-confidentiality-promises-carry-serious-risks.

THE PRE-JOINT SESSION CONFERENCE

For many practitioners who participate in in-person mediations, the option of having a pre-joint session meeting with the mediator that includes your client is often something that either mediators do not offer, or attorneys decline to participate in. In an online mediation, this may be a mistake. An online pre-joint session conference with your mediator and client can serve many purposes:

- It allows the client and the attorney an opportunity to practice on the videoconferencing platform.
- The client is given an opportunity to meet the mediator and speak directly with them in a private and less-stressful setting than the day of mediation.
- The mediator has an opportunity to begin to establish rapport and communication with your client.
- Permits everyone involved to work out the pre-mediation jitters and feel comfortable in the online setting.

These benefits should not be underestimated, and if your mediator does not offer a pre-mediation session, it is a good practice to request one.

FINAL PREP FOR MEDIATION

We have discussed extensively what an attorney should do in advance of the mediation day but there remain a few final best practices in the day or so before the mediation.

First, it is a good practice to upload all documents, pleading, and exhibits that may be used in the mediation and organize them in separate folders on your desktop so that they are easily identifiable and accessed. Send any relevant documents electronically to the mediator in advance. Remember that a paper file is useless in an online proceeding.

Close all unnecessary programs on your computer and make sure that all confidential information that may be on your computer is hidden when you share your screen. This is one of the most common mistakes made during online meetings. Your computer needs sufficient bandwidth to properly perform during the mediation and having several programs open and running in the background will reduce bandwidth.

Consider the use of visual aids in the online mediation process to make your points. Visuals are especially impactful in a virtual setting, and the use of charts, slides, spreadsheets, and whiteboard applications such as Google Jamboard can be extremely effective and persuasive. Jamboard is not only free and easily accessible (https://jamboard.google.com), but it allows you to type, draw, add pictures, or use color stickers to punctuate and summarize discussions.

Anticipate an agreement and prepare a digital template that can be modified in the mediation as agreements are reached. The template should include any agreements that have been made, even tentatively, prior to the mediation, and your usual boilerplate language. We highly recommend the use of aspirational non-enforceable language to stimulate a cooperative working relationship to implement the agreement.

Have a plan for execution of any agreement that may be reached on the day of mediation, including having a traveling notary on call or an e-signature program at the ready so that you can end with a signed agreement.

■ **ONLINE PRO TIP:** Discuss and decide with your client whether they will be with you in-person for the online mediation session or if they will also be participating from another location. If they will be with you, consider where you will set up, how you will both appear onscreen, and consider having a separate computer up in another room where you can access the mediation to have private conversations with the mediator and/or opposing counsel or others.

MEDIATION DAY

Whether your online mediation consists of one longer mediation session or a sequential series of mediation sessions, on the day of an online session there are several tips for best practices to make the experience successful for all.

Early log in: Be sure to sign on a few minutes early and have your client and team members do the same. Technical issues often occur at the time of signing into the meeting and those few extra minutes will give the mediator an opportunity to resolve them without taking time away from the mediation session itself. An early sign on will also give you a chance to chat with your client and settle them if you are not in the same location. Ask to be placed in a private breakout room with your client or team if you need a moment to have a private discussion.

Practice proper "netiquette": The abundance of online meetings has given rise to a whole new world of proper etiquette in an online setting, otherwise known as "netiquette." A few top tips: (1) always mute your microphone when you are not speaking; (2) do not speak over others, as the audio will not be captured properly in an online platform; (3) remember that you are online and visual at all times, dress for a professional meeting despite the fact that you are remote; and (4) if you are called away from the mediation for any reason, be sure to communicate that fact to the appropriate participants, including the mediator and your client.

Get the phone numbers: Make sure that you have all relevant participant's telephone and/or cell phone numbers in case you need to communicate with anyone outside of the mediation session or if there are technical issues.

Beat the fatigue: Be prepared for "Zoom fatigue" and take breaks when possible. There are four main reasons why video meetings are tiring.

1. Excessive amounts of close-up eye contact is highly intense.
2. Seeing yourself during the video meeting constantly in real time is fatiguing.
3. Video meetings dramatically reduce our usual mobility.
4. The cognitive load is much higher in video meetings.[5]

5. Vignesh Ramachandran, *Stanford Researchers Identify Four Causes for "Zoom Fatigue" and Their Simple Fixes*, Stanford News (Feb. 23, 2021), https://news.stanford.edu/2021/02/23/four-causes-zoom-fatigue-solutions/.

If you can take a break, turn off your video and audio and get up and move around, but do *not* sign off from the meeting unless you are done for the day. Many people find that a break for 30 minutes every three hours is helpful. Keep this in mind for your own performance and comfort and also that of your client.

Consider the niceties: If your client will be participating remote from your location, consider having lunch delivered to them or suggesting that they have food, drink, and comforts at hand. These are niceties that mediators will often provide in person but that go missing in a virtual session.

Talk to your colleagues: If you feel it might be helpful, ask the mediator to set up a separate breakout room where you can have a private discussion with them, your opposing counsel, or both. The separate location does not have to keep you from having important conversations with your colleagues that might move the case forward.

HYBRID MEDIATIONS

As the world emerges from the COVID-19 pandemic, the option of returning to in-person mediations has returned, but with a world now so comfortable online some participants are choosing to participate remotely anyway. They are loath to give up the convenience and other benefits to attend in-person, whereas other participants may crave the personal touch of being "at the table." This will inevitably lead to hybrid proceedings where some participants are in-person and others are remote. In fact, it is anticipated that hybrid meetings of all kinds will become the norm in the post-pandemic world.[6]

With hybrid mediations come complications, both practical, with the technology and set up, and psychological, with people working in two different and unequal formats.

The Practical Issues

The complications of having one or more participants in the same location as the mediator and having others attending remotely via videoconferencing requires a technology and equipment setup beyond what a fully online mediation does. For example, the video feed for any remote participants will require a monitor for each in-person participant to view them or a large screen where the video thumbnails and screen can be seen by all in the room. It becomes even more complicated for the remote participants to properly view all the in-person participants. In addition, audio becomes just as complicated but necessary to ensure that everyone can properly hear the mediation.

The solutions: Thankfully, technology is rapidly catching up with the needs of hybrid meetings, and cameras that transmit a 180- or 360-degree view of the room with integrated microphones and speakers are now available at a variety of price points. In addition, for an additional investment, a conference room can be

6. *The Rise of Hybrid Workplace: A Global Survey of Executives, Employees and Experience Experts, and Knowledge Workers*, Oct. 2020, https://www.webex.com/content/dam/wbx/us/gated/analyst-report/dimensional-research-entering-the-era-of-hybrid-work-cm-2220.pdf.

transformed into virtual tech studio with AI-assisted cameras, microphones, and speakers that make the hybrid meeting feel seamless.

■ **ONLINE PRO TIP:** Many of the community workspaces and rental office suites are installing tech suites in their spaces that are available for rent by the hour or day for your hybrid mediation.

The Psychological Issues

The psychological issues raised in a hybrid mediation are perhaps even more challenging because they can strike at the core of the mediation paradigm as a discussion facilitated by a neutral professional. When the mediator is physically present with one party and their counsel, and the other party is remote, there can be a subtle, or not so subtle, feeling or perception created of favoritism. As the parties' perception of the mediator's neutrality is always a critical component of any mediation process, this is quite a problem and can affect the chances of reaching settlement.

The solutions: As with all things, awareness of the issues presented is the first step in meeting the challenges. The solution lies in strong facilitation and use of inclusive strategies by the mediator. It is far too easy for in-person attendees to dominate the discussion. The mediator must draw the remote participants in, keep them engaged, and ensure their voices are heard, not interrupted, or talked over. At times, the mediator may need to call on in-room or remote participants to ensure that all voices are heard.[7] If you and/or your client will be participating remotely in a hybrid mediation, be sure to properly educate your client about these challenges so that they can make an informed choice. Also closely monitor the session, and your client's feelings about the process, when it comes to these issues, and be prepared to step in and request additional time or attention for your client so they feel included and heard.

CONCLUSION

Although practitioners expressed some trepidation concerning the move to online mediation at the start of the pandemic, the process has proven to be successful and even beneficial for a variety of reasons, including convenience, cost-effectiveness, and safety. As the world moves beyond COVID-19 and the necessity of mediating online, the virtual process, and the hybrid process, will firmly remain options for parties to resolve their differences and bring an end to their conflicts. You and your clients can take advantage of the many benefits of online mediation and work with professionals from around the country and the world who can best help you reach resolution.

---

7. Bob Frisch & Cary Greene, *What It Takes to Run a Great Hybrid Meeting*, Harv. Bus. Rev. (June 3, 2021), https://hbr.org/2021/06/what-it-takes-to-run-a-great-hybrid-meeting.

As with all things, success in online mediation requires preparation. That preparation for attorneys includes not just preparing themselves but also their clients and team members. It is essential to remember, however, that despite the role of new technology in the mediation process, the basic principles remain in place, whether in-person, online, or hybrid. The goal remains to reach resolution and conciliation by focusing on the interests and needs of our clients. Online and hybrid mediation skills are just a few more tools in your practice toolbox.

CHAPTER 5

Using a Limited Scope Approach (Unbundling) to Represent Clients Outside and Inside the Mediation Room

The combined use of unbundled legal services can give otherwise unrepresented parties greater access to justice. By using unbundling, attorneys can expand their practices, gain additional clients and increase their revenue all by helping represent the otherwise unrepresentable.

—Professor Kristen M. Blankley, University of Nebraska

A system based solely on the paradigm of full representation means either a litigant has the resources or luck to obtain beginning-to-end assistance from a lawyer, or is left alone to languish in the inexorable demands of the legal system. Unbundling offers flexibility that benefits the great majority of the public.[1]

—Hon. Michael B. Hyman, Chicago, Illinois

For decades, America's favorite hot drink was brewed coffee served in ceramic mugs. In recent years, coffee has been given a boost in its popularity and sales by changing its preparation and presentation. The coffee industry responded to consumers with new processes, innovative presentations, and creative marketing. This industry remodeling helped stimulate the coffee industry and give it life when many thought the health and fitness craze might devastate it. Just think of single cup servings a la Keurig, the popularity of the "barista," myriad of non-dairy milk options, and the ever-rotating array of seasonal and specialty drink options.

Similarly, approximately 60 years ago, dentists feared that widespread introduction of fluoride would render dental services obsolete. Rather than defensively

1. ADA: Flouride: Topical and Systemic Supplements (2021) https://www.ada.org/en/member-center/oral-health-topics/fluoride-topical-and-systemic-supplements, noting specific endorsements.

reacting to battle the fluoride movement, the dental profession embraced this discovery with the theme "The American Dental Association supports regular brushing with fluoride toothpaste as a necessary component of twice-a-year dental checkups for overall dental hygiene."[2]

Changing its image from tooth drillers to managers of preventive dental health preserved and revitalized the dental profession.

Family lawyers have much to learn from these tales of flexible reinvention. We have an opportunity to buff up our inventory of service products to rise to the very challenges that appear to threaten our livelihoods. Consumers are choosing to do without lawyers because of the high economic barriers of entry (cash deposits called retainers), loss of control, perceived pejorative attitudes and condescending treatment by lawyers, and fear of lawyers being deal breakers and family wreckers. More than half of these self-represented litigants could afford to hire a family lawyer but choose not to. Rather than blame the public, overcrowded and underfunded courts, the organized bar, or the press, family lawyers can revitalize their own economic futures by exploring new and more responsive ways of meeting consumer demand and increasing their profitability.

UNBUNDLING: RETHINKING HOW TO PACKAGE AND DELIVER LEGAL SERVICES

The Traditional Full-Service Package

Most of us offer one legal service product: the full-service representational package of legal services. Upon being hired by a client and without otherwise limiting services, we explicitly or implicitly undertake to provide the following services:

- Gathering facts
- Advising the client
- Discovering the facts of the opposing party
- Researching the law
- Drafting correspondence and documents
- Negotiating with the other lawyer (or unrepresented party)
- Representing the client in court

Although not all services are performed in every engagement, both clients assume that we, as tactical captains, will decide what services are needed and who will perform them. In some states, these assumptions are even codified in the Statement of Client's Rights and Responsibilities. It is also assumed that we, not the client, will perform these services on behalf of the client. While the client

2. For a comprehensive overview of unbundling rules, see Noble & Porter, Beyond Mediation: Conflict Coaching, Final Report Online Mediation Task Force (Aug. 2021). See also An Analysis of Rules That Enable Lawyers to Serve Self-Represented Litigants: A White Paper by the ABA Standing Committee on the Delivery of Legal Services (2014). Among topics discussed are rules authorizing limited scope services, communications between counsel and parties, document preparation, and appearance and withdrawal in court.

may be a resource for factual information, we are responsible for doing all of the work. In fact, many of us discourage involvement of the client in preparing correspondence or written court documents. (Some of us even fail to send the client copies of all correspondence.) And once at the courthouse, it is clear to everyone that this is a lawyer-directed production.

In full-service representation, the client has the right to approve decisions regarding the final settlement and to be informed about the progress of the case as it goes along. At its very essence, much like hiring a surgeon to handle an operation while the patient is under anesthetic, the client selects a lawyer based on a client's feeling of trust in the lawyer's competence and judgment. If either the competence or the judgment is questioned to the point of undermining client confidence, the client's remedy is to go it alone or hire another lawyer—probably also operating under the full-service representational package. In return for the responsibility of controlling the case management and doing the work, lawyers and clients contract for the lawyer to be paid for the work performed, generally on an hourly basis. Applying pure economic motivation, the lawyer makes more money if more lawyer work is done. Clients, while suspicious of this motivation, generally trust lawyer integrity and judgment, and because they view full service as increasing the quality of legal services, clients sign on for this model—until they lose confidence, run out of money, or both.

Some of us often "unbundle" by employing a cost-benefit analysis to determine which services we should provide to a given client. For example, we might decide which depositions to take and who will take them. Because we fear malpractice claims should the client later be unhappy, defensive over-lawyering to do all possible work becomes more common—with clients paying the bills. Over-lawyering doesn't run up costs for just one spouse. The other spouse must defend and will often choose to escalate in response. Such over-lawyering can pollute the value system of an entire legal community, becoming the "safe and prudent" standard of customary law practice under the guise of protecting clients' rights.

Unbundling Defined

Unbundling (also called *limited scope, "do it yourself"* or *discrete task representation*) offers clients a middle ground between dispensing with us altogether and signing on for the full-service package. With our help, the client determines which services are to be performed by the client, which services are to be performed by the lawyer, and the extent or depth to which we perform the designated services. The division of these tasks should be clearly and specifically spelled out in the initial attorney-client engagement letter. Here are 17 service categories:

1. Legal advice: office visits, telephone calls, fax, mail, email, virtual
2. Advice about availability of alternative means to resolve the dispute, including mediation and arbitration
3. Evaluation of the client's self-diagnosis of the case and advice to the client about legal rights
4. Guidance and procedural information for filing or serving documents
5. Reviews of correspondence and court documents

6. Preparation and/or suggestion of documents to be prepared
7. Factual investigation: contact of witnesses, public record searches, in-depth interview of the client
8. Legal research and analysis
9. Discovery: interrogatories, depositions, requests for document production
10. Plans for negotiations, including simulated role playing with the client
11. Plans for court appearances made by the client, including simulated role playing with the client
12. Backup and troubleshooting during the trial
13. Referral of the client to other counsel, an expert, or a professional
14. Client counseling about an appeal
15. Procedural assistance with an appeal and assistance with substantive legal argumentation in an appeal
16. Preventive planning and/or legal checkups
17. Other agreed-upon services

We only have the responsibility to perform those services that are specifically checked off and authorized by the client. We are not entitled to payment for services that have not been checked off unless the limited scope arrangement is modified in writing by both lawyer and client. In the same vein, if the client makes ineffective or self-destructive decisions or actions in handling (or not handling) a task for which we are not responsible, the client cannot blame or take legal action against us. Rather than being treated paternalistically, clients are afforded the control to choose the scope of engagement and must therefore live with the result.

Family lawyers are currently offering a number of new service products to serve both self-represented litigants and represented clients. After reviewing some of these common unbundled services, the balance of this chapter will focus on our limited scope role representing clients as a consulting lawyer outside the mediation room as well as a limited role of being at mediation sessions without necessarily being counsel of record for the rest of the case.[3]

Attorney Coach: Educator and Advisor

The 2016 IAALS study, Cases without Counsel, surveying experiences of self-representation in U.S. Family Courts, found that what most hurt litigants without lawyers was the lack of legal advice.[4] While court forms and procedures have been simplified so that working people can process divorce papers themselves, processing a divorce without some legal advice can adversely affect the life of the self-represented litigant (often referred to in the archaic Latin as *Pro Se Litigant*).

---

3. For a more comprehensive discussion of limited scope services in family law matters, see FORREST MOSTEN & HON. ELIZABETH POTTER SCULLY, UNBUNDLING LEGAL SERVICES IN FAMILY LAW (ABA, 2017); Mosten & Traum, *The Family Lawyer's Role in Preventive Legal and Conflict Wellness*, 55 FAM. COURT REV. 26 (2017); Forrest S. Mosten, *Unbundled Legal Services Today—and Predictions for the Future*, 35 FAM. ADVOCATE 14 (2012).

4. IAALS, Cases without Counsel: Research on Experiences of Self-Representation in U.S. Family Court (2016).

The ABA study found that, compared with people who had a lawyer's help, self-represented litigants received lower child and spousal support and less temporary relief through pendente lite orders, lived with outdated orders due to getting fewer modifications, and did not take advantage of tax breaks due to receiving less advice on tax consequences. Equally important, self-represented litigants knew less about alternative dispute resolution (ADR) and used it less frequently than people who were represented by lawyers. This means that although self-represented families got their divorces more easily and cheaply, conflict and parenting deficiencies were not addressed as adequately as if the agreements had been mediated or the parties had been taught how to resolve disputes in the future by lawyers serving an educational role in regard to diffusing conflict. By serving as a client legal coach (attorney coach), we can offer self-represented litigants a non-threatening and less-expensive alternative. Clients decide when, for which issues, and at what depth they want to consult with their lawyers. Accustomed to handling the whole case or not helping a person going through divorce, we must be willing to alter our expectations about decision-making, fees, and handling of the nuts and bolts of the case.

How can attorney-coaches provide value to our clients by delivering such limited service for limited fees? Here are a few suggestions:

- We can help a client calculate income and statute-allowed deductions, exemptions, and hardships and then print out statutory guidelines for support. This will provide the client with a reality check and help the client prepare for direct negotiations with the other spouse or a court hearing without our being present.
- We can help our unbundled clients fill out court forms. Even with simplified forms, experience and training are needed to complete them properly. A wrong check box can adversely affect our client's rights. As attorney-coaches, we can assist laypersons who otherwise would be flummoxed or who often make self-destructive choices.
- Going to the courthouse can be frightening and overwhelming. As attorney-coaches, we can orient clients on such things as where to park, which courtroom to go to, and how much time to allocate, and double-check that all forms and copies needed for a court hearing are prepared, the filing fee is ready, and other requirements have been met. We can also educate them about what information court staff is and is not permitted to share, coach them on the right moment to approach court staff, and warn them that if court staff declines to provide information or cuts an interaction short they should not necessarily take it personally.
- Figuring out budgets for post-divorce expenses is a daunting process. An attorney-coach, we can help a client budget for and talk through the inevitable choices that living in two households entails.
- Clients may need the help of other professionals, such as accountants, therapists, vocational counselors, or financial planners. As an attorney-coach, we can help the client assess the need for these professionals and offer alternatives for referral.

Red Flag Warning

In a 2013 unbundling presentation, Toby Rothchild, executive director of the Legal Aid Foundation of Los Angeles, and Wendy Wen Yun Chang, a lawyer who represents lawyers in legal malpractice actions, described the types of clients that pose challenges for unbundling:

- The Principled Client: claims to be acting on "principle"
- The Great Expectations Client: expects to triumph on every issue
- The Emergency Client: every task becomes a last-minute crisis
- The Coy Communicator: withholds pertinent information
- The Control Freak: unable to let go of tasks or delegate
- The Client with Cognition Issues: may lack understanding of relationship
- The Client Who Cannot Handle It: needs broader attorney support
- The "Paralawyer" Client: micromanages attorney work
- The Favor Client: Scope creep as result of requests for extra help

- Clients often need emotional support. As attorney-coaches, we can help clients get through their reactions, which can paralyze them or escalate the conflict. By referring clients to the literature on the stages of an emotional divorce (denial, resistance, anger, acceptance) and the various types of divorce (Maccoby and Mnookin's four types of divorce—spousal divorce, parental divorce, economic divorce, and legal divorce),[5] as legal coach, you can help normalize your clients' experience.
- As an attorney-coach, you can discuss legal issues and give advice on legal position that the client should take. You can provide the client with a duplicated statute (such as the factors considered in permanent spousal support) or give the client an article, such as one describing the choice between accepting a buyout or reserving court jurisdiction on defined benefit plans. Like a physician prescribing a particular medication, you can improve client decision-making just by providing resources you are aware of.
- If you have a client library, you can recommend books, websites, or DVDs to help your client. For example, the State Bar of Wisconsin's DVD *Your Divorce Deposition* may be a tremendous resource in helping a client prepare for taking or defending a deposition. Similarly, the film *Split* produced by Ellen Bruno and the websites www.uptoparents.org and www.ourfamilywizard.com can be invaluable in educating clients who are trying to represent themselves.
- You can be available to answer the client's questions and concerns. Just having you available throughout the divorce process often makes it easier for a self-represented litigant to get through the divorce.

5. Eleanor E. Maccoby & Robert H. Mnookin, Dividing the Child: Social and Legal Dilemmas of Custody 103, 300 (1992).

General Conflict Management Client Coaching

This chapter discusses legal coaching within limited scope representation within the family law context. It is important that you be aware of (if not actively explore) conflict coaching in a more general context.

The coaching specialty of conflict management coaching—also known as conflict coaching—has steadily emerged within the field of ADR and should be of special interest to attorneys. Toronto-based Cinnie Noble, one of the world leaders in conflict management coaching, describes this process as follows:

> Coaching is partnering with clients in a thought-provoking and creative process that inspires them to maximize their personal and professional potential. Coaching is an ongoing relationship which focuses on clients taking action toward the realization of their visions, goals, or desires. Coaching uses a process of inquiry and personal discovery to build the client's level of awareness and responsibility and provides the client with structure, support, and feedback.[6]

Unlike sports coaching, conflict coaching, like many other types of coaching, does not entail advising people on what to do to improve their actions and reach their goals. Rather, one of the cornerstones of the field of coaching is the self-determination of the client, and one of the main skills of trained coaches is the use of powerful questions that increase the insight and awareness that help people help themselves.

Conflict management coaching may be used instead of or in tandem with mediation in a number of ways:

1. As a pre-mediation process, to help clients anticipate and prepare for any challenges that may impact their ability to effectively participate in the process or otherwise engage with the other party
2. As a post-mediation process, to help clients in the aftermath of a settlement agreement to address any unresolved matters and identify ways to manage ongoing interactions
3. To help clients improve their negotiation skills and their comfort and confidence to actively participate in mediation
4. To provide a self-reflective method that helps clients interact in sessions with increased proficiency and confidence

You can also use professional coaching to strengthen your own mediation and negotiation skills, to adapt to the new lawyering roles, and to integrate those roles to expand your law practice.

Although the balance of this chapter focuses on your craft of offering limited scope legal services to your clients, training in conflict management coaching or engaging a conflict management coach will accelerate your own development in this field.

---

6. Cinnie Noble, *Conflict Coaching, A New ADR Technique, Ontario Bar Associations' Alternative Dispute Resolution Newsletter*, vol. 17, no.1 (Dec. 2008).

Coach or First Class?

In addition to giving advice and being a teacher, you can help a client wrestle with the central issue in unbundling: if problems arise, should the client continue to self-represent with you as a coach, should you convert the lawyer-client relationship into a full-service engagement, or should the client seek alternative counsel? Just as a patient diagnosed with cancer is inexperienced in determining the best medical treatment, a self-represented litigant needs the attorney-coach's advice about which lawyer role to use. Therefore, we must provide advice to help the client understand how limited scope coaching and full service differ and the costs and benefits of various options.

To begin, we must help the client assess his or her legal needs by answering three questions: (1) Is a lawyer needed at all? (2) If so, for which tasks? (3) How will the lawyer-client relationship be structured? Determining the scope of the coaching relationship requires a blend of education, negotiation, and shared control.

Education is a two-way street. We must educate the client about the benefits of using (and paying for) our experience, knowledge, and skill on a limited basis while the client remains in charge of case strategy and implementation. This education flows naturally from a discussion of the client's needs.

- Is the assessment conference the only client-lawyer meeting, or will another meeting be planned now or be left to client discretion?
- Are meetings calendared in a pre-scheduled recurring framework or pursued on an "as needed" basis?
- Will the client handle every aspect of self-representation (fact gathering, discovery, correspondence and pleadings, negotiations, court appearances), or will some of these tasks be delegated to you?
- We also can educate the client about the extent of any service you might provide as a limited service attorney coach. For example, our client may want to handle (with limited lawyer coaching) all court filings, discovery, negotiations, and court appearances short of trial but have the lawyer convert roles from coach to lawyer of record at the trial itself. Our client can educate us as well. In other words, the client must clarify his or her goals, values, experience, and ability to handle various tasks, given the time and money available. Based on what we learn from each other, *the lawyer and client decide together whether to establish a coaching relationship and to what extent.*

Coaching the Rich and Vulnerable

When you think of coaching, you probably think about helping a middle-income self-represented litigant process a divorce without complex life-threatening issues. However, coaching is also being requested more and more by professionals and those who earn well over $100,000—people who can afford the full package, want to both save money and keep lawyers out of their divorces!

Mary earned $500,000 a year as a corporate executive. She had totally supported her husband for three years and now was being harassed by him at work and home.

Mary did not want a lawyer speaking to Todd. As with Mongo in ***Blazing Saddles***, a lawyer's presence and power might only enrage Todd and send him more out of control. So, Mary customized and limited her lawyer's work. The limited scope lawyer drafted the restraining orders, and her legal assistant accompanied Mary to the court, where Mary processed it herself. The lawyer guided Mary through the criminal complaint process and consoled her when the prosecutor rejected the case. The lawyer was on call during the Christmas holiday when Mary called from the Caribbean to report that Todd was in her house removing items: "What should I do?" The lawyer advised Mary concerning a lump-sum buyout of her spousal support liability and drafted the final agreement, which Mary and Todd negotiated in a bar. Was this frustrating professional work? Yes. Could the lawyer have helped Mary more if he had been the full-service counsel of record? Yes. Could he have made more money, and could Mary have afforded it? Yes and yes. Were limited unbundled services what Mary wanted and was willing to pay for? Yes.

This mutual process lessens the conflict of interest that naturally arises when we advise a potential client about retaining our services. Some clients' rights advocates say that a client should have a lawyer's advice in negotiating a contract for legal services due to the financial and role complexities in that relationship. Are we as family lawyers the best person to advise our clients as to whether our services are reasonable and necessary and if so what financial terms are appropriate? Should we advise our potential clients on this business transaction? In the unbundled situation, the attorney-coach still has a financial conflict in advising whether the client needs further coaching. However, because coaching implies that someone other than the coach (the client, a different lawyer, or another professional) may handle the legal services recommended by the coach and because the coach's fees are much lower, the conflict of interest is greatly reduced.

Negotiation Coach

In this coaching role, the negotiation on a variety of issues can take place with the client and the other spouse directly, between the client and the other spouse's lawyer, between the client and child or other member of the client's family (including in-laws, grandparents, grand uncles and aunts, or other involved stakeholders and decision-makers), with a court clerk, with an IRS agent, with a former lawyer, or with a present significant other. The client can be negotiating with anyone involved in the family maelstrom and may need help in the process.

By working with our clients in understanding their underlying needs and goals and anticipating those of the other spouse, we can help our clients develop priorities and clear objectives for their negotiations. The rest is downhill. As coach, we can educate the client about the psychological profiles of the parties and teach the client basic negotiation principles such as determining each party's underlying needs and negotiation techniques such as how to formulate an offer.

The major coaching functions for negotiation include the following.

Teaching divorce dynamics: Using this coaching function, we educate our clients about general divorce dynamics that may give our clients additional insight into their current situations. If we can teach our clients about the four distinct divorce relationships mentioned earlier (emotional, physical, financial, and legal), our clients may find it easier to understand the negotiation process.[7] For example, if the spousal (emotional) divorce is almost complete, the couple will probably be less raw and can focus on other issues. If all four divorces are at early stages, there will be more work to do on all fronts. Similarly, teaching the client about the long-term effect of anger may provide a perspective that makes it easier for the client to get through the divorce.[8]

Assessing the legal strengths and weaknesses of each party's position: This is a traditional lawyer function. Instead of merely sharing this information with the client to obtain settlement authority, helping the client learn this assessment makes it available for the client's use in discussions with his or her spouse.

Analyzing the personalities of the parties, communication dynamics, emotional and financial leverage: These insights are utilized by experienced negotiators, and we need to transfer this experience to our clients for use at the family dining table or restaurant, when the spouses are hammering out a deal themselves. In short, skilled lawyers have the ability to insightfully read our clients, opposing parties, counsel, and others involved in and affected by a negotiation. In addition to our own experience, we probably have direct knowledge of and access to negotiation resources that can help.

We can be invaluable in helping a client understand negotiation dynamics. By sharing our impressions and teaching clients how to appreciate and empathize with the underlying needs and goals of their spouses, we can help our clients to maximize their effectiveness in formulating and presenting their proposals. Overall conflict can be reduced by helping our clients recognize the behaviors of their spouses that pushed the clients' buttons and understand what destructive behaviors a spouse may unleash in reaction to the client. As one client admitted after a coaching session, "I want to thank you for 'beating me over the head' this morning. I needed it. I began to see the whole picture more clearly again . . . what was happening to me and the level I was permitting myself to sink to. I didn't like the picture at all. I am going to start writing the letter [to my wife's lawyer], which I think you'll be pleased with."

Teaching negotiation theory and techniques: The only negotiation training to which many family lawyers have been exposed has been OJT (on-the-job training). That is all that many family lawyers who are naturals in negotiation think

---

7. Judith S. Wallerstein & Sandra Blakeslee, Second Chances: Men, Women, and Children a Decade after Divorce 7–8 (1989). ("Divorce is the only major family crisis in which social support falls away [W]hen a man and a woman divorce, many people tend to act as if they believe it might be contagious. The divorced person is seen as a loose cannon. We have names for them: rogue elephant, black widow. Despite the widespread acceptance of divorce in modern society, there remains something frightening at its core.").

8. Carrie Menkel-Meadow, *Toward Another View of Legal Negotiation: The Structure of Problem Solving*, 31 UCLA L. Rev. 754, 818–21 (1984).

that they may need. The recent boom in negotiation training and literature has made less talented lawyers more knowledgeable and competent in negotiation skills and generally has made the naturals even better. Regardless of formal training, we can give our clients a customized crash course in the relevant negotiation skills needed to aid a client in reaching his or her goals. This project is greatly facilitated by having a collection of client-friendly negotiation books and tapes available for study. See the Appendices for a fuller discussion on developing and maintaining a client library in your office or on your website.

Developing a negotiation plan: Regardless of the techniques and interventions that the client actually displays during the negotiation, experts in this field generally concur that the quality of the negotiation plan and the degree of pre-meeting preparation are the keys to a successful outcome.[9] Coming up with an initial settlement position (what to ask for) is often the most difficult task facing a lawyer representing a client in a negotiation. It is no less difficult (probably more so) for us to help a client develop a plan with several backup positions and prepared responses for anticipated concerns raised by the other spouse.

Preparing through role playing: Most law schools emphasize role playing for teaching law students essential practice skills such as client counseling, negotiation, and trial practice. In effect, we can become the client's clinical instructor by rehearsing a negotiation and then giving constructive feedback to the client's performance (often recorded) to prepare for the real thing. We can do this type of rehearsal in front of the client's friends or even office staff to get comments that might help the client.

One method of preparing the client for negotiation is to role-play the scene in advance. Clients can play themselves, and we can play the other spouse or other negotiation participants. Both client and coach stay in role and try to work out the issue(s) at hand. This exercise helps the client practice by saying the words that will affect the outcome during the real negotiations as well as to anticipate at least some reactions of the other spouse. Another negotiation preparation technique is to have the coach and client reverse roles: the client plays the other spouse, and the coach plays the client. This role reversal can be very illuminating, increasing understanding of the other's needs and concerns by placing oneself in another's shoes. The client can also see what to do or not to do because the client gets to react to proposed actions as if he or she were on the receiving end. This exercise is a cousin to the mediation technique of reframing (also called "looping" or "reflecting": repeating the client's words, demonstrating that the client's needs and concerns are understood).

Consulting in mid-negotiation: Although remaining on the sidelines, the coach often remains available by telephone during (or shortly after) a spousal meeting to serve as a resource and emotional support for the client. Being "on-call" not only can provide the client with concrete help, but being able to ask

---

9. Stephanie I. Kimbro, Lawyers Mut. Liab. Ins. Co. of N.C., Unbundled Legal Services: Risk Management Handouts of Lawyers Mutual (2010). *See* www.lmic.com and contact Kim Spirito (spiritok@lawyersmutual.com), vice president of Loss Prevention and Claims to discuss access to the video and supporting materials.

for a "lifeline" from a coach can produce an important sense of support and confidence for the client. Depending on your comfort level and your relationship with the client, you as the attorney might even feel comfortable providing your personal cell phone number in order to be able to offer live text message support in a subtle yet swiftly responsive fashion.

Court Coach

Historically, courts have been seen as the private preserve of the legal profession. The unwanted children of the court system, self-represented litigants, often do not speak the correct language, dress in appropriate uniform, or know where to stand or when to speak—or not to speak. They are perceived as being unprepared and taking too much court time. So it is not surprising that many feel they have already been burned due to their status as a self-represented litigant.

Nevertheless, people represent themselves in record numbers, and they certainly want (and are willing to pay for) help from lawyers who are willing to provide it. We can accommodate self-represented litigants by helping them with many concrete tasks:

- Ghostwriting court pleadings and briefs or reviewing and editing the client's court submissions
- Organizing, arranging, and marking documents for court exhibits
- Advising clients and helping them prepare appropriate pretrial motions
- Drafting or reviewing the client's written work needed for a court hearing, educating the client about court procedures and giving advice, such as explaining the right to challenge the judge assigned to the case and the timing and considerations that might go into that decision, when to act, and what to say
- Helping the client prepare opening and closing statements and direct and cross-examination; ghostwriting, reviewing, or simulating court conditions through role playing; and staying available for telephone consultation during last-minute preparations and while the client is in court

Fear of Malpractice as a Barrier to Unbundling

Under current ethical rules and case authority, malpractice exposure and vulnerability to professional discipline frighten many lawyers away from experimenting with unbundling. Malpractice exposure exists for lawyers who render incomplete advice or who fail to give needed advice in areas ancillary to the client's presenting problem. For example, a lawyer's failure to sufficiently advise a client who comes in for a worker's compensation claim about a potential third-party claim may give rise to a malpractice action.[10] This malpractice exposure increases when the client comes in for a limited time and explicitly restricts the lawyer's time and activity in unbundled situations. If legal research is required and the lawyer is authorized to spend only 30 minutes, a rushed or an inadequate job might lead to

10. Rudolf v. Shayne, Dachs, Stanisci, Corker & Sauer, 8 N.Y.3d 438, 442, 867 N.E.2d 385, 387, 835 N.Y.S.2d 534, 536 (2007).

wrong advice. The exposure is increased by the fact that clients receiving unbundled service are extremely vigilant about lawyer overbilling.

Those clients choosing discrete task representation are often schooled in competitive shopping for lawyer services and have a do-it-yourself mentality. Such clients may be inherently mistrustful of lawyers, extremely stingy about paying legal fees, or both. We need to make sure that we are not compromising our ethical duties as attorneys when performing unbundled services. To give you comfort, Lawyers Mutual, a leading lawyer malpractice insurance company, not only does not discourage its policy holders from offering unbundled legal services, but encourages them to do so in a competent and responsible manner. Toward that end, in 2014, Lawyer's Mutual produced a one-hour video highlighting best practices of unbundling, *Debunking the Myths of Unbundling*.[11] The State Bar of Oregon's malpractice plan has taken a similar position of support for responsible unbundling since 1997.[12]

Another ethical problem surfaces when a lawyer coaches the self-represented client on negotiation strategy and scripts the client in how to talk with the other party who is represented by counsel. With regard to representation of the opposing party, the California State Bar has issued a formal ethics opinion holding that this "scripting" violates the rule of professional responsibility prohibiting indirect communication with a represented party.[13] Such a rule conflicts with the organized bar's stated policy of encouraging client coaching and widening legal access. Lawyers who ghostwrite clients' correspondence and court documents to help improve the quality of the work at a fraction of the cost may also face liability and judicial condemnation. Although Colorado is an unbundling-friendly jurisdiction, a federal district judge in that state excoriated a lawyer who ghostwrote court pleadings for a self-represented litigant and indicated that such conduct may be punished by sanctions or contempt for committing a fraud on the court.[14] Such statements by judicial officers can have a chilling effect on lawyers who are considering unbundling and who desire to service clients within the clients' ability to pay.

Notice of Limited Scope Role

Some of the challenges facing our attempts to unbundle and serve as a coach to unrepresented litigants are that other lawyers or judges may not be aware that we are representing a party in a limited scope role or they are unaware of the tasks, issues, or court processes to which our role is limited. This can create service of process/notice issues. It mean that a judge may require clarification of the scope of your

11. *See* Nichols v. Keller, 19 Cal. Rptr. 2d 601 (Ct. App. 1993); *see also* Peter Spero, *The Attorney's Duty to Advise Beyond Scope of Representation,* L.A. Daily J., Dec. 19, 1994, at 7.

12. Kimbro, *supra* note 9.

13. California State Bar Comm. on Pro. Resp., Formal Op. 1993-131 (1993). This opinion is based on Model Rules of Professional Conduct Rule 4.2 (prohibiting a lawyer from directly or indirectly communicating with a represented party).

14. The law varies from state to state in terms of whether limited court appearances are permitted. For a state-by-state directory of rules governing unbundled services, see www.americanbar.org/groups/delivery_legal_services/resources/pro_se_unbundling_resource_center/court_rules.html.

representation on the record, or not permit us to appear in court just for one hearing or to prepare court pleadings without become a full counsel of record.[15] Also, other lawyers may become confused or reluctant to deal with our client on the same issues or with us on other issues. Such reluctance is understandable if we do not communicate clearly the existence and details of the scope of our engagement.

While many jurisdictions have not yet formally acknowledged the concerns of unbundled legal service providers, the California Judicial Council has addressed this problem head on by developing a set of unbundling-friendly rules and family law forms to permit lawyers and their clients to give clear notice to other lawyers and judicial officers. The form, Notice of Limited Scope Appearance (FL-950), is provided in the Resources section. This form has several benefits:

1. It is filed with the court and served on other lawyers so that actual notice is perfected.
2. The form permits "vertical unbundling," which means that the client and lawyer can allocate tasks and such allocation is binding on the court and other lawyers. For example, the lawyer might limit his or her scope to negotiation only. In such case, the client would be responsible for all other tasks.
3. The form also permits "horizontal unbundling," which means that issues or different court appearances can also be allocated between lawyer and client. For example, the lawyer might handle all tasks and court appearances in respect to retirement plans and the client is responsible for all other issues. Or the lawyer might attend an initial hearing involving several substantive issues. Once that hearing is concluded, the lawyer has no further responsibility.
4. The form also provides that the client agrees to sign a substitution of attorney, relieving the lawyer when the scope of work is completed. When a client fails or refuses to do so (which happens rarely), the California Judicial Council has developed forms for a limited scope attorney to withdraw without a hearing if there is no written objection and a form for clients to make such objections—leaving the decision of relief of counsel up to the court.

Even if your state does not have such forms, you can develop your own based on the California template as well as work toward obtaining such forms in your jurisdiction in the future. However, without a court rule or ethical opinion permitting limited scope, there may be uncertainty in your jurisdiction. To check unbundling rules state by state, see www.americanbar.org/groups/delivery_legal_services/resources/pro_se_unbundling_resource_center/court_rules.html. For a resource library of state by state recommended forms, see https://www.srln.org/node/1483/resource-sample-unbundled-attorney-retainer-agreements-multi-state-2020.

Using an Unbundled Approach Outside the Mediation Room

The first step is for you to make it clear to your clients (and potential clients) that you are available and interested in helping them through a mediation without becoming full counsel of record. Clients will appreciate your willingness to be a

---

15. *See* Nichols v. Keller, 19 Cal. Rptr. 2d 601 (Ct. App. 1993); *see also* Peter Spero, *The Attorney's Duty to Advise Beyond Scope of Representation*, L.A. Daily J., Dec. 19, 1994, at 7.

consulting lawyer in mediation. First, while many people may want to mediate, fear of being overpowered by the other party or a lack of confidence in their ability to hold their own may weigh against entering mediation. Hiring us on a limited scope basis can alleviate or at least reduce this fear. Second, although our assistance may be appreciated, clients often want to keep our time to a minimum to save costs. Working outside sessions can accomplish that. So instead of billing four hours for a three-hour session (assuming a half hour for travel time), we can limit the time to under an hour for session preparation and de-brief with the client. We can remain on call for a possible telephone or email conversation if our client faces a question or a problem during the mediation session.

Some of the key tasks in helping clients when you do not attend the session include:

1. Help the client set an agenda that will meet his or her concerns. We can help frame the issues so that when the mediator calls for the agenda, the client is ready.
2. Make sure the client can handle the proposed format of the mediation. Some mediation participants can stay focused for a four-hour session; others wear out after 90 minutes.
3. Help your client prepare an opening statement that is effective and within the client's ability to deliver. For example, some mediation parties need to write out every word and maybe even read their opening statement, others can refer to their draft, reading occasionally, some may only need an outline, and still others will speak from the heart. Help a client use this opportunity to speak in aspirational terms and objectives rather than use the statement to make a negotiation demand. For example, instead of saying, "I want $3,500 per month in child support," the client can learn to say, "I hope you and I can ensure that the children continue to have sufficient resources to meet their needs." You can even play the role of mediator or other party and offer the client an opportunity to practice the statement and then offer some gentle hints for improvement.
4. Make sure the client has backup documents prepared and available at the mediation with sufficient copies for the other party and the mediator.
5. Alert the client to the possibility of bringing important people to the mediation. For example, if the client's father has been bankrolling the family or is owed outstanding loans, having the father attend a session might pay dividends. If the father's presence could inflame the situation, this dynamic needs to be discussed before a client suggests that he attend. If another party is attending the session, ethical prohibitions against accepting compensation from third parties should be addressed by parties, attorneys, and the mediator in advance, and appropriate notices and waivers should be signed according to mutual agreement and comfort levels.
6. Make sure your client has copies of statutes, cases, or other information to share at the session. For example, if an issue will be the interest rate applied to a deferred payment, provide various options for presentation at the session Department of Labor rate of inflation, bank or mortgage rates, current investment rates of family bonds, for instance.

7. Make sure budgets, income information, and schedules of assets and debts are collected with backup documentation and are ready for discussion.
8. Discuss primary and second negotiation options on each issue so that client is ready.
9. Help client link issues together or be willing to concede a point if the other party agrees to a reciprocal concession.
10. Read the summary letters prepared by the mediator so that we know how progress is being made and what trade-offs are being considered.
11. Be ready to draft or review interim, partial, or temporary agreements.
12. Alert the client to be vigilant about when it might be best for us to attend a session.
13. Work with the other party's lawyer to defuse conflict and find compromise positions in support of the mediator's efforts. Be willing to write letters to the mediator or participate in conference calls to move the mediation along.
14. Be ready to suggest the addition of other professionals to help the process. The addition of a neutral forensic CPA or financial planner might cut through unproductive and expensive discussions.
15. Be ready to suggest an ancillary process to take place within the mediation to break an impasse or accelerate progress. For example, if the parties cannot seem to work out a school schedule after several sessions, consider bringing an evaluator or parenting coordinator to conduct a confidential mini-evaluation to provide a nonbinding recommendation after interviewing the parties, children, significant others, teachers, coaches, and other persons (collaterals).
16. If the mediation is being conducted on Zoom or other online platform, prepare the client to handle Zoom logistics and special confidentiality concerns. See Chapter 4.5 by Susan Guthrie on representing clients in online mediations.

Using an Unbundled Approach in the Mediation Room

Even though you may not be representing your client in court proceedings before or after the mediation, your limited role can be expanded to being in the room at mediation sessions with your client. Such increased service may be cost-effective for your situation in any of the following situations:

1. Your client refuses to make any decisions or agreements in the mediation until speaking with us. Advise client to be careful about making impulsive agreements or saying yes when he or she does not understand the ramifications of a decision, However, some parties hide behind the absence of their lawyer to do nothing—frustrating the other party and putting the mediation at risk.
2. When client is stumbling through sessions and making bad deals or blowing up good deals, our presence might make a big difference.
3. When client explicitly asks us to come or where the other party has announced his or her intention to bring a lawyer.
4. The mediation seems to be stalling or taking too long or the expense is getting out of hand. In such situations, we can expedite the process, resulting in savings of money and time.

5. A deadline has been imposed by the court or another reason has come up (e.g., a deadline is looming to sign up for application to a school, escrow is closing on the sale of a house, or health insurance coverage is running out).

If a decision is made to attend sessions with our clients, several ground rules should be followed to maximize your effectiveness:

1. Always give notice to the other lawyer and to the mediator that you are coming to a mediation session. Client might be the one to give notice to the other party and the mediator. Showing up unannounced is not only discourteous but also could cause the other party to retaliate in some way or at least reduce high ground and ability to convey trust to the mediator and to the parties.
2. Ask the mediator how to help when we are in the room. The mediator might indicate that client's active role in speaking might kick-start the agreement-making process. On the other hand, the mediator might believe that a quiet, steady presence on our part would anchor progress already being made.
3. Ask the other lawyer how we can best work together. Find out if the other party has needs and concerns that we might be able to address.
4. Ask client before our arrival and continually check your client's temperature to make sure that client is comfortable with our input. Remember that the parties and mediator had been a system before our arrival, so our presence (and that of the other lawyer) may significantly change the dynamics—and not always for the better.
5. Support the mediator overtly in session and privately with your client. To help your client, do not show how smart you are or how the mediator is not up to the job. We are not getting paid by the word or the number of times we are proven to be correct. What counts is the ultimate result. Try coming up with brilliant solutions and paving the way for your client or the mediator to present the solution. We can receive our acknowledgment and credit through the gratitude of our client in graduating from mediation with an agreement.
6. If we have a limited scope role, the best way to get fired is for the mediation to terminate prior to a settlement being reached. Therefore, it would be foolhardy to threaten litigation unless certain conditions are met. Termination of mediation has major costs for the client and the entire family, so our job is to do everything possible to keep the process going forward and prevent premature or preemptive threat or termination of the process.

PRACTICE TIPS

1. Any unbundled legal service products we choose to offer can supplement (not necessarily replace) our central existing product—representing clients in litigation.
2. By offering limited scope services to clients who would otherwise self-represent, we will be receiving revenue from clients who otherwise would not have hired a lawyer.

3. By serving as an unbundled client coach, we can provide guidance, information, and support to self-represented litigants without having the responsibility of being counsel of record.
4. We should develop our assessment skills to help clients decide whether to use discrete task lawyering or to hire us as counsel of record in a full-service package.
5. Customize coaching so that the level of lawyering fits the needs, ability, and value system of each client.
6. Education is a two-way street. As coach, educate the client; the client educates us on what working relationship is desired and will work best.
7. In drafting correspondence, the client can initiate drafts for us to review; conversely, prepare drafts to be sent by the client. In some situations, the client will ask us to send a letter on law office letterhead to provide more gravitas, where we can do so clarifying our role as a consulting or limited scope representative.
8. Before a negotiation, offer the client an opportunity to consult to develop a strategic plan and to role-play making and responding to offers.
9. Consider being a court coach to help prepare a client to go to trial on his or her own.
10. Lawyers who offer mediation-related services often receive calls from prospective clients and colleagues. These callers may be interested in the concept of unbundling generally or in specific service products offered by our office. By organizing materials in advance to include in packets, send out these educational and marketing materials quickly as well as minimize staff cost.
11. Malpractice carriers in many states (e.g., Minnesota) have developed forms and publications offering guidance about unbundled legal services. Check with insurance carriers in your jurisdiction for these useful resources.

CHAPTER 6

Representing Clients in Mediation with a Collaborative Lawyering Approach

Lawyers involved [in Collaborative Practice] are as committed to the resolution of the issues as are the parties. The Collaborative Process centers on a discovery of personal needs and interests and how those are prioritized by each spouse.

—Nancy J. Cameron, *Collaborative Practice: Deepening the Dialogue* (2014)

The previous chapter discussed how we to help mediation participants effectively without taking on the full role as counsel of record. This chapter will incorporate the values, protocols, and roles of collaborative lawyering while serving as consulting lawyer or unbundled coach in mediation.

COLLABORATIVE LAWYERING

Collaborative Law is an unbundled service that limits the scope of legal services by all lawyers contracting to bilaterally withdraw in the event that the matter is litigated. Collaborative Practice shares a core mediation principle; namely, that the process should empower the parties and make their interests central. Not only are lawyers less adversarial toward each other, but they also join together to ensure that the negotiation belongs to the parties. The lawyers expressly sign on to treat their own clients and the other party in a respectful and peaceful manner for the collective benefit of all members of the family.

While a Collaborative Law process generally does not include a mediator (with some exceptions, as neutrals can be invited to facilitate the process at times), it dovetails nicely with mediation to the extent that Collaborative Lawyers sign on to the following peacemaking principles:

- Respect and dignity for the other party and other professionals
- Direct and open communication with the other party and professionals

- Voluntary and full disclosure of relevant information and documents necessary to make agreements
- Commitment to the healing of the family
- Use of interest-based negotiation to try to meet the needs of both parties

Be a Beacon of Hope

One of a mediator's greatest attributes is to be the one person in the room who has an optimistic demeanor and belief that regardless of the conflict, progress toward an agreement, if not a written settlement, is possible.

The mediator does not need to be so lonely. As lawyer for one of the spouses, you can be a second beacon of hope.

When the other spouse or lawyer makes an outrageous offer, try to find the nugget of movement upon which to build. When your offer is rejected or gutted through an aggressive modification, shrug it off and come up with another proposal with more chance of acceptance.

If you are the target of verbal abuse, literally "turn the other cheek" and don't respond in kind.

Your rose-colored vision and grounded behavior will not only model positive negotiation behavior for your client, but also get you the respect of the other side and appreciation (and help) from the mediator.

Collaborative Law encourages the respectful use and cooperation of lawyers, mental health professionals, and financial professionals on behalf of divorcing families. The world's largest collaborative organization, the International Academy of Collaborative Professionals (www.collaborativepractice.com) is based on an interdisciplinary approach involving some or all of these professionals, and its mission is "to transform the way families resolve conflict by building a global community of . . . consensual dispute resolution professionals.[1] This practice encompasses many models, all informed by a unified goal of family conflict resolution through collaboration and consent among all professionals involved.

Collaborative Law puts a buffer between the parties and the courthouse by taking away the customary lawyer tools of threats and court action. The absence of such power and leverage tactics permits parties to focus on their own needs and those of people in their lives (children, business associates, members of their religious community, for instance) to build agreements. Whereas in mediation, we make participants aware of the risks and disadvantages of litigation alternatives

1. The principles of collaborative practice on the website of the International Academy of Collaborative Professionals (www.collaborativepractice.com) state, "While Collaborative lawyers are always a part of collaboration, some models provide child specialists, financial specialists and divorce coaches as part of the clients' divorce team. In these models the clients have the option of starting their divorce with the professional with whom they feel most comfortable and with whom they have initial contact. The clients then choose the other professionals they need. The clients benefit throughout collaboration from the assistance and support of all of their chosen professionals." IACP, *Standards and Ethics*, 2018, https://www.collaborativepractice.com/sites/default/files/IACP%20Standards%20and%20Ethics%202018.pdf.

to incentivize settlement; in Collaborative Law, we incentivize settlement by also contractually eliminating the litigation alternative, at least for the professionals involved in the process. The Clients always have the right to go to court with other professionals.

In the collaborative process, a contract, the participation agreement, provides for the inadmissibility of collaborative communication and documents. Privacy and confidentiality incentivize many clients to turn to mediation as well. Evolving regulations surrounding the inadmissibility of collaborative practice communications do clarify that some data may still be discoverable, as in Alabama, the District of Columbia, and other jurisdictions adopting section 17 of the Uniform Collaborative Law Act, "a collaborative law communication . . . is not subject to discovery and is not admissible in evidence," however, "evidence or information that is otherwise admissible or subject to discovery does not become inadmissible or protected from discovery solely because of its disclosure or use in a 'collaborative law practice.'" The participation agreement, which can be a private agreement among parties and professionals or a court order, helps further assuage parties' concerns. The disqualification clause in a participation agreement is a safe "container"[2] for the parties and professionals to use in working out issues without the imminent, looming specter of litigation.[3] As we discuss later in this chapter, such disqualification of mediation consulting lawyers can benefit mediation participants as well.

Why You Will Get More Work by Offering a Collaborative Approach

When Woody first started his mediation practice in 1979, he lived off the crumbs referred by other family lawyers. Over time, the flow of family law referrals has reversed. More recently, Lara's practice in New York has experienced the same reverse referral-flow shift. Mediators have become major referral sources for family lawyers for several reasons:

1. Many divorcing spouses make their first call to a mediator. Competent and trained mediators routinely encourage mediation participants to consult an attorney at some point in the process.
2. When making a referral for their clients, mediators want to select attorneys who will support the mediation, not blow it up. When referred lawyers have collaborative training, the mediator can facilitate an agreement with the expected help of lawyers who understand and value mediation principles and do not have one foot in the courthouse and the other in the mediation room. New mediators, who might not yet know attorneys in their community with relevant training, often refer parties to attorneys with listings in the directories on the IACP or other local collaborative practice websites, trusting that the approach of lawyers focused on such work aligns with the spirit of a mediated process.

---

2. *See* Pauline H. Tesler & Peggy Thompson, Collaborative Divorce (2007).

3. To train as collaborative lawyer, we recommend taking a basic course in collaborative training and several advanced collaborative training courses, studying the growing literature, and joining a local interdisciplinary collaborative practice group.

3. If we have a practice that favors consensual dispute resolution rather than litigation, mediators know that we are a prime referral sources for them. If we also offer a collaborative approach, this increases the expectation of mediators in our community that a referral to us might be reciprocated in the future.

For an in-depth exploration of how collaborative practitioners have developed successful practices, Woody Mosten and Adam Cordover's seminal volume, *Building a Successful Collaborative Law Practice*, offers a comprehensive survey of practitioner experiences and recommendations.

How to Use a Disqualification Agreement in Our Mediation Representation Work

At the beginning of a mediation, in determining what role lawyers will play, many mediators offer a protocol for how parties can maximize their use of lawyers during the mediation process. Mediators differ in whether they will offer any protocol or whether they will provide lawyer recommendations.

From the Consultant Lawyer

I did not know what to expect when I agreed to schedule 15 minutes to be jointly interviewed by the parties (with the mediator present) to potentially serve as consulting lawyer for one of the parties. Other than their names and their participation in mediation, I knew nothing about their family or the specific issues in the matter.

After a brief introduction by the mediator, the parties asked me a variety of questions, ranging from my background working with specific types of financial issues to whether I delegate work to associate lawyers to the billing increments that I utilize in determining charges. We did not get into discussion of any details or specifics in their matter.

As a mediator, I am no stranger to joint introductory meetings with parties to generally discuss the mediation process and whether I would be a good fit to work with both parties; however, this was different. The parties were looking to hire consulting lawyers that not only would be a good fit for each individual party but would be a good fit for the overall mediation process.

I was pleased to learn (a few hours after the joint interview), that one of the parties wished to hire me as his consulting lawyer. Working on this matter, I have found the joint interview process to be a "confidence building measure" for the parties within the mediation process. By jointly interviewing potential consulting lawyers from one list that they created together and utilizing a fully transparent process for selection, there would be no surprises for either party. In addition, this interview process provided the parties with joint control over all of the professionals involved in the process.

The trust building through the joint interview process has set the tone and contributed to the parties' desired transparent and collaborative process in mediation.

Jeffrey Jacobson is a Certified Family Law Specialist through the State Bar of California Board of Legal Specialization. He limits his practice exclusively to consensual dispute resolution, serving as Collaborative Lawyer, consulting lawyer, and mediator. He is a leader in the Los Angeles collaborative and family law community.

The following is a template protocol that we proactively provide to mediation parties early in the process. We offer it for consideration, not as to what is required, but as a summary of possible issues our clients (actual and potential) should consider in their relationship with us. After each point of the template protocol, we discuss some issues and alternative approaches for you to consider.

1. **If either of you wants to consult an attorney, you will let the other party and the mediator know promptly.** Under the law in most states, anyone (even a party in mediation!) has the absolute right to consult an attorney at any time. The fact that a party in mediation sees an attorney can be a private and confidential event between the party and the lawyer. The content of the communication between lawyer and client is statutorily privileged in virtually all jurisdictions. This means that without the provisions offered by this template protocol, the traditional and legally supported view is that if a mediation party wants to consult a lawyer, that is a private confidential decision and act and the other party or the mediator need never know.

In fact, in determining the standard for confidentiality of limited scope representation, California has parted company with many other states by providing complete confidentiality for anyone using an unbundled lawyer. Neither self-represented litigants nor their limited scope attorneys need to inform the court or the other party or lawyer if documents were prepared by or with the help of a lawyer. Specifically, according to the 2021 California Rules of Court, Rule 5.425 (f) an attorney who contracts with a client to draft or assist in drafting legal documents as part of a family law proceeding but does not make an appearance in the case is not required to disclose within the text of the document that he or she was involved in preparing the documents. That being said, Rule 5.425 (d) still notes, more generally, that "a party and an attorney must provide the required notice of their agreement for limited scope representation by serving other parties and filing with the court a Notice of Limited Scope Representation," making the family law drafting provision a notable exception. A few other states permit drafting assistance without disclosure; for example, Illinois Supreme Court Rule 137 makes it clear that an attorney may assist a person who is representing herself in drafting or reviewing a pleading or other paper without making a general or limited scope appearance and without the attorney signing the pleading or other paper. Missouri Rule 55.03(a) and Montana Rules of Civil Procedure 11 also permit a lawyer to draft pleadings or motions for self-represented litigants without signing the documents or disclosing lawyer involvement.

However, most states (Florida and Colorado being the leaders) have opted for an attorney disclosure protocol: self-represented litigants must to inform the court and the other party when a lawyer is providing ghostwriting help on court documents. In some states, this duty falls upon the lawyer to proactively provide such disclosure.

So why does this template protocol swim upstream against the legal current? The reason for this protocol is to support transparency of communication between the mediation parties and with the mediator. Providing the other party and the mediator with notice if a lawyer's advice may come into play serves several positive mediation goals.

First, many mediation parties who start without lawyers are afraid that the other party is getting legally coached from the sidelines to the disadvantage of the party going it alone. Such fear can escalate into paranoia or even to a premature termination of mediation out of fear of being outplayed by a "lawyer in the closet." By agreeing to this notice provision, the fearful party is on notice and can seek his or her own legal consultation, if he or she so chooses. A less positive consequence is that such a provision could deter one or both parties from consulting an attorney out of fear that by doing so, two lawyers might wrest control away from the parties in the mediation.

You Consulted a Lawyer? Process Betrayal

When Lara, as mediator, embarked on her first mediation session with Daniel and Meredith, she knew that the conversation would be emotionally charged. The parties had been married for twenty years, with three beloved pets between them and two beautiful homes that they had poured their hearts into renovating and decorating. Meredith was a significant earner while Daniel had tended to home and hearth. Daniel had just lost his mother, and had hoped he would not lose his marriage as well. The first mediation session was fraught. While soft tones of patience and understanding echoed in the room, the grief was palpable. Despite the atmosphere, the parties were able to honor one another in their exploration of mutual needs and acknowledged their disparate income realities. Just before the conclusion of the first session, where much progress had been made and a number of equitable distribution terms had been outlined, Meredith lightly mentioned "well, the lawyer that I consulted with did not tell me that my business profit share might be calculable as part of spousal support calculations." Daniel froze. It was not about the numbers. "You consulted a lawyer? I thought we were mediating. This is complete betrayal. You are a liar. I thought we were in an amicable process. I need a lawyer now. This was a waste of time." And he stormed out.

The parties did continue with mediation, and after a number of sessions and draft revisions, with the assistance of review attorneys, signed a global settlement that left each of them whole and able to move forward with their individual lives. However, the heartache that Daniel experienced upon discovering that Meredith had consulted with counsel in advance of that first session never fully subsided, and came up session after session. Had there been a protocol for Meredith letting Daniel know right away, or in advance of pursuing such a consultation, no one would have been blindsided and the initial energy of trust and respect might have been preserved.

Second, by alerting the mediator that lawyers will be consulted, the mediator can strategically plan to work with the parties to better address their concerns and provide more neutral information as requested by either party. If lawyers are to become involved after the parties have already engaged with mediation, the mediator can help improve selection and integration of the lawyers into the process as allies for settlement.

What is your approach to a prospective client who consults you and asks whether he should agree to this protocol offered by the mediator? We suggest that you inquire of your prospective client:

1. What is your understanding of the protocol for use of lawyers in mediation proposed by the mediator? Do you have a copy in writing?
2. What are your concerns or questions about this protocol?
3. Would you like to know what options there are to this protocol?
4. Would you like to discuss the benefits and downsides of the protocol proposed by the mediator and options we have discussed so that you can compare?

You also need to share any professional reservations or support that you have in working with a prospective client under the template protocol. If the mediation party is in favor of sharing attorney-client meetings and communications but you are not comfortable working with this approach, the most professional thing to do is turn down the assignment. However, it is important that you do so in a way that still empowers the client to make his own decision about agreeing to use of the protocol provided by the mediator or modified by agreement.

2. You will consult mediation-friendly consulting lawyers, unless a different agreement between the parties is made, and I have your authority to provide referrals of possible consulting lawyers to either of you without compromising my neutrality.
3. The purpose of this aspect of the protocol is to give mediation parties that have engaged with the mediation process prior to retaining attorneys the advantage of selecting a lawyer who will maximize the opportunity for settlement. We should consider two factors: the amount of mediation-supportive training we might have (or are planning to obtain) and the proven success record we have with a particular mediator.

A mediation participant, as any person engaging with a conflict resolution process, has the right to select any attorney of her choice. Actually, some parties may want to select an aggressive litigator to create leverage and power in an effort to get the best deal possible. A downside of selecting an adversarial attorney is that such pressure could result in an impasse or mediation termination rather than agreement. Yet, it is still the client's choice.

The underlying basis for an agreement requiring the parties to work with attorneys who have mediation or Collaborative Law training may be more obvious to clients than it is to lawyers. While many litigators do represent clients in mediation, those lawyers with mediation or collaborative training offer clients two advantages. First, these lawyers often understand the mediation process at a more sophisticated level. They know from training (and perhaps through experience as a mediator) what strategies and perspectives the mediator may be using. Such a lawyer will have training on how to prepare clients to give their opening statements; build an agenda; and even better, negotiate with the mediator. A second advantage of lawyers trained in mediation and Collaborative Law is that such lawyers generally support client-centered decision-making and may provide excellent support for their clients going through the challenges of mediation.

Basic training qualifications for an effective mediation friendly consulting lawyer in mediation include:

- Completion of a 40-hour family mediation training
- Completion of a two-day minimum basic Collaborative Law training
- Active membership in a collaborative practice group

If you do not meet these training qualifications presently, you might find available mediation training through mediation training programs or collaborative training from members of the International Academy of Collaborative Professionals (www.collaborativepractice.com) or your local Collaborative Law Group. In California, Collaborative Lawyers are listed in online rosters on https://collaborativepracticeeastbay.com/find-a-professional/, www.lacfla.org, and www.cdsoc.com, to name a few. In New York, collaborative attorney profiles can be found on websites such as www.nycollaborativeprofessionals.org and www.licdp.com, and mediation-friendly consulting attorneys can be found at www.nysmediate.org.

Mediators generally want to minimize risk of lawyer domination or adversarial posturing that often occurs when lawyers enter the mediation process. Past success of a lawyer with the mediator is one indication of lowered risk. Also, as experts in their field, mediators know which lawyers work well with them and have the skills and perspectives that result in satisfied clients. In light of this, a mediator might be best suited to recommend a consulting attorney, or a few consulting attorneys, to one or both of the participants in that mediator's process, and the mediator might seek acknowledgment and understanding from the participants that such recommendations are simply part of that mediator's process, without impact on that mediator's neutrality.

Some of the lawyering qualities that mediators appreciate through experience are to be knowledgeable and supportive of the mediation process, responsive to client needs, open and respectful to the other party, and nimble and creative in supporting a client-based solution that may fall outside the legal parameters. If we work to develop these qualities, more mediator referrals may be on the way.

Despite all of the preceding, mediators deeply value the participants' ownership over their process. If parties have retained attorneys prior to engaging with the mediation process, or if they truly feel strongly about seeking attorney review with lawyers that are not "mediation friendly" for personal reasons, mediators may feel comfortable proceeding as long as there is transparency about the involvement of such attorneys and consent between the parties, agreeing to proceed with a mediated process despite the retention of attorneys channeling a different ethos.

4. You and your client need to discuss and agree as to whether all communications with your attorney will remain confidential or whether you will share the advice if it provides information or different perspectives than have been discussed in mediation. As discussed earlier, the attorney-client privilege permits clients to keep all attorney-client communications confidential. This essentially protects secrets clients might tell you. In mediation, the fear of

secrets or the actual secret strategies can cause some lack of trust between parties that may destroy the possibility for successful mediation. Therefore, in evaluating whether you would participate in such a protocol of disclosure, you must decide whether your long-standing devotion to the lawyer-client privilege can give way to having your client share what you have told him or her with the other party and the mediator.

But why should you give up this highly protected legal privilege of confidentiality? What are the advantages of your client sharing these otherwise privileged and sacrosanct communications?

The key is transparent information and informed decision making. For example, what if during a mediation session for which you were not present, the parties are considering $1,500 a month in child support? You are representing Mom, who happens to be the primary custodial parent, and your calculations show $2,200 a month in child support. You have also told your client that you cannot see any legal reason why she should accept less than $2,200.

What would be the advantage of your client not sharing this otherwise privileged advice with Dad and the mediator? Perhaps, your client does not want to anger Dad or has other issues that she wants to negotiate that dwarf the importance of the $700 difference in child support.

What would be the advantage to your client of her sharing your advice with Dad and the mediator? First, Mom would not have to keep a secret. Secrets beget more secrets, and secrets beget fear, which in turn begets preemptive aggressive moves, termination of mediation, or both. Second, Mom could share your advice in a mediation session and Dad might agree with your assessment, resulting in an agreement (perhaps on modified terms). And third, if Dad does not agree, at least he is informed of what Mom has learned from you and they can discuss the issue of child support with the benefit of this fuller information.

5. Once you engage an attorney, you need to discuss and agree whether the mediator should send summary agreements to the attorney, whether the mediator may communicate with the attorneys, and whether such communications shall be confidential or disclosed to the other party. It is becoming commonplace for mediators to send out summary letters following mediation sessions. These letters are also known as minutes or progress notes. These summary letters contain agreements reached in session, discussions that resulted short of agreement, assignments for either party, and the mediator's observations and recommendations for substantive agreements and for an improved process. For example, in a summary letter, the mediator might state:

> You agreed to arrange transitions of parenting care in a way that would reduce conflict during the transition itself. Toward that end, you agreed to always greet each other in a friendly way, not conduct business (negotiate children's events or finances) during the transition, and, for the parent dropping off, to say good-bye and kiss the children in the car before the transition and to leave as quickly as possible to reduce the loyalty conflict of the children during these important

> moments. You also agreed to try and arrange drop offs and pickups at school or activities so that only the parent starting parenting time would be present. I called these "blind transitions."

These summary letters are not binding. They are used to help parties remember what happened during sessions and serve as a structured anchor for out-of-session work. If parties want these agreements to be enforceable and binding on them, they would need to each sign a written agreement that contains the "magic word" of being a binding agreement, admissible and enforceable by the court.

It is important for you to be aware of these letters sent your clients by the mediator for two reasons. First, it gives us a heads-up as to what is going on the mediation so that we can discuss midcourse corrections with our clients. Second, and equally important, if we are fully engaged during the agreement-making process, we can appreciate and understand the trade-offs leading to a final agreement so that their agreement review is more accurate and supportive than if we are coming in from the cold.

If either of you want your attorney to attend a mediation session, this may occur without the agreement of the other party. However, the party intending to have his or her lawyer attend must give at least three days' notice to the other party and to you so that the other party may bring her or his lawyer. If a set time for a mediation is not convenient for either lawyer, it is agreed that the date of the mediation will be changed to accommodate both you and your client and both lawyers. You may be accustomed to attending mediation with your client to offer protection and advice and to be in charge of the negotiation. This occurs most often in cities and regions in which mediation is viewed as a late-stage process in litigation consisting of a single session presided by a third-party neutral (generally, a retired judge or a veteran litigation lawyer) who evaluates the strengths and weaknesses of each party's position and gives directive recommendations for compromise settlement terms. This view of mediation is often accompanied by the mantra "A good settlement is one that makes both parties equally unhappy."

The preceding view of mediation is heavily steeped in an "old paradigm" view of negotiation and settlement. This "old paradigm" is rights-based and lawyer-centered, and settlements are seen as compromises reached primarily to avoid the uncertainty of litigation.[4]

The mediation process underlying this protocol is very different from a collaborative approach. First, rather than assuming that a mediation will be a one-time conference or hearing, it is based on sequential sessions. Each of these sessions is two to four hours in duration. Rather than assuming that a global agreement will be reached at the end of a session, the sequential session model prepares parties and lawyers to work toward an agreement over time rather than pressuring everyone to come up with an agreement by the end of the session.

Although lawyers often attend sequential sessions with their clients, the protocol discussed here is designed for the many situations in which parties attend

---

4. Leonard L. Riskin & Nancy A. Welsh, *Is That All There Is? "The Problem" in Court-Oriented Mediation*, 15(4), GEORGE MASON L. REV. 863–932 (2008). Riskin and Welsh describe mediation as lawyer and legal culture-dominated in much the same way as described here.

sessions with the lawyers absent or on the sidelines. The protocol is designed to accommodate a smooth and nonthreatening procedure if one party wants a lawyer to attend a session. Notice is given to prevent fear and pressure. Also, once one party has decided to have a lawyer, two changes in the mediation process result. First, the other party is afforded the same opportunity to attend. Second, scheduling must accommodate both lawyers in addition to the parties and mediators—no session will be scheduled without the entire mediation "team" present. Clients are essential members of this team!

Mediation Disqualification Agreement

As discussed earlier, the key element defining collaborative practice is the attorney disqualification clause. This definition is ratified by the Uniform Collaborative Law Act, state statutes, court cases, and by virtually all of state and local Collaborative Practice Law Groups.

The same benefits of an attorney disqualification clause can apply to lawyers involved in the mediation process. By agreeing to terminate services upon the termination of mediation or initiation of court action, you create a barrier to the courthouse steps. Your client may always avail himself of court action, but if your client does, he or she will need to hire another lawyer.

We firmly believe in the mantra "Every day out of court is another day out of court!" We have seen many seemingly intractable situations somehow work themselves out through further discussion and modification of the mediation process. However, once the Maginot Line of a contested court hearing is crossed, the unintended consequences and harm are usually far worse than imagined.

Many clients will not be comfortable with this disqualification process. They either want the negotiation leverage that threats sometimes provide or do not want to start looking for another attorney should mediation terminate. It is not uncommon for clients to have such concerns. After all, they are often mediating the biggest deal of their lives with someone with whom they may have little trust and a poor negotiation history. Your mission, should you choose to accept it, is to be open to the possibility of working with such a disqualification clause, should the client want it. A sample clause is provided in the Resources section. Because over 60 percent of court-ordered mediations result in full settlements (even higher in self-selected mediations), the odds are that no litigation will be necessary anyway. And if despite the odds, parties should initiate litigation, there are many litigators from whom your client can choose. Your true focus should be in making mediation the last stop on the dispute resolution highway. If your involvement with a disqualification agreement can smooth the path for mediated agreement (or help the client feel better about that possibility), we suggest that you familiarize yourself with the disqualification option and consider accepting engagements involving this option.

Use of Other Collaborative Professionals in Mediation

If you have some experience in representing clients in mediation, you should be well versed in the involvement of therapists working as mediators, co-mediators child specialists, or other roles. Therapists can also enter the mediation process as evaluators, consultants, and treating therapists for the parties and their children.

Financial professionals also are involved as neutral or party consultants, providing opinions about business valuation, marital lifestyle, or cash flow analyses for support as well as advice on tax issues. Financial planners can help with the preparation of budgets and explanation of the long-term financial ramifications of particular settlement proposals, and insurance or real estate professionals offer help in obtaining appraisals and necessary policies.

One of your key goals should be to find those professionals who have substantive expertise as well as knowledge of and commitment to the mediation process. We have found many child custody evaluators who are directive toward the parties and resistant to mediative roles. The same is true of many financial professionals who are ingénues to the mediation process.

A resource in your community for professional recommendations in mediation are the mental health and financial professionals listed on your local collaborative practice website (for the collaborative practice groups in your area, consult www.collaborativepractice.com.) Most of the professionals listed have had mediation training and experience. The following are some of the roles these professionals play in collaborative practice that can be adapted for mediations.

Divorce Coach/Process Facilitator/Communications Coach

Many collaborative practice groups require divorce coaches to be licensed therapists from a variety of backgrounds: clinical psychologists, social workers, and marriage and family therapists/counselors. These collaborative divorce coaches may be in addition to parenting coaches consulted by the parties. While their roles may differ, the following are some descriptions of how you might involve a collaborative divorce coach in a mediation.

To manage and contain emotions, coaches can work directly with the parties to help them and their children get through the divorce process with a minimum of pain and long-term negative impact. Rather than providing therapy to treat disorders or produce long-term behavior change, coaches educate and support the parties through the divorce crisis period. The coach avoids using diagnostic labels or getting caught up in symptoms and complaints. The coach is looking for positive "can-do" solutions to help the client overcome emotional barriers to reaching agreement.

Experienced mediator and coach David Kuroda LCSW in Los Angeles sets out the following clear, limited goals for coaches:

- **Identify and prioritize client concerns.** Help the client identify his or her concerns and emotions and assist in helping the client to share these emotional issues with his or her spouse. At the same time, help each client understand and appreciate how his or her own power and behavior impacts the spouse. The coach can give tips to the client to modulate the impactful behavior to reduce reactions from the other party. In the tradition of the prolific Dr. Murray Bowen, coaches can help parties reduce the emotional reactivity toward each other by helping them to "differentiate"—get some distance from the emotional enmeshment of the parties so that they can think things through rather than react with tantrums or cold withdrawal.

- **Prepare the client to succeed in the mediation process.** The coach can teach the client what to expect in joint sessions and how to maximize progress by giving ideas about how best to work with lawyers and other professionals as well as with his or her spouse. Discuss and rehearse for the emotional fallout of seemingly "safe" legal and financial issues. The coach can help the client normalize common emotional reactions and make problems seem solvable by showing how most people going through divorce deal with them. For example, coaches can discuss how most people are caught up in roles and communication patterns that did not work in the marriage and will not work in the divorce negotiations. By identifying such patterns, the coach can help the client avoid such negative repeated interactions altogether, take a detour if they come up, or minimize the reaction if the pattern comes up during a session.
- **Catch the client doing well.** It is somewhat of a miracle that anyone going through divorce is able to be mature, reflective, and nonreactive with the person that they are divorcing during the most important negotiation in their lives! If there is ever a time to regress or act immature, this is it. Yet, we expect parties to mediation to be at their best—or even better than their best. Rather than try to remake the client going through one of life's toughest challenges, coaches often try to identify the positive and constructive behaviors exhibited by the client, point them out, and encourage the client to do it again. Coaches can help parties recognize their best personal attributes and call on them during this family crisis.
- **Educate the client about tested parenting and communication guidelines and help them practice.** Coaches can teach parties what to say and not say to each other and to their children as well as how to say it. Coaches can effectively use Web resources such as www.uptoparents.org or films such as *Split* by Ellen Bruno as learning tools to improve behaviors. Coaches can also recommend books for children of divorcing parents to read, based on their developmental age and literacy level, such as *Two Homes*, *Dinosaurs Divorce*, and *Why Do Families Change?*, to name a few.
- **Educate parties about the impact of different parenting plans; help the client select the most appropriate plan and discuss the plan with the other spouse.** There are wonderful books (e.g., *Mom's House, Dad's House*) and court-sponsored websites about parenting plans.[5] Coaches can review this material with clients and help them make sense out of them.
- **Assess and screen for signs of domestic violence, child abuse, or other forms of coercive control.** In addition to their process skills, many coaches have undergone specialized training related to domestic violence and can play an invaluable role in screening and providing protections within the collaborative process. Coaches also are attuned to child-related issues that can be addressed within the privacy of the collaborative process.

---

5. The Arizona State Court website is a useful model that can be used outside Arizona as well, http://www.azcourts.gov/portals/31/parentingtime/ppwguidelines.pdf.

- **Contribute to the communication and teamwork of the collaborative team.** Coaches can play an invaluable role in coordinating the efforts of different professionals and facilitating teamwork.
- **Provide emotional support for the client during and between mediation sessions.** Mediation sessions can be overwhelming even for the strongest of divorcing parties. Some legislation allows parties who are ordered by the court to attend mediation (especially alleged victims of abuse) to have nonlawyer resource persons available to lend support. Coaches are trained to handle outbursts and breakdowns and prevent premature termination of the process. Some parties can contain their behavior during sessions, yet need a shoulder to cry on or helpful hints between sessions. Coaches can be invaluable in that role.

Child Specialist/Co-Parenting Coach

While a mental health professional with child specialist credentials may serve in the broader role as coach for one party or as a neutral more generally, the parties may choose to engage a child specialist in addition to parties' individual coaches. In such engagements, the child specialist is generally a neutral resource for the parties and their children. Information about the child's point of view or suggestions about co-parenting strategies are likely to be heard and respected more fully when they emanate from a qualified neutral person as opposed to the other party.

In the limited role as neutral child specialist, the mental health professional is the "voice" for the child(ren). The child specialist's main focus is to keep the children's concerns and needs at the top of the agenda and to maximize the children's sense that they are being heard by the adults who are handling the reorganization of their family. In joint meetings with the parents, the child specialist can take a family history and assess the parental concerns and the parenting needs of the parties. The specialist may use a number of data collection instruments, including parent and child questionnaires, psychological written testing, and review information such as parental and children emails, report cards, medical records, videos and photos, and reports from other professionals.

In serving a facilitative, non-evaluative role, the child specialist can help the parents set boundaries and lessen derogatory or pejorative behavior toward the other parent, handle concerns about parental incapacity due to substance abuse, improve and increase consistency on discipline, diet, bedtime, homework, and coordination of activities, handle the appropriate integration of new romantic partners, and help the parties reduce their conflict in front of the children.

The child specialist can serve as a consultant for the children and can educate the parents and answer their questions about children's needs in general based on the specialist's training and experience as well as research. In meetings with children, the child specialist can explain to the children how their parents are handling the divorce in a child-centered way, describe the divorce process to the children, create a sense of comfort and safety for the children, and provide honesty and transparency toward what is happening in their lives. Child specialists can also make assessments and work with the children in reducing their risks from divorce and increasing their resilience and ability to adapt during this stressful and often disruptive period in their lives.

In addition, the specialist translates the children's needs for the family in one of several ways:

- Meeting directly with the children and reporting their needs to the parents alone or in a five-way feedback session involving attorneys and coaches
- Discussing the children's needs with other therapists, teachers, and "collateral providers" of the children (e.g., nanny, sports coaches, tutors, clergy) and reporting back through a written report and or feedback session
- Facilitating the children's direct involvement with the parents

Sometimes, even with the involvement of a child specialist, parents will have unresolved disputes over key parenting issues. Confidential or nonconfidential evaluation, whether comprehensive or focused on one issue, can also be conducted within or in conjunction with the mediation process.[6]

Financial Professionals

The use of neutral financial professionals (e.g., CPAs, financial planners, tax lawyers, pension specialists) rather than separate experts retained by each party is common in mediation. Every collaborative financial professional has undergone at least the basic course in collaborative practice and often has taken advanced courses in collaborative practice, mediation, and conflict resolution. Collaborative financial specialists also attend dispute resolution conferences and typically participate in ongoing collaborative and mediation study groups. This means that in addition to their financial expertise, these specially trained financial professionals are skilled at active listening, discussion facilitation, and interdisciplinary teamwork.

Some of the typical duties of financial professionals include:

- Gathering and organizing financial documents
- Developing a statement of assets and liabilities-marital balance sheet
- Preparing a marital standard of living analysis
- Running hypothetical computer searches for statutory guidelines for child and spousal support
- Analyzing cash flow (income and living expenses for each party and expenses for the children in each home)
- Determining imputed income for non-income-producing investment property and for support purposes
- Performing present value calculations for deferred streams of income such as spousal support, defined benefit plans, and annuities
- Analyzing ability of each party to purchase a new residence or the need to sell the family residence

6. Forrest S. Mosten, *Confidential Mini Evaluations: Another ADR Option* 45(1) FAM. L. Q. (ABA Spring 2011).

- Preparing written financial disclosures for each party
- Valuing and distributing retirement assets
- Valuing business interests
- Providing advice on income tax filings, capital gains, support deductibility, and other tax issues
- Determining college expenses and recommending financial plans

Neutral financial professionals can provide financial advice and analysis for the parties in an impartial way. Financial professionals contribute their views of the common financial interests and goals of both parties and creatively develop options for review by the parties, lawyers, and mediator. Financial professionals can be active participants in the negotiation process, offering financial perspectives and input on various proposals. They can provide analysis and practical advice for long-term outcome of proposed financial agreements. For example, they can factor in inflation, increased needs of parties and children, and return on investments and can help parties identify and evaluate various settlement options.

The key role of financial professionals is to educate the parties. As there are many technical and nuanced concepts and terms, a competent financial professional will patiently explain (in understandable language, not "accountant-ese") what the concepts mean, what work is needed, who will do the work, and how the work fits into the overall resolution of the divorce.

One of the key roles you can play as a consulting attorney is to be a resource of ideas and personnel. By incorporating the people and concepts of collaborative practice and involving professionals who have a demonstrated commitment to non-adversarial divorce, you increase your value not only to your client but also to the mediation process.

PRACTICE TIPS

1. Build relationships with collaborative and mediation-friendly professionals in your area. Get to know their strengths, weaknesses, specialties, and demeanor. The more professionals you know, the better able you will be to suggest people who are a good fit for a given case.
2. Don't be afraid to import concepts, roles, and interventions from Collaborative Law into your mediations when appropriate.
3. Obtain informed consent when involving a collaborative professional in your mediation. Define the collaborative professional's role carefully and explicitly.
4. Enlist the input of the collaborative professionals in determining how they might best be used to solve a particular problem or impasse.
5. Be prepared to discuss your preferred qualifications for a consulting attorney and draw from the ready pool of collaboratively trained attorneys in your community.
6. Study the aspects of attorney disqualification in collaborative cases and consider importing them into your representation of mediation parties.

7. Attend trainings, seminars, and conferences in Collaborative Law. If you do not have formal training, complete a reputable training program. Read practice building books such as Building a Successful Collaborative Family Law Practice (Mosten & Cordover).
8. Prepare your client to raise the issue of an agreed-upon protocol for using collaborative attorneys at the start of mediation so that the other party is less likely to engage a litigator to serve in that role.
9. Utilize collaborative websites as resources for mental health and financial professionals to get involved in mediation.
10. Even if the other party or mediator resists, remain flexible, tolerant, and collaborative in your approach toward noncollaborative behavior.
11. Consider involving interdisciplinary professional experts in mediation, outside of the collaborative arena.

CHAPTER 7

Setting Up the Mediation

"Alone we can do so little; together we can do so much."

—Helen Keller

SELECTING THE MEDIATOR

Once a decision has been made to mediate, the next step is to determine who the mediator will be. Mediators have different professional orientations and take a variety of approaches. We must advise our clients about the importance of selecting the appropriate mediator and take steps to ensure a fair process that will meet our client's needs.

Finding the expert: We need certain expertise to ensure that our client's consent to the mediation is appropriately informed. We need to be aware of and conversant in different mediation orientations and philosophies (e.g., evaluative vs. facilitative). For example, if an evaluative approach is not likely to further settlement in a particular case, the substantive expertise and litigation or judicial experience of the mediator—while valuable in a courtroom—may not be enough to get the parties to the finish line. We should also know the field of locally available mediators well enough to speak to the skills and orientation of possible mediators, their reputations in the community, their levels of experience, and any particular skill sets they offer that might be relevant to the dispute at hand. If we don't have this information, we need to poll our trusted colleagues, review mediation organization, court roster, and individual mediator websites, and gather information about potential mediators just as we would if we needed a referral to an attorney in a different practice area. Matching the matter at hand to the best suited mediator can be one of the most important ways in which we represent and support our clients as they embark on an effective mediation journey.

Cultural competence: If our clients' lives hold unique demographic elements, where identity affiliations may have process implications, we should look for cultural competency. Successful cross-cultural interactions require mutual awareness of cultural differences and respect for these differences. Culture is not merely a function of a person's region of origin; cultural identity can be shaped by a multitude of factors, including without limitation faith, ethnicity, race, physical abilities, educational background, class, gender, sexual orientation, geographical location, the language or languages spoken in the home, and profession. Culture influences perspective, and differences in perspective can lead to conflict. A mediator's ability to navigate the cultural differences among disputing parties, or to understand the cultural similarities that govern a particular family's values and inform the parties' decisions, is paramount for success of dispute resolution. Cultural competence (i.e., the capacity to navigate cultural differences effectively) is an essential aspect of the mediation toolkit. "Cultural competence is about acknowledging implications of cultural differences for a dispute and its outcomes, and then transcending them in a respectful and productive manner to arrive at an optimal resolution for all disputing parties."[1]

An Uneven Playing Field Doesn't Mean Ending the Game

Jim and Marta wanted to get married. Marta had been the housekeeper for Jim and his first wife before their separation. (Remember *Down and Out in Beverly Hills*?) Jim wanted a premarital agreement, and Marta wanted anything that Jim wanted. Jim wanted to mediate the agreement to cut out the lawyers.

Sounds imbalanced? It was. Language difficulty, financial naïveté, immigration problems, and deep infatuation spelled out duress if not coercion. If you ran away from this one as either a lawyer or a mediator, no one would blame you. But Marta and Jim wanted to get married. Jim wanted the agreement to provide for his children and to protect himself from a possible divorce. All they both wanted was help.

The first challenge as mediator was to work with Jim to allow him to understand why it was in his best interest for Marta to have a lawyer and an interpreter at the sessions. At his request, Woody took on the assignment of finding Marta a lawyer and accompanying her to the lawyer interviews. Four interviews later, Marta had a lawyer who was both independent from and supportive of the mediation. The lawyer was the key to the mediation. Three sessions later, Jim had his agreement, and he and Marta have their new life together.

Vetting for Training: Many family law mediators are retired judicial officers or family law litigation veterans. Although their substantive knowledge may be impressive and their instincts about likely litigation outcomes finely honed, these family law experts may be new to facilitative mediation and/or may not have received appropriate mediation training. In some states, family law and divorce mediators receive training over a 40-hour period, at a minimum. However, in many states, the mediation profession is not formally regulated and certification norms are not uniform. It is important that mediators receive comprehensive training that provides them with a basic understanding of the nuances of mediation, imparts key skills, and helps ensure that mediators live up to the promise

1. Dave Aschaiek, *The Mediator's Toolkit: Cultural Competence: Transcending Culture Differences in Mediation*, MEDIATE.COM (Dec. 5, 2011). *See also* Allan Barsky, David Este & Don Collins, *Cultural Competence in Family Mediation* 13(3) MEDIATION Q. (Spring 1996).

of mediation and meet the clients' needs. We can do our due diligence on behalf of our clients and ensure that our selected mediator has been adequately trained.

Match the Needs of Both Parties: Not only should we keep in mind the needs, preferences, and temperament of our own client, but we should attempt to meet those of the other party as well. We need to find out from our client what kind of approach he or she feels is most likely to resonate with the other party. For example, our client may be far along into the process of grieving the loss of the relationship, ready to settle, and committed to mediation. The other side, however, may be more emotionally raw and less comfortable with the idea of getting a divorce, let alone starting mediation. In such a situation, we may wish to maximize chances of the other side coming to the table and staying there by selecting a mediator with a facilitative, gentle approach or personality type likely to appeal to the *other* client.

Discuss Options with Your Client: Once we have researched which mediators are available and formed some preliminary opinions about who might be a good fit and why, we should talk this through with our client. We must set aside sufficient time for this crucial conversation. Send the client links to internet information about potential mediators you have found. Compare and contrast each potential mediator's strengths and weaknesses to help your client make an informed choice. Explain information about the potential mediators and how this information might affect the client's mediation experience. If we have an existing professional relationship with the mediator, we need to disclose and discuss that fact with the client. A clients need to know that a professional mediator will not favor them just because the mediator knows and respects her lawyer.

Some clients will take the initiative and come up with a mediator or mediators on their own. We should encourage clients to do this. One of the goals of mediation is to place power in the participants themselves, and if clients believe they have participated actively in the selection of the mediator, they will be empowered, invested, and generally more optimistic about the mediation process.

Letting the Other Spouse/Counsel Nominate a Mediator

Schooled in the trench-warfare mentality of litigation, you may be accustomed to jockeying for tactical advantage over even the most technical and minute issues: jurisdiction, venue, judge, evaluator, and even location of the settlement talks (your office or theirs). As in most process decisions involved in setting up a mediation, we generally favor using the mediator proposed by the other side. Because resolution of settlement terms in mediation are ultimately consensual, a client rarely will be harmed by the choice of the mediator. Remember, unlike judges and arbitrators, mediators do not make binding decisions. Moreover, our primary goal is to set up the mediation so that the parties can work out their problems and come to a fair settlement. It is possible to get so bogged down in trying to game the logistics of the mediation that the opportunity to mediate gets lost. All of the strategic micromanagement in the world won't make a difference if the parties never get to the table!

Also, as an attorney, we can model for clients how they should approach the dispute, and we can have a profound impact on the parties' attitudes merely by setting a tone that is conducive to the mediation. Flexible, accommodating behavior by counsel models an agreement-making mode that increases settlement momentum for the parties. There are, of course, circumstances in which specific factors render deferring to the other side's choice of mediator impractical or unwise. We should exercise a veto if we suspect a proposed mediator has a demonstrable connection or favoritism toward the other party or lawyer. What if the other lawyer has worked with this mediator ten times and you only once? What if the other lawyer and the mediator are golfing buddies? What if the other lawyer and the mediator have spoken together on a recent continuing education panel? What if the mediator's office is in the same building or suite as the other lawyer? These factors could cause concern that the mediator favors the other party, and in some cases, such suspicions might be valid. However, several safeguards built into mediation favor letting it go.

First, mediators build their practices based on their reputations for neutrality and fairness. Most mediators are zealously committed to preserving this reputation and will themselves decline a matter that poses a conflict to these principles.

Second, mediators have a growing obligation to disclose prior contact with lawyers and parties. In some locales, mediators specifically list all the matters in which they have previously participated with each counsel and often circulate that list in the same packet as the mediation agreement. Retired judicial officers tend to be especially vigilant of this issue and comfortable disclosing prior matters involving counsel. Detailed, unsolicited disclosure itself should give our client a feeling of comfort concerning the mediator's integrity. (Of course, a failure to disclose or a "fudge" disclosure could raise major concerns.)

Third, if the mediator ever does display bias in favor of the other side, we can end the mediation immediately. Although such delayed termination could result in wasted mediation fees and possibly hurt settlement momentum, it is generally preferable to get the mediation started in the first place rather than delay or not have the mediation at all.

Fourth, if a party expresses a concern about bias, the mediator may be consciously on guard and may even increase his or her vigilance for fairness. Because the other lawyer proposed the mediator, we and our client can gain comfort that, if the mediator presses the other spouse during the mediation, the mediator is exhibiting appropriate balance and deserves respect and increased credence.

Barring specific information tending to indicate that the other party's choice would do our client palpable harm, we may presumptively favor using the other party's recommendation. Instead of constantly maneuvering to improve our client's position, our test should be "If it doesn't hurt my client, *let it go*." This may be a novel and frightening approach to many lawyers who worry that their zealousness may be called into question if they miss a single opportunity to control a decision. But if we have worked collaboratively with the other party's attorney before, or have worked with the nominated mediator before and feel good about the mediator's integrity, fairness, process experience, reputation, and competence in the area of dispute, it is probably best to let the issue go.

The Mediator Nominating Process

Generally, the mediation setup process is facilitated when the party or lawyer most resistant to commencing mediation has the option of nominating the mediator. However, the resisting lawyer may be inexperienced in mediation and may not have the knowledge to make a nomination. In addition, the other lawyer may be busy, skeptical, (or lazy) and willing to let us make the nomination. In such situations, we should be careful not to abuse the trust reposed in us by the other side. We should discuss our intended process with the other lawyer and attain consent along the way to avert any accusations of manipulating the process. Aligning with the other lawyer as our partner starts with the selection process and can continue until the settlement agreement is signed, and beyond.

The first step in mediator nomination is to identify the type of mediator background and style that most suits the parties and the nature of the dispute (yes, both parties!). It is then important to assemble background information on each of several possible mediators (three is a good, but not perfect, number), with a gender mix if possible. In addition to a curriculum vitae and the mediator's standard mediation agreement, request a sample of articles written by or about the mediator and any promotional material the mediator can provide. Many family lawyers keep files on a wide and diverse group of mediators so that nominations can be sent out as needed. The nominations should be sent with a cover letter/email making it clear that the other party has the unilateral right to choose among the mediators proposed. We may also clarify the other party's option to reject all three, in which case other names will be provided. The letter should contain a full disclosure of our past professional and personal involvement with each of the nominated mediators. If there are any pending court hearings coming up for this case, we should indicate a willingness to continue the dates of the hearings, preserving the status quo of any current orders, retroactivity, or other issue that may be necessary for the protection of the clients. If agreement cannot be reached on an issue, we should indicate a willingness to address that issue first in mediation. Finally, it is helpful if the other party is offered an opportunity to interview any or all of the nominated mediators (with your client paying half the cost). Of course, our client should also have the right to interview any mediator selected by the other party.

A cutting-edge protocol for selecting a mediator is to permit the clients to interview potential mediators with both lawyers present during the interview session. Using Zoom or another online platform, mediator interviews can be as short as 10 to 20 minutes so that four mediators could be interviewed in a single Zoom hour. Mediators will rarely seek compensation for this cameo appearance, although practices may vary. Some questions that can be asked of the mediators include:

- Where did you get your mediation training?
- How long have you been practicing mediation?
- What training have you received?

- What have you learned in your training that will help us in this mediation? Do you have unique cultural competencies or attributes that give you greater insights into the dynamics this family might be facing?
- How many mediations have you done with consulting attorneys?
- Are you a member of a local Mediation Practice group, and what have you learned from that group that will help you help us in this mediation?
- Are you a mediator member of your State Mediation Organization, a national organization such as the Academy of Professional Family Mediators, or other Professional Mediation Groups?
- Have you ever been through a divorce or are you a child of divorce? If so, how did you handle it? Do you bring your personal experiences into your practice as a mediator?
- What are the biggest risk factors in the mediation ahead for us?
- How do you balance power when one party has greater wealth or income? How do you balance power when cultural dynamics inform a communally learned and preserved imbalance?
- What biases do you have about divorce and what parties should or should not do?

Designing the Process

Setting up a mediation can be as simple and straightforward as the parties and lawyers want it to be. Certain steps can enhance the success of a mediation, and pitfalls can abort it from the start.

Approving the Mediation Agreement

Most (if not all) competent mediators require the parties to sign a written mediation contract before any negotiation takes place. Such an agreement contractually protects confidentiality (some states preserve mediation confidentiality by statute even without agreement), spells out the mediator's basic rules, and provides for payment of the mediator's fee. (See the sample mediation agreement and the model standards in the Resources section.)

While every clause is subject to negotiation, the "let it go" standard also applies here. Mediation agreements vary from mediator to mediator. We and our client should review the agreement closely so that we are familiar with both the text and consequences of the provisions of the mediator contract. However, unless the agreement contains language that is prejudicial to our client or omits some protection that cannot be dispensed with, diluted, or obtained down the road, it is usually far better to just sign the agreement and move to the next stage of the mediation. Haggling over ground rules has killed many potential mediations that could have helped the families involved.

Orientation with the Mediator

In elementary school, many of us learned the lesson of the five Ps—Prior Preparation Precludes Poor Performance. The same is true in mediation. Many lawyers' only experience with mediation occurs in the courthouse, where the parties (and often counsel) sit down cold with a mediator, entirely unprepared, and within an hour either reach complete agreement or give up and proceed to court. Because court-annexed mediation has an approximate success rate of 60 percent, many lawyers believe that mediation works quickly or not at all and that the odds are four in ten that a particular case will end up in a contested hearing. Private mediation can work very differently. In 2019, the American Bar Association[2] updated its general dispute resolution statistics to confirm that mediations end in agreement approximately 80 percent of the time, and our own experience and informal survey of competent family law mediators and mediation-friendly lawyers indicate that 85–90 percent of matters starting in private mediation end in a complete agreement. The remaining cases often settle soon thereafter, having used the mediation as a foundation for negotiated agreement or as a forum for streamlining the litigation.

The initial orientation sets the stage for the process and benefits lawyers, parties, and the mediator like. The lawyers and parties benefit by receiving a tour of the mediation landscape so that they know what to expect in the process. In turn, the mediator needs to understand the needs and concerns of both the parties and their lawyers to better design, convene, and facilitate the mediation.

Telephone/Zoom Conference Call

At a minimum, counsel should arrange to have a joint conference to set up the date(s) of the mediation and the briefing schedule and to determine who should be at the table, how food is to be arranged (if the session is taking place in person), the time of day, and other administrative details. We should consult with our client as to whether having the parties join that conference call is important. Of course, the other party or lawyer may feel differently about such client involvement and you may need to work this out or just "let it go" and handle it in accordance with the other side's comfort level.

Setting the Date for the Mediation

The success of a mediation may depend on when it is scheduled and how much time is reserved for the mediation itself. The goal should be to set the mediation for the earliest possible date while allowing sufficient time for the parties and counsel to prepare adequately. Lawyer attitudes toward mediation are just as important as openings on everyone's calendar. Lawyers who are experienced in representing clients in mediation understand that the probability of success at the mediation is very high if it is scheduled before further acts or posturing or conflict (involving parties or counsel) extinguish interest/motivation in settlement.

Actually, the long wait for a courthouse mediation appointment or an impending hearing date may be a primary motivation to initiate private mediation. If lawyers are going to be meeting with the mediator along with their clients and/or be present at the mediation sessions themselves, no more than two to six weeks

---

2. American Bar Association, *How Courts Work*, Sept. 9, 2019, https://www.americanbar.org/groups/public_education/resources/law_related_education_network/how_courts_work/mediation_advantages/.

should elapse between the date of agreement to mediate and the commencement of mediation. If the parties will be mediating without lawyers, it is often possible to commence mediation within a few days. More mediators are being trained every year and the supply of qualified mediators is increasing.

This increased supply offers more choice and makes waiting weeks or months for an opening less acceptable. In any community, the top echelon of mediators will always be in high demand and the waiting time for them will be the longest. The involvement of such highly regarded mediators does in fact increase the odds that a case will be resolved in a satisfactory manner. However, lag time between agreement to mediate and the start date may decrease the chances of settlement, cause the mediation to be more protracted or conflictual, or increase the risk that the mediation never actually begins. Balancing the best choice of mediator with an accelerated start date is a key area of mediation strategy for lawyers.

Invite All Parties to the Table

Here is one of Woody's mediation stories:

> My client was the son of a powerful industrialist. Father and son were co-owners of the company but wouldn't talk with each other. They sent faxes even though their offices shared an adjoining wall. The presenting reason for the spat was that Howard, the dad, had been rude to his son's wife. My client, Steven, and his father started fighting—but so did Steven and his wife—which led him and his business litigator into my office.
>
> Steven loved and hated his father. He didn't want to stay in business with his father, but was equally agitated that his estranged wife was keeping the children from seeing their grandparents. Steven did not have much love for Howard's new wife (who was the same age as Steven).
>
> Before starting work on the divorce, I spent considerable time with Steven and his business lawyer to get their approval to initiate an invitation to Dad, his new wife, and Steven's sister to mediate their future as a family and as business owners. With the changing and widening context that included all of the players, Steven had an opportunity to improve his overall legal health (not to mention stomach lining) as well as simplify the divorce negotiation. In my role as dispute resolution manager and negotiation coach, creating two negotiations instead of one may have been unorthodox—but it created opportunities for long-term solutions.

Format

There are two general formats in family law mediation: single-session and multisession. When clients are selecting a mediator or participating in designing the format of the mediation, they need to understand the information set forth visually on the following chart.

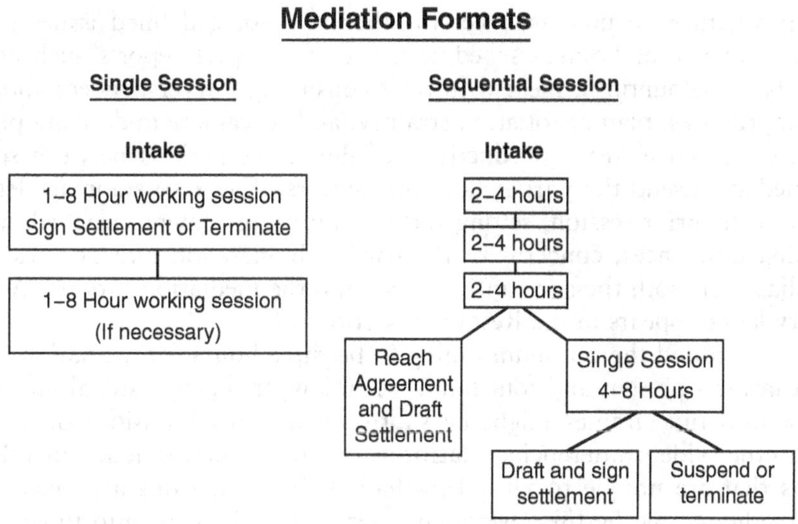

Reprinted from Forrest S. Mosten, *Mediation Career Guide*, Jossey Bass, 2001,

Traditionally, most civil mediations are set up to take place in a single session. Sometimes these sessions can last days and nights—exhaustion often contributes to settlement as much as skill. Another choice is to have a series of shorter sessions (two to four hours each). Mediators may send out summary letters following each shorter session; these letters serve as minutes/notes and outline the agreements made and the remaining open issues. The parties continue to meet in shorter episodic sessions pending full agreement or termination. In planning your mediation, you can offer either model or a combination of the two. In the hybrid model, parties usually begin with sequential sessions. If an impasse develops, the parties can try to resolve it in a single-session marathon.

Single-Session Format. In the single-session model, parties and counsel generally meet at the appointed date and time and mediate until an agreed-upon end time (unless agreement is reached sooner) or until an agreement is reached or an impasse on one or more issues blocks further progress. Sometimes exhaustion, the need for further information or reflection, or other factors cause the mediation to adjourn for the day, with a set date agreed on to finish up the agreement. Mediators differ as to whether the mediation session concludes when a document is drawn up and signed by the parties or an agreement in principle is reached on all issues with the drafting of a formal settlement agreement or court order to follow.

Multisession Format. In the multisession model, after the mediation orientation and any private sessions with the mediator to prepare for the first joint working session, the parties and mediator (and lawyers if they shall attend sessions) work out a schedule of sessions ranging from one and a half hours to four hours in length. The goal for each session is to accomplish as much as possible, with the understanding that the parties will continue their work and hold additional meetings until all of the issues have been resolved. Between sessions, the parties gather documents, meet together to resolve defined issues (such as personal property or holiday schedules), wait for expert reports such as home appraisals or accountings, meet with their consulting lawyers, reflect about possible compromises, plan negotiation strategy, and reevaluate underlying priorities and positions. To increase productivity of the recess periods between sessions, many mediators send the parties (and the lawyers, if agreed) summary letters or minutes of the prior session, setting forth tentative agreements reached, areas of continuing differences, concerns of the parties, homework, and observations of the mediator on both the substantive issues and the mediation process. A sample summary letter appears in the Resources section.

We have found the optimum timing to be three hours for mediation sessions without lawyers present and four hours when lawyers participate, although these recommended time frames might be shortened in virtual sessions on Zoom or through other videoconferencing platforms due to "Zoom fatigue" or other distractions that are unique to virtual mediation. If the sessions are much shorter than three hours, by the time everyone is seated (tardiness is unfortunately quite common) and discussions have occurred about additions and corrections to the last summary letter, new or emergency concerns have been raised, or a topic has been started to develop underlying concerns and options and to explore the consequences of an issue, little time is left to allow for resolution. If three hours is too long for our client or for some reason the session runs out of steam, we can instruct our client to be vigilant and ask whether a session can end early (hopefully without charge). This mediation interruptus can occur regardless of the length of session but seems particularly frustrating to the parties if they have just started when it is time to leave. Since many professional mediators, like therapists and unlike most lawyers, book back-to-back sessions, parties generally do not have the option of continuing past the stop time. Actually, caution your client against staying beyond the time set for the appointment. Early in our careers, we all experienced the impact of no ending time. In one situation, after reaching the end time, the parties agreed to buy another 30 minutes of the mediator's time, then another and another—finally extending the mediation five additional hours for a total seven-hour session. Agreement was reached, but everyone's previous plans and nervous systems were shot! We have all vowed "never again" and we have (for the most part) kept that vow. If lawyers are present at the mediation, time for sessions should be increased between 50 and 100 percent for several reasons. One is the simple reality that there are more people in the room to talk—and most lawyers are good talkers. Second, a major purpose of having lawyers present is to give clients the opportunity to consult with their lawyers on the spot, and such consultations can often run to 30–45 minutes when a difficult issue is involved or when emotions are running high. When one side is conferring, the mediator may meet with the other side or it may just be dead time. Finally, in addition to bringing up additional issues and fully (sometimes too fully) advocating their clients' positions, lawyers might increase the conflict in the mediation room, requiring extra time to reach resolution.

Hybrid Format. As in most models, the two major formats are subject to innovative alteration or may be combined into a hybrid format. For example, the parties alone may commence mediation in a multisession format without their consulting lawyers. When the parties get close to final agreement and need a little boost over the last hurdle, a single closing session with counsel may be scheduled. On the other hand, if the parties meet lawyers in a single session, the parties may work together better than anticipated. In such a situation (or just to save money), the parties may agree to meet in multisession format with the mediator and without counsel, each side reserving the right to include counsel in sessions down the road.

PRELIMINARY PRIVATE PLANNING (PPP) SESSIONS

Some training programs advocate starting with private meetings, and there is extensive couples' therapy literature in support of the concept that starting with individual sessions establishes comfort and rapport with each participant and allows the parties to raise and explore issues privately before dealing with them in open session. Mediators who begin with private sessions try to induce movement in each party's attitude and negotiating position by getting them to "earn" the opportunity to meet directly with the other party. They implement the Edelman (*The Tao of Negotiation*) theory of facilitating agreement by having both individuals reevaluate and reflect to weed out or modify their own unreasonable positions before negotiating directly with the other side. In New York State, the Office of Court Administration has endorsed pilot training programs that encourage mediators to schedule private pre-mediation sessions prior to joint session work in order to implement screening tools, primarily geared toward determining mediation readiness and mediation appropriateness.

Family mediation clients seem to want and expect more early direct contact with the other party—largely because direct contact is one major difference between mediation and litigation. The most common and traditional mediation format is to start with the parties meeting jointly with the mediator. This process is taught in most mediation training programs and is utilized in community and private mediations. Meeting directly with the mediator makes both parties feel a part of the process, creates or reinforces trust that there will be no secrets or hidden agendas, and allows the parties to negotiate directly with each other rather than through a shuttle messenger.

We recommend a cross between the two models, incorporating the approach of Dwight Golann, who in his 2014 book, *Sharing a Mediator's Power: Effective Advocacy in Settlement*, argues strongly for lawyers to take a preventive planning role, including encouraging the mediator to counsel a client on how to approach bargaining. After having a joint orientation meeting with both parties (or a conference call with the lawyers), we suggest that the mediator meet with each party individually for a private session (one to two hours; if the consulting lawyer attends, two to two and a half hours are reserved for the private session).

During the private sessions, clients are encouraged to raise any concerns they may have about the mediation process; the behavior and attitude of the other spouse; and their views about the emotional, financial, parenting, or financial issues in the mediation. This time is used for the mediator to learn the facts of the case and to help the clients prepare for the negotiations by gathering documents and getting information from professionals and institutions (e.g., bank records, insurance rates, retirement benefits, listing reimbursement claims). These sessions provide an educational opportunity for the client, as well as a moment to pause and contemplate uninformed initial positions. The mediator's role as reality agent, testing each side's position with legal information, research findings, and practicality, can even result in the client independently eliminating certain positions in advance of the first joint session. Prepare clients to be open to the mediator's help to better achieve their goals, see how some of their goals may conflict with each other, and explore options and reassess positions. The mediator may start pointing out the areas of commonality and the values the parties share. These private sessions can be used to reinforce basic negotiation skills that clients can learn, helping both sides think about what they want to present during the joint session and how to make such a presentation. Finally, clients can benefit from such private time to assess whether the mediator will truly listen to and understand our client's underlying concerns. Clients should know that the mediator can be available for additional private time to discuss questions and concerns during or between sessions.

We need to help our clients decide whether the mediation should commence with joint or private preliminary planning sessions. If private sessions are agreed upon, lawyers can orient their clients about what can be accomplished and help clients be prepared to articulate concerns and develop goals and positions subject to the mediator's input. If you attend the private session, you can be a supportive resource for your client by raising issues that may have been forgotten, asking questions that your client previously asked you, articulating your client's position from your perspective, and raising your own concerns as consulting lawyer about the process or the negotiation.

For example, you may want to reaffirm that all tentative and preliminary agreements are to be subject to the overall agreement that you, as consulting lawyer, want to review carefully. You may want to emphasize your desire to receive all summary letters or other correspondence directly, your availability to the mediator, and your commitment to be an ally to the mediator throughout the process. If attending a private session, we must continue to remember that we are still guiding our client through a constructive process, and that this is not an opportunity for us as "client advocates" to present argumentative briefings in an attempt to bend the mediator to our client's side. The private sessions are a step in the collective mediation process seeking to structure a constructive negotiation between the parties, and it is critical that if we have an opportunity to participate in the private session together with our client, we further that goal.

Even if you haven't used this approach before, be open to reflecting on your process. For example, New York mediator Daniel Burns had never used preliminary private planning sessions during his 25-year career, but after attending Woody's advanced mediation training in 2014, he endorsed this strategic approach as a new feature of his mediations, and a number of other mediators throughout New York state, such as Alla Roytberg and Lara, have followed suit.[3]

3. Daniel R. Burns, *Preliminary Private Planning Sessions—Do They Work?*, https://burnsmediation.com/tag/daniel-r-burns/page/3/ (last visited Aug. 3, 2022).

MEDIATION BRIEFS

Generally, briefs are utilized in the single-session format, but nothing prevents counsel from agreeing to submit briefs in the multisession format as well. Lawyers who have not participated in mediations may treat the use of briefs as perfunctory or be wary of revealing their legal theories and/or supporting facts. Some lawyers may propose that briefs be sent confidentially only to the mediator and not be shared with the other side. This wariness may be caused by a trial lawyer's desire to preserve the surprise factor (e.g., "the loaded gun") or by skepticism about the potential success of mediation combined with desire to keep legal bills low.

There are no hard-and-fast rules about what a mediation brief should contain. Often, like a trial brief, it contains an outline of the disputed legal and factual issues and a summary of the submitting party's position on each disputed issue. Because mediation is not litigation, a helpful and effective mediation brief might also cover other topics of relevance in the mediation context. For example, it can contain specific proposals for resolution of each disputed issue and an explanation of why the proposed resolution is fair, workable, and responsive to the interests of both parties. It can explain the nonfinancial emotional or financial interests or concerns of the submitting party. It can address what obstacles have prevented settlement of the dispute. It also can address the nature of the past and contemplated future relationship between the parties.

Once mediation has been agreed upon (or ordered by the court), view it as the last dispute resolution process in the case—the end game during which the case *will* be settled. Success rates of mediation back up this more hopeful view. Therefore, if briefs are utilized, do not hold back; utilize research and careful drafting to use the mediation brief as a tool to persuade the other party. Do not write your brief directed solely at the mediator or even the opposing lawyer. In mediation (as in all negotiations), the real judge and jury, the last decision-maker, the relevant audience is the other party. The mediation brief should be drafted with the other spouse in mind: what will persuade that party? The brief should also be submitted far enough in advance for the other spouse to discuss it with his or her lawyer, accountant, family, and other respected people. Try to work out a protocol with the other lawyer so that the mediation briefs can be sent directly to the other spouse to expedite the reflection and reassessment process and to absolutely confirm that the briefs will be seen and studied by the parties.

COSTS OF THE MEDIATION

Just as knowledge of a lawyer's hourly rates and the amount of required retainer is insufficient to plan for the total cost of a lawyer's fee in divorce litigation, such information by itself is insufficient to determine a mediator's total fee. The variables that determine the total fee are the complexity of the legal and financial issues and the emotional and negotiation chemistry of the parties. Sizable assets may not necessarily mean a prolonged mediation, particularly when no community business exists and most of the assets are in cash or other liquid assets that are not difficult to value and allocate. A negative asset case may be far more difficult because every dollar may affect basic living needs. As to emotional and negotiation variables, naked conflict is never pleasant and will extend the mediation time. However, other less overt styles of the parties may even be more difficult.

If parties are midscale in both complexity and style, experienced mediators generally estimate one full day for a single session or three to six shorter scheduled sessions. Although complex and emotional cases may take more than ten sessions, it is more common that parties without children, complex assets, or difficult dynamics can resolve their dispute in one to three sessions. In the multisession format, it generally takes one hour of outside mediator time for every session, allowing for telephone calls with parties and counsel, contact with experts, drafts of summary letters, and review of correspondences and other documents sent by the parties.

A handout detailing mediation expenses is useful in educating clients before they start mediation. Such knowledge helps avoid sticker shock, and understanding the variables that run up mediation fees might help your client reflect about and change his or her behavior to a more helpful mode. A template estimating typical mediation fees is included in the Resources section.

Who Pays the Mediator?

Who will pay the mediator's fees is often a subject of major negotiation and sometimes is a hurdle to starting a mediation. The two most common options are for each party to pay half the total fees and for the parties to pay proportional to their respective gross incomes. Many lawyers believe that the contribution of the parties should be equal to give each spouse an equal stake in the outcome of the mediation and also to level out an imbalance of power so that the less affluent spouse need not be apprehensive that the mediator might kiss the hand that feeds the kitty. Some variations in fee arrangements include reserving the final allocation of the mediator's fee for negotiation within the mediation or decision by the court if necessary. The spouse unable to pay could receive a preliminary advance distribution from the marital estate or even a personal loan from the other spouse to pay the fees. Of course, parties can borrow or otherwise obtain fees from extended families or by other means. Many mediators accept credit cards, and the parties can then negotiate that obligation along with other marital debts.

Even if the parties agree to pay equally, it may be necessary for you to negotiate that the obligation be joint and several (causing one spouse to pay the bills of the other defaulting spouse) or if the mediator must look to each spouse separately for that spouse's share of the bill. Of course, just as in lawyers arranging other services and experts, it is good practice for your client, rather than you personally, to be directly and exclusively financially liable for the mediator's fees.

Under the second option, the parties make unequal contributions to the mediator, yet each spouse has some financial stake. If one spouse is totally without funds, the other spouse may pay or merely advance all of the mediator's fees. In such a situation, there may be resentment on the part of the paying party and fear about fairness on the part of the spouse paying less than half or nothing at all. It is important to address these concerns with your client, the other side, and with the mediator before the start of the session. Professional mediators are quite accustomed to these unequal payment arrangements. Once retained, experienced mediators rarely, if ever, think about how much each side is paying and do not favor the party paying the bill while it is current. Few mediators can avoid negative countertransference against parties who do not pay as promised, which can affect a mediator's impartiality and effectiveness, and some will reschedule sessions if fees are not fully paid in advance.

Another nuance of payment of mediation fees deals with the common situation in which one party meets privately much more with the mediator than does the other party. We generally recommend that parties pay equally for both parties' time regardless of any time imbalance. The mediator is using time with one party to help *both* parties reach an agreement. In fact, if the other party is eating up the clock, you can advise your client to be grateful: it is far better for the mediator to deal with these concerns than have the situation blow up. Of course, if parties cannot see the benefit of equal payment, you can negotiate with the mediator to have all joint sessions paid equally (or another way) and have each party billed separately for their individual time with the mediator in person, on the phone, or by email.

Methods of Payment

Mediators differ in the payment arrangements they offer. Hourly charges are most common. Some mediators bill by the day, and others negotiate a flat fee with certain parameters, such as $2,000 per day up to 7 p.m. and then hourly. For many years, the noted alternative dispute resolution (ADR) firm of Gregorio, Haldeman, Piazza & Rotman in San Francisco charged a flat fee and is available for a 24-hour day (rarely used because everyone else is exhausted, but a very compelling marketing tool). Some mediators (generally lawyer/mediators) charge for out-of-session time; others do not. Some mediators ask for an advance deposit to be applied against hourly charges; others require clients to pay the current charges and the remaining deposit is applied to the final bill.

Many mediators do not even send bills but are paid in full at the beginning or end of each session. (There are vibrant conversations at mediator conferences as to whether payment at the beginning or end of a session is better practice, from both a business standpoint and to maintain momentum within the session.) Therapist/mediators are accustomed to billing for a 45- to 50-minute hour and so may charge for three and a half sessions for a three-hour mediation session.

Most mediators are open and not defensive about discussing their fee arrangements. There is a general spirit of disclosure and informed client consent about which mediators receive training and which mediators are generally committed.

THE SITE OF THE MEDIATION

The mediator's office is the obvious first choice—it is neutral. Some mediators do not have offices, but rent only their working space without access to sufficient breakout rooms or other amenities; some reside in other cities and are traveling to a locale to mediate a dispute. In such situations, parties with sufficient means may elect to rent space at a hotel, another consensual dispute resolution firm, a court reporter's office, or some other space to ensure neutrality. Perhaps one has access to a colleague's office that can be used. However, it might come down practically and economically to using your office or your colleague's. [We often call the other lawyer our "collaborative colleague," particularly when we both sign a disqualification clause (see Chapter 6).] (Of course, some mediators have fully virtual practices and all meetings occur via Zoom or another videoconferencing platform, eliminating these scheduling logistics.)

Again, when scheduling an in-person mediation, you should invoke the "let it go" mantra. If the other lawyer has sufficient space and wants to host, you should agree to travel there, as long as you work out a number of logistics. You must be assured that the mediator has exclusive use and control of a room of sufficient size to accommodate all parties, counsel, and others present for the mediation. The room should contain a whiteboard, a flip chart, or other settlement-inducing features that the mediator might request. You, as the visiting lawyer, and your client should have exclusive use of another room with a door that closes, ensuring privacy. The mediator, you, and your client should all be given access to telephones, fax, and wireless internet facilities. You should be assured that your messages and documents will be delivered promptly, with confidentiality protected. The hosting lawyer should commit to not taking telephone calls that interrupt mediation work, going through email or snail mail, directing staff, or otherwise conducting customary office business that would interfere with the mediation. In short, as with other process issues, it is important for you to discuss any concern that might make someone uncomfortable and to attempt to approximate a neutral setting to the best possible extent.

In recent years, online mediation has taken hold throughout the family mediation community as well, informing the development of an entire international task force to provide training accordingly. For the many nuances and strategies involved in online mediation, see Chapter 4.5 by Susan Guthrie.

FOOD AND DRINK: AGENTS OF COLLABORATION

Unlike the courtroom, where litigants are restrained from bringing in food or beverages with the threat of bailiff intervention, mediations, especially when taking place in person, should provide a nurturing atmosphere. It is harder to dislike those with whom one has broken bread. The arrangements for providing caloric and tasty sustenance should be discussed explicitly and not left for the day of the mediation.

Mediation authority Laurence Boulle addresses the ritual importance of food and drink in his book *Mediation: Principles, Process, and Practice*:

> Mediators may also provide food, drink and other refreshments which can be "ritually" served in a way which shows respect for and the equality of all parties present. Consumption becomes a common activity, participated in equally by all participants, which temporarily distracts attention from the negative features of the dispute during the settling-in phase.

The following discussion assumes a single-session format (even if such session is designed to last several days). In the multisession model, unless mediations are scheduled online, the meetings are generally at the mediator's office, which is accustomed to providing drinks, cookies, candies, and other tide-overs. During day-long sessions, there are usually four feedings: breakfast, lunch, midafternoon snacks, and evening food.

Space permitting, the ideal setup is to have a neutral food room that all parties and lawyers can enter at any time to replenish their plates. The host is responsible for having the food set up, ice freshened, and cleanup completed. Some of the most important settlement discussions are initiated casually while participants engage in the common goal of enjoying the repast. The positives of a generous spread go beyond creating a warm atmosphere and putting people together. If personal needs are provided for, the participants will not need to go off-site and have hunger as an excuse to leave early or to blame for an inability to focus on the issues.

Who is to arrange and pay for this catering? The options are the lawyers, the parties, or the mediator. Although we usually suggest that the lawyers be given the responsibility for arranging the meals, the food negotiations themselves are fun (especially when the clients are paying) and help you and your colleague test out your working collaborative relationship. The office host may provide local purveyors and caterers. We have had many lawyers report that the task of arranging and feeding both parties and lawyers felt good and contributed to the day's settlement success. Other mediators opt to arrange for and provide the food, under the theory that the subtle, reciprocal social obligations created between guest and host and between joint guests can grease the wheels of the negotiation and help things proceed more smoothly.

Setting up the mediation properly and preparing for it diligently not only will increase the odds of success but also will expedite a settlement process that reduces conflict and lowers the parties' costs. If you play a proactive role in getting the mediation setup, you will help settle a case and help start the family healing process.

PRACTICE TIPS

1. Take care in selecting the mediator and support the client by gathering and presenting information about possible mediators.
2. Consider any information you have about the needs of the other party and counsel that impact mediation selection.
3. Unless the mediator is clearly incompetent, unqualified, or there are favoritism concerns, agree to the one proposed by the other party.
4. "Let go" of unimportant issues in setting up the process. Reassure the client that flexibility is not weakness.
5. Establish a collaborative team approach with the opposing lawyer in setting up the mediation; you are both allies in the quest for amicable resolution—even if you differ on the issues or in your views of the parties.

6. Make it easy for the other side to try mediation; provide full background information of proposed mediators and disclosure of your past contact, give the other side wide control, and be willing to continue court actions to schedule the mediation.
7. Educate your client and the opposing party and lawyer about the 85–90 percent success rate in private mediation—far higher than the 60 percent in court-annexed mediation.
8. Do not cut corners or hold back important facts or law in preparing for the mediation.
9. Schedule the mediation as quickly as possible with sufficient time for preparation—one to six weeks should be the range.
10. Select the best mediator the parties can afford; be willing to compromise that choice to begin the mediation more quickly.
11. Explain the difference between the single-session and multisession mediation formats and propose the format or hybrid that best serves your client.
12. Use the time between sessions to the client's advantage: review the negotiation process, gather documents, revise positions, and prepare for the next session.
13. Schedule sufficient time for each mediation session; double the time allotted if lawyers are present.
14. Make sure your client understands how much the mediator is being paid, when payment is due, what the client is paying for, and what additional fees are expected and when. Urge mediators to offer a written estimate of their costs.
15. Define allocation of payment between the parties.
16. Try to use a neutral site, but invoke the "let it go" principle if the other lawyer wants to host.
17. Think about strategic options to arrange for food and drink.
18. Discuss the advantages of having a private session with each side before commencing the mediation.
19. Discuss the advantages of having you attend the sessions.
20. Direct your mediation brief and verbal presentation at the other party—not at the opposing lawyer or mediator.

CHAPTER 8

Building an Agreement Your Client Can Live With

"A mediator I was working with recently told me that he saw a well-known divorce attorney talking to a client in one of the corridors of the court house where I practice. This attorney was telling his client that mediation will not work. He told his client to only do what he told him. He also said that the client should not make any decisions unless it is agreed to by the attorney. This is a recipe for disaster and failure. If the client is encouraged to go into mediation with that closed mind attitude, then it is doomed to fail."

—Henry Gornbein, "How Lawyers Can Sabotage Mediation," Huffington Post, 2012

Once the mediation is set up, lawyers can work proactively with their clients, the mediator, and the other party's lawyer to further the goals of the mediation. Mediation's popularity is largely due to the availability of lawyers and other divorce professionals who are willing and prepared to be team members. The overall purpose of attorney involvement is self-evident: to offer information, advice, and assistance to ensure that clients are protected and their underlying needs and goals maximized. The consulting lawyer's assignment, however, is far different from the role of zealous courtroom advocate. The lawyer's ultimate job in mediation is to help the client complete the mediation successfully, resulting in an agreement that feels fair and workable to the client based on the reasonably available information. The lawyer's job is not to negotiate for the last dollar, vindicate every single one of the client's legal rights, or look under every last stone. Leaving some money on the table or passing up possible legal protections may be worthwhile to the client if the overall agreement satisfies other needs, such as finality, preservation of an amicable parenting relationship and healthy children, or privacy. Informed consent means that the client is the one who makes these decisions.

Clients can choose to have the lawyers heavily involved in the mediation, attending and participating actively in the mediation sessions. Clients can also choose to "go it alone" during the sessions themselves and keep attorneys in reserve, even if the lawyer could have elevated the client's comfort level during the mediation and/or affected the settlement terms. In mediation, the client is in charge—not only of the ultimate settlement but also of whether, when, and how to use the attorney's services. (An unbundled approach, its nature, and its ethical ramifications are discussed in Chapter 5.)

In a 2014 article, John R. Phillips, a former chair of the ABA Dispute Resolution Section, summed up conflicting roles of the lawyer in mediation: "Advocates often err on the side of extremes, either trying to control the mediation process or sitting idly by, expecting the mediator to be knowledgeable and effective in soliciting information from the parties to bring about compromise."[1]

ADVISOR AND COACH

When mediation participants hire legal counsel, most are seeking both advice and emotional support. Even though a mediator might provide comprehensive information and a full menu of possible options and consequences, clients often want to know what their lawyers recommend because such a recommendation is neither neutral nor impartial but viewed as supporting the client's goals and needs. While a mediator may point out, for example, that a healthy family system collectively benefits everyone in it, the attorney's concern may focus on the client's individual interests, which a mediator cannot ethically emphasize.

Many clients are unwilling to try mediation without the backup advice of their own lawyer. However, clients' feelings about retaining counsel for mediation are often ambivalent. Clients want support and protection but also worry that lawyers will take over the mediation such that the lawyers will control their future—or worse, blow up the mediation altogether. At times, clients who have started the mediation process after pursuing other options with their lawyers find themselves so exhausted by the roles that controlling lawyers have played that both parties terminate their relationships with the controlling lawyers and proceed through mediation unrepresented. Many people choose mediation specifically for the self-empowerment and control it affords, and they don't want to have to convince a lawyer to support the resulting agreement or be told how shortsighted or stupid their actions have been. And they certainly don't want to spend their children's college funds fighting each other.

On the other hand, going through a divorce is frightening, stressful, and profoundly unsettling. It is the single largest and longest-lasting financial transaction most people ever experience. Parties are deciding critical issues involving every aspect of their lives when their judgment is clouded by emotion. Both spouses fear the unknown—how will their lives turn out—as well as the known—few families live as well after a divorce, children are put at emotional risk, and it takes a long time to recover. It is normal and appropriate for divorcing spouses to be afraid, and fear creates reluctance or less confidence to mediate.

1. John R. Phillips, *Making the Best Use of Mediators and Their Role*, ABA Dispute Resol. Mag. 26 (Summer 2014).

Consulting family law attorneys offer clients the opportunity to enjoy the self-determination and other benefits of the mediation process without sacrificing the security and comfort of having received independent legal advice. Competent and caring family lawyers make it possible for clients to have the best of both worlds.

Educating and Advising on the Client's Legal Position

Just as in full-service representation, a major job for the consulting family law attorney is to identify legal issues, educate the client about the law, and help the client formulate legal positions. Clients who benefit from this preparation:

Tend to be far more effective in negotiation sessions.

1. Are not surprised by new legal information and have a chance to process it and adjust expectations in advance.
2. Have a greater sense of mastery over the subject matter on the table.
3. Are able to articulate vital issues with greater confidence and focus, and are equipped to recognize and respond to issues raised by the mediator and the spouse. If the client hears assessments of the law and/or the merits of a given position that diverge from their attorney's assessment, the client can explore and resolve those differences during the session with counsel, or both.

Informed consent requires information—the more the better. Input from counsel facilitates critical thinking and improves the quality of client decisions.

Franklin Garfield and Frederick Glassman offer the following insights about early lawyer involvement: "The vast majority of parties who choose to mediate their cases have an incomplete and incorrect knowledge of the law. If they are involved early in the process, consulting attorneys can largely remedy this problem."[2]

Compiling the Client's Financial Information and Assessing Needs

Given that the exchange of detailed financial disclosure statements is a prerequisite for a divorce in most jurisdictions, a customary mediation assignment calls for each party to prepare a written statement of assets, debts, income, and expenses and bring it to the session to facilitate discussion of financial issues such as support, division of property, and allocation of debt. Seldom does the mediator have time to personally prepare financial disclosures for mediation clients. Even if time did permit mediator involvement in preparation of financial disclosures, it is questionable whether such help would be consistent with the mediator's neutral role. Clients have fiduciary obligations to make their own full and fair financial disclosures to the other spouse, and mediators are not equipped to verify or investigate the disclosures made. Most clients would benefit from having their lawyer make sure all expenses are included, all potential assets and income are identified, and all backup information is exchanged between parties.

---

2. *In the Beginning: Independent Counsel's Place in Dissolution Mediation*, L.A. DAILY J., Feb. 14, 1994.

We may also suggest that the client receive help from a CPA, financial planner, or budget-savvy family member or friend. Various designations have developed in recent years for financial professionals who work with divorcing parties (e.g., Certified Divorce Financial Analyst (CDFA), Certified Financial Divorce Practitioner (CFDP), Certified Financial Divorce Specialist.) Another resource is https://www.collaborativepractice.com/members or your local collaborative practice group to find financial professionals trained in client-centered interdisciplinary services (including mediation and collaborative law).

Often all the lawyer does is review the financial data and communicate approval to the client. The lawyer does this by briefly quizzing the client to verify that the client truly understands the situation and that the information is complete and well put together. This act of confirming accurate financial information is reassuring to clients participating in mediation, and its importance should not be understated. Just as people are willing to pay for health checkups and feel better when the doctors tells them that everything is fine, mediation participants are willing to pay a consulting attorney to review basic financials and receive a clean bill of financial health. Lawyers can anticipate the questions the spouse or mediator will ask and help the client prepare an explanation. This not only helps clients feel prepared, but also can streamline the mediation sessions. Although lawyers routinely work with financial forms and are not daunted by them, many clients become intimidated, bogged down, procrastinate, and hit major emotional roadblocks when faced with the financial disclosure forms and worksheets. For clients emerging from a marriage in which the informal division of labor located financial information and decision-making power in the other spouse, this may be their first foray into budgeting, a skill that will be crucial in the future. Our support can give clients much-needed confidence not only in their ability to participate effectively in mediation but also in our professional services and judgment.

Obtaining the Documents Needed to Make an Informed Decision

A major criticism of mediation in family law matters is that spouses might make lifelong decisions based on inadequate information and limited financial disclosure given a waiver of full discovery. A spouse who lacks material information about property (both assets and liabilities) or income can be deprived of essential rights designed to provide a fair standard of living and distribution of the marital estate. Whether discovered before or after an agreement is reached, playing with half a deck or having the cards dealt from the bottom of the deck creates mistrust in the other spouse and the mediation process. This may in turn lead to a challenge to the finality or enforceability of the agreement, further conflict or litigation between the spouses on other issues, or, even, possible claims against the professionals involved.

Consequently, many family lawyers routinely advise their clients to postpone even considering mediation on financial issues until formal discovery, governed by the traditional statutory process, is completed. Such discovery can range from a simple demand to fill out required court forms for income and property with documentary backup to a formal demand to produce full-scale interrogatories, legal requests to produce documents of the other party, subpoenas on third parties (banks, employers, family members), and depositions of witnesses that can go on from a few hours to many weeks.

Lawyers know well that a failure to conduct adequate discovery can lead to their own malpractice exposure. This exposure often leads to defensive over-lawyering and a negative attitude toward mediation early in the process. However, research has demonstrated that the best use of mediation is early in the process, before positions become entrenched and brutal battles (including those over discovery) can dissipate resources and inflame conflict, as noted in a widely cited 2007 exploration by Kenneth F. Dunham in *Is Mediation the New Equity*. In a nuanced conclusion summarizing the findings of a 2009 ABA Taskforce on Improving Mediation Quality, John Lande noted that most participants "preferred scheduling mediation sessions to occur after 'critical' discovery is completed but before discovery is fully completed," confirming that financial disclosure is a necessary baseline that empowers parties to engage in the process, but that engaging in protracted discovery battles before beginning a mediation process can undermine the collaborative nature of the process.

To reconcile the need for adequate disclosure with the benefits of early use of mediation, clients need to be informed that such financial disclosure is required whether mediation is used or not. Informed consent is also the foundation of a successful mediation. It is important to advise less knowledgeable spouses about their rights to full discovery of their financial lives. Receiving documents and other backup is not just a legal entitlement, but a necessary element in good mediation participation. The more knowledgeable spouse is often the party pushing for mediation, partly to maintain the more powerful position inside the mediation room by muting the role of lawyers and the litigation process, including formal discovery. Yet, it is ironic that the more powerful spouse actually benefits by making early full financial disclosure with documentary backup. The more powerful spouse can then demonstrate a good faith commitment to fairness that will expedite the mediation. The other party and the mediator need sufficient information to have meaningful discussions—the prelude to reaching a fair agreement. Such disclosure will also increase the comfort level of the less powerful spouse's attorney and accelerate the review and approval process. Finally, once agreement is reached, such financial disclosure is like an insurance policy for the more powerful spouse's reliance on the finality of the agreement reached in mediation. Such disclosure, in addition to the involvement of counsel by the less powerful spouse, will increase (if not guarantee) court approval of the agreement and virtually obliterate any attempt to set the agreement aside at a later date. States such as California and Florida, and certain counties in New York, have mandatory financial disclosure forms or other requirements of mutual financial disclosure that are nonwaivable preconditions for obtaining a judgment of dissolution of marriage or legal separation.

In California mediations, parties use the mandatory forms for income, expenses, and property developed by the California Judicial Council. The parties prepare their own forms and exchange them during the fact-gathering process. The same forms (generally updated) are finalized and exchanged as a condition for obtaining a judgment of marital dissolution. In New York, many mediators use net worth statement forms provided by the unified court system to outline party income, assets, expenses, and liabilities, but the use and filing of these forms is not mandatory in all counties. Sample forms from California and New York are available in the Resources Section of this book.

In the Utah Rules of Civil Procedure, Rule 26.1 mandates that parties disclose most of their essential financial information in order to allow for early mediation, well before formal discovery is required. This rule encourages transparent exchanges of financial information before parties become entrenched in their positions, optimizing the landscape for successful mediation.

It is important to pave the way for full disclosure even before mediation commences. If the parties are communicating directly with each other, the less-powerful spouse should be advised to express the expectation that the other party will provide disclosure early in the mediation process, providing ample time for review and potential consultation with a certified divorce financial analyst if further support is needed. The more powerful spouse should be advised to start gathering documents and to put them in an indexed mediation notebook (resembling a trial notebook, in electronic drop box or paper form) so that both spouses, the mediator, and counsel can work from that shared information. Such a notebook should include tax returns, bank and stock statements, real estate deeds, purchase and improvement information, credit card and other debt details, reimbursement claims, and the like.

Sample Mediation Notebook Contents

- Tax returns—personal (last three years)
- Tax returns—corporate (last three years)
- Cash disbursements analysis reports
- Summary of household expenses
- Summary of child-related expenses
- Schedule of assets and debts
- Narrative from Richard Moore regarding management of the community estate
- Real estate deeds
- Deal memorandum and MCA contract
- "Celebrity Goodwill: Enjoy It While It Lasts: It's Not an Asset" by F. Expert, Esq.
- Documentation of loan to brother
- Greenpeace donation
- Pension plan
- Corporate records
- Real property and furniture
- Contingent tax liability

Even with expectations for disclosure in place, some parties delay or resist providing financial documents. Reasons for such delay or resistance might vary. While some families might be experiencing a financial power and control dynamic, other reasons for delay or resistance might be cultural, or due to the exposure of intergenerationally intertwined family finances. Every effort should be made to work out these problems early in the mediation. Most experienced mediators are capable of assuming the role of case manager as well as facilitating settlement terms. Even if the court process is invoked to compel production of documents or obtain other discovery, many states require in-person or telephonic meetings between counsel before any motion is filed. These meet-and-confer conferences can be conducted with the mediator. Sometimes the mediator can be helpful in facilitating negotiation between the lawyers on the exchange of financial documents.

Therefore, in situations of discovery impasse, concern should be raised with the mediator either by the spouses or by a letter from consulting counsel. Even if the parties may have started without counsel, if a looming financial discovery battle appears on the horizon, rather than throwing in the towel on the mediation and having the entire case head to court, it is preferable for the lawyers to attend a mediation session devoted to resolving this discovery issue. Even if resolution is not achieved, with the help of the mediator, counsel can work out an agreement to bifurcate the proceeding—the exchange of financial documents may be separated from resolution of other issues in mediation. The discovery problem can be decided by a judge or an arbitrator, and the mediation can continue with other issues not affected by this problem, such as parenting, personal property, and disposition of the house. As an alternative, the parties involved can reach an agreement to stay committed to the mediation process but take a recess or suspension in the negotiations until the discovery dispute is resolved.

Review of Documents

In helping the client evaluate and formulate a negotiation position, lawyers can review legal documents such as deeds, promissory notes, employment contracts, partnership agreements, and prior court orders, among others. The principal task is to educate the client about what the documents mean, identify which documents are important, and advise the client as to how to use the documents during the mediations. It is important for the lawyer and client to have a clear agreement on what documents the lawyer will review and in what depth. As in other aspects of discrete task representation, the client is ultimately in charge of the lawyer's scope of representation. However, we have the right (and perhaps the duty) to advise the client about the dangers of unduly restricting our work and to refuse to undertake an assignment unless it can be done so competently so that the client is reasonably protected.

Monitoring the Progress of the Mediation

There are two views on when a participant in a mediation should engage counsel. The first school of thought argues that the lawyer should not be brought in until after the parties have reached an agreement. The lawyer's function is then to review the terms and drafting of the agreement and to play a technical role in processing the agreement already reached. The underlying support for the "review only" role is that the parties are capable of reaching their own agreement with the mediator and that earlier participation by lawyers will only muck it up and be a deal breaker. Further, by waiting until the end, the parties can make substantial progress and simply fine-tune the agreement once lawyers are involved. The second view on timing the lawyer's involvement is that by waiting until after an agreement to involve a lawyer, mediation participants make deals without full information. When the lawyer has a concern about a deal point and recommends renegotiation of that portion of the deal as it is discussed in the mediation, the client is faced with a major dilemma. If the client follows the lawyer's advice and reopens negotiations, the other spouse might react by feeling betrayed and accusing the other party of bad faith. As a result, the cost of the mediation will increase, or the other spouse might walk away from the mediation process entirely.

We see merit in both views. We have seen mediations sabotaged by adversarial attorneys who over-negotiate and push people around. In one court-referred mediation in New York where Lara served as the mediator, one of the parties had an explosive altercation with his own attorney during a joint mediation session over the lawyer being aggressively adversarial when the client himself wanted to collaborate, and the party fired his attorney mid-session, causing the session to conclude and subsequently resume with new counsel. We have also seen mediations virtually start from scratch after lawyers began reviewing an agreement in which they had no prior input. Everything else being equal, we favor having the parties start the mediation without lawyers present but having the mediator send summary letters to counsel if the parties so authorize. Parties should be encouraged to consult counsel early and often. In this way, even if they are not in the actual mediation room, attorneys become an integral part of the process. If after review of a summary letter or consultation, the lawyer is concerned about a particular pending issue or the direction of discussions, that view can be raised by the client or directly by the lawyer through a letter to the mediator or to opposing counsel. The parties and mediator can then deal with the concern head-on and resolve it in the agreement.

Once the review process starts, it generally goes more smoothly because the lawyers are familiar with and have participated in the agreement.

To Caucus or Not to Caucus?

Once the mediation starts, lawyers should be familiar with the mediator's policy about holding private confidential caucuses (meetings with only one party present). Some mediators, concerned that it makes the subjectivity of the mediator too powerful a factor in the process and creates mistrust, oppose any use of caucus and insist that all communications be in joint or open session. Other mediators routinely use caucuses to establish rapport and help make sure parties feel heard. Some mediators have different policies for cases where lawyers participate in mediation than for those where parties attend mediation sessions without lawyers present. While some lawyers feel very strongly about whether or not to caucus, usually it works out best if such process decisions are left to the mediator, with client input. It is important that your client know whether caucusing will take place, whether such communications will remain confidential or can be shared with the other party, and how to use caucuses to the best negotiating advantage.

Caucus Tips for Clients

When the mediator asks to speak to the other party, leave quickly without attitude and do not try to get the last word in. If the mediation is taking place online, accept any requests to be moved into a private breakout room promptly.

While alone outside the mediation room or in your virtual breakout room, do not obsess about what the others are discussing. Try to relax and shake any anger or tension. The mediator may be working with the other party on issues you cannot control.

If the caucus lasts longer than anticipated, be patient. You could be benefitting from the discussion taking place.

If the mediator requests a caucus with you, acquiesce politely and let the mediator direct the conversation.

Be candid with the mediator. If the caucus is confidential, trust the mediator to keep your secret. If it is not, trust the mediator to use appropriate discretion in handling your confidences. If you are bursting at the seams, it will not hurt you to express sadness, anger, or other emotions to the mediator.

If you are uncomfortable with something the mediator says or does, bring it up with the mediator.

If you feel you are losing control during a joint session, ask for a break and a private caucus with the mediator.

If you have a settlement proposal but are unsure about certain aspects or how best to present it, ask for a caucus and run it by the mediator.

LAWYERS AT THE MEDIATION TABLE

More frequently, family lawyers are present with their clients during mediation sessions. In some states, court-annexed mediations even require that lawyers attend. Although mediation still offers parties the opportunity to communicate directly and generate their own agreement, having the lawyers present at the table may be the added help that brings a settlement home.

When Lawyers Should Be Present

Assuming that the mediator (or court/organization) permits the lawyers to participate in the session, in the following situations, it is advisable for clients to be accompanied by their lawyers:

- One or both parties will not start or continue mediation without counsel present.
- One or both lawyers will not permit their clients to start or continue mediation without counsel present.
- Due to a gross imbalance of power, sophistication, knowledge, or emotional readiness, the mediator recommends that counsel be present.
- After considerable effort, an impasse develops on one or more issues and the lawyers could be catalysts for settlement.

- The issues or timing of the mediation impacts ongoing litigation or court management of the cases, and the lawyers' input would be helpful.
- Direct communication between the parties is so disruptive or harmful that the support and buffering of lawyers would be helpful.

A general guide is that absent harm, the parties should be encouraged to work first without lawyers. However, if any of the preceding criteria kick in or there is doubt about whether lawyers should be involved, the prudent (but more expensive and time-consuming) path is to have the lawyers present. It is critical to understand that these concerns should not threaten the life of the mediation. When things get tough or technical, many lawyers or clients pull the plug prematurely. Instead of terminating or considering lawyer involvement to be the demise of a mediation, consider it another approach or format of a mediation in progress.

The Role of Lawyers at the Session

There are three basic ways in which lawyers participate in mediation discussion. First, the lawyer speaks for the client, much as in traditional negotiations. This occurs when the client feels overwhelmed by the other party or when the lawyer cannot surrender control. The second approach is for the parties to conduct the discussions with the lawyers remaining rather mute, in the background of the process. Here the lawyer serves as an advisor, a coach, and a legal expert resource but does not change the dynamics of the direct party negotiation. Third, the lawyer and client are both members of a negotiation team, and either speaks at any time. The team power may not necessarily be equal.

In his 2014 book *Sharing a Mediator's Powers: Effective Advocacy in Settlement*, Dwight Golann suggests that you combine roles by asking the mediator for advice in formulating a settlement proposal. In his review of this book, John R. Phillips cites Golann's proscription that if a mediator is reluctant to take authorship of a proposal, the mediator may be willing to endorse the proposal as a good-faith step that the other party should consider reciprocating.[3]

All three models are in play at mediation tables around the country. In fact, we have mediated and served as mediation counsel in all three formats—sometimes all three during the same mediation or even during the same session. It is important for you to educate the client about the choices available and for the client to be involved in deciding what role you should play.

During a session, when in doubt, listen more and say less. Many mediations are thrown off track by lawyers who believe that their clients want or need them to be highly assertive, articulate, and controlling. Clients might even say that's what they want—but what they really want is to end up with a mediated agreement that meets their needs. No matter how silver tongued a lawyer is in the session, if eloquent words derail the process, the lawyer is not doing her job. This does not mean lawyers should give away the store. Clients deserve agreements that are fair to them and that meet their needs. If the mediation is not going well,

3. *Id.*

rather than walking out or giving in, find a way to reshape its direction with fresh ideas for settlement or structure of negotiations (e.g., designating time to brainstorm creative solutions, exploring an apology, suggesting other dispute resolution processes).

Many family lawyers find it difficult to share control with a mediator. Because mediators have no ultimate decision-making authority, some lawyers either dismiss their input or struggle with them over procedural and substantive issues, large and small. Successful mediative lawyers use the mediator as an ally and a process coach. Quite often the mediator can provide important insights, information about the other side, and recommendations for what to say and how to say it effectively. By having a neutral perspective and being trusted by both sides, a mediator can be a helpful third member of your team.

Finally, many family lawyers, comfortable with other lawyers and familiar with pitching an argument to a judge, will direct comments primarily to the mediator and secondarily to the other lawyer. Big mistake! The real decision-makers are the parties. Effective lawyers in mediation address the other party as often as possible. If the other party buys the pitch, you've almost made the sale. However, the other co-judge in the room is the client. Don't forget to take care of the emotional and informational needs of the client. Use the mediator to help inform, educate, and persuade clients. Often clients finally hear what their lawyers have been trying to say when they hear the same thing from the mediator.

A helpful part of the lawyer's role is reviewing summary letters of each session that the mediator may send to parties and counsel. A sample letter from a consulting attorney to a mediator, commenting on a mediation summary letter, is included in the Resources section.

USE OF EXPERTS

In selecting a mediator, it is important to ascertain the prospective mediator's views and customary practice with regard to outside experts. Many family lawyers are accustomed to using neutral experts, and this option works particularly well within the mediation context. When each side retains its own expert, the expense to the family is doubled and the two professionals' results (all too often advocating the client's best-case scenario) are often compromised at some point. In many high-asset and complex marital estates, the professional fees of the dueling forensic accounts dwarf the fees of both lawyers..

By utilizing a neutral third-party expert, both spouses can benefit. The fees are reduced for the following reasons: The parties are paying one expert, not two. By agreeing consensually on the expert, cooperation by the parties in complying with the expert's requests may be increased, reducing conflict and expense. Rather than catering only to the client who hired the expert, the professional is retained through the mediation and will make judgment calls neutrally, starting with a more middle-ground report that facilitates follow-up negotiation. Finally, because both parties are involved in selecting the expert, rather than hearing from the other side's hired gun or having the expert imposed by the court, the expert's findings may be better accepted by the parties.

Lawyers can play a major role in the use of experts in mediation. First, by supporting the initial use of a neutral expert, lawyers might elicit their clients' consent to a process that could be instrumental in resolving the major issues in the case. The only risk to a client is the possible future cost of retaining his or her own experts if the matter is not resolved. While possible, this additional cost rarely occurs. Each client can take comfort knowing that unless otherwise agreed upon, the neutral expert's report and written work product are confidential and inadmissible by statute, or such confidentially can be agreed to at the outset. Also, even if the neutral report is detrimental to the client, the results are not binding and can be the starting point for negotiations at the mediation table. The client retains control to negotiate, negotiate, and continue to negotiate until a satisfactory resolution is reached—no result will be imposed.

Lawyers can be of great help in identifying potential experts for the client to propose at the mediation table, and the selection can be negotiated by counsel in or out of session. Choosing an expert consensually rather than having one appointed by the judge affords clients the opportunity to meet the expert in advance separately in the expert's office, jointly with both spouses in the expert's office, or with the mediator in session. If either party feels uncomfortable, the parties can agree to continue interviewing until they both agree. We can also advise our client as to the recommended scope of the expert's services and even assist in the negotiation and/or drafting of the joint engagement letter. We have found that experts generally prefer to have lawyers and clients absolutely clear about what work is expected and what the cost might be. Rather than engaging the expert for a soup-to-nuts job, the parties may agree to unbundle the expert's work and use services on a tiered step-by-step basis.

For example, if the parties agree to jointly retain a vocational counselor to evaluate one spouse's earning capacity neutrally, perhaps the counselor could meet with that spouse for two hours, do two hours of job research, and report back to the parties and mediator with a brief letter. If this amount of work does not settle the issue, the parties may then want the counselor to administer standardized vocational assessment tests and prepare a detailed written report (still confidential unless otherwise agreed upon) or even come to a mediation session to discuss the findings. As an alternative, one vocational counselor could perform a confidential mini-evaluation, reserving the right for either party to compel a formal evaluation with another vocational counselor, whose report would be sent to the court if not resolved in mediation.

The same unbundled approach could be used with any type of expert. The parties retain control and calibrate their use of expensive professional services, opting first for the least-invasive, least-protracted, least-binding, and least-expensive approach. Regardless of the approach taken, we can help our client understand and interpret the significance of the expert's report and advise our client as to a workable negotiating position, using the report as one external, objective measure of reality.

THE LAWYER AS NEGOTIATION COACH

Most family lawyers are skilled negotiators. The lawyer coach can teach the client some of the essentials of negotiation theory and give supervised individual training to the client in preparation for the mediation session. As a start, superb books on negotiation are available that the client can be encouraged to read and discuss with friends or with you. (A list of these books is included in the Resources section.) Viewing videos on negotiation and actual mediation sessions might give clients an appreciation for the process and some ideas on how to approach the discussions.

Helping the client develop creative options and a plan for the negotiation may be one your most important roles. In her groundbreaking article "Toward Another View of Legal Negotiation," Professor Carrie Menkel-Meadow makes a persuasive case that thorough and creative negotiation planning, not style of presentation, is most effective in achieving negotiation success. We can help our client assess the strengths and weaknesses of various proposals and develop not only an initial proposal but also backup proposals based on anticipated responses. Mediators often report that the most difficult job is not convincing the other side of the merit of a particular proposal, but having one party (either party) actually put a proposal on the table that the party can live with. By providing the client with a negotiation plan in advance, the consulting lawyer can help the momentum of the mediation and help the client in the process.

Understanding itself may not be enough to do the job. Another function of the consulting lawyer is to walk the client step-by-step through the negotiation process that will occur in the mediation. A role play where we take on the role of the other spouse might help the client articulate underlying concerns and proposals for each anticipated issue. Clients benefit greatly from this dress rehearsal and report greater comfort and familiarity with the issues once the curtain goes up at the mediation.

PRACTICE TIPS

1. Educate your client about the difference between legal information provided by the mediator and your advice recommending a particular course of action.
2. Collaboratively determine with your client what scope of service you will provide during the mediation, what tasks the client will perform, and what discrete tasks you will perform.
3. Make sure your client completes a financial budget, income information, and property and debt schedules and is conversant about the information set forth on the forms; determine who will complete the forms (your client, a CPA, a financial planner, or you).
4. Make sure your client fully discloses all relevant income and property information and that you receive adequate disclosures from the other side.
5. If you represent the more powerful, more knowledgeable spouse, urge early and full financial disclosure—it may be the key to a mediation's success and finality.
6. You are not a potted plant. As consulting lawyer, you can offer input to your client's opposing counsel and directly to the mediator.
7. Acknowledge and praise clients when they are successful in representing themselves in mediation. Clients need your support as well as your guidance.

8. Instead of immediately filing for court relief, if an impasse develops on document production, failure to attend a deposition, or any other discovery issue, use the mediator as a case manager to mediate an expedited process.
9. Review important legal documents and advise your client about their meaning and importance in the mediation. Make sure your client keeps you in the loop so that you receive the documents *before* agreements are made in mediation.
10. Make a deal with your client about how often lawyer and client will communicate, who will initiate contact, and how proactive you should be.
11. If outside experts are needed, consider using a neutral expert rather than having both parties retain their own. You can be helpful in determining the level of the expert's service and fee and in interpreting findings for your client.
12. To stimulate negotiation, consider confidential mini reports (discussed in detail in future chapters) from experts so that the parties get a feel for an expert's opinion.
13. Help your clients understand the negotiation process, develop a strategic plan, and simulate the negotiation process ahead of time. Be a negotiation coach.
14. Remember, your job as a consulting lawyer in mediation is to help your client *complete* a fair agreement that the client believes is fair—not to win legal points or get the last dollar in the negotiations.
15. Protect your client in a manner that supports and honors the process they have chosen.

CHAPTER 9

Reaching Agreement

If an agreement is reached, mediators can try to create an atmosphere in which the parties savor their successes together. This can include congratulatory and complimentary statements by the mediator, stressing the hard work and sacrifices made by all involved and the ways in which agreements the parties have reached are preferable to their court or other alternatives.

—Douglas N. Frenkel and James H. Stark, *The Practice of Mediation: A Video-Integrated Text*, 3rd ed. (2018).

The goal of mediation is to help parties discuss their concerns with the concrete purpose of reaching agreements that can be carried out by the parties voluntarily (or enforced by a court, if necessary). In this chapter, we explore the approaches, skills, and tools to help you help your clients achieve this goal.

TYPICAL DIVORCE AGENDA

After dealing with immediate emergency issues, the next step is to establish an agenda of issues to be covered to ensure that important concerns and needs can be raised. In a comprehensive (parenting, support, and property) mediation, a customary agenda may include the following:

- Personal conduct and separation issues such as agreements regarding intimacy (between the parties or third persons), physical separation of the households (who will move from the family home, how, and when), living together in the same home, physical safety, diminishing emotional enmeshment and establishing boundaries between the parties such as limiting repeated and lengthy telephone calls or unannounced visits, curtailing derogatory remarks, handling relationships with extended family and friends, and other issues and concerns raised by the parties
- How the parties will handle negotiation of issues outside mediation sessions and deciding which issues and in what format such out-of-session discussion will take place
- Immediate issues concerning parenting time

- Immediate issues concerning support, payment of current debts, and management of assets
- Decision-making over issues involving the children and labeling legal custody (e.g., sole, primary, joint, or no label at all)
- Setting up a workable parenting schedule for the future, including holidays, vacations, and special days
- Identifying, valuing, and allocating assets and debts
- Long-term child and spousal support
- Miscellaneous issues such as filing taxes, life and health insurance, filing court documents and ancillary documents such as deeds, partnership resignations, QDROS for retirement vehicles, the involvement of grandparents and new significant others, the preservation of cultural or religious traditions, and so on

A client handout for a template divorce agenda is included in the Resources section.

Each client should be prepared to start working issue by issue and building the overall agreement step by step. Success is incremental—gained in baby steps. If lawyers are in the mediation room, they should try to recognize and positively acknowledge even the smallest indications of agreement and overlook many of the setbacks. Our belief and support for our client that there will eventually be full agreement plays an important role in building an agreement.

AGREEMENT READINESS

AT THE MEDIATION TABLE

TIT FOR TAT

Despite the best motives, sometimes the other side plays dirty. What do you do?

Robert Axelrod's brilliant book *The Evolution of Cooperation* may offer an approach based on his extensive game theory research.

Axelrod has two important tips. First, cooperation maximizes overall economic wealth for each party and for all parties collectively. Parties who cooperate each get more than those that compete for individual gain.

Second, if the other party plays dirty, the best way to maximize ultimate cooperation is to retaliate, fast! The purpose of retaliation is not to punish but to motivate the dirty player to return to cooperation. It turns out that if one waits to respond to uncalled for defections, there is a risk of sending the wrong signal. The longer defections are allowed to go unchallenged, the more likely it is that the other player will draw the conclusion that defection can pay . . . by responding right away, it gives the quickest possible feedback that a defection will not pay.

Balancing quick retaliation with an unwavering commitment to cooperation is a major challenge.

While we provide tools for effective bargaining around the mediation table, we stress agreement readiness as a necessary condition for building an agreement. Are the parties ready to settle, or are they still infatuated with their own positions?

Here is the key to assessing agreement readiness. If either or both parties are constantly saying "yes . . . but . . ." to their lawyers, the mediator, and/or to each other, each party needs more work to achieve readiness. For example:

Husband: "I am willing to agree to return the children at 7 p.m. *but she never has them ready on time for pick-up.*"

Wife: "I would get them ready on time *but he is usually so late in arriving that I will no longer worry about the agreed time for pick-up because he never is there on time.*"

The key to overcoming the "yes . . . buts . . ." is to ask our own clients to be responsible and accountable for their own behavior and request reciprocity from the other party.

IDENTIFY AND ACKNOWLEDGE INITIAL POSITIONS OF THE PARTIES

An essential tool for us to help our clients and their spouses get past their positions is for us to identify, acknowledge, and be able to restate the *positions* stated by both our client and the other party. This process demonstrates that we understand and empathize with what a party says she/he wants. Such identification and acknowledgment builds trust and rapport that are essential for reaching agreements.

Husband: "I want the house sold now so I can get my share of the equity."

You: "It is my understanding that in order for you to be able to have use of your share of the house proceeds you would like it sold as soon as possible."

Ask the parties to acknowledge that they need a new approach to solving their problem.

Until parties understand and indicate an awareness that they are open to exploring a new option (other than their own), they can "yes . . . but . . ." and they might remain stuck.

Spouse 1: "I want the house sold now."

Spouse 2: "I want to have us own it together for the next 12 years until the children all graduate high school."

Lawyer: "It sounds like you both agree that neither of you is willing to accept the other party's position. Am I right?"

Spouse 2: "Yes."

Spouse 1: "Yes."

Lawyer: "Do I also understand that you both want to work out the house in mediation rather than have a judge do it?"

Spouse 2: "Yes."

Spouse 1: "Yes."

Lawyer: "Since you agree that you want an agreement and neither of you is willing to accept the other's position, the only way I know is for you both to agree to a new third way—not yours [Spouse 1], or yours [Spouse 2]. Are you each willing to *try* to find that third way?"

Spouse 2: "Yes."

Spouse 1: "Yes."

Lawyer (to the mediator or other lawyer): "Do either of you have a sense as to how to get us back on track?

When you are attending a session, ask parties, the other lawyer, and the mediator for permission to propose an alternative or offer a suggestion.

If we wish to avoid or reduce resistance to any ideas or advice that we would like to offer to help, we can try this preliminary step of *asking for permission* before giving advice:

Lawyer: "You seem very set on your views about the house. I have an idea that I'd like to explore. Would you like to hear it?"

Spouse 1: "Yes."

Spouse 2: "Yes."

Lawyer: "All right. I can't promise you that this will solve the problem or that either of you will like it. But regardless of the outcome, are you willing to hear the entire idea and at least consider it?"

Spouse 1: "Yes."

Spouse 2: "Yes."

Lawyer: "What would you think of the possibility of Spouse 1 finding a way to buy out Spouse 2's share of the equity at today's value (we would need an appraisal), have Spouse 2's share bear interest at an agreed amount, have principal and interest accrue with no monthly payments, and permit Spouse 1 an agreed amount of time to pay off this amount or sell the house? There are several details to work out, but what do each of you think of this overall concept?"

Try using this tool with your own client, with the other party, and the mediator. If neutral experts are invited to participate in the session, try this tool when such experts offer recommendations as well.

ENCOURAGE GROUND RULES

Structure is a safety net for parties who are drowning in conflict. Mediators are trained to have the parties agree to clear boundaries in their behavior toward each other and reflect those boundaries in agreements. For example, mediation ground rules may include no cell phones or name calling in the sessions. Lawyers can encourage clients to not only abide by ground rules but ask to establish additional ground rules, if needed. When conducting sessions via Zoom, ground rules might include closing other browsers with open tabs, turning off notifications and switching on "do not disturb" settings, or avoiding checking emails during the session.

A key issue in virtually every divorce mediation is what the ground rules are for parties to communicate with each other in sessions and outside. While it is common for many mediators to convey Party A's offer to Party B, whenever possible you should be supportive of having the parties present their own offers directly to each other. Stating all terms and provisions of their own proposals encourages the parties to "own" every position they take during negotiations. When the parties say the words themselves, the proposals better reflect their needs. Equally important, as one party listens to an offer being presented by the other party, a working trust may begin to build.

Although many lawyers feel more comfortable if they remain in private caucuses with their clients and have the mediator convey offers back and forth, if the mediator communicates the offer from the other party, the party hearing the offer is at least one step removed. In addition, direct party communication also prevents possible distortions or errors by the mediator in relaying the positions of the parties.

Some mediation participants are reluctant to present their own offers. Many feel inadequate or unprepared to articulate their own negotiating positions. Others may be excellent negotiators at work or at a car dealership but fall apart when negotiating with their former spouses.

In order to maximize the parties' success in presenting their own offers to each other, we can coach our clients to help them determine what they want and how to ask for it. Framing an offer is a difficult challenge—so is finding the right way to communicate the offer so that it will be heard and considered by the other party. We should be willing to spend planning time with our clients prior to a proposal being communicated.

In addition, we should coach a client who is receiving an offer. We can "preview" an offer by helping our client to listen closely to the offer and not to interrupt or lose control. We can also offer an opportunity to meet after our client hears the details of an offer to discuss the pros and cons and to prepare a response.

With this type of help, parties appreciate having their own voice in the mediation and having the direct and unfiltered opportunity to assess the behavior and position of the other party.

RED FLAG RULE

This is a ground rule that you can suggest to prevent things from getting out of hand:

> Lawyer: "So, I understand you and your spouse are planning to divide up the family photos next Saturday between 2 and 3 p.m. while the children are with their friends, and you have asked for some guidelines. Can we focus on one rule?"
>
> Client: "Yes."
>
> Lawyer: "If either of you feels uncomfortable during the selection process, either of you may raise your hand and say that the 'red flag is up.' A raised flag means that discussion is over for the day. Neither of you may call the other later that day to try and reengage. No reason needs to be given for the flag raising so you can't argue over the reason. You can also raise the red flag verbally if either of you is uncomfortable during a phone conversation. If there is a problem, you can discuss it with either of us (lawyers) or with the mediator. Are you both comfortable with this ground rule?"
>
> Client: "Yes."

Lawyer: "Do you have any questions or concerns about it? If not, do you feel comfortable raising the red flag ground rule at your next session?"

Client: "Yes."

The red flag rule might help some parties more than others. The red flag option might be most helpful to parties who express collaborative intent but find themselves emotional or overwhelmed when faced with a critical decision-making moment or triggering topic.

INTEREST-BASED NEGOTIATIONS

A key approach for negotiation is a focus on the interests of the parties. Interest-based negotiation derives from Fisher Ury and Patterson seminal book, *Getting to Yes: Negotiating Agreements without Giving In.* Interest-based thinking is quite different from the type of negotiation traditionally used by litigators, which reflects the adversary system and is focused on the vindication of legal rights. Inherent within this "old paradigm" is a view that lawyers are in charge and that if the other side won't compromise sufficiently, courts always produce the best justice. Power, leverage, and fear are the levers used to create self-doubt in the other party to push for compromise. The conflict is seen as a zero-sum game in which every dollar paid to the other side comes out of our client's pocket.

As the focus of this adversarial approach is to maximize the financial gain on each issue, there is little or no consideration of or value ascribed to the ongoing future relationship between the parties in determining a successful outcome of the negotiation. The assumption is that both parties will be equally unhappy about the result and that somehow they will go on with their lives, heal or not heal, but the impact of the negotiation on the long-term viability of family relationships is rarely contemplated head-on.

Under the new paradigm of interest-based negotiation, the focus is to dig below the stated positions of the parties to identify and meet underlying interests and concerns as opposed to legal positions. The goal is client-centered, not lawyer-centered, decision-making. While financial considerations are important, factors such as impact on the emotional functioning of the parties and children, speed of resolution, control over result, and costs of the negotiation are factored in, and it is in these realms that common ground can often be identified. The input and advice of nonlawyer experts such as therapists and financial professionals are considered just as or more important than lawyer expertise. As in the old paradigm, negotiators try to create dissonance in the other party to reflect upon their positions. The difference is that instead of using threats and fear of litigation as the sole means of creating dissonance, interest-based negotiators create dissonance by exploring each party's BATNA, that is, Best Alternative to a Negotiated Agreement. Win–win scenarios are not only possible but common. Candor and transparency in communication are viewed as essential to build the trust necessary to reach effective agreements, and the process defines the long-term relationship between the parties as valuable and worth preserving to the greatest possible extent.

DE-POSITION WITH POSITIVE SELF-INTEREST

Interest-based negotiation may seem like a great thing . . . but do you have just a bit of doubt whether you can pull it off or whether the other side will play with you?

Here is a strategy that we bet will work (most of the time).

Be smart, not nice. Start with the self-motivation of your client or the other side in order to negotiate. And rather than challenging, accept what each person says . . . people generally trust others who value, acknowledge, and don't challenge them at the start.

Let's see how this works. Your client is the wife who wants to stay in the house. Husband wants it sold. You know if it gets to court, no one can predict the outcome.

How do you help your client be open to another possibility other than staying in the house? Here it goes . . .

1. Restate wife's position: "I understand that you want to stay in the house."
2. Give (hypothetically) what she says she wants: "For our discussion today, let's pretend that husband agrees for you to stay in the house."
3. Transition to the positive self-interest of your client getting what she wants: "So if you now are not fighting about whether you get to stay in the house, how do you benefit from such an outcome?"
4. As client gives her underlying concerns and needs, go one by one and keep asking for more—never challenge them regardless of how unrealistic or unworkable they might be: I will benefit by:
    - "Staying in the housing market as I could not otherwise qualify."
    - "Making money as the house appreciates."
    - "Having stability by staying in the same neighborhood."
    - "Making my husband keep his word."
5. For each of these underlying concerns and needs, reframe them mutually so they could lead to other options and be accepted by the other side as well.
    - "Find a way to continue owning your own home."
    - "Increasing your current assets with sound investments."
    - "Making sure that you and your children maximize your stability and minimize chaos through the separation process."
    - "Building trust with your husband by being accountable to promises and commitments."
6. After restating all of these reframed concerns and needs, ask your client for the following commitment: "If I could assure you that we will focus on each and every one of your needs and concerns as you stated (in #5), would you be open to exploring a solution other than staying in this house. Just be willing to explore, you do not have to accept this option."

Your client (or the other side in a negotiation) may not say "yes" every time, but you may be surprised with how many yeses you get.

Try this baby step; it just might work.

The fact that the new paradigm is a departure from the traditional lawyer-centric, adversarial approach does not mean that the law is invisible in an interest-based negotiation. Educating clients on legal reality is part of client-centered decision-making and securing informed consent to proposed solutions. Knowing about the law matters, but it should not dictate any particular result or define the best result for each family. Issues such as determination of a parenting plan and spousal support, moreover, involve so much discretion by judicial officers so that the "legal" result (especially over the long term) is difficult to predict.

You're Not the Judge—The Clients Are

When families operate within the court system, the rule of law prevails. Most lawyers are comfortable with, if not totally supportive of resolution within the legal system. In mediation, the parties may arrive at a solution that is personally idiosyncratic or governed by values and authority that might be far different from the law. If it makes sense to your client, and seems fair, practical, and enforceable, when do you stop being a naysayer and start being supportive?

We know of a mediation for a couple who had a clear agreement providing for a sexually open marriage; each partner was free to engage in unlimited sexual opportunities outside the relationship. Problem: Sharon fell in love with a new partner and wanted to move out. Keith had promised to give Sharon $200,000 from his separate estate in case of a breakup but felt his promise was null and void due to her desire to move out and stop having sex with him.

The parties spent several sessions discussing the intricate (and intimate) details of their contract and the consequences of breach. Was it within the contract that Sharon could be away from Keith for more than a week at a time? Was she required to leave a phone number? When she was at home, was it OK to email her lover from the marital bedroom? Was it bad faith for her lover to coach her in the negotiations?

No judge would have listened to this private, legally *irrelevant* stuff. Few lawyers would engage in negotiations over these points! However, this was Sharon and Keith's life. Through mediation, they were able to work out a deal that was fair to them and made sense to them.

In a joint holiday card, they both wished their mediator well and indicated that they were still the best of friends.

In preparing our clients for negotiations in mediation or participating in agreement building ourselves, we should be respectful and open to considering the positions of *both* our client and the other spouse on any given issue. Mediators are trained to then reframe those stated positions in an effort to tease out the underlying interests behind them. However, lawyers can participate in this reframing as well. One of our greatest assets in a mediation is our ability to bond with the other party and lawyer so that our ideas and proposals will get a fair hearing. If we can reframe the positions of both our client *and* the other party in a fair way that points out mutual interests, this bonding and trust building will accelerate.

As explained in *Getting to Yes*: "Interests motivate people. They are the silent movers behind the hubbub of positions. Your position is something you have decided on. Your interests are what caused you to so decide."[1,2]

Interests can be substantive (e.g., housing, financial security), emotional (e.g., anger, fear, anxiety, revenge), relationship (e.g., with children, with former

1. Roger Fisher, William Ury & Bruce Patton, Getting to Yes: Negotiating Agreements without Giving In, ch. 3.
2. *Id.*

spouse), or process related (e.g., momentum, feeling heard). Once a lawyer has worked with the mediator and other attorney to help uncover both clients' interests, it is crucial to link the mutual interests of both parties so that they can build from commonality (e.g., both clients want to keep the children in the same neighborhood, both want to live close together to facilitate parenting, both want certainty and finality, etc.).

After identifying the mutual interests, we can help our client brainstorm options for resolution. Brainstorming is having each party think of all possible options and put them on the table. After all options are put on the flipchart (or Google Docs, Jamboard, or screen-shared Word document in a Zoom mediation), you can help the mediator and parties prioritize and evaluate the identified options based on criteria such as cost, impact on children, privacy, speed of resolution, and impact on the future relationship of the parties. The parties talk through the positives and negatives of each option. This discussion is what can lead the parties to agreement.

AT THE MEDIATION TABLE

YOU CUT—I'LL CHOOSE

During the dark hours of a mediation, when an impasse looms, the parties can collaborate to build a hypothetical dummy model of resolution—putting off for a while who will get what. The mediator uses a "what if?" approach. Both parties want the same thing, such as the house, so they work out all the terms—without initially deciding who will get each portion. More often than expected, the positive energy from the model building can break the impasse, making it easier to resolve who will get what.

There are quirks, however. In a mediation, deferring the decision as to who will get the house, a couple built a dummy model on a house buyout. In the dummy model, it was agreed that the light fixtures (including an expensive chandelier) would stay with the house at no cost to the party who would eventually be awarded the residence. Well, when Sara found that she could not afford the house monthly nut, she chose the tax-free buyout—and surrendered the right to stay in the house to Joe. But here's the rub: Her parents had given the couple the chandelier as a housewarming gift. Sara was willing to give up the house but not the chandelier. An angry session later, Joe agreed to buy her a new chandelier if and when Sara ever bought another house and if she was not involved in a romantic relationship at the time of purchase! Quirky? Yes. But also a done deal!

NORMALCY AND SOLVABILITY

In a divorce, spouses will often concentrate on their own misery and pain, ignoring the condition of the other spouse. Or, a spouse will actually blame the other spouse for his/her pain. One twin set of tools to stop the blame game is to help parties see that the presenting problem is normal for other divorcing couples and the problem is solvable.

Husband: "If I agree to let Wife live in the house, the kids will never want to spend time with me. I think it would be better if we just sold the house and each of us purchases new residences."

Lawyer: "Many Dads have this same concern, and they find ways to establish a new home for the children who enjoy their time just as much as with Mom in the family residence.

Use professional articles and research to offer commonality: Objective criteria or expertise can often settle an argument. If Spouse 1 says a four-year-old should not have overnights and Spouse 2 wants overnights, rather than pushing anyone to compromise, we might say:

"Would either of you be interested in what child development research says about this issue? If so, I have an article by______. Let's look at her findings and recommendations." Lawyers can do the same thing by referring to mediation research on process issues. A summary of highlights of mediation research is included in the Resources section.

EXPERIMENT AND TEST OUT SOLUTIONS

Mediation allows parties to privately and confidentially experiment and test out agreements without fear of establishing a binding legal precedent. Agreements can be time limited and reviewed for viability within days or weeks. Agreements can also be modified to take into account the impact of new agreements. We can reassure our client that there is no final binding agreement until all the parts are cross-stitched into a whole written agreement subject to review and final signatures. However, if both parties choose to make incremental final agreements on bifurcated issues, we can let our client know that we would support such incremental agreements (if appropriate) and help draft them in a timely way.

INVOLVEMENT OF CHILDREN

Participation of children in a mediation session is controversial and subject to mediator discretion. Dr. Florence Bienenfeld, a noted mental health professional, strongly urges the involvement of children: Including children in the mediation process gives them an opportunity to hear, to be heard, and to gain perspective about the difficult situation in which they find themselves. Most children leave the mediation session less burdened and better fortified for whatever will happen to them.

Dr. Bienenfeld is not alone. There has been a worldwide shift in attitude toward children's involvement in parental conflicts. When we began practicing, the general consensus was that any direct involvement in the parental dispute was inappropriate and harmful to children. The United Nations, as well as state agencies and private child education and advocacy groups are increasingly recognizing a child's right to be heard in matters that affect that child, as echoed in former prime minister of Portugal Antonio Guterres' 2019 Remarks on the 30th Anniversary of the Convention on the Rights of the Child. Research and expert opinion support this increased respect for the child's voice.

Professor Cassandra Adams argues that mediation is an appropriate and beneficial method of addressing and listening to the voices of children. She argues that a holistic mediation process that includes the voices of parents and children will promote the integration of interests and recommends specific child-oriented education and training for mediators who handle family law issues.

Children generally do not participate in the negotiating and bargaining stages of mediation. Before children are invited to a session, discuss this issue carefully with clients. It must be worked out whether siblings should come in together or separately and/or whether the parents should also be present. Each client should get assurance from the mediator that the children must want to be present and that they are not to be given the impression that they are responsible for the decisions being made by their parents or that they have the power to veto or alter their parents' agreements. Each client should know that mediators are trained to reassure the children that their parents are choosing the peaceful and less-destructive option of mediation in large part because their parents love them. Often by meeting the mediator and actually sitting in the mediation room, children fill in their concrete reality of what is happening at the mediation, which can help ameliorate their fears and concerns.

In the case of many older adolescents and adult children, parents more readily choose to have them sit at the mediation table and participate as important participants or as resources for their needs and desires (which are important to their parents) or about factual matters such as the operation of the family business or investments. While children should never be given the impression that they get to decide issues affecting them, a teenager's buy-in after the opportunity to be heard may make the difference between a parenting plan that is workable and one that isn't. Noncompliance with parenting agreements can be most challenging when teenage children are involved, so their buy-in can be invaluable.

STARTER TOOLBOX FOR REACHING AGREEMENTS

Here are some sample tools (by no means exhaustive) for you to start using immediately the next time you attend a mediation session.

Emotional Reframing: Use this tool to capture the feelings that your client or the other party has expressed. She/he will feel heard and appreciate your sensitivity, which instills confidence and reduces fear.

> Spouse 1: "Spouse 2 never brings Josh home on time."
>
> Reframe: "You must be frustrated/angry/worried when this happens."

Bifurcate Divorce Issues: Salvage Agreements, Plan for Contained Litigation: Some mediations just will not settle all issues. Rather than throw out the progress and good work, one strategy is to use the progress and goodwill developed in the mediation to isolate the issues to be litigated and join the mediator to write up the agreed issues for a final settlement. This tool will not only remove the "all or nothing" scenario but also permit parties to get resolution in a rational manner. The lawyers and mediator can work with the parties to work out which issues will be litigated and how they will be litigated. For example, within the mediation process, parties can work out expedited and limited discovery as well as how the spouses will interact with each other and the children through the end of litigation. Parties can also agree to return to mediation after the judge makes a decision to discuss how to live with the decision (often needing clarity), heal, and plan for the future.

NEGOTIATING WITH THE MEDIATOR

Unlike a judicial officer, a mediator's role and interventions can be greatly influenced by the requests and needs of the parties. As our client's representative, we can take a proactive role in negotiating with the mediator during negotiations in a number of ways:

1. If our client expresses that she is not being given the opportunity to present her concerns or facts, we can request the mediator to make additional time either during the sessions or in stand-alone private sessions.
2. If we or our client believe that the discussion in mediation is not considering necessary legal, financial, or parenting criteria or factors, we can supply the mediator cases, statutes, articles, reports, or other material to enhance the quality of the discussion.
3. If the format being used is not meeting the needs of our client, we can request a process modification. For example, the time between sessions may need to be compressed or delayed, the length of the sessions may need to be increased or reduced, your client may need more breaks, perhaps the other party is taking too many breaks, our client needs more or fewer ground rules, and so on.
4. If our client is making impulsive decisions or cannot make any decisions at all, we should contact the mediator to discuss a possible change in approach.
5. If the mediator is a flabby drafter, we may request that the lawyers jointly draft agreements and other documents.
6. If the parties have reached agreements on key issues, we may ask the mediator to suggest writing up binding partial agreements and have those agreements turned into enforceable court orders.

There are many other issues in which lawyers can weigh in tactfully and collaboratively. Remember, we are not potted plants. Most competent mediators welcome the input and suggestions of lawyers who are knowledgeable and supportive of the process. Clients are spending considerable money and reliance on the mediation process and a key part of a lawyer's job is to make sure that the process is working to its full capacity.

WORKING WITH MEDIATOR PROPOSALS

While the goal of mediation is to facilitate agreements by direct negotiation between the parties, sometimes snags develop. We have discussed how working in separate caucuses or having lawyers play a more active negotiation role can accelerate agreement.

Another strategy to break impasse is the use of a mediator settlement proposal. If the parties are stuck on one issue or are having difficulty linking an overall settlement, many mediators are willing to provide their own proposal for settlement.

A mediator proposal can work in several ways:

1. The proposal may be suggested by the mediator or requested by the parties.
2. The proposal can mirror a court resolution or reflect an integration of proposals by the parties.
3. The proposal can be offered take it or leave it or as a catalyst to more negotiation.

During bargaining, be vigilant about the timing and use of mediator proposals. If a mediator proposal is offered too early, it can cut off creativity and exchange of ideas that might morph into a settlement with such directive intervention by the mediator. If impasse hardens and parties start saber rattling or packing their briefcases, a mediator proposal could come too late.

In selecting a mediator, one aspect of a lawyer's due diligence is to learn whether and how a proposed mediator uses this tool of mediator-generated settlement proposals as a last stage effort. If the mediator is flexible about how mediator proposals are used, we might discuss their possible use with our client, the other lawyer, and the mediator.

If we and/or our client begin to feel that the discussions are stalled on any particular issue or an overall agreement, we can raise the possibility of using a mediator proposal with the other lawyer and the mediator. However, it is important to be clear about how the process will work and how the mediator's neutrality and trust can be preserved during and after the mediator proposal is presented.

A lawyer might consider using the following protocol in setting up and implementing a mediator proposal:

1. Request that the mediator neutrally describe the state of negotiation. This can be done privately with the mediator or with the other lawyer.
2. Request that the mediator set out areas of agreement in joint session.
3. The mediator should set out issues (and sub-issues) that need further work in joint session.
4. Hopefully, the mediator will then check in with parties as to their reaction to the mediator's sense of agreed issues and those that need work and invite other areas that need work to achieve overall agreement.
5. Discuss with the mediator what facts or objective criteria are needed to bridge the gap.
6. Discuss whether there are additional decision-makers who should be involved in receiving, reviewing, and responding to a mediator proposal.
7. Discuss whether the parties are ready hear the mediator proposal at the session itself or whether the mediator should send a proposal by email in days following session.
8. Make sure that it is clear that the mediator proposal is not "take it or leave it" but rather a compilation of the mediator's ideas as to what might meet the interests and concerns of the parties.

9. Request that the mediator prepare a written term sheet that lists all agreed-upon issues, all issues to be subject to a mediator proposal, and a detailed proposal by the mediator as to each issue.
10. Discuss whether the mediator proposal will be presented in joint session or separately with the parties.
11. Make sure that there is ample time to discuss questions and concerns with the mediator, either jointly or privately.
12. Be nimble to use mediator proposal either to completely resolve issues or kick-start further bargaining.

"NOTES FOR MY MEDIATION"

During a particularly tense mediation, the wife was reading this poem to herself sotto voce. She had written the words in a mood of hopeful prayer to give her comfort through several stressful and important weeks for every member of the family. This poem can be sent to clients in the mediation packet or handed out during a difficult mediation.

Notes for My Mediation

Stay centered/relaxed/focused.

Concentrate on positive aspects of this process. We will get through it and it will end.

Change is difficult, requires patience and perspective. The bigger the change the greater the requirements. The outcome will be a good one.

Our mediator understands the dynamic and can help—let the mediator, who has been through harder mediations and has the experience, help.

This process requires tolerance, forgiveness, and going the extra mile.

I will continue to be responsible for myself and try to do well for our child, who is my major focus.

I can only control myself.

I will respond to my spouse's anger and judging with perspective and forgiveness.

I will not allow my spouse to hurt or anger me through words or actions.

I will not react personally or negatively to my spouse.

I will continue to act affirmatively whenever possible.

My spouse cannot help it and is not acting out of malevolence or intentional hurtfulness.

I will continue to act with integrity, sensitivity, and with my eye on the goal of completing the process with the best possible outcome.

I will keep my eye on the prize of peace.

I deserve it and have worked hard for it.

I believe I will come out of this a stronger, better person.

I believe God will help me and take care of me.

My Vision:

There will be a time within the next year when I will catch myself smiling or laughing without even thinking about it.

I will wake up with a mind and heart clear of fear of the unknown and the unanticipated financial and emotional threats that now burden my life and relationships.

I will return to being an innately happy person who values recreation, relaxation, and relationships.

I will be able to regenerate.

I have carried the burden for many years; I can continue to carry it quietly for another few weeks. It has been a long road. I can keep going a little bit longer. I have done a good job. I will get to the end and start a new beginning.[3]

3. Editor's Note: Poem submitted by attorney Forrest Mosten. Identity of the author is withheld by request. Salient facts are fictitious. Published in the *Family & Conciliation Courts Review*, January 1996.

CHAPTER 10

Reviewing and Drafting Mediated Agreements

(V)irtually all divorce mediators, lawyers or not, now urge both husband and wife to consult their own lawyers before, during or after the mediation. The role of such "outside" lawyers also is unclear. Just how deeply must they delve into the bases of the mediated agreement? One danger, of course, is that some reviewing attorneys undermine a mediation by inappropriately imposing an adversarial perspective. But sometimes a strong adversarial impetus is just what the client needs.

—Leonard L. Riskin and James E. Westbrook,
Dispute Resolution and Lawyers, 2nd ed., 1991

It is generally accepted that the family lawyer's major role in mediation is to review and give approval to the settlement agreement and court documents. We should inform our clients at the outset that nothing is binding until the final agreement is signed by both parties and notarized, or signed and submitted to the court. This encourages flexibility and creativity in negotiations. Once signed and notarized, in some states, or signed and submitted to the court, in other states, the agreements entered in mediation can become enforceable court orders with the same validity as any order negotiated directly between lawyers or rendered by a judge. This impending legal finality often makes spouses anxious about the consequences of an enforceable contract or court order, and their concerns about nearing the end of the mediation process can cause clients to reconsider elements of the agreements, both major and minor. The impending finality, ironically, can also be a catalyst for emotional turmoil. Fear and uncertainty about the future can overcome the euphoria of having reached agreement and the anticipation of moving past conflict and on to the next chapter of their lives. It is definitely a nerve-racking time!

Clients are not the only nervous ones. With the increasing trend in many jurisdictions to grant mediators and other alternative dispute resolution (ADR) neutrals immunity from malpractice liability, the reviewing family lawyer may be the only pocket (deep or shallow) to which a dissatisfied or remorseful client can later look in a malpractice action or bar complaint. Because clients rely on lawyers more in the review process than at any other time in mediation, clients are dependent on the sometimes-conflicting lawyer roles of supporting the client's deal and vigilantly protecting the client's legal and financial position now and for the future. It is no wonder that lawyers also grow nervous as signing time approaches. Lawyer anxiety may be intensified as clients put time and emotional pressure on the reviewing lawyer to churn out settlement documents quickly, to be meticulous in reviewing deal points and draft language, and to keep the fees low. After all, one of the chief client motivators in choosing mediation is to expedite their divorce process and save money—and high bills from the consulting lawyer can defeat that purpose. In settings where the lawyers did not participate in the mediation sessions and are learning of the agreed-upon terms for the first time, this review process can be particularly intense—and may be expensive.

Juggling conflicting goals and demands is not a new skill for most family lawyers. It is indeed possible to render competent and needed services, to provide legal information and advice, and to be supportive of the client's productive work at the mediation table. We are no strangers to dealing with client's remorse. We are skilled at holding deals together when they begin fraying at the seams. We perform these feats week in and week out— on the agreements that we negotiate ourselves. The big challenge in mediation is to rise to the challenge of keeping your client's deal together—especially when you may be critical of the terms reached or believe that your client "gave away the store." It is very tempting to indulge in comparisons between the agreement brought in after mediation and the hypothetical "best case scenario" deal that "might have been" obtained had the lawyer been the client's negotiating arm from the beginning or had the final terms been left to the court to decide.

The "let it go" mantra that worked so well in working with opposing counsel in setting up the mediation can also be applied to reviewing an agreement. It is our duty, as well as the client's expectation for us, to point out problems that we find. We would never suggest that a reviewing lawyer ignore present or future difficulties that the agreement might cause the client. However, *how* we inform the client about these difficulties is as critical as the substance of the critique.

First, assess the weight and magnitude of a deficiency and communicate it accurately to your client, with thoughtful consideration to tone and word choice. Some problems are minutia, others are ticking time bombs, and still others are fires presently raging out of control. Not all of your valid concerns are raging fires! Many lawyers review an agreement by sending a client a letter exhaustively detailing every possible problem in the proposed draft settlement agreement or redlining the document with so many comments that the original draft barely remains intact. Many lawyers edit a draft agreement so profusely in order to protect themselves against possible client's complaints or claims rather than to better help the client understand the agreement or to obtain a materially improved agreement. The information delivered to the client may be the same in both approaches. The first approach is lawyer-centered, and the second approach is client-centered. Client-centered approaches usually work better, especially for mediation participants who have grown accustomed to an empathic client-centered process in dealing with their mediator and expect and appreciate a similar client-centered manner from their reviewing lawyer.

Your concerns about the presented agreement should be balanced, as much as possible, by your appreciation for the benefits to the client that have been achieved in the mediation building the agreement.

Consistent with the traditional law school approach that focuses on finding every imaginable problem, many lawyers are obsessive about pointing out everything that may *not* work. Unlike a law school exam showcasing issue spotting for the sole purpose of identifying flaws, pointing out the favorable aspects of a proposed agreement as well not only makes the client feel more confident about their mediation performance (we are not suggesting unrealistic pandering) but also communicates a more realistic overall assessment of the agreement. In the mediation classes that we teach, we have many times encountered mediation trainees who have raised their hands and said:

> I wish the world was as rosy as you paint it. In the real world [i.e., the trainee's perceived world], people don't want to pay for gratuitous solicitous comments from me. My clients think that I am pandering to them. My clients want my straight opinion about the agreement's defects. They know the good aspects; after all, they negotiated it.

Many lawyers (and other people too!) unequivocally attribute their own worldview to others and are shocked to learn that their view is not universally held. Most people keep agreements. Most clients do not expect their lawyers always to be right. They expect us to try to understand their concerns and to try to do right by them, given the circumstances. And we have found that clients like and are willing to pay for affirmations about benefits of the mediated deal.

Be open and ask about the client's motivations and actions that led up to making the agreement. Be curious, not judgmental. Ask: *why?* For example: "*Why* did you agree that your spouse could be awarded her car worth $20,000 without requesting an equal amount ($20,000) of marital property or an equalizing payment of $10,000 from her share of the house proceeds?" The client may not have been crazy to give up dollars that were possible to obtain by negotiating further or by taking the case to trial. The client may have received equalizing dollars in other issues of the agreement or may have chosen to give up dollars for expeditious closure, for a better parenting relationship, for payment of a moral debt, or for some other nonmonetary reason. Be careful not to ask about the agreement in a way that implies or telegraphs disapproval until you understand the trade-offs leading up to the final agreement from the client's point of view.

REVIEW SUMMARY LETTERS AND HAVE YOUR CLIENT PREPARE A MEMORANDUM

If not present at a mediation session, a lawyer should carefully review any summary letters from the mediator as a first step in reconstructing the history of the negotiations. We should ask our client to prepare a detailed email or memo that (1) gives the client's view of the trade-offs and (2) articulates the client's view of the benefits of the agreement as well as any concerns the client might have.

The summary letters and client memo are excellent supplements to the draft agreement or deal memo prepared by the mediator in our review of the agreement. Many agreements are clear enough that a lawyer's comments can be contained in a balanced letter to the client. Even in the simplest agreement, it is important for us to ask our client to schedule a meeting, in person or on Zoom, and engage in a face-to-face consultation to go over the agreement clause by clause.

Child support agreements can last ten years or more, and spousal support awards can last decades—for example, $2,000 a month for ten years is $240,000 in support payments alone! With this type of present and future impact on their lives, most clients benefit from a personal meeting with their trusted legal professional to discuss the terms and ramifications of the agreement. Clients need to understand the consequences, legal and practical, of their agreement and need our help reality testing to make sure the agreement is workable. Be sure to initiate a preventive discussion to help the client consider and handle future family-relationship issues. Also, we can diagnose other legal soft spots facing the client in the future and recommend preventive solutions. (See Chapter 11.)

In addition to the issues you have spotted, most clients have some questions or concerns of their own in regard to the agreement. If we take on the assignment of reviewing settlement agreements, we owe it to our client to set aside sufficient time during which there can be a wide-ranging discussion about the agreement and how it will impact our client's life after the settlement is signed.

Even the clients who are the biggest penny pinchers generally find this review conference to be well worth the fees that you charge. If there is resistance to paying for additional time, one response you might consider can be something like:

> Very few homeowners like paying 6 percent to a real estate broker to sell a house. However, the stakes are high enough, so most people consider the broker's commission to be a necessary cost of selling a house. You are now entering into the most important agreement of your life, and I have found that my clients benefit greatly from sitting down with me before signing on the dotted line. We both have done a great job in keeping your fees down to this point, and now we are almost at the finish line. Just consider this review to be a necessary cost of getting a divorce.

Will There Be a Writing? What Is the Product of Successful Mediation?

Mediation grew out of a desire for a more holistic, less adversarial process for divorcing families. In her 2014 article, Rebecca Aviel stated: "There is ample room in family law for expertise without advocacy, for the exercise of legal judgment and skill without full-fledged partisan loyalty to an individual client."[1]

Typically, family law mediations result in Separation Agreements, Stipulated Judgments, Stipulations of Settlement, or Marital Settlement Agreements, which resolve pending issues contractually and/or via court order, and a final binding

---

1. Rebecca Aviel, *1099 Counsel for the Divorce*, 55 Bos. Coll. L. Rev. (Sept. 2014).

writing is something that the participants value and expect (terminology may vary from state to state).

Many other mediation participants, however, may just be seeking information or clarifying discussions and neither need nor expect a writing of any kind. For those turning to a mediator for post-judgment parenting matters, this is exceedingly common. To some, the demand that an agreement be reduced to writing can in and of itself evoke resistance or imply lack of trust.[2]

Spouses may have diametrically opposed hopes and expectations about their mediation's purpose and technical outcome. One spouse may enter mediation hoping for reconciliation (the "leaning in" spouse) and the other may enter mediation expecting and hoping for a final, enforceable divorce decree (the "leaning out" spouse). Dr. William J. Doherty of the University of Minnesota has found that 30 percent of couples coming into marital therapy are "mixed-agenda" couples: one spouse is leaning out and the other spouse is leaning into the relationship.[3] While the number of mixed-agenda couples entering mediation or coming into our offices is probably lower than 30 percent, most experienced family lawyers are familiar with this dynamic.

It is by no means a foregone conclusion that a final, enforceable, written document will be the result of mediation. Consider the following range of possible outcomes:

1. A discussion with the mediator that leads to the parties returning to the marriage.
2. A referral by the mediator to discernment counseling to explore whether both parties wish to commit to couples counseling.
3. A Reconciliation Agreement that may include a referral to a couples counselor and may also include parenting and financial issues requiring review and drafting by an attorney.
4. A Post-Marital Agreement that will be a binding private agreement with the assumption that the parties will remain married. Physical separation may be contemplated or provided for in such an agreement. In most states, attorney representation is encouraged or required for such agreements, especially where spousal support rights are affected.
5. A Temporary Physical Separation, with or without a written agreement.
6. A Long-Term Separation: with Memorandum of Understanding (Non-Enforceable Private Separation Agreement). Given that the parties do not want this agreement to be involved in court enforcement, the lawyer level of review may vary from very light to very involved.
7. A Long-Term Separation: with Enforceable Private Separation Agreement. In some states, mediators, even if they are lawyers, are not permitted to draft final documents.[4]

---

2. *See* DOUGLAS, FRENKEL & STARK, THE PRACTICE OF MEDIATION, 2nd ed. 287–88 (2013).

3. WILLIAM DOUGHERTY, DISCERNMENT COUNSELING TRAINING MATERIALS (2015).

4. Tim Pierce, Ethics Counsel for the State Bar of Wisconsin, wrote the following in 2010 about lawyers drafting final documents.

Utah Ethics Opinion 05-03 (2005) opined:

8. A Marital Settlement Agreement or Separation Agreement with No Filed Court Documents. The difference between an MOU and a Marital Settlement Agreement or Separation Agreement is that the agreement is considered an enforceable binding document, which many mediators are not permitted to draft and that needs greater review by the parties' lawyers.
9. A Public Marital Settlement Agreement with Filed Court Documents and No Final Decree. Many states permit bifurcation of the divorce proceedings so that parties can finally resolve all parenting and financial issues and obtain a partial court decree/judgment while reserving the dissolution of marital status for a later second or further decree/judgment.
10. A Court Decree/Judgment of Marital Dissolution (Divorce) with Public Terms of Settlement. In some states, the terms of the marital settlement or separation agreement are merged into the decree/judgment so that there is no necessity of a Marital Settlement Agreement. In other states, the Marital Settlement Agreement or Separation Agreement is submitted to the court and either adopted as a Court Judgment/Decree or as an Exhibit to the Judgment/Decree.
11. A Court Decree/Judgment of Marital Dissolution (Divorce) with Private Terms of Settlement. In order to protect privacy of financial and other settlement terms, some states permit the parties to obtain a Judgment/Decree of Marital Dissolution resolving some or all of the financial and parenting terms and reserving the balance of the terms for a completed and signed private judgment/decree to be held by the parties and not filed in court at the time the first Decree/Judgment is approved. In turn, the terms contained in the private judgment are not subject to court enforcement unless and until the private judgment is submitted and approved by the court. In our experience, the vast majority of such private judgments/decrees are never filed with the court since parties tend to comply with such terms without court assistance.

When a lawyer-mediator, after a successful mediation, drafts the settlement agreement, complaint, and other pleadings to implement the settlement and obtain a divorce for the parties, the lawyer-mediator is engaged in the practice of law and attempting to represent opposing parties in litigation.

Likewise, Ohio Ethics Opinion 2009-4 (2009) stated:

> At issue is whether upon completion of a domestic relations mediation and preparation of a mediation report, a lawyer-mediator may prepare necessary legal documents, such as petitions, decrees, and ancillary documents, for filing by or on behalf of one or more of the parties to a domestic relations proceeding. Examples of these documents might be a Separation Agreement, Shared Parenting Plan, Petition for Dissolution of Marriage and Decree for Dissolution of Marriage, Ohio Child Support Guidelines Worksheets.
>
> A domestic relations lawyer-mediator who goes beyond preparing the mediation report, which is required of the mediator by law and rule, into the preparation of necessary legal documents for filing by or on behalf of the parties to a domestic relations proceeding is engaging in a legal representation subsequent to the mediation.

These opinions reflect the generally agreed-upon consensus that the preparation of pleadings or other documents for filing in court constitutes the practice of law.

It is important to discuss what outcome the client wants from the mediation and the level of review and drafting that may be required.

Is the Mediator a Lawyer?

If you take a survey of all people who mediate family issues in your community, you may find that most family mediators are not lawyers, and many of these mediators do not have a professional license. Most of these mediators do not draft enforceable final documents. This is due to both training, custom, and state laws that define drafting of final documents as the practice of law and requiring licensed lawyers to perform that function.

Therefore, when mediators who are not authorized to draft mediate your client's matter, your workload in review and drafting will be significant and you need to estimate the scope of your work and fees accordingly.

Even if the mediator is a licensed lawyer, that mediator's role in drafting depends on your jurisdiction. Some states prohibit any mediator, including those with law licenses, from preparing documents beyond a confidential and informal Memorandum of Understanding (MOU) or other type of summary. The rationale behind such a prohibition against mediator drafting final documents is that lawyers who mediate assume a neutral, nonlawyer role in dealmaking, but drafting is seen as converting that neutral role into a dual representation role[5] in which the parties have conflicting interests.

In states that permit lawyer mediators to draft binding agreements, there are two basic schools of thought. The first is that while drafting may constitute the practice of law, the mediator can appropriately draft if parties provide an informed consent conflict of interest waiver and are encouraged to consult and retain independent lawyers to review and supplement such drafting.[6] The second does not define a mediator's work as the practice of law and permits a lawyer- mediator to draft final agreements as a neutral scribe, a practice explored at length in Robert K. Collins' 2016 article, *The Scrivener's Dilemma in Divorce Mediation.*[7]

---

5. Dual representation (a single lawyer representing the conflicting interests of two parties) is viewed as unethical in most jurisdictions as violative of ABA Model Rule of Professional Conduct, 3-310 (C)(1) and (C)(2).

6. Leading states permitting lawyers to draft final documents as intermediaries are Massachusetts (Massachusetts Bar Association—Ethics Opinion No. 85-3), New York (New York State Bar Opinion 736, 2001), and Utah (Utah Rule of Professional Responsibility 2.4)

7. Maine and Oregon are leading states permitting mediators to draft as neutrals with certain conditions.

Rule 2.4 Lawyer Serving as Mediator

(a) A lawyer serving as a mediator:

(1) shall not act as a lawyer for any party against another party in the matter in mediation or in any related proceeding; and

(2) must clearly inform the parties of and obtain the parties' consent to the lawyer's role as mediator.

(b) A lawyer serving as a mediator:

Having competent lawyer mediators draft as either a neutral or intermediary can benefit clients, since the person who facilitated the negotiations between the parties can often most accurately capture the spirit and substance of the parties' agreements. In addition, using the mediator's draft as a point of departure can reduce the number of disputes between counsel over agreement terms, and permits the mediator to facilitate resolution of any such disagreements. Mediator drafting is also consistent with the desire of many mediation participants to have a "one stop shop" with attendant lower transaction costs.

---

(1) may prepare documents that memorialize and implement the agreement reached in mediation;

(2) shall recommend that each party seek independent legal advice before executing the documents; and

(3) with the consent of all parties, may record or may file the documents in court.

(c) Notwithstanding Rule 1.10, when a lawyer is serving or has served as a mediator in a matter, a member of the lawyer's firm may accept or continue the representation of a party in the matter in mediation or in a related matter if all parties to the mediation give informed consent, confirmed in writing.

(d) The requirements of Rule 2.4(a) (2) and (b) (2) shall not apply to mediation programs established by operation of law or court order.

Maine accomplished the task in 1993 by adding the following provisions to its version of 2.4 which is identical to ours:

(c) The role of third-party neutral does not create a lawyer-client relationship with any of the parties and does not constitute representation of any of them. The lawyer shall not attempt to advance the interest of any of the parties at the expense of any other party.

(d) The lawyer shall not use any conduct, discussions or statements made by any party in the course of any alternative dispute resolution process to the disadvantage of any party to the process, or, without the informed consent of the parties, to the advantage of the lawyer or a third person.

(e) When acting as a mediator, the lawyer shall undertake such role subject to the following additional conditions:

(1) The lawyer must clearly inform the parties of the nature and limits of the lawyer's role as mediator and should disclose any interest or relationship likely to affect the lawyer's impartiality or that might create an appearance of partiality or bias. The parties must consent to the arrangement unless they are in mediation pursuant to a legal mandate.

(2) The lawyer may draft a settlement agreement or instrument reflecting the parties' resolution of the matter but must advise and encourage any party represented by independent counsel to consult with that counsel, and any unrepresented party to seek independent legal advice, before executing it.

(3) The lawyer shall withdraw as mediator if any of the parties so requests, or if any of the conditions stated in this subdivision (e) is no longer satisfied. Upon withdrawal, or upon conclusion of the mediation, the lawyer shall not represent any of the parties in the matter that was the subject of the mediation, or in any related matter.

See also Robert K. Collins, *The Scrivener's Dilemma in Divorce Mediation: Promulgating Progressive Professional Parameters*, 17 Cardozo J. Conflict Resol. 691 (2016), https://larc.cardozo.yu.edu/faculty-articles/45.

THE LEVEL OF REVIEW

Just as lawyers who unbundle their services to coach self-represented litigants need to determine the extent of their service, so do lawyers who take on the assignment of reviewing mediation agreements. The scope of representation must be defined explicitly between lawyers and clients to avert misunderstandings and increase client satisfaction. It is not unusual for a client to call a lawyer, wanting a full review within a low budget and a request that the reviewing lawyer provide a fee cap of not more than a few hundred dollars. While it may be possible to do a review within the requested budget, it is crucial for both the client and lawyer to understand what a *full review* means. As with all areas of ensuring competence, if a lawyer is presented with a limited review budget that would not permit the lawyer to provide competent service, the lawyer should consider turning down such an engagement rather than taking on malpractice exposure or a dissatisfied client (or both!) for performing inadequate or incompetent service.

This point bears repeating. Client-centered control and decision-making has its limitations. Although the client has a right to negotiate the level of service and fees, a lawyer also has the right to decline to perform the requested services if unable to do them in a competent manner. If we indicate a need for legal research before giving an opinion, our client has a right to limit the research time to, for example, two hours. If we agree to work under those conditions, we have made a deal that defines the parameters of our work for this professional task. We do not need to promise to have a full answer, or in fact any answer, within that limited time period. Our client pays for our best efforts and may be rewarded with a full answer (with the hope that it supports the client's desired outcome) that we may reach in less than two hours. The client might not get the right answer that more exhaustive research could have yielded. But as long as the client understands the basis of the bargain, he or she has a right to make an informed choice.

What if the client wants to limit research to 15 minutes, wants the agreement reviewed with a supporting letter in one workday, or walks in at 4 p.m. on a Friday without an appointment and wants custom drafting of a step-down spousal support order in 30 minutes—while we keep another client waiting for a scheduled appointment? In each situation, to ensure competence, we have the right to pass on the assignment or to demand conditions under which competent performance is possible. The client has a choice to accept our conditions (or an agreeable compromise) or to look elsewhere for professional assistance. It is a two-way relationship, and both attorney and client must agree to the scope and expectations of the assignment. Between the extremes of dealing with unreasonable working conditions or telling the client to look elsewhere, there is a wide area for a compromise about the scope of a lawyer's review. For example, we can do a full legal audit and look at every check and bank statement of the other spouse for the last three years or merely look at an income and expense court form or do something in between. We can provide four optional clauses for each deal point or merely read the proposed draft for glaring unfairness or technical mistakes—or do something in between. We can insist that the client have an independent CPA to calculate tax liability and future capital gains or indicate that there may be tax liability and the client should consult appropriate professionals or do something in between. These are clearly judgment calls about the scope of review that the lawyer should raise for joint decision-making between client and lawyer.

In contrast to the pure unbundled form of providing discrete task service in which we are not full counsel of record, here there are two differences. First, we may or may not be the lawyer of record who is responsible to the client for court litigation as well as the mediation. Second, the task of lawyer service is clear: review the agreement and advise the client accordingly. Even if we are counsel of record expected to provide "full service," it is rare that we perform every task or take on each task in 100 percent depth. A full service lawyer is likely dispense with taking depositions or limit the number of depositions taken, and we rarely ask every possible question within any one deposition. When we litigate, we don't subpoena *every* possible witness for each hearing and may dispense with live witnesses altogether. We rarely document by letter every conversation we had, or every request by our client. Simply, few, if any, clients can afford to pay for perfect and complete lawyering, and it is rarely cost-effective, requiring weighing the dollars expended for the marginal benefit gained.

Lawyers and clients can agree that the only task the lawyer will perform is reviewing the mediation agreement. Filing documents, making court appearances, conducting discovery, or handling the range of other lawyering functions can be excluded by contract. However, we still may be liable for any negligence in performing the tasks agreed to be within the scope of representation: review of the mediated agreement.

The late Geoffrey Hazard, a recognized authority on legal ethics opines that a lawyer can limit the scope of representation ethically, but also cautions about maintaining professional competence:

> If a lawyer says, "What I will do for you is review the papers and tell you if you have a claim, but I'm not going to take the case on," I can't see why that's troublesome. Many lawyers do it, and many clients would like to know that you can engage a lawyer to do this alone. But if I agree to make an opening statement, but only to spend five minutes giving it; or if I agree to do a real estate mortgage but not to do any personal property security matters in a commercial transaction, that would be improper. If the limitation is inconsistent with what a reasonable lawyer could plausibly suggest he's going to do for the client, it's a limitation of liability in disguise, and is unethical. And lawyers are always responsible for advice that they give.[8]

Therefore, if a lawyer negligently advises a client on an issue that comes up during review, even if the lawyer scope was properly limited, that lawyer may be subject to malpractice liability.[9]

---

8. Geoffrey C. Hazard, W. William Hodes & Peter R. Jarvis, Law of Lawyering (4th ed., 2021).

9. You should be aware of the 2012 California Supreme Court case *Cassel*. In *Cassel*, the court held that mediation confidentiality extends to all lawyer–client communications conducted during mediation, even outside the presence of the mediator. This means that a client is precluded from tes-

DRAFTING THE AGREEMENT

Because many mediators will not or cannot by law draft the actual settlement agreement or draft any court documents,[10] one of the consulting lawyers may have to take on that job. In such situations, the mediator generally will provide a memorandum of understanding (MOU) reflecting the essential deal points. The quality and depth of that memo varies depending on the professional background and skill of the mediator. Mediators preparing an MOU often keep the memo brief and to the point, explicitly deferring the legal drafting to lawyers. Depending on their training orientation, family law experience, drafting skills, and the law in various states, many lawyer/mediators also do not draft agreements, and the depth and clarity of their deal memos vary widely. Generally, the binding and enforceable effect of the mediation settlement is also deferred until the parties and counsel approve and sign thc final legal agreement.

In drafting a settlement agreement from a deal memo, the "let it go" mantra should kick in. It may be tempting for a lawyer to try to improve our client's position by resolving all uncertainties in drafting choice in favor of our client, putting the burden on the other lawyer to catch the problem and start a negotiation over drafting. Unfortunately, the authors all have been involved in mediations that resulted in "successful agreements in principle," only to have the drafting process take months and dwarf the original mediation costs in negotiation dollars and acrimony. Therefore, in drafting, proactive restraint should be the standard. If new terms are deemed necessary to carry out the intent of the agreed-upon deal reached in mediation, try to limit proposed new terms to what is minimally necessary to remedy a wrong or fix a perceived problem. Even more seriously, we must make every effort not to change or water down deal points the parties agreed to in mediation about which we are less than enthusiastic. Again, the purpose of drafting is to *complete* the mediation, and often this means pulling punches and not seeking advantages that you might have won had you negotiated the deal yourself.

As in drafting agreements arising from direct lawyer negotiation, best practice and professional civility dictate that we clearly point out any changes from the deal memo in a cover letter and/or a redlined version of the proposed draft to the other party's lawyer and the the mediator. This means that we should use a computer program that invites the other lawyer and party to insert proposed modifications directly on the draft. Call up the other lawyer and run by new terms to obtain agreement or to work out compromises before sending out the redlined

---

tifying about wrongful advice provided by the lawyer—which virtually eliminates most malpractice claims. This holding has been vastly criticized by consumer groups and the plaintiff malpractice bar and has generated proposed legislative responses. Also, the *Cassel* court may have been viewing mediation as a single session rather than sequential sessions over weeks or months. Many questions remain about whether a court would uphold the *Cassel* result if you were to provide negligent advice in your office several weeks after a joint mediation session rather than in a conference room with the mediator working in the same office suite.

10. Many drafting issues involve professional responsibility for mediators with law licenses and other issues involving mediators without a law license in respect to the unauthorized practice of law.

draft. In mediation, it is also helpful to consult with the mediator before sending out drafts to the parties to get a preview of the mediator's reaction.

If snags in drafting occur, schedule a meeting with the other lawyers (and sometimes the parties as well) to meet with the mediator (or have a Zoom or telephone conference call) to discuss drafting issues before a full draft is sent out. Consider copying the mediator on correspondence between counsel so that the mediator is up to speed in dealing with the lawyers or parties if drafting questions arise.

Due to the problems inherent in having one side's lawyer do the drafting, reviewing lawyers should be open to having the mediator neutrally draft the settlement documents (particularly if the mediator is also a family lawyer). If lawyers are not attending the mediation sessions, they can advise clients to request that the mediator neutrally prepare the initial draft of the agreement. The advantages of this approach are that having worked with the parties, the mediator is intimately familiar with the parties' agreement. Second, being trusted as impartial, the mediator's attempts at neutral drafting will most likely be very middle ground. A fair and balanced initial draft of the agreement may obviate adversarial posturing between that could cause delay and cost—often putting the mediation into jeopardy. The option of having the mediator do the initial drafting is often very attractive to mediation participants who have developed a trusting bond with the mediator. Even when lawyers were present at the sessions and are fully aware of the agreement terms, having the mediator do the drafting increases the chances that a writing will actually be completed and signed. Of course, it is always an option to have the agreement drafted and signed on-site to prevent later remorse or backtracking. However, also factor in the importance of giving the client time to reflect on the terms and have a chance to read and reread proposed language. While obsessing over drafting and backing out of deals are clear risks, so is putting excess pressure or duress on a client to sign and then have the client experience "buyer's remorse." Your support for the client to "think about it" rather than sign a deal exhausted after many hours of negotiating is particularly important considering the reluctance of courts to set aside mediated agreements.[11]

Sharing Boilerplate Early: "Boilerplate" is legal slang for the customary/template clauses that appear in most agreements. Lawyers often have their own pet boilerplate and may have different perspectives on what boilerplate is and what constitutes "new negotiation." One way to address this is to have both lawyers share their pet boilerplate early. In this way, settlements may not be held up once the final substantive points are resolved.

Single Text—Track Changes: One of mediation's great benefits is limiting or eliminating turf issues between parties and professionals. Some traditional lawyers refuse to share "electronic drafts" via email due to a desire to control the drafting process, fear that metadata might reveal privileged or work-product protected information, or even fear that the other lawyer or party might tamper with or change the draft. To move above this game playing and increase collaboration, consider a consensual process that has everyone working off one document and

11. *See* James B. Coben, *Litigation About Mediation: A Case Study in Institutionalization*, ABA Dispute Mag., Jan. 2022.

using color (not just "red" changes). Tracked changes are often helpful to this kind of process. Develop a culture of sharing editable Word documents or working in a joint Google Docs, Dropbox, or other format, so as to avoid cumbersome PDF file exchanges. This will feel more mediative, and the drafting will probably go faster and obviate the need for elaborate letter writing.

Don't Forget Aspirations and Cultural Context

It is customary for lawyers to limit drafting to provisions that can be enforced by a court. This means that "nonenforceable terms" are often viewed as irrelevant, surplusage, or, worse, contrary to or undercutting the effect of enforceable provisions.

As indicated earlier in this chapter, there are many reasons for parties to be in mediation other than walking out with an agreement that can be enforced in court. One key motivation is to identify and memorialize the aspirations and intent of parties even when agreements are not reached. Such language can remind parties of the context of their discussions.

You can provide an important service if you support the work of your clients around the mediation table by accurately incorporating nonenforceable terms.

Some common examples include:

1. Imprecise, intangible, but meaningful aspirations of the parties. Such aspirations may include a desire to act "cooperatively," "supportive," child-centered," or otherwise positively toward the other party.
2. Set out the fact that an issue has been discussed but that no agreement has been reached and memorialize the positions of the parties. Example: *Husband is willing to pay 30 percent of any bonus as additional spousal support. Wife is not willing to accept 30 percent of any bonus of the husband as additional spousal support. No agreement has been reached and the issue shall be reserved for future discussion in mediation or shall be determined by the court. The positions of the parties in respect to this issue may/may not be considered by a court in resolving this issue.*
3. Describe an agreement and indicate that the parties do not want such agreement to be the subject of any court enforcement. Example: *Each party intends to contribute to the college expenses of the children in the amounts that each party is capable and desirous of paying, and neither party nor the children may enforce this clause in a court of law.*
4. The parties can decide which issues will be discussed or reevaluated in the future. Example: *The parties currently agree that the children shall live in the Springfield School District. This issue shall be evaluated by the parties returning to mediation on or before January. The criteria for such evaluation shall be. If no additional agreement is reached, during such reevaluation, the children shall continue to attend school within the Springfield School District unless there is a court order to the contrary.*
5. If relevant, memorialize any consultations with religious or community leaders that informed certain decisions, often surrounding parenting, as a reminder to the parties that their determination was grounded in a shared value system guided by specific cultural ideals and parenting intentions.

This expanded view of "proper" drafting may feel foreign at first. However, as lawyers gain more experience in the jurisdiction of mediation in which the interests and needs of the parties supersede state law and court procedure, drafting in this manner might provide unanticipated comfort and satisfaction.

To Sign or Not to Sign?

If the parties choose to use a mediator to help them negotiate their own agreement, should a lawyer be willing to sign the final judgment as lawyer for the party? If the lawyer refuses, is the client left with a nonbinding or an unenforceable document negating time and money invested in mediation?

Although there is no hard-and-fast answer, it is essential that we raise the question of signing at the outset of the lawyer–client relationship. Whether our signature (or lack thereof) affects the validity of the agreement or affects our malpractice exposure is a gray area and varies by jurisdiction. Some lawyers won't sign or will condition their signatures with the words "Approved as to Form Only" or other such limitation. The essence of professional responsibility and liability is whether the lawyer provided advice and assistance that was negligent. If we believe an agreement is not in the client's interest, *we and our client* cannot negotiate a compromise that will satisfy us, and our client chooses to go forward, we must clearly communicate our reservations in writing to our client and should not sign the agreement in *any* form. If the other party requires a lawyer's signature, the client is then in a position of trying to find another lawyer or signing the agreement without a lawyer's signature. The other party then must decide whether to go ahead with the deal. In any event, we will have one unhappy client, and we should not be surprised if we also have an unpaid fee, poor review, or worse!

The best way to avoid this problem is to have early involvement in the mediation so that the lawyer is a co-architect of the ultimate agreement. As Garfield and Glassman write:

> If they are involved early in the process, consulting attorneys can serve the interests of the mediator and their respective clients by discussing tentative agreements with their clients, addressing collateral issues that ultimately need to be resolved, but that may not be particularly controversial, and documenting the agreement the parties have reached in order to keep the process moving forward.[12]

Eventually, all agreements must be documented; parties will end up with a comprehensive judgment of dissolution of marriage and perhaps a marital settlement agreement as well. There is no reason to postpone preparation of those documents until the end of the process. Preparing successive drafts of documents that will eventually embody the parties' final settlement accomplishes a number of important goals. First, it gives the parties an opportunity to see their tentative agreement expressed in the formal provisions of the settlement agreement or

12. Franklin Garfield & Frederick Glassman, *In the Beginning: Independent Counsel's Place in Dissolution Mediations*, L.A. DAILY J., Feb. 14, 1996, at 7.

judgment. Second, it enables the consulting attorneys to collaborate with respect to a whole host of issues that are subsidiary to the parties' main agreement, but important nonetheless. The provisions added by the consulting attorneys to the draft document may range from "boilerplate" provisions to provisions that may be considered "standard" or "customary" to provisions that serve mainly to supplement the parties' general agreement with important detail.

If consulting attorneys are involved in the process from the outset, it is very likely that the final agreement will turn out to be "better" for both parties than if consulting attorneys are retained only at the end to "review" an agreement that is a fait accompli. By the end of the process, the parties are heavily invested in the agreement they have negotiated. Even if there are problems that will predictably lead to friction later on, the parties generally come to their attorneys for *approval* of what they have already done. While it may not be fair to say that the parties want their attorneys to do no more than rubber-stamp the deal, the parties are generally resistant to the idea of lawyers blowing up a deal. They want the consulting attorneys' review of the agreement to be quick and inexpensive; they want to be reassured that they have succeeded in negotiating a favorable agreement. Rarely, unless assailed by doubts, are clients genuinely interested in being told that their agreement may be ill-advised in any significant respect.[13]

The public's confidence in mediation depends, to a large extent, on the competent yet nonintrusive involvement of lawyers in the review process. Many divorcing spouses will not enter mediation without such review. Once invested in the process, people need their lawyer's expertise to feel informed and confident that the agreement worked out in mediation is indeed in their best interest.

PRACTICE TIPS

1. Advise your client that nothing is final until the agreement is signed and that review and possible renegotiation and clarification of terms are part of the mediation process.
2. Be clear about what constitutes a "review," what specific tasks you will do, and what is expected of the client to make your review successful.
3. Work out your level of review: is this a full audit of every aspect of the divorce, or does the client just want you to refine drafting language?
4. Balance your support of the client's efforts and the need for improvement of agreement terms.
5. Never suggest starting from scratch or chastise the client for making poor decisions in the mediation process or trying to negotiate agreement without you. Take what was mediated and build an improved agreement.
6. Do not indulge in a wholesale rewrite of the agreement. Be judicious in what you criticize and what you leave alone.
7. Actively inquire and develop a full understanding of the history of the negotiation and your client's reasons for agreeing to specific trade-offs. Review

13. *Id.*

all mediator summary letters and compare them to the proposed written agreement.

8. Set aside plenty of time for the client to ask questions and share concerns. Your client's sense of having been supported is just as important as your competent legal and practical advice.
9. Be clear about what documents you will be drafting from scratch compared with reviewing the work of the mediator or other attorney.
10. Be gracious, whenever possible, in deferring to the neutral drafting of the mediator and assuming that the mediator is competent to draft.
11. Let it go: Do not tussle with the other lawyer about who will draft the documents and whose language is "better."
12. Do not "overdraft" or consistently write in favor of your client. Attempt to write the deal points in acceptable language for both parties. Lengthy drafting negotiations and/or delay often undercut the goals of your client.
13. Use one text drafting with Word, Google Docs, Dropbox, or another program that invites and permits redlining and tracked changes (modifications on the text). Take some time to familiarize yourself with the evolving platforms and programs in common use in your professional community so that you can confidently function using the one your counterpart suggests or prefers. Surrender the control that PDF affords you for the collaboration of a single text. (If you work from a single document such that all revisions are public, make sure that you do not use that document for private communications with your client, and be aware of the issue of metadata.)
14. Be clear at the beginning of your engagement whether you are willing to sign the agreement and in what form.
15. Offer your suggestions as determined by the parties in mediation. Some parties and/ or mediators prefer that the parties convey the ideas of consulting lawyers, and others prefer direct communication with you.
16. Be prepared to solve any drafting problems with the parties and professionals in a collaborative and nonthreatening way. Remember: a good job is defined as an agreement based on informed consent resulting from a positive and respectful process.

CHAPTER 11

Preventing Future Conflict

Education and early intervention can help parties flag existing conflicts before they spiral out of control. Preventive lawyering can identify possible issues and avoid conflicts before they occur. When lawyers act preventively, they can maximize opportunities for families.

—Forrest S. Mosten and Lara Traum, *The Family Lawyer's Role in Preventive Legal and Conflict Wellness* (2017)

Getting a divorce does not mean a family is free and clear of family court, or of future disputes. Especially when there are minor children, long-term support payments, or continuing financial entanglements—deferred sale of the family residence, ongoing joint business or investments, deferred compensation, and the like—the parties are likely to need ongoing legal and dispute resolution assistance in the future.

This chapter explores three methods of preventing conflict in the family: incorporating dispute resolution clauses into the final settlement agreement, using preventive mediation to form new family relationships, and maintaining and expanding the legal health of all family members through legal wellness checkups.

DRAFTING FUTURE DISPUTE RESOLUTION CLAUSES

After spending thousands of dollars on lawyer and mediator fees to handle a divorce, most clients are more open to learning about how to prevent future disputes. The goal of preventive planning is to raise concerns and solve problems *before* they reach the level of overt conflict. The operative assumption is that absent emergency, consensual methods of dispute resolution are preferable. Therefore, parties should be advised and trained to try the least invasive method of dispute resolution first when problems arise. Only if the conflict remains unresolved should parties consider ceding additional settlement control by degrees until, as a last resort, they delegate decision-making completely to a third party. Even as more invasive methods are utilized, parties should build in a mandatory return to mediation with the benefit of new information from the more invasive process as a catalyst for a mediated result returning control (or as much of it as possible) to the parties themselves. By "mandatory," we suggest that if one party wishes to return to mediation, the other party has the legal obligation to return to mediation before seeking court relief.

The following are some options we can incorporate into settlements to prevent conflict and to keep the parties away from the courthouse in the future.

Although the enforceability of mediation clauses is not guaranteed in every jurisdiction, courts routinely enforce contractual or statutory obligations to mediate as a condition precedent to litigation.[1] Concerns about enforceability of such clauses are relatively insignificant in practice: "Given the relatively minor time, risk and expense of compliance and the likelihood that noncompliance may be used to block any later clauses, most parties to mediation clauses probably will comply."[2] A sample mediation clause is included in the Resources section.

Written Notice of Dispute

Completing a legal divorce rarely means ending a relationship with a former spouse. Even with a well-drafted agreement and a detailed parenting schedule, opportunities for conflict seem inevitable and unending. Being a parental and business partner with a former spouse may be one of the most challenging relationships in modern life. When the challenges become excessive, explosions can occur in areas such as choosing the children's school, dividing up Thanksgiving, paying for lessons or camp, or figuring out new support if income fluctuates or either party becomes involved with a new spouse or live-in partner. Mediators and lawyers cannot anticipate every eventuality. As many families experienced in 2020 and the years that followed, phenomena such as the COVID-19 pandemic brought many post-judgment families with well-drafted agreements back to mediation, parenting coordination, or court. Hopefully, parties will be able to communicate by telephone or in person and make whatever accommodations or changes are requested. Even if both parties engage in good faith, impasse sometimes still develops. When one party feels aggrieved and believes that a dispute remains unresolved, step one in the dispute prevention chain should be for that party to write a note or letter to the other party, detailing the concern and suggesting a proposal for resolution. This component of resolution by giving the other party "notice" of the problem should become a mandatory step by its express inclusion in the divorce settlement.

Upon receiving notice that there is a problem and considering the proposal for resolution, the recipient can accept the proposal in full, in which case the matter will be resolved. With most divorced couples, even if tensions have escalated to the point of requiring such notice, the dispute ends right here: No more meetings, lawyers, mediators, or judges. The family just carries on.

---

1. James R. Coben & Peter N. Thompson, *Mediation Litigation Trends: 1999–2007*, 1(3) WORLD ARB. & MEDIATION REV. (2011).

2. NANCY ROGERS & CRAIG MCEWEN, MEDIATION: LAW, POLICY, AND PRACTICE § 8:01 (2d ed., 1994). For an example of a dispute resolution clause, *see* Richard Chernick, *Dispute Resolution Assessment and Process Design in Professional Responsibility Disputes*, Amer. Arb. Ass'n (Prof. Resp. Panel/Panel Seminar No. 2, Los Angeles, CA), May 15, 1996.

If the proposal is not accepted, the party receiving the notice should have a contractual duty to respond in writing within a specified time period, setting forth that party's concerns about the proposal. The party receiving the notice and responding within the specified time period should also present an alternative proposal as part of that response. From this point on, either party has the option of continuing the correspondence exercise or calling for the next step: an in-person meet-and-confer session.

Parties Meet and Confer

Following the entry of the decree, divorcing spouses might build in contact by correspondence, telephone, text message, parenting app, online, or in-person meetings to take care of ongoing matters between them. Such joint business can include regular "asymptomatic" parental meetings as well as intermittent accountings to reconcile finances; tote up contributions and reimbursements for post-divorce joint expenses; or to divide up receipts, dividends, or sales proceeds of jointly owned property. These post-divorce meetings are premised on maintaining the legal wellness of the family before issues and "illness" arise—the parties are doing necessary business to meet the ongoing needs of the divorced family even if no current dispute is raging.

The preventive dispute resolution provision to meet and confer is somewhat different. It is designed to kick in when there is a dispute between the parties that cannot be resolved and that might otherwise be headed for court. When the written notice and subsequent correspondence fail to resolve the problem, a personal meeting constitutes the last clear chance to avoid bringing in a mediator or going to court. The judgment should spell out when, where, and how the parties should meet and confer. The party requesting the meeting should offer a choice of neutral sites (unless a mutually agreeable site has previously been worked out) and several possible meeting times within the time period prescribed. The other party should be required to acknowledge the meeting request in writing, but also have the right to choose among options for venue and time. If none of the meeting times is acceptable to the party receiving the notice of personal meeting, that party should have the duty to respond within a specified time frame and to offer several reasonable alternatives.

Shawna and Jim have been divorced for eight years and have a 12-year-old daughter, Sammy. Sammy has been taking dance classes for six years and is on a competitive dance team. It is 2021 and Sammy has been unable to continue attending dance classes because the dance studio requires all children ages 12 and up to have received the COVID vaccine. Shawna would like Sammy to receive the vaccine and continue participating in her activities in a safe and protected fashion, while Jim feels that there is not enough data to support vaccination at the age of 12 and fears that injecting Sammy with a new vaccine might cause long-term risks to her future health and safety. Sammy is distraught and just wants to keep dancing. Shawna and Jim have exchanged numerous text messages, emails, and even a few FedEx'd letters. The exchanges are increasingly hostile, and Shawna is considering vaccinating Sammy unilaterally even as Jim considers petitioning the court for a custodial change in light of Shawna's threats to vaccinate. As required by their agreement, however, Shawna and Jim agree to meet before taking action. Jim emails Shawn, asking that they meet outside at a local park or café that neither of them otherwise frequents in an effort to avoid bumping into neighbors, and suggests that they meet during their lunch breaks from work while Sammy is in a remote learning pod with a few friends so that they can discuss the topic out of her earshot. Shawna agrees to the time frame, notes that she would prefer meeting in the park so that they can have the conversation without masks on, and suggests that they bring and exchange supportive research regarding their positions. Shawna and Jim both confirm their attendance on Tuesday at 12:30 p.m. via email. Upon meeting, though tensions are high, they are able to acknowledge that they are both concerned with Sammy's safety—with Shawna highlighting safety concerns for an unvaccinated child in the short term and Jim highlighting safety concerns for a vaccinated child in the longer term. They also acknowledge that they want Sammy to be able to keep dancing. They agree to meet with Sammy's pediatrician as well as the dance instructor for joint brainstorming and recommendations. The court filing is averted and the family has the opportunity to heal.

Because the vitality and effectiveness of this dispute resolution matrix depends on compromise, integrity, and commitment to manage conflict, the outlined procedures are intended as default fallbacks. The real hope is that the level of trust engendered by both parties' consistent post-separation behavior will enable the parties to circumvent the formalized matrix altogether and set up a quick phone call to talk things over and reach a consensus.

Resolving or even avoiding conflict can pay dividends that benefit the family system in ways small and large.

Required Mediation

If the in-person meeting does not resolve the issue, either party should have the right to compel mediation. One consideration when drafting might be whether to require the use of the mediator who successfully handled the divorce or leave the choice of the mediator up to mutual agreement of the parties. For a host of reasons, one or both parties may have concerns about using the same mediator again. On the other hand, using a mediator with flaws might be better than having the parties start over again. In contrast, the underlying purpose of this mediation clause is to get the parties into mediation and get them there . . . fast! Arguing about the choice of mediator defeats this goal. In the event that the choice of mediator is left to mutual agreement of the parties and the parties cannot agree at the time, such a provision could also provide that "in the event that the parties are not able to agree upon a selected mediator within X number of weeks, a mediator shall be selected/appointed by Y (i.e., a person, an organization, a court, or someone else)."

The clause should specify the minimum amount of mediation required. At the very least, one or two three-hour sessions will get the parties to sit down with a neutral and make an attempt at resolution. If there is progress, additional sessions can be mutually agreed upon. Another view is that there should be three or four required sessions (possibly adding initial private meetings) or a full day in the single-session format.

Finally, the mediation clause should allocate mediation costs clearly. The options for payment discussed earlier apply to future disputes as well, with one change in perspective. Although the higher earner may be willing to advance or pay for mediation costs during a divorce, he or she may be more reluctant to sign on to an open commitment to pay for mediation regarding an undetermined number of issues for the next several years. Due to this concern, parties may be better off agreeing to a fixed split—if not 50–50, then 60–40 or 75–25. It also may be less prudent to have a split based on future comparison of adjusted gross income because this would require a disclosure of income information (maybe involving joint returns with a new spouse) that could cause additional conflict in and of itself or create a scheduling delay.

In about 2005, Woody finished mediating a high-profile, complex matter and he suggested that because the parties had experienced such success they should discuss having a mandatory mediation clause. The wife, the wife's lawyer, and the husband wanted such a clause. The husband's attorney, a well-regarded litigator, stated that although he was very satisfied with how mediation had worked to settle the divorce, he never (and he repeated the word *never*) would permit his client to give up his right to go to court without first trying mediation. While the wife and wife's lawyer pointed out that the clause was neutral and applied to both parties, and that emergency situations were excluded, the person with the veto won! You know the coda of the story. Two years later, the husband wanted the wife to participate in mediation and the wife refused—14 months of virulent and expensive litigation followed.

Confidential Mini-Evaluation (CME)

This process is available when mediation does not resolve either a parenting or financial dispute and the parties might benefit from having a nonbinding confidential expert opinion to defuse the conflict. Initially developed as an alternative to the costly and adversarial formal court custody evaluation,[3] the CME is a balancing act that gives the parties the input of an experienced custody or financial evaluator without the cost, delay, adversarial posturing, and virtually binding decision of imposing a court-appointed evaluator on the family and making the decision part of the permanent court record. The CME evaluator is selected by the parties and will customize the process based on the mutual instructions of the parties, lawyers, and mediator. For example, the evaluator may do the entire evaluation in one day without any home visits, psychological testing, or interviews with collateral witnesses such as teachers, childcare providers, or physicians. To save both time and expense, no written report is prepared. In addition, such written reports often become indelible parts of the family history. They usually expose the least attractive aspects of both parents. Furthermore, such written reports often create smoldering

3. Forrest S. Mosten, *Confidential Mini-Evaluation,* FAM & CONCILIATION CTS. REV. 373–84 (July 1992); and Forrest S. Mosten, *Confidential Mini Evaluations: Another ADR Option,* 45(1) FAMILY LAW Q. (ABA, Spring 2011).

resentment in the parent described, or are used as weapons. The CME evaluator can give oral feedback containing recommendations, and the parties then can use that report to stimulate negotiations. If resolution is not reached, either party can compel a formal evaluation, but the judgment should provide that in any subsequent evaluation or court hearing, the parties are restrained from making reference to the communications or recommendations adduced during a CME.

Although the CME can be started by the parties themselves or by their lawyers, it works best when initiated and conducted in the mediation setting. The settlement clause can require parties to have prospective evaluators come to the mediation (or appear online) for joint audition interviews under the mediator's guidance. The mediator can facilitate negotiations over the final selection and scope of the evaluator's assignment. Being present during the evaluator's oral feedback session along with the parties' lawyers, the mediator can be an objective listener to the evaluator's report and then use that information to help negotiate a resolution. The CME process can be adapted for experts in financial issues as well. Instead of the parties hiring two forensic CPAs to do a cash available report for support or a business evaluation, each of whom might take adversarial positions in submitting lengthy reports replete with bells and whistles, one neutral CPA can be hired on a customized assignment to give an oral report to the parties. The same can be true if the parties need real estate appraisers or vocational counselors to determine suitability for employment, for example.

Mediation Fills the Family Album

Mediation is a malleable, custom-designed process that can adapt to the changes in a divorced family. The first time Kate and Samuel came in, they had one daughter, Rebecca, age two, and a baby on the way. Samuel was involved with Cheryl. A divorce settlement was reached.

Three years later, Kate and Samuel returned, urged strongly by Cheryl, who had a son in her arms. Samuel's company had gone out of business, and he wanted a reduction of the overgenerous support agreement made at the time of divorce.

Four years later, seven years after the divorce, Kate and her new husband, Peter, initiated a mediation when they wanted to move to an adjoining county, radically changing a longstanding joint physical custody arrangement. The move was worked out, with Samuel having additional decision-making control surrounding weekend activities, as well as putting driving responsibilities on Peter and Kate.

After another two years, the family was back, this time with lawyers in the room. Tensions had simmered over driving and lifestyle differences. After two all-day sessions, the parties agreed that Cheryl and Samuel would move close to the other home with a return to an equal time-share arrangement.

While less than a perfect situation, the family has a history of resolution, and only they know when the mediation will recommence. A mediation file rarely closes—yet the timing and format of the next stage to resolve family conflict are subject to later determination.

These CME evaluations permit parties to get the expert information needed to facilitate negotiated agreement without being stuck with an adverse written report that could be submitted to the court. A sample court stipulation for a CME appears in the Resources section.

Formal Evaluation Report

If a parenting or financial dispute does not settle after the results of a CME are reported by the CME evaluator at a mediation session, one of the parties may require the use of a neutral full evaluation as provided in the judgment. The full evaluation capitalizes on the benefits of having one impartial expert instead of two, and because it entails a written report that can be sent to the judge and admitted into evidence, it may provide extra motivation for the parties to settle. On the other hand, because it is an unabridged full-service job, the expert will probably take longer and it will cost quite a bit more than a CME.

As with the CME, the parties should provide for mandatory mediation at the request of one party after the report is complete and before it is submitted to the court. This mediation will give the parties an opportunity to resolve the matter based on the CME expert's findings (for which they probably paid dearly) and before the party feeling wounded goes out and pays another evaluator to prepare still yet another report (unless the dispute resolution clause makes the full evaluator's findings binding on the parties). The opportunity to mediate before sending the report to court allows the family to keep the matter private rather than airing the linen (clean or dirty) in public.

Binding Adjudication

Despite all the good faith efforts, some disputes just won't settle. Some parties need someone to make a decision for them. However, before automatically assuming that the binding adjudicator will be a judge in the public court system, consider several other private options in drafting future dispute resolution clauses.

Arbitration

Although arbitration is binding and enforceable like a court order, the parties can streamline the process to make it faster and cheaper than the court system. The trend is to give the arbitrator virtually absolute power to decide the matter with little right of court review or appeal unless specifically reserved.

The dispute resolution clause can call for all issues to be resolved by arbitration or merely delineate single issues that can be arbitrated with court having jurisdiction to decide everything else. It is customary to designate which rules of arbitration service providers will govern. If you are unfamiliar with the specifics of the designated rule scheme, look it up to make sure it is appropriate for your type of dispute.

When she was still a practicing attorney, Judge Scully reviewed a draft cohabitation agreement that provided for future arbitration of disputes under the rules of a specified major provider. When she looked up those rules, she discovered that although various subsets applied to specific types of disputes, no subset existed for family law, and it was not apparent which set of rules would apply to a family law dispute. Because the goal of these kinds of clauses is to limit areas of future dispute, be mindful that the lawyer is not inadvertently opening new lines of miscommunication.

Also, different arbitrators can be designated to handle different disputes. For example, if a deferred house sale is provided for in the judgment, the parties may agree to a modified step process, such as meet and confer, mediation, full appraisal report, then straight to arbitration, eliminating the CME. In so doing, for this issue only, perhaps they could name a real estate broker at the time of judgment or at the time of the dispute. The same approach can be taken by naming a CPA to arbitrate tax filing, audit, or refund conflicts. In high-conflict custody cases, there is a trend to designate a therapist or another mental health professional to serve as arbitrator or special master to have binding authority over some but not all parenting disputes. For example, the binding decision-maker might decide issues such as holiday and vacation periods, selection of medical providers, and struggles over extracurricular activities, while major decisions, such as location of residence or choice of school, would remain in the public court system.

Private Judges

An alternative to arbitration is a private judge. Very popular in states such as California, Florida, and Texas,[4] this option is providing steady employment for retired judges (and some veteran litigators) and is an available option for those who can afford to pay for more accessible justice. There has been considerable criticism that the popularity of private judging has created two tiers of justice: one for those who can pay and the public court system for everyone else. The disclosure of conflicts of interest potentially created by repeat buyers of the same private judging services is another issue of current public debate; for example, this issue arose in the Brad Pitt–Angelina Jolie divorce and resulted in a published California appellate decision and a new custody trial.

The benefit for the family of providing for a private judge is that the major costs to litigants in the public court system result in complex prehearing court procedures and waiting time to get to and complete the hearing. Some courts are so overburdened that it takes months to schedule a hearing of any sort. Once it has started, the judge may have to bifurcate and trifurcate the proceedings to squeeze in three hours of hearing time per day and four hours several weeks later. It can be very frustrating for parties and lawyers—and very expensive. Private judging offers the speed and customized, streamlined procedures of arbitration with the safeguards of the rules of evidence and rights of appellate review guaranteed in the court system. Many private judges wear their robes, most private trials have a court reporter to preserve the record, and many private courtrooms have been built to accommodate demand. These amenities can be the subject of discussion and drafting in the judgment.

---

4. *See* Jill S. Robbins, The Private Judge: California Anomaly or Wave of the Future? (2012), www.iaml.org; Patricia Fersch, *Will Mediation and Private Judges End the Uncivility of In-Court Family Law Litigation Post Covid?*, Forbes (Jan. 28, 2021), https://www.forbes.com/sites/sap/2022/08/02/how-wr-grace-creates-a-culture-of-diversity-equity--inclusion/?sh=3c7d46a41676.

Once a private judge is selected, the scheduled hearing time is virtually guaranteed to go on that date. The judge works six to eight hours a day without the interruption of other cases—which is more than enough for any trial lawyer! In December, a dad wanted an immediate change of custody because his son had received Fs in four of six subjects in seventh grade. After considerable negotiation and preliminary procedural wrangling in court, in early January, the parties stipulated to use a respected retired judge. By February 1, the parties had completed an eight-day hearing and the child had changed his residence to live with his father.

Mediation to Follow a Binding Decision

Of course, if the parties cannot agree on the terms of arbitration or private judging, the parties can still use the public court system as their binding-decision option. Regardless of which binding option is included in the settlement agreement, it is generally worthwhile to have any decision followed by mandatory mediation if requested by one party after the binding decision is rendered. After beating each other up in a contested hearing and receiving a result that may satisfy neither party, the parties may welcome the return to the mediation process, which helps them restore some control to their lives as well as facilitate healing from the wounds of litigation. Many clients do not realize that even after the judge rules, the parties can generally negotiate a modification of the court order that may better meet their needs and with which they can both more realistically comply.

Many lawyers are unaccustomed to drafting dispute resolution clauses. Traditional litigation mindset has been "We have enough to do in working out agreements on the current disputes. If there are problems in the future, parties can always seek a modification in court (except in final determinations such as property divisions and nonmodifiable spousal maintenance orders) or enforcement actions. Let's just wrap it up fairly and let the future take care of itself." This school of family law may be suspicious of a step-by-step, calibrated approach to future dispute resolutions. The cure may be seen as worse than the disease. Fears of unnecessary hoops and expense when the case might end up in litigation anyway are quite reasonable.

Robert Theobald, a well-regarded futurist and advisor to the Oregon Legislative Task Force designing the court of the future, has said that the essence of professional competence is trying to use one's best judgment in making the very best decisions at the moment given the people involved.[5] It is true that at times, negotiating and drafting future dispute resolution clauses may take more time and money than actually litigating a dispute later. Also, by detailing a step-by-step approach, the parties may incur unnecessary fees and conflict in addition to the costs of litigation. This concern may also be valid.

When presented with that concern, many clients opt to leave everything open or just have a mediation option without any other graduated steps. Yet others, even when advised about the dangers of uncertainty, may choose to invoke

5. Robert Theobald, Opening Address, 1995 Northwest Conference of Association of Family and Conciliation Courts, Nov. 1995.

the calibrated process set out here, a hybrid, or a wholly original concept. In rendering the most competent service, modern family lawyers are keeping their eyes on the road ahead as well as in the rearview mirror—sharing those observations with their clients and working collaboratively to enhance informed client decision-making.

Preventive Mediation

If mediation helps preserve relationships during and after a divorce when parties have differing interests and life paths, the process should also work when the parties form new relationship commitments that modify the family. Preventive mediation may be discussed by divorcing spouses as a way to spare family members (especially the children) future conflict and pain if either spouse breaks up with a new romantic partner. However, the main use of preventive mediation during divorce is to educate both parties and their lawyers in how to stay out of trouble (but not just with each other) after the judgment is entered. Any conflict affecting any member can have a ripple effect on the entire family system.

Preventive mediation is used most frequently in forming committed life partner relationships such as domestic partnerships and marriage or sharing a residence. As exciting and promising as these relationships can be, they are also frightening, especially for divorce survivors and their children. People fear not only an acrimonious breakup (perhaps another one), but also the new problems that might be presented by this new commitment. These concerns go beyond the legal ramifications of sharing income, buying real estate, and having joint bank accounts or obligations to a broad range of issues: "How will I communicate and resolve problems with my new partner (better than I did the last time around)?" "How will we work out budgeting and managing our money?" Will it hurt our new relationship to have separate incomes?" "Should we have a baby? If so, what would that do to our lives?" "How will we deal with controlling in-laws or the need for a sibling to live with us or be supported by us?"

When a neutral mediator facilitates the negotiation of a prenuptial agreement, parties and their lawyers should account for the impact of mediation confidentiality on future disputes. In the event that the validity of a prenuptial agreement is disputed in future litigation, confidentiality statues that protect mediators in some states might render certain evidence inadmissible, making claims more challenging to pursue. Clients participating in a mediated prenuptial agreement process should sign paperwork acknowledging their understanding of such limitations and provide their informed consent before proceeding with the process.

Binding legal agreements may be helpful in protecting against the disaster of a breakup, but what new partners really want is information and guidance about leading a happy and satisfying life together. Maximizing their opportunities for harmony and mutual gain may be far more important to a committed couple than protecting against the ultimate demise of the relationship. At times, securing estate interests for happily functioning blended families, for example, can become the most significant item to consider.

All that having been said, premarital agreements are walking malpractice time bombs. Some lawyers won't do them, and many who will do them charge extremely high fees because of the explosive risk of professional liability years down the road. Regardless of the fees charged, think about the appropriateness and real value of having two lawyers, pledged to get the best financial and legal deal for their respective clients, haggling over terms while their clients are more interested in just living their new lives together. Yes, marriage and cohabitation can entail great risks in case of failure. These issues must be discussed—but how?

Some divorced couples are now consulting mediators when they form new relationships. They want a supportive, relaxed educational setting in which to speak with a professional who wants to help them. They have heard that many family lawyers do not want to handle relationship formations. Even though mediators generally work with divorces, the orientation of healing and looking beyond rights toward underlying needs and concerns is a very attractive alternative to having two lawyers writing letters and running up big bills. Most important, while understanding that they should face problems, most people are afraid of lawyers planting mistrust or doubt about the other party—either to them or the other.

In preventive mediation, client education may be even more important than writing up the agreements of the parties. However, written agreements can actually help relationships! Worrying about the loss of property or financial insecurity in case of a breakup can cause relationship anxiety. The same is true of worrying about the other partner worrying. If people can talk about sex, intimate emotions, and family secrets, why can't they talk openly about money, property, and legal rights? If an agreement can ameliorate fears and then be put in the drawer, it can actually strengthen the relationship—as long as the process of making the agreement doesn't do too much damage. To be married by clergy, some religions require a couple to participate in education and counseling about the responsibilities and pitfalls of marriage. The overriding goal is that such education may make a marriage stronger and more durable.

Preventive mediation is based on the same principles. It is interesting that the same lawyers who use mediation for divorce rarely think of mediation when they have a client who is trying to save a marriage,[6] getting married,[7] or blending a family in a nonmarital relationship. Part of the problem is that the client calls and says, "I'm getting married; I need help with a premarital agreement." The client's presenting request often determines the lawyer's actions, which might differ greatly from those flowing from the mediative approach of attempting to uncover the client's underlying goals and concerns—many of which have nothing to do with legal rights. However, after articles by attorneys such as Sandra Rosenblum and Judith Nesburn, increasingly popular books such as Laurie Israel's *The Generous Prenup: How to Support Your Marriage and Avoid the Pitfalls*, and writings by Woody have entered the mainstream, preventive approaches to family building have gained popularity.

---

6. *See* Laurie Israel who writes and practices in the area of marital mediation http://www.ivkdlaw.com/practice-areas/marital-mediation/.

7. Sandra M. Rosenbloom & Judith C. Nesburn, *Isn't It Unromantic? Collaboratively Negotiating Pre- and Post-Nuptial Agreements*, http://www.judithcnesburn.com/CM/Custom/artice-collaboratively-negotiating.asp.

Ethically and practically, the lawyer's role in a preventive mediation is the same as in a dispute mediation: help the client achieve a result maximizing the goals and concerns that improve the client's life—which may or may not coincide with maximizing legal protection. A mediator can set the proper tone for doing this important business without intruding on the romance. The mediation can also cover wills, durable powers of attorney, deed drafting, and other estate planning needs, which often go hand in hand with marriage planning. As explored in other writings by Woody and Lara, "a preventive lawyer, like a doctor, helps clients: 1) identify symptoms that could undermine the client's legal health, 2) address 'chronic' issues that might periodically resurface, and 3) avert conflict at every possible opportunity."[8] When structuring a new marriage or family, a holistic, preventive view of marital and estate planning logistics can offer invaluable education, thoughtful legal planning, and successful conflict prevention.

The recognition for marriage education, including informed consent for agreements, has spawned at least two successful Bar-sponsored preventive programs in addition to the activity in practitioners' offices. Under the leadership of former chair Lynne Gold Bikin, for example, the ABA Section of Family Law launched a partnering program designed to educate citizens before making committed relationships.[9]

If a client is reluctant about using and paying for a mediator for a premarital agreement, consider using a collaborative approach in building an agreement. In addition to choosing an interdisciplinary option and utilizing the values and guidelines of collaborative practice discussed in Chapter 6, this approach prevents much resentment that often is the fallout of one party wanting the agreement and the other being either neutral or opposed. Rather than having a lawyer draft a one-sided agreement to maximize the interests of the client and then sending it over with the message (either overt or covert) "Please sign this, sweetheart," both parties are involved in a facilitated meeting to fashion the concepts of the agreement and construct it together. Both collaborative lawyers can then jointly draft the agreement so that much of the heat of these transactions is avoided.[10]

Other Uses of Preventive Mediation

In addition to helping form a romantic relationship, preventive mediation can be conducive to forming a new parent–child relationship. Adoptions often cause tension and fraying among the participants. For example, as an alternative to working only through lawyers, mediation is a suitable process for having the birth parents, adoptive parents, and other concerned biological or adoptive family members iron out concerns with the guidance of their lawyers. In surrogate

---

8. Forrest S. Mosten & Lara Traum, The Family Lawyer's Role in Preventive Legal and Conflict Wellness (2017).

9. American Bar Association, Section of Family Law, Partners Curriculum Manual for Teachers at Overview (1996). ("Partners teaches students about the legal system as it impacts on marriages, families, and children. It also teaches basic relationships that can withstand the normal stresses of the daily interaction of family life.").

10. For more on Collaborative Teams and process approaches, see Mosten & Traum, *Interdisciplinary Teamwork in Family Law*, 56 Fam. Court Rev. (2018).

situations, for example, a sister is sometimes the birth mother, which results in the adoptive mother's family of origin being intimately involved in the future of that child—and not without conflicting interests. Finally, family businesses are rife with potential strife. Preventively working out parent–child and sibling issues while at the same time formulating business goals and agreements is a perfect application of mediation.

These opportunities for preventive mediation often arise from presenting problems around conflict—to wit, the present divorce. We have all run across conflicts involving parents and adult children, siblings, or quarrelling business partners. These sad cases are often symptomatic of underlying relationship dynamics that cry out for resolution—or at least workable arrangements supported by agreements. Such matters also can benefit from the use of an intergender lawyer-therapist co-mediation team, just as medical triage teams offer interdisciplinary response teams to help ensure that all challenges are uncovered and prevented or resolved. A family experiencing the resolution of conflict may also be more open to learning about methods for preventing conflict and maintaining legal health in the future.

Preventive Legal Wellness Checkups

Mediation offers many benefits for resolving and managing conflict, but even its most ardent proponents concede that a successful mediation is focused on settling a current dispute, not on helping people have happier, more satisfying lives. Research has failed to suggest that mediation brings about long-term behavioral change in the participants, as Timea Tallodi calls for more interpretive qualitative studies in her 2019 book *How Parties Experience Mediation* to explore whether long-term relationship changes occur as a result of mediation. Compared with the process of psychotherapy, client contact with a professional in mediation is superficial compared to a psychodynamic relationship.[11] Some mediation authorities, such as Robert A. Baruch Bush, Joseph P. Folger, and Gary J. Friedman, talk about mediation as a transformative experience.[12] Such transformation, when and if it occurs, may or may not be the motivation that propels people into future mediation and is not likely to occur unless the presenting dispute is settled in a fair and satisfying manner. Two esteemed mental health colleagues with whom Woody has co-mediated, the late Dr. Constance Ahrons and Dr. Mary Lund, have stated: "Mediation is not necessarily a growth experience. Fasten your seat belts and get ready for a rough ride. The best you can hope for is for it to stop hurting when it's over. Then you can start healing."

---

11. Joan Kelly et al., *Mediator and Adversarial Divorce: Initial Findings from a Longitudinal Study, in* Divorce Mediation: Theory and Practice 465–66 (Jay Foldberg & Anne Milne eds., 1988). "The mediator intervention was not powerful enough to selectively reduce major psychological distress beyond the passage of time."

12. Robert A. Baruch Bush & Joseph P. Folder, The Promise of Mediation: Responding to Conflict Through Empowerment and Recognition 20–21 (Jeffrey Z. Rubin ed., 1994); Gary J. Friedman, A Guide to Divorce Mediation: How to Reach a Fair, Legal Settlement at a Fraction of the Cost 365–66 (1993).

Having muted expectations for long-term behavior change through mediation is important in helping clients be satisfied with the progress they do achieve. Once resolution is achieved, having used mediation can significantly and positively impact a participant's future life. The benefits of saved money, expeditious finality, preserved privacy, salvaged relationships, and feelings of satisfaction rather than victimization can facilitate improved personal lives for the participants and/or limit any damage caused by the dispute that would be compounded by the transaction costs of resolution.

The legal wellness checkup is an unbundled service that we can use to improve the legal health of clients at every stage of representation. Just as a doctor will examine a lump on your nose even though the presenting problem is a stye in your eye, a preventive lawyer will inquire about a client's overall legal health when trying to solve the specific problems—for example, divorce, support or custody modification, or adoption—that brought the client into the office. The legal checkup can be brief, such as one question: "Do you have a will?" The client's answer can initiate a client–lawyer dialogue that focuses on the importance of having an up-to-date will, a durable power of attorney, beneficiary designations, and other related documents. It is the client's choice to take any action or have any legal work done. If work is desired, the client must decide whether to prepare documents without assistance, use the family lawyer who diagnosed the problem, or hire another lawyer or financial planning professional. Providing such services can entirely transform a family lawyer's practice or simply be incorporated into existing practices in various ways, ranging from "including preventive dispute resolution clauses in separation agreements, drafting preventive relationship agreements, including follow-up executor clauses in agreements suggesting that clients return for legal health checkups, to encouraging clients to use family legal hotlines sponsored by bar associations and courts.[13] Preventive lawyering can complement a crisis-based practice" or become a practice of its own.[14]

If we actively ask other questions concerning our client's life, the discussion can be more wide ranging. Such questions could include the following:

- "I notice that your expenses seem to be exceeding your available cash of about $1,000 a month. How do you plan to solve this problem?"
- "You mentioned that you sometimes are feeling depressed these days—and that intensifies when the children are at their mother's home. What thoughts do you have about feeling better?"
- "I am delighted to hear that you and Jim are moving in together. You looked great together the last time he was in the office with you. He has custody of his three children, right? Do you have any concern as to how this might affect your relationship with your former spouse, his former spouse, or your own children?"

---

13. *See* Jane C. Murphy, *Access to Legal Remedies: The Crisis in Family Law*, 8 B.Y.U. J. PUB. L. 123 (1993).

14. *Id.*

- "You really do work long hours! I am sorry to hear that this work stress comes home with you. What are you going to do about it?"

Probing these hot spots through concerned lawyer–client conversation can encourage the client to think about possible solutions. The client need take no action at all. As a preventive lawyer, we have fulfilled an important function just by raising the questions. The client has the right to ignore advice, cut corners, or make stupid or self-destructive choices once these questions are on the table. The client is ultimately in charge of the information and options provided by the lawyer in regard to legal health.

In addition to spontaneous conversation that sparks preventive counseling, many lawyers use preventive checklists to guide the conversation. Invented by Louis M. Brown, the internationally recognized father of preventive law, such checklists are available in a variety of sources. Sample checklists are provided in the Resources section.

People are more than willing to pay for a medical wellness checkup on a regular basis. They will go to their doctor's office for these checkups even if they have no current symptoms or pain. They do not expect the doctor to find a problem. In fact, they are delighted and will pay their bill when given a clean bill of health. Why do lawyers generally believe that acute problems must be present before clients need to see us? Some preventive family lawyers schedule the next office visit before the client leaves the office—when the client has been proclaimed legally healthy! Others have implemented nonlitigation calendars that prompt the lawyer to contact the client on a periodic basis or on the occurrence of significant client events through life cycle dates or events that resulted from the executory provisions of the settlement agreement.

With respect to life cycle events, the nonlitigation calendar can be set to trigger client contact one year before, six months before, three months before, and one month before important dates in the client's life, including the age of retirement eligibility, matriculation of children to a new school or college, and the date each child attains majority.

When negotiating or mediating custody and support agreements, educate the parties about the possibility of having wellness checkups with the mediator on a regular basis. Generally, these checkups can be scheduled on a six-month or one-year basis. The contract specifies that the parties come to see the mediator even if there are no presenting problems. The appointment is generally one hour long, but if there is a pressing issue, more time can be booked. On occasion, spouses complete a wellness checkup without any repressed or latent issue arising. In that case, the parties deservingly get a clean bill of health and support from the mediator that they are doing well. However, usually something comes up—often parties save their concerns for the checkups, knowing that their discussion will be monitored and managed by the mediator and not get out of hand. These regular discussions can preempt and solve problems before they ripen into expensive and destructive conflict.

Sample Notice-Triggering Events for Nonlitigation Calendar

October 1, Year 1 Settlement completed that provides that the client reside in the family house until the oldest child, Mary, is 18 (on September 15, Y3). The youngest child (Johnny) is at local elementary school and will matriculate to middle school in February Y4.

October 2, Year 1 The preventive lawyer makes all of the following entries in the office's nonlitigation calendar.

January 15, Year 2 Write client concerning upkeep and expense of house.

October 1, Year 2 Write client about house and general status. Remind client about buyout date and monitor efforts to save money for possible buyout. The mortgage interest is 9 percent on date of the judgment (October 1, Y1). Check current interest rates for refi possibilities. Remind client of wellness checkup.

January 15, Year 3 Monitor buyout or sale progress. Discuss initiating negotiations with other spouse (either directly between the clients or through counsel).

May 1, Year 3 Monitor buyout or sale progress. Remind client to bring in listing agreement or any sales documents before execution and financing. Discuss seeking extension of September 15 deadline.

August 1, Year 3 Monitor house sale listing or buyout. Final check to ascertain if court action to extend deadline is required.

September 1, Year 3 Final monitoring of house sale listing or buyout.

October 1, Year 3 Write client to schedule wellness review re residence, insurance, estate planning, and status of possible career change.

PRACTICE TIPS

1. Work toward future dispute resolution processes that will not only resolve disputes but also prevent conflict from developing.
2. Erect barriers to the courthouse so that, absent an emergency, filing in court is a last rather than first resort.
3. Encourage parties to work out problems themselves and to surrender control to an outside decision-maker only once other options have been attempted unsuccessfully.
4. Include both a written notice and a personal meet-and-confer requirement for parties to use in resolving future disputes themselves.
5. Build in required mediation as the first and primary dispute resolution process.
6. Have parties return to mediation after more invasive processes such as expert evaluations, arbitration, and court. Parties can regain control by mutually modifying imposed decisions and begin to heal after conflict.

7. Use a confidential mini-evaluation (CME) to retain privacy and control and to cut costs in parenting and financial disputes.
8. Provide a safeguard for the parties not to file an expert's report with the court until the findings can be a basis for a mediated agreement.
9. Arbitration can be used on single issues or for an entire case, with the possible exception of child custody.
10. Consider using a private judge to select the best decision-maker, expedite a hearing, and possibly save overall costs.
11. New family relationships can benefit from using preventive mediation. Marriage, adoption, and family business are prime candidates for using mediation to form and monitor the new relationships.
12. Provide legal wellness checkups to keep clients healthy legally and to provide a new source of revenue.
13. Establish a nonlitigation calendar to monitor ongoing client events and to remind clients to come into the office for a regular legal checkup.

CHAPTER 12

Be a Peacemaker

There is a great and growing desire for change in the world; change that ushers in a renewed commitment to ethical and spiritual values, that resolves conflicts peaceably, employing dialogue and non-violence, that upholds human rights and human dignity as well as human responsibility.

—Tenzin Gyatso, H. H. the XIVth Dalai Lama, 2008

You now have the perspectives, concepts, and skills to work with clients, mediators, and other professionals to produce informed, fair, and lasting agreements. You also have an opportunity to establish a lucrative and sustainable professional practice effectively representing clients in family mediation. As you cultivate your practice in the years to come, your skills will continue to develop and evolve and you will inspire the next generation of family lawyers.

This is good. This is very good. But it is not the end of our journey. Frankly, if over the next 20 years you merely support your clients through the pursuit of divorce settlements more effectively and build a profitable practice, you will still be following the same path that traditional divorce professionals have been treading for decades. What would you need to do to take your professional identity to the next level? Not just to glide, but to soar?

We have an opportunity to both help families and improve our own lives that goes far beyond settling divorces and making our livings more sanely. Just as the absence of war does not constitute peace, helping divorcing people stay out of court does not make you a peacemaker. If we reach just a bit further—reach inside ourselves to become true peacemakers—we have a profound chance to transform the lives of the families we serve as well as our own. When you reach the last page of this book, today, start thoughtfully and deliberately down a peacemaking path.

WHAT IS A PEACEMAKER?

According to Merriam Webster, a "peacemaker" is "one who makes peace especially by reconciling parties at variance."[1] *Reconciliation* is "the act of causing

1. Merriam-Webster Online.

two people or groups to become friendly again after an argument or disagreement or the process of finding a way to make two different ideas, facts, etc., exist or be true at the same time."[2] Peacemaking, therefore, as we envision it, is an active process. Peace does not just happen. It is the product of concrete and deliberate words, acts, and choices. Harmony is, at its essence, allowing individual voices to combine with clarity and resonance and ring out together, creating a collective whole. It requires listening. It requires hearing. It requires responding to, incorporating, enhancing, and complementing the sounds around you. The individual voices are essential. If any individual voice is weak or silenced, the resulting music will be anemic, and it is in the collective interest to restore and amplify it.

Harmony in the family means that the system as a whole functions well and that each person in that system functions within it. When we choose to be peacemakers, we commit ourselves to working deliberately toward a world in which we function together as the sum of individual voices, each of which is integral to the beauty and success of the whole.

Many lawyers are peacemakers; many are not. Peacemakers can be litigators, teachers, negotiators, or client counselors. Lawyer peacemakers come from all backgrounds, and there is no litmus test to earn your peacemaker card. Being a peacemaker is not defined by what role you play, but by how you actively restore and create harmony in your interactions with clients, colleagues, opposing parties, children and other members of the family, judges, court staff, witnesses, experts, and others in your community, as well as your clients' communities, which might differ from your own.

Peacemaking is not a process but a set of values, personal attributes, goals, and behaviors that guide and illuminate your work. In other words, your core values as expressed through your work as a family lawyer will define whether you are a peacemaker. Peacemaking means devoting lawyering efforts to the improvement and repair of the parties' individual lives, repair of their relationships, and prevention of future conflict, with deference, consideration, and respect for who the parties are, where they come from, and what their needs might truly be.

So where should you begin? The following are some points of departure.

Foster Mindfulness

Peacemakers cultivate personal peace and mindfulness and harness their core values and strongest personal attributes. They have been inspired to do so since Leonard Riskin wrote of the importance of this practice in his groundbreaking book on ADR and lawyers, over 25 years ago. Although he has made many other important contributions to our field, perhaps his most enduring hallmark is his work on mindfulness. Riskin defines mindfulness as "being aware, moment to moment, without judgment, of one's bodily sensations, thoughts, emotions, and consciousness. It is a systematic strategy for paying attention and for investigating one's own mind that one cultivates through meditation and then deploys in daily

2. *Id.*

life."[3] Mindfulness concentrates on helping us to do our jobs better by acquiring compassion as well as helping us provide professional distance so that we do not get caught up in the emotions and reactivity of our clients, and it frees us from habitual mindsets that hinder our creativity in negotiation or in the courtroom. As we strive to better understand and appreciate the unique cultures and family dynamics that inform the lives of our clients, mindfulness offers an increased opportunity to pay even greater attention.

Clark Freshman extended the significance of mindfulness work to negotiation at large, noting that

> Mindful negotiation training could include training people to label positional impulses as they arise rather than acting on them. Existing meta-analyses suggest negotiators fail to identify opportunities for trade-offs in nearly half of their negotiations. Training negotiators to note a "competing impulse" before rejecting a potential trade-off may cut this tendency substantially.[4]

In recent years, the concept of mindfulness has flooded social media and challenged us to infuse every aspect of our lives with intentionality, from the way we eat to the way we observe a sunset to, now, how we engage with our professional practices and clients.

Identify Your Core Values

Another of our field's most inspirational thinkers, Nan Waller Burnett, hails from the mental health field. Her groundbreaking book *Calm in the Face of the Storm* devotes each of its 365 chapters to a peacemaking value and how to better understand it and apply it in our work. Exploring these core values to identify which ones resonate most with you will help you formulate a peacemaking signature.

Examples of Use of Key Core Values

Empowerment—People should have control over their own destinies and reduce their dependence on professionals, courts, and other experts.

Cooperation—People work more effectively and are more satisfied when they are working together.

Fairness—People should get a fair shake out of life, and human action and institutions should be designed with fairness as an outcome.

Satisfaction—Although the customer may not always be right, what clients say and believe about their satisfaction is important in evaluating professional service.

---

3. Riskin, Leonard L. "Mindfulness: Foundational Training for Dispute Resolution." *Journal of Legal Education*, vol. 54, no. 1, 2004, pp. 79–90. *JSTOR*, http://www.jstor.org/stable/42893839. Accessed 30 Aug. 2022.

4. Clark Freshman, Adele M. Hayes & Greg C. Feldman, *The Lawyer-Negotiator as Mood Scientist: What We Know and Don't Know about How Mood Leads to Successful Negotiation*, 2002 J. Disp. Res. 1 (2002).

Options—People do better with choice. Do you take the time to make sure that you and those around you have choices for everything from what to have for breakfast to how to obtain and finance healthcare?

Creativity—The process of carving out time and devoting energy to create new ideas and opportunities is a value in and of itself.

Hope—Having a belief in the possible and believing it should be shared with others who are paralyzed with fear and pessimism.

Reconciliation—Actively seek out to apologize to others or to accept a heartfelt apology from someone who has hurt you or someone you care for.

Transformation—Believe that you and others can change for the better. In the divorcing context, such transformation can be facilitated and accelerated by the way the divorce is resolved.

Rational Problem Solving—People can find solutions by thinking through and talking about difficult issues.

Peacemaking—Peace and the act of being peaceful way toward those in pain and conflict are values to which you should devote time and energy.

Although Burnett's book is intended to encourage spiritual growth and intrapersonal comfort, you can adapt peacemaking values for your work with clients and professional colleagues. Burnett uses her daily themes as a loom on which she weaves a living definition of peacemaking. We have selected some of Burnett's daily themes and connected them with our vision of peacemaking values to offer strategies for integrating peacemaking in your work at the negotiation table and in collaboration with other family law professionals. As you review each value, read each of the steps aloud and then write out your answers as you develop them. Take proactive steps to discuss these values with colleagues at conferences and lunches, and with friends and family in person and online. This is not a one-time conversation—it will develop and evolve throughout the rest of your legal career.

1. Explain each value and its importance in your work.
2. Think about how you share and communicate each value with clients and colleagues and how you implement each value in your work.
3. Ask yourself how each value can impact the process that you utilize to create settlements.
4. Reflect on how you can implement each value into expanding the services that you offer to clients to increase your profitability.
   A. **Peacemaking:** Do you believe that peace and the act of being peaceful toward those in pain and conflict are values in and of themselves? What impact can your direct application of peacemaking have on negotiations between divorcing spouses and on meeting their children's needs? Do you talk about peace with your clients, colleagues, clients, and staff and share with them a vision of peace in the world that goes beyond your

professional practice? Do you design your office to invoke and foster peace for everyone who comes through the doors?

B. **Empowerment:** Do you believe that your clients should have control over their own destiny and should reduce their dependence on professionals, courts, and other experts? How do you develop protocols to help your clients gain such empowerment over their own parenting and financial decisions? What can you say and do to assist clients to gain empowerment given your expertise, experience, and power as a professional? How do you ensure that the other lawyer can be empowered to fully participate at the negotiation table? How do you use your commitment to client empowerment on your website, at initial meetings, and during other opportunities to grow your practice?

C. **Cooperation:** Do you believe that people work more effectively and are more satisfied when they are working together? What can you do to encourage your clients to cooperate with their spouses, especially when your clients are not feeling cooperative? How can you better cooperate with your colleagues in sharing practice materials that you have developed and referring cases that you choose not to take on?

D. **Fairness:** How do you believe that fairness for everyone in the divorcing family fits in with your work? How do you approach your clients with the importance of "fairness" (as opposed to just getting the issue behind them)? What standards do you utilize to measure fairness in a divorce on any one issue and in a global settlement package? How do you react when you perceive that you have been treated unfairly by a colleague or a client?

E. **Satisfaction:** How important is the client's expressed (and unexpressed) satisfaction with the final settlement and with your competence, efforts, and fees in evaluating your professional services? How do you assess the satisfaction of clients? How do you reach out to your colleagues to determine whether they are satisfied with you in handling their referrals and working with you on cases?

F. **Options:** How do you ensure that clients have a full array of options, opportunities, and help to make good, informed choices? How do you employ options to determine different professional roles or fee structures that you make available to potential clients? Are you open to options that your staff can use to approach their working day and prevent burnout?

G. **Creativity:** As you start each day, what efforts do you make to approach people and problems in a different and exciting way? What innovative methods do you use to support clients to design their own solutions creatively? When you host a meeting at your office, what new ideas do you employ to make everyone comfortable and to set the stage for a successful settlement?

H. **Hope:** Do you have a positive view of the future, especially when the past has been negative? How do you share that forward-looking belief with others who are paralyzed with fear and pessimism? What strategies have you put in your toolbox to motivate clients with hope during setbacks in negotiations? After investing time and money to develop your practice, if you hit setbacks or a flat growth period, how do you remain hopeful for your own successful and meaningful future?

I. **Reconciliation:** What approach do you use with your clients to help them stay in or return to a relationship in their families? How do you actively encourage your clients to explore the possibility of apology and forgiveness? How do you reach out to apologize to clients, colleagues, and others when you believe you have caused hurt or acted badly? How do you accept a heartfelt apology or express forgiveness from a colleague who has hurt you in your professional life?

J. **Transformation:** How do you encourage your clients to change for the better during or after a divorce? How do you accelerate your own professional and personal change regarding interaction with your family law colleagues and ideas and developments generated in your field? How do you continually breathe new life into your law practice so that it remains cutting edge and stimulating for you?

K. **Rational Problem Solving:** How do you bring about solutions to seemingly intractable problems by thinking through and talking about difficult issues? How do you motivate discussions when tough issues or a gulf between positions verge on impasse? How do you increase your profitability when you want to take more time for vacations and self-renewal (to prevent burnout) when the costs of running a law practice continue to escalate?

L. **Trust:** What are your feelings about the importance of building trust between your client, who may be hostile to his or her spouse, and that spouse, to create lasting agreements and healthy relationships? How do you initiate or reestablish trust with other lawyers? How do you react when you believe that your trust has been betrayed by a member of your staff or by a colleague?

M. **Compassion:** How do sympathy and concern for the misfortune of others impact your daily work? How do you demonstrate compassion for your client, the other party, and the other lawyer? If colleagues are struggling with their clients or with you in your case or in their personal lives, how do you express compassion for them?

You may have other core values that are not on this list, such as love and belief in family/children; devotion to a divine being or religion; commitment to economic justice and fair distribution of wealth; preservation of natural resources and our planet; or the eradication of tyranny, mass disease, or other social ills. Whatever your core values may be, think about how you can incorporate them into your work as a family lawyer. Take a few minutes to think about these additional core values and how they impact your career and the people you wish to help.

Actively Prevent Future Conflict

Perhaps the greatest difference you can make as a peacemaker is to add conflict prevention to your lawyering work. By the time people enter into mediation, something has already failed—a dispute has escalated to the point that it requires a mediator's intervention. Just as doctors try to prevent relapse or recurrence and promote future health when treating symptoms of illness or disease, it is our duty and opportunity to help clients minimize future recurrence of conflict and maximize future harmony. We can do that using tools such as dispute resolution clauses in contracts between parties, agreement implementation calendars to remind parties about what they have agreed to (and find out if additional facilitation is necessary), and conflict-wellness checkups (for examples, see www.mostenmediation.com/legal/wellness.html) as discussed in Chapter 11.

Apply Peacemaking to Your Daily Lawyering Work

You are in charge of whether to take the next step in moving toward peacemaking rather than just settling cases. If your choice is affirmative, the following are some avenues in which you might walk your peacemaking walk.

Get Training in Mediation and Collaborative Law

If you have spent most of your professional career learning substantive family law, how to write court motions, and how to better conduct cross-examination, you may need to go back to school to learn new skills and perspectives. If you invest the time and money to do so, you will be learning more than the curriculum in your bulky training manual. Relationships you form during training seminars can give you support in your new career path. You will have shared experiences and a common set of skills.

During the training, pay attention to the other participants as much as to the material and process. Arrive early and stay late as much as possible given your other responsibilities. Be open to invitations to go off-site for lunch or an evening meal. Treat training like a trip out of town so that you are not distracted by calls or other obligations of your practice. Follow up after the course with other training participants. They can be your core for a study group or structured reading program about representing clients in a peacemaking way. As more training opportunities migrate into the virtual space, you can access an interstate and international array of training programs from the comfort of your home or office and continue to build skills and relationships without much logistical duress.

Collaborate with Peacemaking Lawyers, Mediators, and Other Professionals

Generally, peacemaking lawyers are generous to colleagues. Be ready to accept an invitation to observe as a fly on the wall, attend a meeting or conference of a local interdisciplinary organization, or adapt the practice materials of others to your evolving family law work. And be sure to return the favor. The input by another lawyer or mediator about your performance in a recent case can be invaluable to you.

Reciprocal feedback can bring new ideas and approaches to your colleagues' work. Follow up on the help from your colleagues with acknowledgment of their generosity. Send them clippings or forward email links that you believe will be helpful to them. Building your practice and reputation can bear fruit for decades to come.

Honor Your Colleagues

In this book, we have suggested the following mantra when reviewing mediated settlements: "Let it go!" This means that "winning," rather than pushing every technical point or making sure that no money is left on the table, means making sure that your client understands trade-offs and is comfortable with the overall deal.

The same "let it go" mantra applies to working with other lawyers in your community. You might observe that a lawyer has intimidated your client; let it go. If you hear the other lawyer misstating the rules for calculating capital gain on a family residence, let it go. Letting it go does *not* mean that you will be negligent or dilatory in making sure that your client gets proper information or is treated respectfully. Letting it go *does* mean that the goodwill and relationship of colleagues may mean more in the long run (including this case) than "calling out" someone and causing a loss of face or respect. Private debriefing sessions are the place to discuss what worked and what can be done better next time. Gentle humor can be an invaluable and disarming method of making a point about civility without attacking or putting someone on the defensive.

After one challenging settlement conference at Judge Scully's office when she was still in practice, knowing that the opposing attorneys had traveled far and were likely to get stuck in rush hour traffic if they drove straight home, she invited them to the restaurant downstairs for a drink. Everyone was able to move beyond the intractability and frustrations of the day and enjoy one another's company and insights in a spirit of mutual respect and collegiality. One of the opposing attorneys, who had been practicing law for over 30 years, commented at the end of the evening that this was the first time he had ever received this kind of invitation from another attorney after a settlement conference. Try to make deposits of positive acknowledgment and good acts and minimize withdrawals due to unnecessary conflicts or control struggles. It is a difficult balance, but one from which you and your family law colleagues will benefit.

Contribute to Family Law Organizations

In working with colleagues on issues of importance to our field, perhaps you have experienced or observed turf struggles and adversarial wrangling over issues that affect us and the public. Our colleagues have strong views about issues that can be viewed from different perspectives. Regardless of the importance of any one issue, it is important that we dialogue rather than confrontationally debate these issues (see Linda Ellinor and Glenna Gerard, *Dialogue* 1998).

How we speak with each other is no less important than the points we want to make. We need to watch the tone of our public discourse on listservs and during organizational outreach. We should stress our commonality and form alliances with other organizations and professionals regardless of differences over any one issue. Just like at the table with our clients, our model is more than what we say. Collaboration with colleagues has its own rewards, many of which reveal themselves only over time.

One doesn't have to hunt for concrete opportunities to work positively with family law colleagues toward common goals. There are nonprofit family law organizations in most communities that need committed, ethical support, and help. Promoting access to family law services for the indigent and working poor is one way in which collaborative efforts by family law professionals can effect positive change.

YOUR NEXT STEPS IN USING PEACEMAKING TO IMPROVE AND EXPAND YOUR PRACTICE

As lawyers, we often suggest to the parties we serve that they consider the "next steps" to take in implementing their agreement. A pledge to take "next steps," especially when those steps are specific and concrete, is an essential key to making key changes. Here are some "next steps" to transform your lawyering work into peacemaking:

1. Make peacemaking your life's work. Talk about it; study it; create a personal mission statement. Create a career plan and articulate a vision for your role in the field—5, 10, 20, and 30 years from now.
2. Perform a peacemaker impact study in the work you do. Evaluate every projected plan to gain skills, help your clients, or build your practice by whether and how such a plan reflects peacemaking.
3. Add new roles or services within your current job or practice to enhance peacemaking. For example, think about how to educate members of your local bar association Family Law Section about peacemaking or consider developing a mentoring program to help local lawyers who are going through disputes with each other or in their personal lives.
4. Become a preventive conflict-wellness thinker and provider. Use the preventive legal wellness checkup when clients first come in and after you have helped them achieve a settlement. Test settlement terms by how they will help restore future peace in the family.
5. Constantly reflect on your own professional behavior and monitor your humility and openness to new approaches. Make sure you treat your staff, court clerks, and clients' meddlesome extended family members with the same respect you offer to esteemed colleagues and others you value highly.
6. Embrace others through the implementation of peacemaking values. This can be a challenging and often lonely profession. We need mutual help and support—and to be reminded daily of the core values that shape our work, improve lives, and contribute to our society.

APPENDIX A

Model Standards of Practice for Family and Divorce Mediation (2000, amended 2012)

CONVENING ORGANIZATIONS

The Association of Family and Conciliation Courts
The Family Law Section of the American Bar Association
National Council of Dispute Resolution Organizations (NCDRO)

OVERVIEW AND DEFINITIONS

Model Standards of Practice for Family and Divorce Mediation

(As adopted by the NYSCDM Board of Directors, May 2002; updated May 2012)

Family and divorce mediation ("family mediation" or "mediation") is a process in which a mediator, an impartial third party, facilitates the resolution of family disputes by promoting the participants' voluntary agreement. The family mediator assists communication, encourages understanding and focuses the participants on their individual and common interests. The family mediator works with the participants to explore options, make decisions and reach their own agreements.

Family mediation is not a substitute for the need for family members to obtain independent legal advice or counseling or therapy. Nor is it appropriate for all families. However, experience has established that family mediation is a valuable option for many families because it can:

- Increase the self-determination of participants and their ability to communicate;
- Promote the best interests of children; and
- Reduce the economic and emotional costs associated with the resolution of family disputes.

Effective mediation requires that the family mediator be qualified by training, experience and temperament; that the mediator be impartial; that the participants reach their decisions voluntarily; that their decisions be based on sufficient factual data; that the mediator be aware of the impact of culture and diversity; and that the best interests of children be taken into account. Further, the mediator should also be prepared to identify families whose history includes domestic abuse or child abuse.

These Model Standards of Practice for Family and Divorce Mediation aim to perform three major functions:

1. To serve as a guide for the conduct of family mediators;
2. To inform the mediating participants of what they can expect in mediation;
3. To promote public confidence as a process for resolving family disputes.

The Model Standards are aspirational in character. They describe good practices for family mediators. They are not intended to create legal rules or standards of liability.

The Model Standards include different levels of guidance:

Use of the term "may" in a Standard is the lowest strength of guidance and indicates a practice that the family mediator should consider adopting but which can be deviated from in the exercise of good professional judgment. Most of the Standards employ the term "should" which indicates that the practice described in the Standard is highly desirable and should be departed from only with very strong reason. The rarer use of the term "shall" in a Standard is a higher level of guidance to the family mediator, indicating that the mediator should not have discretion to depart from the practice described.

The New York State Council on Divorce Mediation adopted the Model Standards of Practice for Family and Divorce Mediators with Comments (Model Standards). The Comments are considered a part of the Model Standards. Upon renewal and as a condition of membership, all Members, Mediator and Accredited, when acting as mediators, agree to support and aspire to these Standards and to abide by the Model Standards, and shall be held to the Standards for ethical and disciplinary purposes.

Standard I

A family mediator shall recognize that mediation is based on the principle of self-determination by the participants.

A. Self-determination is the fundamental principle of family mediation. The mediation process relies upon the ability of participants to make their own voluntary and informed decisions.
B. The primary role of a family mediator is to assist the participants to gain a better understanding of their own needs and interests and the needs and interests of others and to facilitate agreement among the participants.
C. A family mediator should inform the participants that they may seek information and advice from a variety of sources during the mediation process.
D. A family mediator shall inform the participants that they may withdraw from family mediation at any time and are not required to reach an agreement in mediation.

E. The family mediator's commitment shall be to the participants and the process. Pressure from outside of the mediation process shall never influence the mediator to coerce participants to settle.

Standard II

A family mediator shall be qualified by education and training to undertake the mediation.

A. To perform the family mediator's role, a mediator should:
   1. have knowledge of family law;
   2. have knowledge of and training in the impact of family conflict on parents, children and other participants, including knowledge of child development, domestic abuse and child abuse and neglect;
   3. have education and training specific to the process of mediation;
   4. be able to recognize the impact of culture and diversity.

B. Family mediators should provide information to the participants about the mediator's relevant training, education and expertise.

Comment: The requirement that family mediators shall have "knowledge of family law" means that the mediator shall have a thorough understanding of child custody law, the Child Support Standards Act, spousal maintenance law and equitable distribution law, Family Court proceedings, and divorce procedures, and training and continuing education to gain knowledge and skills about family economics. Family economics includes budgeting, income identification and definition, income taxes, health and life insurance issues, estate rights, assets and debt definition, valuation and distribution and related tax issues.

Standard III

A family mediator shall facilitate the participants' understanding of what mediation is and assess their capacity to mediate before the participants reach an agreement to mediate.

A. Before family mediation begins a mediator should provide the participants with an overview of the process and its purposes, including:
   1. informing the participants that reaching an agreement in family mediation is consensual in nature, that a mediator is an impartial facilitator, and that a mediator may not impose or force any settlement on the parties;
   2. distinguishing family mediation from other processes designed to address family issues and disputes;
   3. informing the participants that any agreements reached will be reviewed by the court when court approval is required;
   4. informing the participants that they may obtain independent advice from attorneys counsel, advocates, accountants, therapists or other professionals during the mediation process;
   5. advising the participants, in appropriate cases, that they can seek the advice of religious figures, elders or other significant persons in their community whose opinions they value;

6. discussing, if applicable, the issue of separate sessions with the participants, a description of the circumstances in which the mediator may meet alone with any of the participants, or with any third party and the conditions of confidentiality concerning these separate sessions;
7. informing the participants that the presence or absence of other persons at a mediation, including attorneys, counselors or advocates, depends on the agreement of the participants and the mediator, unless a statute or regulation otherwise requires or the mediator believes that the presence of another person is required or may bebeneficial because of a history or threat of violence or other serious coercive activity by a participant.
8. describing the obligations of the mediator to maintain the confidentiality of the mediation process and its results as well as any exceptions to confidentiality;
9. advising the participants of the circumstances under which the mediator may suspend or terminate the mediation process and that a participant has a right to suspend or terminate mediationat any time.

B. The participants should sign a written agreement to mediate their dispute and the terms and conditions thereof within a reasonable time after first consulting the family mediator.
C. The family mediator should be alert to the capacity and willingness of the participants to mediate before proceeding with the mediation and throughout the process. A mediator should not agree to conduct the mediation if the mediator reasonably believes one or more of the participants is unable or unwilling to participate.
D. Family mediators should not accept a dispute for mediation if they cannot satisfy the expectations of the participants concerning the timing of the process.

Standard IV

A family mediator shall conduct the mediation process in an impartial manner. A family mediator shall disclose all actual and potential grounds of bias and conflicts of interest reasonably known to the mediator. The participants shall be free to retain the mediator by an informed, written waiver of the conflict of interest. However, if a bias or conflict of interest clearly impairs a mediator's impartiality, the mediator shall withdraw regardless of the express agreement of the participants.

A. Impartiality means freedom from favoritism or bias in word, action or appearance, and includes a commitment to assist all participants as opposed to any one individual.
B. Conflict of interest means any relationship between the mediator, any participant or the subject matter of the dispute, that compromises or appears to compromise the mediator's impartiality.
C. A family mediator should not accept a dispute for mediation if the family mediator cannot be impartial.
D. A family mediator should identify and disclose potential grounds of bias or conflict of interest upon which a mediator's impartiality might reasonably be

questioned. Such disclosure should be made prior to the start of a mediation and in time to allow the participants to select an alternate mediator.

E. A family mediator should resolve all doubts in favor of disclosure. All disclosures should be made as soon as practical after the mediator becomes aware of the bias or potential conflict of interest. The duty to disclose is a continuing duty.
F. A family mediator should guard against bias or partiality based on the participants' personal characteristics, background or performance at the mediation.
G. A family mediator should avoid conflicts of interest in recommending the services of other professionals.
H. A family mediator shall not use information about participants obtained in a mediation for personal gain or advantage
I. A family mediator should withdraw pursuant to Standard IX if the mediator believes the mediator's impartiality has been compromised or a conflict of interest has been identified and has not been waived by the participants.

Standard V

A family mediator shall fully disclose and explain the basis of any compensation, fees and charges to the participants.

A. The participants should be provided with sufficient information about fees at the outset of mediation to determine if they wish to retain the services of the mediator.
B. The participants' written agreement to mediate their dispute should include a description of their fee arrangement with the mediator.
C. A mediator should not enter into a fee agreement which is contingent upon the results of the mediation or the amount of the settlement.
D. A mediator should not accept a fee for referral of a matter to another mediator or to any other person.
E. Upon termination of mediation a mediator should return any unearned fee to the participants.

Standard VI

A family mediator shall structure the mediation process so that the participants make decisions based on sufficient information and knowledge.

A. The mediator should facilitate full and accurate disclosure and the acquisition and development of information during mediation so that the participants can make informed decisions. This may be accomplished by encouraging participants to consult appropriate experts.
B. Consistent with standards of impartiality and preserving participant self-determination, a mediator may provide the participants with information that the mediator is qualified by training or experience to provide. The mediator shall not provide therapy or legal advice.
C. The mediator should recommend that the participants obtain independent legal representation before concluding an agreement.

D. If the participants so desire, the mediator should allow attorneys, counsel or advocates for the participants to be present at the mediation sessions.
E. With the agreement of the participants, the mediator may document the participants' resolution of their dispute. The mediator should inform the participants that any agreement should be reviewed by an independent attorney before it is signed.

Standard VII

A family mediator shall maintain the confidentiality of all information acquired in the mediation process, unless the mediator is permitted or required to reveal the information by law or agreement of the participants.

A. The mediator should discuss the participants' expectations of confidentiality with them prior to undertaking the mediation. The written agreement to mediate should include provisions concerning confidentiality.
B. Prior to undertaking the mediation the mediator should inform the participants of the limitations of confidentiality such as statutory, judicially or ethically mandated reporting.
C. The mediator shall disclose a participant's threat of suicide or violence against any person to the threatened person and the appropriate authorities if the mediator believes such threat is likely to be acted upon as permitted by law.
D. If the mediator holds private sessions with a participant, the obligations of confidentiality concerning those sessions should be discussed and agreed upon prior to the sessions.
E. If subpoenaed or otherwise noticed to testify or to produce documents the mediator should inform the participants immediately. The mediator should not testify or provide documents in response to a subpoena without an order of the court if the mediator reasonably believes doing so would violate an obligation of confidentiality to the participants.

Comment: If any person, organization or agency working in the area of mediation maintains or operates under rules which are more restrictive than the rules provided in the Model Standards for confidentiality, their rules shall supersede the Model Standards as they are considered a minimum.

Standard VIII

A family mediator shall assist participants in determining how to promote the best interests of children.

A. The mediator should encourage the participants to explore the range of options available for separation or post-divorce parenting arrangements and their respective costs and benefits. Referral to a specialist in child development may be appropriate for these purposes. The topics for discussion may include, among others:
   1. information about community resources and programs that can help the participants and their children cope with the consequences of family reorganization and family violence;

2. problems that continuing conflict creates for children's development and what steps might be taken to ameliorate the effects of conflict on the children;
3. development of a parenting plan that covers the children's physical residence and decision-making responsibilities for the children, with appropriate levels of detail as agreed to by the participants;
4. the possible need to revise parenting plans as the developmental needs of the children evolve over time; and
5. encouragement to the participants to develop appropriate dispute resolution mechanisms to facilitate future revisions of the parenting plan.

B. The mediator should be sensitive to the impact of culture and religion on parenting philosophy and other decisions.

C. The mediator shall inform any court-appointed representative for the children of the mediation. If a representative for the children participates, the mediator should, at the outset, discuss the effect of that participation on the mediation process and the confidentiality of the mediation with the participants. Whether the representative of the children participates or not, the mediator shall provide the representative with the resulting agreements insofar as they relate to the children.

D. Except in extraordinary circumstances, the children should not participate in the mediation process without the consent of both parents and the children's court-appointed representative.

E. Prior to including the children in the mediation process, the mediator should consult with the parents and the children's court-appointed representative about whether the children should participate in the mediation process and the form of that participation.

F. The mediator should inform all concerned about the available options for the children's participation (which may include personal participation, an interview with a mental health professional, or the mediator reporting to the parents, or a videotape statement) and discuss the costs and benefits of each with the participants.

Standard IX

A family mediator shall recognize a family situation involving child abuse or neglect and take appropriate steps to shape the mediation process accordingly.

A. As used in these Standards, child abuse or neglect is defined by applicable state law.

B. A mediator shall not undertake a mediation in which the family situation has been assessed to involve child abuse or neglect without appropriate and adequate training.

C. If the mediator has reasonable grounds to believe that a child of the participants is abused or neglected within the meaning of the jurisdiction's child abuse and neglect laws, the mediator shall comply with applicable child protection laws.

1. The mediator should encourage the participants to explore appropriate services for the family.
2. The mediator should consider the appropriateness of suspending or terminating the mediation process in light of the allegations.

Standard X

A family mediator shall recognize a family situation involving domestic abuse and take appropriate steps to shape the mediation process accordingly.

A. As used in these Standards, domestic abuse includes domestic violence as defined by applicable state law and issues of control and intimidation.

B. A mediator shall not undertake a mediation in which the family situation has been assessed to involve domestic abuse without appropriate and adequate training.

C. Some cases are not suitable for mediation because of safety, control or intimidation issues. A mediator should make a reasonable effort to screen for the existence of domestic abuse prior to entering into an agreement to mediate. The mediator should continue to assess for domestic abuse throughout the mediation process.

D. If domestic abuse appears to be present the mediator shall consider taking measures to insure the safety of participants and the mediator including, among others:
   1. establishing appropriate security arrangements;
   2. holding separate sessions with the participants even without the agreement of all participants;
   3. allowing a friend, representative, advocate, counsel or attorney to attend the mediation sessions;
   4. encouraging the participants to be represented by an attorney, counsel or an advocate throughout the mediation process;
   5. referring the participants to appropriate community resources;
   6. suspending or terminating the mediation sessions, with appropriate steps to protect the safety of the participants.

E. The mediator should facilitate the participants' formulation of parenting plans that protect the physical safety and psychological well-being of themselves and their children.

Standard XI

A family mediator shall suspend or terminate the mediation process when the mediator reasonably believes that a participant is unable to effectively participate or for other compelling reasons.

A. Circumstances under which a mediator should consider suspending or terminating the mediation, may include, among others:
   1. the safety of a participant or well-being of a child is threatened;
   2. a participant has or is threatening to abduct a child;

3. a participant is unable to participate due to the influence of drugs, alcohol, or physical or mental condition;
4. the participants are about to enter into an agreement that the mediator reasonably believes to be unconscionable;
5. a participant is using the mediation to further illegal conduct;
6. a participant is using the mediation process to gain an unfair advantage;
7. if the mediator believes the mediator's impartiality has been compromised in accordance with Standard IV.

B. If the mediator does suspend or terminate the mediation, the mediator should take all reasonable steps to minimize prejudice or inconvenience to the participants which may result.

Standard XII

A family mediator shall be truthful in the advertisement and solicitation for mediation.

A. Mediators should refrain from promises and guarantees of results. A mediator should not advertise statistical settlement data or settlement rates. B. Mediators should accurately represent their qualifications. In an advertisement or other communication, a mediator may make reference to meeting state, national, or private organizational qualifications only if the entity referred to has a procedure for qualifying mediators and the mediator has been duly granted the requisite status.

Standard XIII

A family mediator shall acquire and maintain professional competence in mediation.

A. Mediators should continuously improve their professional skills and abilities by, among other activities, participating in relevant continuing education programs and should regularly engage in self-assessment.
B. Mediators should participate in programs of peer consultation and should help train and mentor the work of less experienced mediators.
C. Mediators should continuously strive to understand the impact of culture and diversity on the mediator's practice.

APPENDIX B

Phrases for Active Listening and to Prevent Miscommunication

Phrases for Miscommunication

Ordering	"You must." "You have to." "You will."
Threatening	"If you don't, then . . . " "You'd better or else."
Preaching	"You should." "You ought." "It's your duty."
Lecturing	"Here is why you're wrong." "Do you realize . . . "
Giving Answers	"What I would do is . . . " "It would be best if you . . . "
Judging	"You are argumentative . . . lazy . . ." "You'll never change."
Excusing	"It's not so bad." "You'll feel better . . ."
Diagnosing	"You're just trying to get attention." "What you need is . . ."
Prying	"When?" "How?" "What?" "Where?" "Who?"
Labeling	"You're being unrealistic . . . emotional . . . angry . . ."
Manipulating	"Don't you think you should . . ."

Phrases for Active Listening

Encouraging	"Can you tell me more?"
Clarifying	"How did this happen?"
Summarizing	"Let me see if I understand what you just said."
Acknowledging	"I can see you are feeling very angry right now."

Open Questioning	"Why? What would you like to see happen?"
Responding	"I see it this way. How do you see it?"
Soliciting	"I would like your advice about how we can resolve this."
Normalizing	"Many people feel the way you do."
Empathizing	"I can appreciate why you feel that way."
Reframing	"I understand that you feel ___ when he/she ____."
Validating	"I appreciate your willingness to be here."

Reprinted with permission from Ken Cloke, *Mediation: Revenge and the Magic of Forgiveness.*

APPENDIX C

Divorce Mission Statement

Divorce Mission Statement *

A mission statement for your divorce is your compass guiding you away from conflict and toward peace. There will be many tempting distractions during your divorce. Your mission statement will keep you on track.

You can use the following ideas to craft your divorce mission statement. Select the ideas that resonate most with your core values. Click on as many as you'd like to create your mission statement and then print it below:

At the end of my divorce, I want the following to be true:

- ☐ I was kind and honest throughout the entire process.
- ☐ My children have two supportive parents committed to co-parenting.
- ☐ We did not have to go to court to settle our divorce.
- ☐ We spent as little money as possible on our divorce, preserving assets to be split between us versus paying lawyers.
- ☐ Our financial responsibility was divided fairly.
- ☐ I still respect my former spouse and our relationship is friendly, cordial and civil.
- ☐ I realize my marriage was not a complete mistake and value the years I was with my spouse.
- ☐ Our children understand and are reminded that our divorce is not their fault.
- ☐ I am committed to being cooperative and respectful when my spouse engages with the world as a single person (dating, working, making new friends, etc.).

- ☐ I took responsibility for any feelings of abandonment, rejection, fear, anger, grief and guilt I had, without blaming or shaming my spouse.

I will make sure that the above statements are realized by doing the following:

- ☐ I will ask for advice from people who are a positive influence, and then follow that advice.
- ☐ I will put my children's best interests above my own.
- ☐ I will take care of myself physically and emotionally.
- ☐ I will forgive myself and my spouse for getting divorced.
- ☐ I will focus on moving forward rather than getting bogged down in the past.
- ☐ I will accept situations rather than manipulating outcomes.
- ☐ I will focus on what is important, both short term and long term.
- ☐ I will use written goals and journaling to track my progress.
- ☐ I will not use my divorce to be punish toward myself or my spouse.
- ☐ I will not consider divorce as something that I need to recover from; rather something I can heal through.

Your divorce mission statement will serve as a reminder of who you want to be at the end of your divorce. Keep it handy. You will need these reminders when things get tough. The hard work of staying in touch with your mission, and realigning your behaviors to fit with your mission, will be worth it.

*Diana Mercer and Katie Jane Wennechuk, *Making Divorce Work* (2010)

APPENDIX D

Sample Agreement for Consulting Attorney Services

*Note: The roles of consulting attorneys can vary. Some consulting attorneys fully represent parties throughout a mediation process that involves attorneys in the mediation room, while other consulting attorneys advise clients behind the scenes in between sessions or in their review of proposed agreements prior to signing. When creating your own agreement for your practice, it is important to tailor that agreement to the needs of the given client and limit the scope of your promised representation to the exact role that you agree to play. Fee structures and other expectations should be adjusted accordingly and laid out in a clear and transparent manner.

I. LAW AND MEDIATION OFFICE OF [ATTORNEY]*

ATTORNEY FEE AGREEMENT

I have read the attached Attorney Fee Agreement completely and understand its contents. . I have initialed each page and signed the last page to indicate my understanding and agreement of the terms.

I agree to the following financial arrangement with THE LAW OFFICE OF [ATTORNEY], attorney at law, for limited scope legal services in a family law matter.

Unlike many attorneys, [ATTORNEY] does not require an advance retainer. He only charges for his professional time expended. I agree to provide a valid credit card and to maintain available credit for such card at all times that is sufficient to pay each monthly invoice. I authorize [ATTORNEY] to charge my credit card and to be fully paid for the full amount of my bill for legal services and costs each month and for the final bill if such billing is within 30 days of the last billing. I understand that an itemized statement for services rendered will be provided to me after the card is charged indicating the amount charged on the client's credit card and I understand that such charges will be made before I see the invoice and at any time I have the right to discuss or contest any itemized charges made on the credit card or to convert to a payment arrangement other than use of a credit card that is mutually agreed between Mr. Mosten and me.

Initial Deposit: 0

Fees

[ATTORNEY]: $ ______

Client Initial ___

____________ ____________________________

Date CLIENT:

____________ ____________________________

Date [ATTORNEY],

LIMITED SCOPE ATTORNEY

SERVICES TO BE PERFORMED

CLIENT hereby engages ATTORNEY to provide all legal services reasonably required to represent CLIENT in connection with the MATTER (hereinafter called the "MATTER"), described on the first page of this Agreement. Under no circumstances will ATTORNEY represent CLIENT in any court appearances or adversarial proceedings of any kind. CLIENT agrees that this refusal by ATTORNEY to participate in court appearances is best for my case and is in my financial best interest. I understand that if the other party initiates an adversarial proceeding and/or I believe that it is in my interest to file an adversarial proceeding, CLIENT acknowledges that additional fees may be necessary to engage a litigator and for services by ATTORNEY to effectuate such transition of representation. Upon mutual agreement, ATTORNEY will make a Limited Scope (unbundled) Appearance in a court action for the sole purpose of filing initial pleadings (Petition or Response) and/or to file a Stipulation or Judgment containing agreements reached by the parties. Upon mutual agreement, if a litigator is engaged, CLIENT may continue to engage ATTORNEY to provide legal services to with CLIENT and the litigator to manage the litigation and to enhance settlement opportunities.

II. FEES

(a) As compensation for all services performed pursuant to this agreement, CLIENT agrees to pay to ATTORNEY at the basic hourly rates set forth on the Schedule.

(b) ATTORNEY shall charge CLIENT for any and all work or time spent by ATTORNEY on CLIENT'S behalf, including but not necessarily limited to, telephone calls, drafting and/or reviewing correspondence, preparation of documents, legal research, conferences whether or not with CLIEN and Mediations (including travel and waiting time.)

(c) Time for all legal personnel, including but not limited to ATTORNEY, associates, paralegals and legal assistants, is charged in minimum increments of .20 hours. Any minimum time charges for a specific task noted on the first page of this Agreement are subject to periodic change in the same manner provided for the basic hourly rates as set forth in Section 2(a) above.

(d) All time spent in connection with the MATTER by the legal personnel designated by ATTORNEY to handle the MATTER shall be billed to CLIENT in accordance with Section 2.

III. COSTS

(a) CLIENT agrees to pay to ATTORNEY, in accordance with this Section 3, all costs and expenses incurred in this MATTER. Such costs and expenses may include, without limitation, long distance telephone calls, messenger and delivery services, postage, travel expenses such as mileage, parking, airfare, meals and hotel accommodations, which shall be in addition to the hourly rates for travel time, photocopying and other reproduction charges, process server fees, filing fees and other charges assessed by courts and other public agencies, investigator's fees, expert's fees, or consultant's fees, and other similar items.

IV. BILLINGS

(a) ATTORNEY shall render to CLIENT statements on a monthly basis setting forth an itemized detail of the services rendered on CLIENT'S behalf for fees and reimbursements to which ATTORNEY is entitled on account of legal advice given or services rendered under this Agreement. The amounts indicated to be due and owing on statements shall be paid forthwith and in any event not later than 10 days after each statement is rendered. ATTORNEY's invoice shall clearly state the basis thereof, including the amount, rate and basis of calculation (or other method of determination) of ATTORNEY fees.

(b) The Court may order payment of ATTORNEY fees and costs by one party to the other. If any such award is made on CLIENT'S behalf and payment is received by ATTORNEY's office, it shall be credited to CLIENT'S account. CLIENT will always remain primarily responsible and liable for all of ATTORNEY fees, costs and disbursements.

(c) If the CLIENT makes an appointment with an ATTORNEY and cancels less than seventy-two hours in advance of said appointment, the CLIENT will be charged the full cost of the appointment. For example, if the appointment is scheduled for one (1) hour, CLIENT will be billed for the entire hour if CLIENT fails to cancel the appointment within 72 hours.

V. DISCLAIMER

ATTORNEY has made no promises or guarantees to CLIENT concerning the outcome of this MATTER and nothing in this Agreement can be construed as such a promise or guarantee.

VI. TERMINATION OF REPRESENTATION

CLIENT shall have the right at any time to terminate the services of ATTORNEY hereunder upon written notice and ATTORNEY shall immediately after receiving notice cease to render additional services on CLIENT'S behalf. Should CLIENT elect to exercise such right, ATTORNEY agrees to cooperate with CLIENT in facilitating the orderly transfer of CLIENT'S files and records to CLIENT or CLIENT'S new ATTORNEY. Such termination shall not relieve CLIENT of the obligation to pay the fees due to ATTORNEY for legal advice given, services rendered and the disbursements made prior to termination.

If CLIENT fails to meet any of CLIENT'S obligations under this Agreement, ATTORNEY shall have the right to terminate this Agreement, and CLIENT shall take all further steps, including without limitation the execution of any documents necessary to complete ATTORNEY discharge or withdrawal. The right of ATTORNEY hereunder is subject to those created by statute or recognized by the rules of professional conduct.

SINCE ATTORNEY SHALL NOT BE ATTORNEY OF RECORD FOR THE CLIENT IN ANY COURT PROCEEDING, EXCEPT ON A LIMITED SCOPE BASIS, THE FAILURE OF CLIENT TO FULLY AND TIMELY PAY INVOICES FOR PROFESSIONAL SERVICES RELIEVES ATTORNEY FROM PERFORMING ANY FURTHER LEGAL WORK ON BEHALF OF THE CLIENT UNTIL PAYMENTS ARE CURRENT AND A MUTUAL ARRANGMENT HAS BEEN AGREED BETWEEN ATTORNEY AND CLIENT.

UPON TERMINATION OF THE SERVICES FOR WHICH ATTORNEY HAS BEEN RETAINED, CLIENT AGREES TO SIGN A SUBSTITUTION OF ATTORNEY FORM RELIEVING ATTORNEY FROM ANY FURTHER RESPONSIBILITY IN THE MATTER. UPON BOTH ATTORNEY AND CLIENT SIGNING THE SUBSTITUTION OF ATTORNEY FORM, ATTORNEY SHALL FILE THE FORM IN THE COURT AND SEND A COPY TO THE CLIENT AND TO ANY OTHER PARTIES OR COUNSEL. CLIENT WOULD THEN HAVE THE OPTIONS OF REPRESENTING HIMSELF/HERSELF OR MAKING ARRANGMENTS WITH ANOTHER ATTORNEY.

RETURN OF CLIENT'S FILE—Throughout the representation, ATTORNEY shall send client copies of work produced and correspondence and documents received from other parties. Before giving documents to attorney, CLIENT should make copies so that at all times CLIENT has a duplicate file. Due to a limitation of storage space, at the conclusion of the matter for which ATTORNEY is retained, Client shall have the right to possession of the entire client file including documents produced by ATTORNEY and other parties and all client personal and business documents, except attorney work product (notes, memoranda, and the like). Any email communication between the parties shall not be part of the file that will be returned to client.. Client should save all such communication either on a computer or print out copies If WITHIN 60 DAYS FOLLOWING THE CONCLUSION OF THE MATTER, CLIENT does not pick up file at the client's expense (ATTORNEY will not pay to messenger or pay to copy the file), ATTORNEY has the right to destroy the file and all of its contents without further notice to the client.

VII. ATTORNEY FEES

Should it be necessary to institute any legal action for the enforcement of this Agreement, the prevailing party shall be entitled to receive all court costs and reasonable ATTORNEY fees incurred in such action from the other party.

VIII. BINDING ARBITRATION

It is understood that any dispute as to legal malpractice, that is as to whether any legal services rendered under this contract were unnecessary or unauthorized or were improperly, negligently or incompetently rendered, will be determined by submission to arbitration as provided by California law, and not by a lawsuit or resort to court process except as California law provides for judicial review of arbitration proceedings. Both parties to this contract, by entering into it, are giving up their constitutional right to have any such dispute decided in a court of law before a jury, and instead are accepting the use of arbitration.

IX. RIGHT TO HAVE ANOTHER ATTORNEY REVIEW THIS AGREEMENT

CLIENT acknowledges the right to consult with another attorney or advisor before signing this agreement. Upon signing the agreement without an attorney, Client agrees that he/she understands every provision of this agreement, including the Arbitration provision and agree to each provision and to the agreement as a whole.

ADDENDUM RE LIMITED SCOPE REPRESENTATION WITH A COLLABORATIVE APPROACH

You have retained our firm to advise you in connection with your Divorce process in which you and your spouse each has your own lawyer, and all have a shared commitment to avoid litigation. The process primarily entails informal discussions and conferences for purposes of settling all issues. Each party and his or her lawyer agrees to adhere to honesty, constructive problem solving efforts, and mutual respect for the integrity of the people and the process.

As I will not represent you in court in any adversarial proceedings whether or not a formal Collaborative Process is signed, the terms of this Addendum and reference to the Collaborative process apply to any form of dispute resolution in which I participate as your lawyer.

Scope and Duties

Assuming your spouse agrees to proceed via the collaborative process using a trained collaborative lawyer, I will represent your interests through the final settlement and filing of a judgment of dissolution. *My representation of you as a collaborative and limited scope lawyer differs in some important respects from conventional representation by a litigation lawyer. Please read particularly carefully* the following section describing my responsibilities, and yours, in collaborative representation under this agreement. Your retention of me as your Collaborative Divorce lawyer is a "limited scope retention." You are retaining me specifically to assist you in reaching a comprehensive agreement with your spouse or partner, and for no other purpose. You retain the right to terminate the Collaborative Divorce process at any time and go to court, *but doing so ends my representation of you.* If your spouse should elect to go to court, this also terminates the Collaborative Divorce process, and you would need to retain litigation counsel to assist you in court. Accordingly, my representation of you and your retainer agreement with this firm are subject to the following:

I will not be your lawyer of record, except for purposes of filing the Judgment and necessary court forms.

My representation is terminated by any party's decision to litigate, *whether or not it was your decision.*

I will not represent you or assist in any litigation against YOUR SPOUSE should the Divorce process end before complete settlement. However, I will cooperate with you in transferring your file to new counsel.

I will not be called by you to give evidence in any family law litigation against YOUR SPOUSE, nor will I testify if called as a witness.

I will keep you fully informed about the settlement process and will not negotiate a settlement of any issue without your participation and consent. I or my staff will promptly respond to your inquiries.

You acknowledge and agree that for so long as you participate in the Collaborative Divorce process, you are--for that time only-giving up your right to unilateral advocacy in the process by your own expert(s), and your access to the court system for resolution of issues. However, you may terminate the Collaborative Divorce process at any time if you wish to seek remedies from the Court.

You acknowledge and agree that for so long as you elect to participate in the Collaborative Divorce process, you are--for that time only-giving up your right to formally object to producing any documents or to providing any information to the other party, if in my professional judgment the document(s) or information is relevant, material, non-privileged, and the kind of information a reasonable decision-maker would want to have available in order to make an informed decision on an issue in your family law matter.

To this end, you agree to make full disclosure of the nature, extent, value of -and all developments affecting -your income, assets and liabilities. You authorize me to fully disclose all such information which in my discretion must be provided to your spouse and his or her lawyer. *If you should decline to make disclosures I regard as necessary, I am bound by the lawyer-client privilege to keep such information confidential. However, I will, in my discretion, withdraw as your lawyer, or terminate my representation in that situation.*

Your spouse is not a party to this Agreement, and is not a "third party beneficiary" of this Agreement, nor are you a third party beneficiary of any agreements between your spouse and his/her counsel. My legally enforceable obligations are to you alone; the legally enforceable obligations of your spouse or partner's lawyer are to him or her alone; and the signing of the Collaborative Divorce participation documents do not create new professional obligations enforceable by a party who is not represented by the lawyer.

The Collaborative Law/Collaborative Divorce process (those terms are used interchangeably in this document) depends upon good faith participation by both parties. *A dishonest or unscrupulous party could take advantage of the Collaborative Divorce process for delay or advantage in litigation.* Neither I nor any collaborative lawyer can guarantee that their client will in fact adhere to the good faith undertakings that are made formally in writing at the start of the process. Remedies against your spouse or partner for bad faith might possibly be available subsequently in court under relevant family law provisions, but might or might not actually remedy the consequences of bad faith behavior in the Collaborative Divorce process. My commitment to you is that I will alert you to any suspicion of bad faith and recommend termination of the process if I suspect bad faith. Similarly, I will either withdraw as your counsel or terminate the Collaborative Divorce process, at my election, if it appears to me that you are unwilling or unable to meet your good faith commitments in the Collaborative Law process. In signing this agreement, you are authorizing me to withdraw or terminate the Collaborative Law process if, in my judgment, you are failing to participate in good faith. *In signing this agreement, you agree that a persistent failure and/or refusal by you to participate in good faith will constitute your decision to terminate my representation, will constitute a "constructive" termination of our attorney-client relationship by you, which I will implement.*

I may recommend that you and your spouse work with mental health coaches, and/or a neutral financial consultant. Where emotion runs high collaborative coaching may be essential for the Collaborative Divorce process to work effectively. Occasionally it is necessary to bring a mediator in for a time to assist if an impasse persists. In signing this Agreement you acknowledge your understanding that if such additional professional resources are in my professional judgment necessary, you have the right to decline to retain additional collaborative professionals. You also acknowledge and agree that should you so decline, it may not be appropriate to continue the Collaborative Divorce process.

You and I both retain the right to withdraw from this contract if either of us feels we cannot abide by the principles of Collaborative Divorce or that the collaborative process is not functioning satisfactorily, by notifying the other in writing.

No lawyer can guarantee that this process will be effective in resolving your issues. Success is possible only if you and your spouse share a commitment to respectful, honest, efficient, and direct consensual resolution of all issues.

While most couples who elect the Collaborative Divorce process arrive at a full resolution of all issues, some do not. If overall resources (yours and your spouse's) are strained, you should consider carefully whether to allocate limited resources to the Collaborative Divorce process if doing so would impair your ability to retain conventional legal counsel in the event you and your spouse were not able to reach full agreement using the collaborative process.

Candid communication and cooperation among professional team members is essential for effective process management by the collaborative professional team and is a central component of the service we are able to provide. It is not possible for us to provide collaborative representation at the standard we consider appropriate without an understanding that we will communicate confidentially with other professionals, in our discretion, for the sole purpose of helping you and your spouse to reach a satisfactory and appropriate agreement using the collaborative process. These communications are made solely for the purpose of facilitating effective negotiations by improving communications at the collaborative table. The content of such professional process management communications will not necessarily be shared with you. *No communication will ever be made of any matter that you direct shall be kept private by me.* References and notes concerning confidential process management communications among professional team members, if any, will not be maintained as part of your file, and *as a condition of our representation of you*, you agree that they are not part of your file, and that you will not request disclosure of or access to any such confidential team process communications or summaries of such communications (if any), either from me or via any third party or institution. You agree that you will make no effort to introduce any such confidential process communications into any proceedings, whether in court or otherwise.

Collaborative lawyers often engage in continuing education, writing, and training to improve the quality of Collaborative Divorce services, including discussions of experiences in actual cases. You agree that I may discuss your case for such educational purposes provided no information about you or your family is disclosed that could identify you.

If your spouse declines to proceed in a collaborative divorce process, these provisions regarding collaborative divorce will not be applicable.

I HAVE READ THE ABOVE PROVISIONS CONCERNING COLLABORATIVE REPRESENTATION AND AGREE TO THEM

Date_________________ Client______________________________

AGREEMENT REGARDING MEDIATION CONSULTING ATTORNEY SERVICES

You have retained me to advise you, Agreement for Consulting prepare documents, and negotiate on your behalf as mutually agreed in connection with your mediation. This retention is premised on your stated desire to avoid litigation.

Scope and Duties

My representation of you as a consulting lawyer in mediation differs in some important respects from conventional representation by a litigation lawyer. *Please read particularly carefully* the following section describing my responsibilities, and yours, in my mediation consultation representation under this agreement.

Some of the duties that I shall perform as your mediation consulting attorney include:

1. Legal advice: office visits, telephone calls, fax, mail, e-mail;
2. Advice about availability of alternative means to resolve the dispute, including mediation, collaborative law, various forms of negotiation and arbitration;
3. Legal research and analysis;
4. Guidance and procedural information for filing or serving court documents;
5. Help select mediator;
6. Help you prepare and plan for mediation sessions and develop negotiation strategy and approaches;
7. Review of correspondence and court documents prepared by my office, the mediator, your spouse's lawyer, or others;
8. Prepare and/or suggest documents to be prepared by my office, the mediator, your spouse's lawyer, or others;
9. Communicate with the mediator, your spouse's lawyer, or other persons by phone, email, or in person;
10. Attend mediation sessions and negotiate on your behalf as requested;
11. Refer you to other counsel, expert, or professionals as needed and authorized; and
12. Other duties as we may agree.

Your retention of me as your lawyer is a "limited scope retention." You are retaining me specifically to assist you in reaching a comprehensive agreement with your spouse or partner, and for no other purpose. You retain the right to terminate the mediation process at any time and go to court, ***but doing so ends my representation of you.*** If your spouse should elect to go to court, this also may terminate the process, however, mediation can continue while court proceedings are in progress. If any request for a court hearing is made, you would need to retain litigation counsel to assist you in court. Accordingly, my representation of you and your retainer agreement are subject to the following:

- I will not be your lawyer of record, except for purposes of filing the Judgment and other necessary non-adversary court documents. I will be filing a Notice of Limited Scope Representation with the court indicating that I will handle all issues in your divorce through negotiation or mediation and that all court notices will be sent to me. The notice will indicate that you are solely responsible for representing yourself in court unless you retain litigation counsel
- I will not represent you or assist in any litigation against YOUR SPOUSE should the mediation process end before a settlement is reached. However, I will cooperate with you in transferring your file to new counsel.
- I will not be called by you to give evidence in any family law litigation against YOUR SPOUSE, nor will I testify if called as a witness.
- I will not negotiate a settlement of any issue without your participation and consent. I will promptly respond to your inquiries.
- You may terminate the mediation process at any time if you wish to seek remedies from the Court.
- You agree to make full disclosure of the nature, extent, value of—and all developments affecting—your income, assets, and liabilities. You authorize me to fully disclose all such information which in my discretion must be provided to your spouse and his or her lawyer. ***If you should decline to make disclosures I regard as necessary, I am bound by the lawyer-client privilege to keep such information confidential. However, I will, in my discretion, withdraw as your lawyer.***

The mediation process depends upon good faith participation by both parties. ***A dishonest or unscrupulous party could take advantage of the mediation process for delay or advantage in litigation.*** Neither I nor any lawyer can guarantee that their client will in fact adhere to the good faith undertakings that are made formally in writing at the start of the process. Remedies against your spouse or partner for bad faith might possibly be available subsequently in court under relevant family law provisions, but might or might not actually remedy the consequences of bad faith behavior in the mediation process. My commitment to you is that I will alert you to any suspicion of bad faith and recommend termination of the process if I suspect bad faith. Similarly, I will withdraw as your counsel if it appears to me that you are unwilling or unable to meet your good faith commitments in the mediation process. In signing this agreement, you are authorizing me to withdraw if, in my judgment, I feel you are failing to participate in good faith.

- I may recommend that you and your spouse work with mental health professionals, and/or a financial consultant or other professionals. Where emotion runs high or where there are minor children, the involvement of therapists may be essential for the mediation process to work effectively. In signing this Agreement you acknowledge your understanding that if such additional professional resources are in my professional judgment necessary, you have the right to decline to retain additional professionals. You also acknowledge and agree that should you so decline, it may not be appropriate to continue the mediation process or for me to remain as your lawyer.

- No lawyer can guarantee that mediation process will be effective in resolving your issues. Success in mediation is possible only if you and your spouse share a commitment to respectful, honest, efficient, and direct consensual resolution of all issues.
- While most couples who elect the mediation process arrive at a full resolution of all issues, some do not. If overall resources (yours and your spouse's) are strained, you should consider carefully whether to allocate limited resources to the mediation process if doing so would impair your ability to retain conventional legal counsel in the event you and your spouse were not able to reach full agreement.
- Candid communication and cooperation among professionals and the mediator is essential for effective process management which is an important component of the service I am able to provide. It is not possible for me to provide representation at the standard I consider appropriate without an understanding that I will communicate confidentially with other professionals, in my discretion, for the sole purpose of helping you to reach a satisfactory and appropriate agreement using the mediation process. These communications are made solely for the purpose of facilitating effective negotiations by improving communications at the mediation table. The content of such professional communications will not necessarily be shared with you. ***I will not communicate any matter that you have directed me to keep private.*** References and notes concerning confidential process management communications among professionals if any, will not be maintained as part of your file, and ***as a condition of our representation of you***, you agree that they are not part of your file and that you will not request disclosure of or access to any such confidential team process communications or summaries of such communications (if any) from me or from any third party or institution. You agree that you will make no effort to introduce any such confidential process communications into any proceedings, whether in court or otherwise.

I often engage in continuing education, writing, and training to improve the quality of my professional services, including discussions of experiences in actual cases. You agree that I may discuss your case for such educational purposes provided no identifying information about you or your family is disclosed.

I HAVE READ THE ABOVE PROVISIONS AND AGREE TO THEM. I UNDERSTAND THAT I HAVE THE RIGHT TO HAVE THIS AGREEMENT REVIEWED BY ANOTHER ATTORNEY OF MY CHOICE BEFORE I SIGN BELOW.

Date__________________ Client______________________________

Date__________________ Attorney______________________________

APPENDIX E

Sample Estimate of Consulting Lawyer Fees

ESTIMATE OF MEDIATION CONSULTING ATTORNEY FEES

Every client has a right to understand and manage the costs of their attorney fees. Even though the costs of my services as your consulting attorney in mediation should be far less than if you engaged a lawyer for litigation purposes, the expenses can add up.

Some mediations can be concluded in one session and others may require ten sessions or more.

The factors that will impact the cost of your attorney fees are:

- Willingness and ability of the parties to negotiate fairly and efficiently with each other;
- The Level of conflict and communication problems;
- Complexity and Emotionality of Parenting Issues
- Size and Sophistication of the Financial Estate and ability and willingness to disclose assets and liabilities
- Collaboration and Expertise of Lawyers and Other Professionals
- Ease of Scheduling and Willingness to Follow My Recommendations

The following estimate of attorney costs should give you an overview of the cost structure. Remember: These are only ranges and your situation may be very different.

Initial Consultation	1-2 Hours
Review of Parenting and Financial Situation	1-4 Hours
Attendance at Private Preliminary Planning Sessions	0-3 Hours
Attending Working Sessions	0-20 Hours

3-4 Hours Each Session	
Average 3-5 Sessions	
Email and Phone Communication with Mediator, Client, Other Lawyer, Experts, and Other Persons between Sessions	0-10 Hours
Review Mediator Summary Letters	1-5 Hours
Draft Petition and Initial Court Documents	0-2 Hours
Draft Judgment and Final Court Documents	0-7 Hours
Revise Documents, Facilitate Drafting Issues, and Closing	1-6 Hours
Total Estimated Range of Consulting Attorney Time (Based on 3-5 sessions	4-59 Hours
Additional Professional Time:	To Be Determined

APPENDIX F

Law and Mediation Office of Forrest S. Mosten*

OPTIONS FOR COUPLES CONSIDERING SEPARATION

Many people having trouble in their marriage, are not clear that they want a divorce. Dr. William J. Doherty, of the University of Minnesota, has found that 30% of couples coming into marital therapy are "mixed-agenda" couples: one spouse is "leaning out" and the other spouse is "leaning in" to the relationship.

When family members approach mediators, lawyers, or other Collaborative professionals, it has been my experience that fewer couples have such "mixed agendas" in that separation seems more inevitable However, separation does not have to mean a divorce

As a family centered professional, it is my practice to offer my clients a full range of possible directions for our work together. This range includes the following options:[1]

1. **Provide Discernment information** to explore whether both parties wish to attempt further couples counseling. https://discernmentcounseling.com/;
2. **Referral to a mental health professional** to offer more specialized consultation and treatment of discernment counseling;
3. Discuss and draft **Reconciliation Agreement** to keep the couple intact that may include a referral to a mental health couple's counselor
4. **Post-Marital Agreement:** This is a written agreement to resolve issues of property and support based on a mutual desire to remain married
5. **Temporary Separation Agreement:** The parties will negotiate a physical separation of households and work out temporary parenting and financial issues with a date to reassess whether to explore reconciliation or move toward a more permanent separation or divorce.

1. Some of these options may not be applicable to your situation. It is recommended that you have a consultation with me or another mediator/attorney/Collaborative Professional to understand the benefits and risks of each option in respect to your children, finances, relationships, emotional adjustment, and other factors.

6. **Long Term Separation Agreement (Non-Enforceable and Private Separation).** This process discusses parenting and financial issues in a confidential setting. Any written agreement would not be enforceable by the court
7. Long Term Separation Agreement (Enforceable and Private): Similar to #6 but the parties would be able to rely upon and enforce its terms. The written agreement could either remain confidential or submitted to the court
8. **Judgment of Legal Separation with Private Terms:** This process resolves parenting and financial issues in a confidential manner but also seeks a Judgment (court order) declaring a legal separation to protect the parties against future debts and liabilities and permit parties to acquire separate property in the future.
9. **Judgment of Legal Separation with terms contained in a public court document.** This document looks similar to # 8 but is also submitted to the court for immediate validity and enforceability regarding a Legal Separation
10. **Private Martial Settlement Agreement with No Filed Court Documents.** This process covers parenting and financial issues with a resulting written contract that may be submitted to the court by either party in the future
11. **Private Marital Settlement Agreement with Filed Court Documents and No Final Decree.** Similar to #10 but parties initiate either a Divorce or Separation proceeding but do not complete it. The contract remains private and confidential
12. **Martial Settlement Agreement with Filed Court Documents filed now or later** and a Final Judgment Dissolving Marital Status obtained in an agreed amount of time or deferred. Similar to #10 and 11 with a request that the court grant a divorce immediately, at a specific future date, or at a date determined in the future by the parties or the court
13. **Court Judgment of Marital Dissolution** (Divorce) with Public Terms of Settlement. The parties submit their settlement to the court and obtain a legal divorce.
14. **Court Decree/Judgment of Marital Dissolution (Divorce) with Private Terms of Settlement.** Parties obtain their divorce but the parenting and financial terms remain private and do not become a court order unless one or both parties seeks such court order in the future. The settlement is final and non-revocable.

APPENDIX G

Limited Scope Agreement

*Note: Not only when serving as consulting attorneys in mediation, but more generally (as unbundled practitioners) the roles of attorneys can vary. A limited scope agreement should clearly delineate:

1. What legal services are you providing?
2. What legal services you are NOT providing?
3. What is the client expected to do herself?
4. If a court process is involved, who is appearing on record and who is not?
5. If a negotiation or mediation is involved, what role are you as the attorney playing, if any?
6. How is time being tracked and how are legal services being paid?
7. At what point, if any, does your limited scope representation conclude?

[ATTORNEY],
Limited Scope Attorney

LIMITED SCOPE ATTORNEY FEE AGREEMENT

I have read the attached Attorney Fee Agreement completely and understand its contents. I have initialed each page and signed the last page to indicate my understanding and agreement of the terms.

I agree to the following financial arrangement with THE LAW OFFICE OF [ATTORNEY], attorney at law, for limited scope legal services in a family law matter.

Unlike many attorneys, [ATTORNEY] does not require an advance retainer. He only charges for his professional time expended. I agree to provide a valid credit card and to maintain available credit for such card at all times that is sufficient to pay each monthly invoice. I authorize [ATTORNEY] to charge my credit card and to be fully paid for the full amount of my bill for legal services and costs each month and for the final bill if such billing is within 30 days of the last billing. I understand that an itemized statement for services rendered will be provided to me after the card is charged indicating the amount charged on the client's credit card and I understand that such charges will be made before I see the invoice and at any time I have the right to discuss or contest any itemized charges made on the credit card or to convert to a payment arrangement other than use of a credit card that is mutually agreed between Mr. Mosten and me.

Initial Deposit: 0

Fees

[ATTORNEY]: $______

Client Initial ___

__________ ______________________________

Date JONATHAN GREENACRE, CLIENT:

__________ ______________________________

Date [ATTORNEY],
LIMITED SCOPE ATTORNEY

LIMITED SCOPE CLIENT-LAWYER AGREEMENT

This Agreement is made between Attorney and Client as designated at the end of this agreement.

1. Nature of Agreement. This Agreement describes the relationship between the Attorney and Client.

Specifically, this Agreement defines:

a) The general nature of Client's case:
b) The responsibilities and control that Client agrees to retain over the case;
c) The services that Client seeks from Attorney in his capacity as attorney at law;
d) The limits of Attorney's responsibilities:
e) The immunity from civil liability granted to the Attorney for services not provided by Attorney;
f) Methods to resolve disputes between Attorney and Client;
g) The method of payment by Client for services rendered by Attorney.

2. Nature of Case. The Client is requesting services from Attorney in the following matter:

Dissolution of Marriage______________________________

3. Client Responsibilities and Control. The Client intends to handle his/her own case and understands that

he will remain in control of the case and be responsible for all decisions made in the course of the case.

The Client agrees to:

a) Cooperate with Attorney or office by complying with all reasonable requests for information in connection with the matter for which Client is requesting services:
b) Keep Attorney or office advised of Client's concerns and any information that is pertinent to Client's case:
c) Provide Attorney with copies of all correspondence to and from Client relevant to the case
d) Keep all documents related to the case in a file for review by Attorney.

4. Services Sought by Client. The Client seeks the following services from Attorney:

__x__ 1. Legal advice office visits. telephone calls, fax, mail, E-mail;
__x__ 2. Advice about availability of alternative means to resolving the dispute, including mediation and arbitration:
__x__ 3. Evaluation of Client's self-diagnosis of the case and advising Client about legal rights;
__x__ 4. Guidance and procedural information for filing or serving documents;
__x__ 5. Review correspondence and court documents;
__x__ 6. Prepare and/or suggest documents to be prepared;
_____ 7. Factual investigation: contacting witnesses, public record searches, in-depth interview of client;
_____ 8. Legal research and analysis;
_____ 9. Discovery: interrogatories. depositions, requests for document production;
__x__ 10. Planning for negotiations, including simulated role playing with Client;
_____ 11. Planning for court appearances made by Client, including simulated role playing with Client;
_____ 12. Backup and troubleshooting during the trial;
_____ 13. Referring Client to other counsel, expert or professional;
_____ 14. Counseling Client about an appeal;
_____ 15. Procedural assistance with an appeal and assisting with substantive legal argumentation in an appeal;
_____ 16. Provide preventive planning and/or schedule legal check-ups;
_____ 17. Other:

5. **Attorney's Responsibilities** The Attorney shall exercise due **professional care and observe** strict confidentiality in providing the services identified by a check mark in **Paragraph 4 above. In providing those** services, Attorney SHALL NOT

a) Represent, speak for, appear for. or sign papers on the Client's behalf; b) Provide services in Paragraph 4 which are not identified by a check mark; or c) Make decisions for Client about any aspect of the case.

6. **Amendments and Additional Services.** This written Agreement governs the entire relationship between Client and Attorney. All amendments shall be in writing and attached to this Agreement. If Client wishes to obtain additional services from Attorney as defined in Paragraph 4, a photocopy of Paragraph 4 that clearly denotes which extra services are to be provided. signed and dated by both Attorney and Client and attached to this Agreement shall qualify as an amendment.

7. **Cancellation of Appointment** If the CLIENT makes an appointment with an ATTORNEY and cancels less than seventy-two hours in advance of said appointment, the CLIENT will be charged the full cost of the appointment. For example, if the appointment is scheduled for one (1) hour, CLIENT will be billed for the entire hour if CLIENT fails to cancel the appointment within 72 hours.

8. **DISCLAIMER:** ATTORNEY has made no promises or guarantees to CLIENT concerning the outcome of this MATTER and nothing in this Agreement can be construed as such a promise or guarantee.

9. **TERMINATION OF REPRESENTATION:** CLIENT shall have the right at any time to terminate the services of ATTORNEY hereunder upon written notice and ATTORNEY shall immediately after receiving notice cease to render additional services on CLIENT'S behalf. Should CLIENT elect to exercise such right, ATTORNEY agrees to cooperate with CLIENT in facilitating the orderly transfer of CLIENT'S files and records to CLIENT or CLIENT'S new ATTORNEY. Such termination shall not relieve CLIENT of the obligation to pay the fees due to ATTORNEY for legal advice given, services rendered and the disbursements made prior to termination.

10. Termination If CLIENT fails to meet any of CLIENT'S obligations under this Agreement, ATTORNEY shall have the right to terminate this Agreement, and CLIENT shall take all further steps, including without limitation the execution of any documents necessary to complete ATTORNEY discharge or withdrawal. The right of ATTORNEY hereunder is subject to those created by statute or recognized by the rules of professional conduct.

SINCE ATTORNEY SHALL NOT BE ATTORNEY OF RECORD FOR THE CLIENT IN ANY COURT PROCEEDING, EXCEPT ON A LIMITED SCOPE BASIS, THE FAILURE OF CLIENT TO FULLY AND TIMELY PAY INVOICES FOR PROFESSIONAL SERVICES RELIEVES ATTORNEY FROM PERFORMING ANY FURTHER LEGAL WORK ON BEHALF OF THE CLIENT UNTIL PAYMENTS ARE CURRENT AND A MUTUAL ARRANGMENT HAS BEEN AGREED BETWEEN ATTORNEY AND CLIENT.

UPON TERMINATION OF THE SERVICES FOR WHICH ATTORNEY HAS BEEN RETAINED, CLIENT AGREES TO SIGN A SUBSTITUTION OF ATTORNEY FORM RELIEVING ATTORNEY FROM ANY FURTHER RESPONSIBILITY IN THE MATTER. UPON BOTH ATTORNEY AND CLIENT SIGNING THE SUBSTITUTION OF ATTORNEY FORM, ATTORNEY SHALL FILE THE FORM IN THE COURT AND SEND A COPY TO THE CLIENT AND TO ANY OTHER PARTIES OR COUNSEL. CLIENT WOULD THEN HAVE THE OPTIONS OF REPRESENTING HIMSELF/HERSELF OR MAKING ARRANGMENTS WITH ANOTHER ATTORNEY.

12. RETURN OF CLIENT'S FILE—Throughout the representation, ATTORNEY shall send client copies of work produced and correspondence and documents received from other parties. Before giving documents to attorney, CLIENT should make copies so that at all times CLIENT has a duplicate file. Due to a limitation of storage space, at the conclusion of the matter for which ATTORNEY is retained, Client shall have the right to possession of the entire client file including documents produced by ATTORNEY and other parties and all client personal and business documents, except attorney work product (notes, memoranda, and the like). Any email communication between the parties shall not be part of the file that will be returned to client. Client should save all such communication either on a computer or print out copies **If WITHIN 60 DAYS FOLLOWING THE CONCLUSION OF THE MATTER, CLIENT does not pick up file at the client's expense (ATTORNEY will not pay to messenger or pay to copy the file), ATTORNEY has the right to destroy the file and all of its contents without further notice to the client.**

13. ATTORNEY FEES FOR LEGAL ACTION: Should it be necessary to institute any legal action for the enforcement of this Agreement, the prevailing party shall be entitled to receive all court costs and reasonable ATTORNEY fees incurred in such action from the other party.

14. BINDING ARBITRATION OF DISPUTES: It is understood that any dispute as to legal malpractice, that is as to whether any legal services rendered under this contract were unnecessary or unauthorized or were improperly, negligently or incompetently rendered, will be determined by submission to arbitration as provided by California law, and not by a lawsuit or resort to court process except as California law provides for judicial review of arbitration proceedings. Both parties to this contract, by entering into it, are giving

up their constitutional right to have any such dispute decided in a court of law before a jury, and instead are accepting the use of arbitration.

15. RIGHT TO HAVE ANOTHER ATTORNEY REVIEW THIS AGREEMENT: CLIENT acknowledges the right to consult with another attorney or advisor before signing this agreement. Upon signing the agreement without an attorney, Client agrees that he/she understands every provision of this agreement, including the Arbitration provision and agree to each provision and to the agreement as a whole.

Alla Roytberg, Esq.*
Founding Partner
Mediator
aroytberg@goodlawfirm.com

Lara Traum, Esq.**
Partner Mediator
laratraum@goodlawfirm.com
Admitted to Practice in:
*NY and NJ **NY, NJ and CT

Roytberg Traum Law and Mediation, P.C.
www.goodlawfirm.com

Manhattan & Forest Hills Offices
405 Lexington Avenue, 26th Floor
New York, NY 10174
T: 212-582-5757
F: 888-293-7930
118-35 Queens Boulevard, Suite 400
Forest Hills, NY 11375
T: 718-575-9479
F: 888-293-7930

May 10, 2022

Ongoing Consulting Agreement

Identification of Parties: This agreement, executed in duplicate with each party receiving an executed original via email, is made between Roytberg Traum Law and Mediation, P.C., hereafter referred to as "Attorney," and ____________________, hereafter referred to as "Client."

1. **Nature of Case:** The Client is requesting ongoing consulting services from Attorney in the following matter:

____

____

2. **Client Responsibilities and Control.** Client shall remain responsible for the conduct of the case and understands that he/she will remain in control of and be responsible for all decisions made in the course of the case. Client agrees to:
   a. Cooperate with Attorney or office by complying with all reasonable requests for information in connection with the matter for which Client is requesting services;

b. Keep attorney or office advised of Client's concerns and any information that is pertinent to Client's case;
c. Provide Attorney with copies of all pleadings and correspondence to and from Client regarding the case;
d. Immediately provide Attorney with any new pleadings or motions received from the other party;
e. Keep all documents related to the case in a file for review by Attorney.

3. **Services to Be Performed by Attorney.** Client and Attorney have agreed that Attorney will provide the following services, indicated by writing YES or NO (**Attorney will not perform any services indicated by the word NO**):
   a. ________ Legal advice: office visits, telephone calls, fax, mail, email;
   b. ________ Advice about availability of alternative means to resolving the dispute, including mediation and arbitration;
   c. ________ Evaluation of Client's self-diagnosis of the case and advising Client about legal rights and responsibilities;
   d. ________ Guidance and procedural information for filing or serving documents;
   e. ________ Review pleadings and other documents prepared by Client;
   f. ________ Suggest documents to be prepared;
   g. ________ Draft pleadings, motions and other documents;
   h. ________ Factual investigation: contacting witnesses, public record searches, in-depth interview of Client;
   i. ________ Assistance with computer support programs;
   j. ________ Legal research and analysis;
   k. ________ Evaluate settlement options;
   l. ________ Discovery: interrogatories, depositions, requests for document production;
   m. ________ Planning for negotiations, including simulated role-playing with Client;
   n. ________ Planning for court appearances, including simulated role-playing with Client;
   o. ________ Standby telephone assistance during negotiations or settlement conferences;
   p. ________ Backup and troubleshooting during the hearing or trial;
   q. ________ Referring Client to expert witnesses, special masters or other counsel;
   r. ________ Provide preventive planning and/or schedule legal check-ups;
   s. ________ Other: ____

   ____

4. **Attorney's Responsibilities:** Attorney will exercise due professional care and observe strict confidentiality in providing the services identified by the word "YES" in Paragraph 4 above. In providing those services, Attorney **WILL NOT**:
   a. Represent, speak for, appear for, or sign papers on the Client's behalf;
   b. Become attorney of record on any court papers or litigate on Client's behalf, **and the parties agree that the Client shall disclose on all papers**

prepared with the assistance of Attorney, that the document was "prepared with assistance of counsel".

c. Provide services which are not identified by the word "YES" in Paragraph 4;
d. Make decisions for Client about any aspect of the case;
e. Protect Client's property by means of restraining orders while discovery and/or negotiations are in progress.
f. The Client may request that Attorney provide additional services. If Attorney agrees to provide additional services, those additional services will be specifically listed in an amendment to this Agreement, and initialed and dated by both parties.

The date that both the Attorney and the Client initial any such list of additional services to be provided will be the date on which the Attorney becomes responsible for providing those additional services. If the Client decides to retain the Attorney as the Client's Attorney of record for handling the entire case on the Client's behalf, the Client and the Attorney will enter into a new written Agreement setting forth that fact, and the Attorney's additional responsibilities in the Client's case.

g. **Right to Seek Advice of Other Counsel:** Client is advised of the right to seek the advice and professional services of other counsel with respect to those services in paragraph 3 which are identified with the word ***"no"*** at any time during or following this Ongoing Consulting Agreement.

5. **Method of Payment for Services:**

a. Hourly Fee:

The current hourly fee charged by Attorney for services under this agreement is $475 for the services provided by Alla Roytberg, Esq. and $375 for the services provided by Lara Traum, Esq. Unless a different fee arrangement is established in clause b) of this Paragraph, the hourly fee shall be payable at the time of the service. Attorney will charge in increments of one tenth of an hour, rounded off for each particular activity to the nearest one tenth of an hour.

If, while this agreement is in effect, Attorney increases the hourly rate(s) being charged to clients generally for Attorney's fees, that increase may be applied to fees incurred under this agreement, but only with respect to services provided thirty days or more after written notice of the increase is mailed to Client. If Client chooses not to consent to the increased rate(s), Client may terminate Attorney's services under this agreement by written notice effective when received by Attorney.

b. Payment from Deposit:

For a continuing consulting role, Client will pay to Attorney a deposit of Three Thousand Five Hundred Dollars $3,500, to be received by Attorney on or before ____________, and to be applied against Attorney's fees and costs incurred by Client. This amount will be deposited by Attorney in Attorney's IOLA Trust Account located at Chase Bank, Forest Hills, New York. Client authorizes Attorney to withdraw the principal from the trust account to pay Attorney's fees and costs as they are incurred by Client. There is no interest earned on this Account.

The deposit is refundable. If, at the termination of services under this agreement, the total amount incurred by Client for Attorney's fees and costs is less than the amount of the deposit, the difference will be refunded to Client.

Costs: Client will pay Attorney's out of pocket costs incurred in connection with this agreement, including long distance telephone and fax costs, photocopy expense and postage. All costs payable to third parties in connection with Client's case including filing fees, investigation fees, deposition fees and the like will be paid directly by Client. Attorney will not advance costs to third parties on Client's behalf.

Client acknowledges that Attorney has made no promises about the total amount of Attorney's fees to be incurred by Client under this agreement.

c. Should it be necessary to institute any legal action for the enforcement of this agreement, the prevailing party shall be entitled to receive all court costs and reasonable attorney fees incurred in such action from the other party.

6. **Discharge of Attorney:** Client may discharge Attorney at any time by written notice effective when received by Attorney. Unless specifically agreed by Attorney and Client, Attorney will provide no further services and advance no further costs on Client's behalf after receipt of the notice. Notwithstanding the discharge, Client will remain obligated to pay Attorney at the agreed rate for all services provided and to reimburse Attorney for all costs incurred prior to such discharge.
7. **Withdrawal of Attorney:** Attorney may withdraw at any time as permitted under the Rules of Professional Conduct of the State New York. The circumstances under which the Rules permit such withdrawal include, but are not limited to, the following:

a) The client consents, b) the client's conduct renders it unreasonably difficult for the Attorney to carry out the employment effectively, and c) the client fails to pay Attorney's fees or costs as required by his or her agreement with the Attorney.

Notwithstanding Attorney's withdrawal, Client will remain obligated to pay Attorney at the agreed rate for all services provided, and to reimburse Attorney for all costs incurred before the withdrawal.

At the termination of services under this agreement, Attorney will promptly release all of Client's papers and property to Client on request.

8. **Resolving Disputes between Client and Attorney**
   a. **Notice and Negotiation.** If any dispute between Client and Attorney arises under this agreement regarding the payment of fees, Attorney's professional services rendered to or for Client, and any other disagreement, regardless of the nature of the facts or legal theories involved, both Attorney and Client agree to meet and confer within ten (10) days of written notice by either Client or Attorney that the dispute exists. The purpose of this meeting and conference will be to negotiate a solution short of further dispute resolution proceedings.
   b. **Mediation.** If the dispute is not resolved through negotiation, Client and Attorney will attempt, within fifteen (15) days of failed negotiations, to agree on a neutral mediator whose role will be to facilitate further nego-

tiations within fifteen (15) days. If the Attorney and Client cannot agree on a neutral mediator, they will utilize the fee arbitration process available under New York State law.

9. **Amendments and Additional Services.** This written Agreement governs the entire relationship between Client and Attorney. All amendments shall be in writing and attached to this agreement. If Client wishes to obtain additional services from Attorney as defined in Paragraph 4, a photocopy of Paragraph 4 which clearly denotes which extra services are to be provided, signed and dated by both Attorney and Client and attached to this Agreement, shall qualify as an amendment.
10. **Severability in Event of Partial Invalidity.** If any provision of this agreement is held in whole or in part to be unenforceable for any reason, the remainder of that provision and of the entire agreement will be severable and remain in effect.
11. **Statement of Client's Understanding.** I have carefully read this Agreement and believe that I understand all of its provisions. I signify my agreement with the following statements by initialing each one:
    - a.________ I have accurately described the nature of my case in Paragraph 1.
    - b. ________ I will be responsible for the conduct of my case and will be in control of my case at all times as described in Paragraph 2.
    - c. ________ The services Attorney has agreed to perform in my case are identified by the word "YES" in Paragraph 3. I take responsibility for all other aspects of my case.
    - d. ________ I understand and agree to the limitations on the scope of Attorney's responsibilities identified in Paragraph 4 and understand Attorney will not be responsible for my conduct in handling my case.
    - e. ________ I will pay Attorney for services as described in Paragraph 5.
    - f. ________ I will resolve any disputes I may have with Attorney under this Agreement in the manner described in Paragraph 8.
    - g. ________ I understand that any amendments to this Agreement shall be in writing, as described in Paragraph 9.
    - h. ________ I acknowledge that I have been advised by Attorney that I have the right to consult with another independent attorney to review this Agreement and to advise me on my rights as a client *before* I sign this Agreement.

____

____

(Client)
(Date)

Roytberg Traum Law and Mediation, P.C.
BY: __________________________

Lara Traum, ESQ.
Notice of Limited Scope Representation (California FL-950)

FL-950

ATTORNEY OR PARTY WITHOUT ATTORNEY *(Name, state bar number, and address):*	FOR COURT USE ONLY
Forrest S. Mosten Forrest S. Mosten Limited Scope Attorney 11661 San Vicente Blvd., Suite 414 Los Angeles, California 90049 TELEPHONE NO.: (310) 473-7611 FAX NO. *(Optional):* E-MAIL ADDRESS *(Optional):* ATTORNEY FOR *(Name):* Forrest S.Mosten, Limited Scope Attorney	
SUPERIOR COURT OF CALIFORNIA, COUNTY OF STREET ADDRESS: MAILING ADDRESS: CITY AND ZIP CODE: BRANCH NAME:	
PETITIONER/PLAINTIFF: RESPONDENT/DEFENDANT: OTHER PARENT/CLAIMANT:	
NOTICE OF LIMITED SCOPE REPRESENTATION ☐ Amended	CASE NUMBER:

1. Attorney *(name):* Forrest S. Mosten
   and party *(name):* Unbundled/Limited Scope/Discrete Task/Legal Coaching Client
   have a written agreement that attorney will provide limited scope representation to the party.
2. Attorney will represent the party
   ☐ at the hearing on: ☐ and for any continuance of that hearing
   ☐ until submission of the order after hearing
   ☒ until resolution of the issues checked on page 1 by trial or settlement
   ☐ other *(specify duration of representation):*

3. Attorney will serve as "attorney of record" for the party <u>only</u> for the following issues in this case:
   a. ☒ Child support: (1) ☐ Establish (2) ☐ Enforce (3) ☐ Modify *(describe in detail):*

   b. ☒ Spousal support: (1) ☐ Establish (2) ☐ Enforce (3) ☐ Modify *(describe in detail):*

   c. ☐ Restraining order: (1) ☐ Establish (2) ☐ Enforce (3) ☐ Modify *(describe in detail):*

   d. ☒ Child custody and visitation: (1) ☐ Establish (2) ☐ Enforce (3) ☐ Modify *(describe in detail):*

   e. ☒ Division of property *(describe in detail):*

   f. ☒ Pension issues *(describe in detail):*

FL-950

ATTORNEY OR PARTY WITHOUT ATTORNEY (*Name, state bar number, and address*):
Forrest S. Mosten
Forrest S. Mosten
Limited Scope Attorney
11661 San Vicente Blvd., Suite 414
Los Angeles, California 90049
TELEPHONE NO.: (310) 473-7611 FAX NO. (*Optional*):
E-MAIL ADDRESS (*Optional*):
ATTORNEY FOR (*Name*): Forrest S.Mosten, Limited Scope Attorney

FOR COURT USE ONLY

SUPERIOR COURT OF CALIFORNIA, COUNTY OF
STREET ADDRESS:
MAILING ADDRESS:
CITY AND ZIP CODE:
BRANCH NAME:

PETITIONER/PLAINTIFF:
RESPONDENT/DEFENDANT:
OTHER PARENT/CLAIMANT:

NOTICE OF LIMITED SCOPE REPRESENTATION
☐ Amended

CASE NUMBER:

1. Attorney (*name*): Forrest S. Mosten
and party (*name*): Unbundled/Limited Scope/Discrete Task/Legal Coaching Client
have a written agreement that attorney will provide limited scope representation to the party.

2. Attorney will represent the party
☐ at the hearing on: ☐ and for any continuance of that hearing
☐ until submission of the order after hearing
☒ until resolution of the issues checked on page 1 by trial or settlement
☐ other (*specify duration of representation*):

3. Attorney will serve as "attorney of record" for the party <u>only</u> for the following issues in this case:
a. ☒ Child support: (1) ☐ Establish (2) ☐ Enforce (3) ☐ Modify (*describe in detail*):

b. ☒ Spousal support: (1) ☐ Establish (2) ☐ Enforce (3) ☐ Modify (*describe in detail*):

c. ☐ Restraining order: (1) ☐ Establish (2) ☐ Enforce (3) ☐ Modify (*describe in detail*):

d. ☒ Child custody and visitation: (1) ☐ Establish (2) ☐ Enforce (3) ☐ Modify (*describe in detail*):

e. ☒ Division of property (*describe in detail*):

f. ☒ Pension issues (*describe in detail*):

Page 1 of 3

Form Adopted for Mandatory Use
Judicial Council of California
FL-950 [New July 1, 2003]

NOTICE OF LIMITED SCOPE REPRESENTATION

Legal Solutions Plus

APPENDIX H

Factors Affecting Appropriateness of Mediation, Collaborative Law, and Cooperative Law Procedures

Factors	Unassisted Negotiation Is Appropriate if	Mediation* Is Appropriate if	Collaborative Law Is Appropriate if	Traditional Litigation Is Appropriate if
Ability of parties to assert their interests	parties are able to assert their interests well	(a) parties are able to assert their interests well and/or (b) lawyers can participate in mediation	one or more parties need or want a lawyer to advocate their interests	one or more parties need or want a lawyer to advocate their interests
Parties' resources and willingness to pay for substantial professional services	parties cannot afford and/or desire professional service, possibly because they want to maximize their own decision making	parties can afford and/or desire a limited level of professional service, possibly because they want to maximize their own decision making	parties are willing and able to pay for substantial professional services and willing to pay cost of hiring new litigation lawyers if there is no agreement in collaborative law	parties are willing and able to pay for substantial professional services
Parties desire for neutral third party to manage the process	Parties do not want neutral third party to manage the process	Parties want neutral third party to manage the process	(a) parties do not want neutral third party to manage the process or (b) are willing to hire mediator in addition to lawyers	(a) parties do not want neutral third party to manage the process or (b) are willing to hire mediator in addition to lawyers

Factors	Unassisted Negotiation Is Appropriate if	Mediation* Is Appropriate if	Collaborative Law Is Appropriate if	Traditional Litigation Is Appropriate if
Parties willingness to hire lawyers	parties are reluctant or unwilling to hire lawyers at all or to take the lead in negotiation	parties are reluctant or unwilling to hire lawyers at all or to take the lead in negotiation	both parties are willing to hire lawyers	at least one party is willing to hire a lawyer
Parties desire to keep their lawyer if the case involves contested litigation	not applicable	parties want to be able to keep their lawyers in contested litigation	parties are willing to risk losing their collaborative lawyers if the parties litigate	parties want to be able to keep their lawyers in contested litigation
Parties desire for well-established dispute resolution procedure and practice	parties are not concerned about using a well-established dispute resolution procedure and practice	parties want a procedure that has been studied extensively and that is the subject of well-developed norms and practices	parties are willing to use an innovative procedure that has not been studied extensively and that is not the subject of well-developed norms and practices	parties want a procedure that is the subject of well-developed norms and practices
Risk that a party would take advantage of another	(a) there is a low risk of parties will try to take advantage of each other, and/or (b) parties are capable of representing themselves effectively, and/or (c) parties may hire professionals if needed	(a) there is a low risk of parties will try to take advantage of each other, and/or (b) parties are capable of representing themselves effectively, and/or (c) parties use mediator skilled in managing conflict, and/or (d) lawyers participate in mediation	(a) there is a low risk of parties will try to take advantage of each other or (b) there is a significant risk of parties trying to take advantage and they are willing to risk that the other party would terminate collaborative law as an adversarial tactic	there may be a significant risk that one party would take advantage of another
Risk that a party may want to use litigation	parties are unwilling to make an investment to reduce risk of contested litigation	parties are willing to make a limited investment to reduce risk of contested litigation	there is a low risk that a party will want to use contested litigation	there may be a significant risk that a party will want to use contested litigation

Factors	Unassisted Negotiation Is Appropriate if	Mediation* Is Appropriate if	Collaborative Law Is Appropriate if	Traditional Litigation Is Appropriate if
Need for threat of litigation to motivate a party to act reasonably	a party does not need threat of litigation to motivate another party to act reasonably	a party may need threat of litigation to motivate another party to act reasonably	a party does not need threat of litigation to motivate another party to act reasonably	a party may need threat of litigation to motivate another party to act reasonably
Parties desire to avoid contested litigation	parties prefer to avoid litigation but are willing to use it if needed to protect their interests	parties prefer to avoid litigation but are willing to use it if needed to protect their interests	parties strongly prefer to avoid litigation and are willing to use it only as a last resort	parties prefer to avoid litigation but are willing to use it if needed to protect their interests
Relative preference of settlement pressure and litigation pressure	parties are wary of settlement and litigation pressure but willing to risk litigation pressure	parties are wary of settlement pressure and willing to risk greater litigation pressure	parties are wary of litigation pressure and willing to risk greater settlement pressure	parties are wary of settlement pressure and willing to risk greater litigation pressure

*This table assumes that any lawyers for mediation participants do not attend mediation sessions except as noted.

Adapted from John Lande & Gregg Herman, *Fitting the Forum to the Family Fuss: Choosing Mediation, Collaborative Law, or Cooperative Law for Negotiating Divorce Cases*, 42 Family Court Review 280, 286–87 (2004).

APPENDIX I

Client Information about Collaborative Representation

Elements of Collaborative Representation	Benefits	Risks
Collaborative Guidelines and Principles The collaborative process involves treating each other respectfully and satisfying the interests of all family members rather than trying to gain individual advantage.	• The collaborative process sets a positive tone so that you and your spouse can work to satisfy your interests. • The process can reduce unnecessary and destructive conflict and avoid litigation.	• This process may not produce a constructive agreement if your spouse will respond only to threats, litigation, or a decision by a judge. • The collaborative process may not be appropriate if you or your spouse do not have the ability to participate effectively. • Domestic violence, substance abuse, or mental illness may make the process inappropriate. • You may feel unprotected if you want your attorney to advocate strongly to protect your interests (including your concerns about your children).

Elements of Collaborative Representation	Benefits	Risks
Participation Agreement Requiring Disqualification of Attorneys in Litigation Clients and attorneys sign a Participation Agreement that includes a court disqualification clause, which states that if the parties do not resolve the matter in the collaborative process, neither attorney will represent the parties in any contested litigation between you. If you would want to hire an attorney to represent you in court, you would need to hire another attorney.	• The process can increase the motivation of all parties and attorneys to reach a settlement. If negotiations break down and a law suit is filed, both parties need to hire new attorneys and the collaborative attorneys are out of a job. As a result, everyone in the collaborative process focuses exclusively on reaching agreement. • All parties and attorneys focus on negotiation from the very beginning of the process. • Collaborative attorneys work to negotiate constructively and avoid attacking the other side.	• If the collaborative representation ends, you and your spouse will need to spend additional time and money to hire new attorneys and may lose some information or momentum during a transition of attorneys. After developing a relationship of trust and confidence with your collaborative attorney, you might feel abandoned emotionally and/or strategically at a time of contentious conflict. • You may feel a lot of pressure if your spouse is willing to terminate the process and you want to stay in it. • You should be cautious about using a collaborative process If you do not trust that your spouse will negotiate honestly and sincerely.
Trained Collaborative Professionals The collaborative process may involve a team of collaborative professionals who have specialized training in collaborative divorce skills. Separate divorce coaches help each party to deal with emotional, relationship, and parenting issues. Child development specialists and financial professionals may be hired jointly to provide unbiased information and advice.	• You and your spouse may benefit from using a team of collaborative professionals with different skills. • Collaborative professionals usually have had special training to help promote constructive settlements. • By investing the time and money for professional training, collaborative professionals demonstrate a commitment to constructive negotiation.	• You or your spouse may feel some pressure to use more professionals that you want or feel that you can afford.

Elements of Collaborative Representation	Benefits	Risks
Direct Communication and Decision Making by the Parties Parties are the key decision makers and you communicate directly with each other and the attorneys.	• You and your spouse control the decisions that affect your lives and families. • You and your spouse can discuss both nonlegal and legal issues. • You and your spouse can develop communication skills and learn how to communicate more effectively in the future.	• You and your spouse might increase conflict without making any progress if your communication styles are disrespectful or harmful to each other and you cannot work together constructively.
Voluntary Disclosure of Assets, Obligations, and Important Information You and your spouse make a binding commitment that you will fully disclose assets and will not to hide important relevant information.	• You and your spouse agree to provide each other with full information of marital and separate assets so that you can make informed decisions. • The collaborative process can include a protection against parties' failure to disclose fully. If either party does not make the required disclosures, the agreement can be set aside. • The collaborative process does not use formal court "discovery" processes to investigate the facts of your case. This can save money and avoid conflicts. Discovery does not necessarily produce full information.	• Your spouse may hide assets and other critical information unless you use a formal discovery process.
Confidentiality of Collaborative Process Communications in the Collaborative process are generally confidential and inadmissible in court.	• Confidentiality can encourage you and your spouse to talk openly and reach creative solutions. • Confidentiality permits your family business to remain private by avoiding public testimony in court and keeping sensitive documents out of the public records.	•

Elements of Collaborative Representation	Benefits	Risks
Divorce Process May Save Time and Money The collaborative process may save you and your spouse time and money in handling your divorce. Some courts give collaborative cases priority within their court system and cases may not have to follow strict court schedules.	• The collaborative process can help you reduce the length of negotiations and the cost of your divorce. • You may save money by avoiding litigation procedures. Specialized collaborative professionals can help resolve disputes that might otherwise go to court. • Settlements can be processed quickly in court so that you can move on with your life.	• Collaborative cases can take a long time if there are no court deadlines to keep the process moving. • The use of a team of professionals can increase the cost of your divorce.

APPENDIX J

Sample Letter to Client Discussing Risks of Going into Mediation

Dear Client:

As you know, I am supportive of our attempt to settle your matter in mediation for the many reasons we have discussed, including without limitation reduced cost, increased privacy, greater control over the process, less stress on your ongoing family relationships, and your increased ability to fashion your own agreement. There are processes in place within the mediation which are intended to ensure that settlements are reached knowingly and voluntarily and that everyone feels comfortable with the ultimate resolution.

Before we start mediation, I want to review some key considerations:

1. If you agree to a settlement in mediation, it will be binding and enforceable—just as if we had gone to court and the judge had made orders in your case. The binding nature of a mediated settlement is an advantage, in that it gives you the certainty and finality of a court judgment without having to litigate. However, the binding nature of a mediated settlement also means that it will be extraordinarily difficult and expensive to try and get out of it, even if you later feel that you signed due to duress, fraud of your spouse, or a lack of disclosure. California courts almost always affirm mediated agreements.
2. If your spouse prepares and signs his/her Final Declaration of Disclosure during mediation and you later find omitted or understated assets or obligations, you may not be able to get court relief because mediation confidentiality will preclude introduction of the financial disclosure statement into evidence. We can discuss carving out an exception to this confidentiality, but I cannot guarantee that a court would honor that carve-out later.
3. Mediation confidentiality also limits clients' claims against their own attorneys. For example, if an attorney gives a client negligent advice during a mediation that causes the client to settle on terms that he or she later believes to have been unfair or harmful to your case, the client may not be able to use that advice against the attorney in a malpractice action due to mediation confidentiality.

Feel free to discuss with me any questions you may have as to how proceeding with mediation could impact your later rights.

Yours very truly,

Client Initial ___ Client Initial ___

MEDIATION DISCLOSURE NOTIFICATION AND ACKNOWLEDGMENT

To promote communication in mediation, California law generally makes mediation a confidential process. California's mediation confidentiality laws are laid out in Sections 703.5 and 1115 to 1129, inclusive, of the Evidence Code. Those laws establish the confidentiality of mediation and limit the disclosure, admissibility, and a court's consideration of communications, writings, and conduct in connection with a mediation. In general, those laws mean the following:

- All communications, negotiations, or settlement offers in the course of a mediation must remain confidential.
- Statements made and writings prepared in connection with a mediation are not admissible or subject to discovery or compelled disclosure in noncriminal proceedings.
- A mediator's report, opinion, recommendation, or finding about what occurred in a mediation may not be submitted to or considered by a court or another adjudicative body.
- A mediator cannot testify in any subsequent civil proceeding about any communication or conduct occurring at, or in connection with, a mediation.

This means that all communications between you and me (as your attorney) made in preparation for a mediation, or during a mediation, are confidential and cannot be disclosed or used (except in extremely limited circumstances), even if you later decide to sue me as your attorney for malpractice because of something that happens during the mediation.

I, **CLIENT NAME,** understand that, unless all participants agree otherwise, **NO** oral or written communication made during a mediation, or in preparation for a mediation, including communications between me and you as my attorney, can be used as evidence in any subsequent noncriminal legal action including an action against my attorney for malpractice or an ethical violation.

NOTE: This disclosure and signed acknowledgment does not limit my (as your attorney) potential liability to you for professional malpractice, or prevent you from (1) reporting any professional misconduct by me to the State Bar of California or (2) cooperating with any disciplinary investigation or criminal prosecution of me.

CLIENT NAME: ________________________ Date:______

ATTORNEY: ____________________ Date:______

APPENDIX K

Sample Mediator's Contract

*Note: The agreements in this section have been provided for reference by the authors of this book. That being said, agreements vary from practice to practice, between jurisdictions, and can include a variety of contractual provisions based on different models of mediation. When reviewing a mediator's proposed contract, we suggest you make sure that the contract is clear as to:

1. The neutrality of the mediator
2. The autonomy of the parties
3. The confidentiality of the process
4. The structure and payment of fees
5. The termination of the mediation process

We also recommend that the contract is reviewed by the parties' lawyers, and compare with the contracts of other mediators in your area.

LAW AND MEDIATION OFFICE OF

[ATTORNEY]*

MEDIATION AGREEMENT

I have read the attached Mediation Agreement completely and understand its contents. I have initialed each page to indicate my understanding and agreement of the terms.

I wish to initiate mediation with [ATTORNEY] and agree to the provisions and financial arrangements set forth.

Hourly Rate:

[ATTORNEY]: **$ _______**
Advance Deposit **0**

_______________________ _______________________
Date Name of Party

_______________________ _______________________
Date Name of Party

_______________________ _______________________
Date Mediator: [ATTORNEY]

MEDIATION AGREEMENT

I.

ESTABLISHMENT OF MEDIATION RELATIONSHIP

The undersigned wish to retain the services of FORREST S. MOSTEN to mediate disputed issues. The Mediator is an attorney licensed to practice in the State of California working as a sole Mediator or working conjointly with a professional from another discipline (e.g. a therapist, clergy and/or accountant). All references to "Mediator" apply both to the lawyer Mediator and any other professional serving as Mediator, consultant, assisting the mediator or communicating with the parties in respect to the mediation.

The parties acknowledge that the Mediator has discussed the advantages and disadvantages of the Mediation process and compared that process with being represented by separate attorneys or having the issues resolved through negotiation between lawyers or by a judge in the court.

II.

RIGHT OF INDEPENDENT COUNSEL

During the Mediation, the parties are each encouraged to consult independent counsel at any time. Each party is entitled to the confidentiality of the attorney/client relationship in respect to any communication with an independent attorney. In particular, the parties should consult independent counsel prior to signing any final settlement agreement.

III.

MEDIATOR REPRESENTS NEITHER PARTY

The parties acknowledge that the Mediator does not represent the interests of either party and is acting at all times as a neutral facilitator, not as an attorney for either party. The parties acknowledge that the purpose of Mediation is to facilitate the ultimate resolution and agreement between the parties regarding the issues, problems, and disputes presented in Mediation and that the Mediator does not act as an advocate, representative, fiduciary, or counsel for either party.

IV.

IMPARTIALITY OF MEDIATOR

The parties acknowledge that, although the Mediator will be impartial and that the Mediator does not favor either party, there may be issues in which one party may be reasonable and the other may not be reasonable. The Mediator has a duty to assure a balanced dialogue and to diffuse any manipulative or intimidating tactics.

V.

CONFIDENTIALITY

The Mediator agrees to keep all communication from either of the parties confidential in respect to any third persons, unless express verbal consent is given by both parties. For the purpose of facilitating communication and resolving differences between the parties, each party specifically authorizes the Mediator to meet individually with either party, and each party understands that such meetings are confidential and that the mediator has no duty to disclose the contents of those meetings to the other party. Therefore, the Mediator may meet with one party without the presence of the other, and any communication received in such individual sessions shall be confidential to the non-present party at the Mediator's discretion. Such disclosure of communications is to preserve the neutrality of the Mediator.

The parties agree that Sections 1119, 1121, 1122, 1123, 1125, 1126, 1128 are affirmed as the rules of our mediation and the sections are set forth here.

> The parties are aware that the provisions of Section 1119 of the *California Evidence Code* make all communications during the course of a mediation confidential and inadmissible in evidence in any civil proceeding as a matter of public policy. Section 1119 provides as follows:
>
> (a) No evidence of anything said or any admission made for the purpose of, in the course of, or pursuant to, a mediation or mediation consultation is admissible or subject to discovery, and disclosure of the evidence shall not be compelled, in any arbitration, administrative adjudication, civil action, or other noncriminal proceeding in which, pursuant to law, testimony can be compelled to be given.
>
> (b) No writing, as defined in Section 250, that is prepared for the purpose of, in the course of, or pursuant to, a mediation or a mediation consultation, is admissible or subject to discovery, and disclosure of the writing shall not be compelled, in any arbitration, administrative adjudication, civil action, or other noncriminal proceeding in which, pursuant to law, testimony can be compelled to be given.
>
> (c) All communications, negotiations, or settlement discussions by and between participants in the course of a mediation or a mediation consultation shall remain confidential.
>
> The parties are further aware that Section 703.5 of the *California Evidence Code* provides as follows: "No . . . mediator shall be competent to testify, in any subsequent civil proceeding, as to any statement, conduct, decision, or ruling, occurring at or in conjunction with the prior proceeding [*i.e.*, the mediation]."

The parties are further aware that the California Supreme Court has held in *Cassell v. Superior Court* (2011) 51 Cal. 4th 113 and *Foxgate Homeowners' Assn. v. Bramalea California, Inc.* (2001) 26 Cal.4th 1, that there are no exceptions to this public policy. "To carry out the purpose of encouraging mediation by ensuring confidentiality, the statutory scheme, which includes sections 703.5, 1119, and 1121, unqualifiedly bars disclosure of communications made during mediation absent an express statutory exception."

Admissibility

The parties' agree that any agreement signed by both parties shall be admissible in any legal proceeding, and not otherwise be protected from disclosure, pursuant to the provisions of Section 1119(b) of the *California Evidence Code.* This document is expressly deemed admissible in any legal proceeding and otherwise subject to disclosure pursuant to the provisions of Section 1123 of the *California Evidence Code.* The parties further agree that neither party nor the mediator shall be required to testify in any legal proceeding as to mediation communications in respect to any issues, including communications related to the disclosure documents, and no documents prepared solely for the purpose of mediation shall be admissible in any legal proceeding.

Disclosure of Physical and/or Sex Abuse

The mediator shall not maintain confidential from the other party or to appropriate third parties any communication from the parties that indicates to the mediator any of the following:

1) Ongoing physical abuse of one party;

2) Ongoing or past physical violence or sexual abuse of a minor child;

3) The intention of one party to commit a criminal act endangering the other party or any third party. The parties acknowledge that although the mediator is an attorney licensed in the State of California, communications made in mediation are not protected by the attorney-client statutory privilege and confidentiality if the mediator were acting in the role of attorney and they release and hold mediator from any civil liability or professional ethical violations for disclosing such communication as a mediator which would be privileged of confidentiality.

Mediator reports and communications – Evidence Code Section 1121

Neither a mediator nor anyone else may submit to a court or other adjudicative body, and a court or other adjudicative body may not consider, any report, assessment, evaluation, recommendation, or finding of any kind by the mediator concerning a mediation conducted by the mediator, other than a report that is mandated by court rule or other law and that states only whether an agreement was reached, unless all parties to the mediation expressly agree otherwise in writing.

Disclosure by Agreement – Evidence Code Section 1122

A communication or a writing that is made or prepared for the purpose of, or in the course of, or pursuant to, a mediation or a mediation consultation, is not made inadmissible, or protected from disclosure if either of the following conditions is satisfied:

(1) All persons who conduct or otherwise participate in the mediation expressly agree in writing, to disclosure of the communication, document, or writing.

(2) The communication, document, or writing was prepared by or on behalf of fewer than all the mediation participants, those participants expressly agree in writing, to its disclosure, and the communication, document, or writing does

not disclose anything said or done or any admission made in the course of the mediation.

(b) If the neutral person who conducts a mediation expressly agrees to disclosure, that agreement also binds any other person designated by the mediator to assist in the mediation or to communicate with the participants in preparation for a mediation.

Written settlement agreements reached through mediation – Evidence Code Section 1123
A written settlement agreement prepared in the course of, or pursuant to, a mediation, is not made inadmissible, or protected from disclosure, by provisions of this chapter if the agreement is signed by the settling parties and any of the following conditions are satisfied:

(a) The agreement provides that it is admissible or subject to disclosure, or words to that effect.

(b) The agreement provides that it is enforceable or binding or words to that effect.

(c) All parties to the agreement expressly agree in writing.

(d) The agreement is used to show fraud, duress, or illegality that is relevant to an issue in dispute.

I. When mediation ends – Evidence Code Section 1125

(a) A mediation ends when any one of the following conditions is satisfied:

(1) The parties execute a written settlement agreement that fully resolves the dispute.

(2) The mediator provides the mediation participants with a writing signed by the mediator that states that the mediation is terminated, or words to that effect.

(3) A party provides the mediator and the other mediation participants with a writing stating that the mediation is terminated, or words to that effect. In a mediation involving more than two parties, the mediation may continue as to the remaining parties or be terminated in accordance with this section.

(b) For purposes of confidentiality, if a mediation partially resolves a dispute, mediation ends when either of the following conditions is satisfied:

(1) The parties execute a written settlement agreement that partially resolves the dispute.

This section does not preclude a party from ending a mediation without reaching an agreement. This section does not otherwise affect the extent to which a party may terminate a mediation.

II. Effect of end of mediation – Evidence Code Section 1126

Anything said, any admission made, or any writing that is inadmissible, protected from disclosure, and confidential before a mediation ends, shall remain inadmissible, protected from disclosure, and confidential to the same extent after the mediation ends.

III.

IRREGULARITY IN PROCEEDINGS – EVIDENCE CODE SECTION 1128

Any reference to a mediation during any subsequent trial is an irregularity in the proceedings of the trial. Any reference to a mediation during any other subsequent noncriminal proceeding is grounds for vacating or modifying the decision in that proceeding, in whole or in party, and granting a new or further hearing on all or part of the issues, if the reference materially affected the substantial rights of the party requesting relief.

VI.

RIGHT OF MEDIATOR TO WITHDRAW

The Mediator will attempt to resolve any outstanding disputes as long as both parties make a good faith effort to reach an agreement based on fairness to both parties. Both parties must be willing and able to participate in the process. A mediated agreement requires compromise, and both parties agree to attempt to be flexible and open to new possibilities for a resolution of the dispute. If the Mediator, in his professional judgment, concludes that agreement is not possible or that continuation of the mediation process would harm or prejudice one or both of the participants or that a conflict exists between either or both parties and the mediator (i.e. failure to follow Mediator instructions or failure to timely pay in full for Mediator's services), the Mediator shall withdraw and the mediation shall conclude.

VII.

FOLLOWING THE INSTRUCTION(S) OF THE MEDIATOR

The parties agree to follow the instructions of the Mediator throughout the Mediation process. Such instructions are designed to insure that both parties receive full disclosure and development of factual information and that each party has an equal understanding of such information prior to reaching an agreement. Such instructions may include, but are not limited to: seeking advice from independent counsel; making available children, family members or other persons available for participation in Mediation; providing financial information, such as pay-stubs, bank statements, tax returns or other records; contacting and/or retaining independent experts or third parties (e.g. appraiser, therapist, doctor, employer, escrow, banks and/or stock brokers); or, anything else reasonably calculated by the Mediator that is to insure fairness in the Mediation process.

If either of the parties fail to follow the Mediator's instructions, each party agrees that Mediator may withdraw forthwith and both parties agree to release, hold harmless and indemnify the Mediator from any claim or liability for refusal to continue the Mediation.

VIII.

TERMINATION OF MEDIATION WITHOUT CAUSE

The Mediation may be terminated without cause by either party at any time. No reason needs to be given, either to the other party or to the Mediator. A decision to terminate Mediation must be made in writing. Mediation may not resume following said notification, unless expressly authorized by both parties.

Upon termination of mediation for any reason, the Mediator agrees not to represent either party against the other, in any court proceeding, adversary negotiation, or for any other reason involving a dispute between the parties.

IX.

VOLUNTARY DISCLOSURE OF POSSIBLE PREJUDICIAL INFORMATION

The parties agree that, while Mediation is in progress, full disclosure of all information is essential to a success full resolution of the issues. Since the court process is not being used to compel information, any agreement made through Mediation may be rescinded in whole or in part if one party fails to disclose relevant information during the Mediation process. Since the voluntary disclosure of this information may give one party an advantage that may not have been obtained through the traditional adversarial process, the parties agree to release and hold harmless the Mediator from any liability or damages caused by voluntary disclosure of prejudicial information in the Mediation process that may be used in subsequent negotiations or court proceedings. The Mediator has no power to bind third parties not to disclose information furnished during Mediation.

X.

THE MEDIATOR SHALL NOT TESTIFY

Pursuant to Evidence Code Section 1127, the parties agree not to call or subpoena the Mediator to testify at any court proceeding nor to produce any document obtained or prepared from any Mediation session without the prior written authorization of both parties. If either party issues a subpoena regarding the Mediator or his or her documents, that party shall pay the Mediator his or her current hourly rate for all hours expended and shall pay all reasonable attorney fees of the other party in respect to the response, compliance, or resistance of said subpoena.

XI.

THE MEDIATOR DOES NOT PROMISE RESULTS

Each party acknowledges that, since Mediation is a process of compromise, it is possible that either party might agree to settle on terms that might be considered to be less favorable in comparison to what the party might have received from a Judge after a contested court hearing, or through negotiation in which one or both of the parties have retained legal counsel. The Mediator makes no representations that the ultimate result would be the same in kind or degree as might be concluded through negotiation or a contested trial on one or all of the issues. Any questions concerning fairness should be addressed to the Mediator as they occur. In addition, the spouses should consult with independent legal counsel to review compromises made during the course of Mediation, and all provisions of a final agreement prior to executing the Marital Settlement Agreement and other court documents.

XIII.

REIMBURSEMENT OF COSTS

The parties agree to reimburse the Mediator for any and all costs expended on behalf of the parties that are authorized in advance by the parties. In addition, at the Mediator's option, in place of and instead of charges for domestic telephone calls and long distance telephone calls (not to exceed \$20 per month), postage, mileage, parking and in firm photocopying or reproductions, a surcharge to the client's bill of 4% of the hourly billings per month for said client may be included. Examples of non-included costs are photocopying provided outside the office, messenger and delivery service costs, attorney service costs, witness and expert fees, deposition reporter fees, filing fees and domestic long distance telephone calls exceeding 20 minutes and international telephone calls, which charges shall be itemized on the client's monthly statement in addition to the monthly surcharge.

XIII.

BOTH PARTIES ARE RESPONSIBLE FOR FEES

The parties hereby agree to be jointly and severally responsible for the fees of mediators and staff of [ATTORNEY]. If, for any reason, the fee of the Mediator is not paid within fifteen (15) days of billing, the Mediator reserves the right to unilaterally refuse to render any further professional services for the parties. The parties agree that, in addition to the payment of any agreed upon fees, each of the parties shall be liable for any costs of collecting the total amount of the fee, including reasonable attorney fees for collecting said fees.

XIV.

FEES AND SERVICES

The services of the Mediator include, but is not limited to: Mediation sessions with either party; telephone or office conferences with either party or with third parties; coordination and referral with other resource persons; drafting of letters or court documents; other services performed by the mediator or behalf of the mediation.

Time for the mediator is charged in minimum increments of .20 hours, as set forth in the Schedule.

XVI.

REPLENISHABLE DEPOSIT

If the parties choose not to proceed by credit card or at any time during the mediation, the parties each agree to pay an initial deposit. Parties shall deposit with Mediator an advance deposit to be credited against client's final bill. Parties will pay Mediator monthly in full for services rendered during that month within 15 days of billing. At completion of Mediator's work with Parties the retainer will be credited towards Parties' final bill and the remainder will be refunded to the Parties.

XVII.

BILLINGS

Mediator shall render to Parties statements on a monthly basis setting forth an itemized detail of the services rendered on your behalf for fees and reimbursements to which Mediator is entitled on account of services rendered under this agreement. The amounts indicated to be due and owing on statements shall be paid forthwith and in any event not later than 15 days after each statement is rendered. Mediator's invoice shall clearly state the basis thereof, including the amount, rate and basis of calculation (or other method of determination) of Mediator's fees.

a) Parties and Mediator agree that it is impossible to estimate how much the mediator's fees and costs will be in advance and therefore no prediction of the total bill can be made.

b) If any bill is not paid in a timely manner, Parties agree to pay finance charges at the rate of one percent per month on the outstanding balance.

c) Set payments on a monthly basis can be arranged by agreement of the Mediator and Parties, in minimum amounts set forth on the SCHEDULE.

d) If either of the PARTIES make an appointment with a MEDIATOR and cancels less than **seventy-two hours** in advance of said appointment, the PARTIES will be charged the full cost of the appointment. For example, if the appointment is scheduled for 3 hours, parties will be billed for all 3 hours if you fail to cancel the appointment within seventy-two hours.

XVIII.

BINDING ARBITRATION

a) All disputes between the parties and the Mediator regarding any aspect of our professional relationship will be resolved by binding arbitration administered through the Los Angeles County Bar Association pursuant to Sections 1280 *et seq.* of the Code of Civil Procedure and not by litigation in court. By this provision, we are both giving up our right to have any such dispute decided by a judge or a jury and we are each giving up the right of appeal.

b) The prevailing party in any arbitration between us will be entitled to reasonable attorney's fees and costs. Any litigation or arbitration between us will take place in Los Angeles County and California law will apply.

c) It is important for you to know that under current California law a mediator has complete immunity from suit regarding negligence or malpractice or any other cause of action. This means that you cannot sue our firm for any Mediator or staff member any damage to you arising out of the mediation relationship.

d) Before signing this agreement you have a right to consult an independent attorney about the legal consequences to you of signing this agreement and specifically waiving the right to use the courts in any fee dispute and using arbitration instead.

XIX.

MEDIATOR'S FEES

Should it be necessary to institute any legal action or arbitration for the enforcement of this agreement, the prevailing party shall be entitled to receive all court costs and reasonable attorneys' fees incurred in such action from the other party.

XX.

RETURN OF CLIENT'S FILE

Throughout the mediation, MEDIATOR shall send parties copies of work produced. Before giving documents to the mediator, PARTIES should make copies so that at all times PARTIES have a duplicate file. Due to a limitation of storage space, at the conclusion of the matter for which MEDIATOR is engaged, BOTH PARTIES shall have the right to possession of the entire client file including documents produced by THE MEDIATOR and other parties and all client personal and business documents, except MEDIATOR work product (notes, memoranda, and the like). Any email communication between the parties and the MEDIATOR shall not be part of the file that will be returned to the parties. PARTIES should save all such communication either on a computer or print out copies. **If WITHIN 60 DAYS FOLLOWING THE LAST MEDIATION SESSION OR CORRESPONDENCE TO OR FROM THE MEDIATOR,** and the PARTIES do not pick up file at the PARTIES' expense (MEDIATOR will not pay to messenger or pay to copy the file), MEDIATOR has the right to destroy the file and all of its contents without further notice to the PARTIES. If the parties do not agree as to which party should take the file, the MEDIATOR shall hold file for a maximum of 90 additional days to permit the parties to resolve the issue of possession of the file by voluntary agreement or court order. At the expiration of this additional 90-day period, MEDIATOR has the right to destroy the file without further notice.

EXECUTION OF MEDIATION AGREEMENT

By signing this Mediation Agreement, each party agrees that he or she has carefully read and considered each and every provision of this Agreement and agrees to each provision of this agreement without reservation.

APPENDIX L

Agreement to Mediate: New York

Roytberg Traum
Law and Mediation P. C.

Alla Roytberg
Principal Attorney
Mediator
aroytberg@goodlaw
firm.com

Lara Traum
Associate Attorney
Mediator
laratraum@goodlaw
firm.com

Manhattan Office:
The Chrysler Building
405 Lexington Avenue,
26th Floor
New York, NY 10174
T: 212-582-5757
Forest Hills Office:
118-35 Queens Boule-
vard, #400
Forest Hills, NY 11375
T: 718-575-9479
www.goodlawfirm.com
F: 888-293-7930

PLEASE RESPOND TO THE FOREST HILLS OFFICE

MEDIATION PROCESS SUMMARY & AGREEMENT TO MEDIATE

This is an AGREEMENT between ________________ and ___________, (hereinafter "Participants") and __________ (hereinafter "Mediator") to enter into a mediation with the intent of resolving issues related to: ________ and to create and clarify the mediation relationship and process.

PURPOSE OF MEDIATION

Mediation is designed to enable the parties to discuss and reach informed agreements, where desired, as to the best arrangements for the individuals and the family in a situation where the parties are getting married and interested in negotiating the terms of their pre-nuptial agreement, spouses, partners or parents are living together and are interested in discussing and reaching informed agreements on how to continue in their current relationship or spouses, partners or parents living apart or considering or intending to do so. The Participants understand that it is for the Participants, with the Mediator's concurrence, to determine the scope of the mediation and this will be accomplished early in the mediation process.

ROLE OF THE MEDIATOR

The Mediator's role is to facilitate the Participants' communication and understanding of the issues. The Mediator will assist the Participants in the discussion of the issues by advising them of the decisions to be made and, if needed, possible alternatives. The Mediator will make no decisions but will simply help the Participants make their own decisions.

Although the Mediator is an attorney and draws upon her legal experience, the Mediator will not be providing legal advice or any other legal assistance for either of the Participants in the context of this mediation.

The Mediator shall conduct the mediation in accordance with the professional standards and ethics as promulgated by the Model Standards of Practice for Family and Divorce Mediators, as adopted by the Family and Divorce Mediation Council of Greater New York, New York State Council on Divorce Mediation, the Association of Conflict Resolution, Family Section and the Academy of Professional Family Mediators.

VOLUNTARY

Mediation is a voluntary process, and any participant, or the Mediator may terminate mediation at any time. It is recommended that any concern or dissatisfaction with the mediation process be discussed as soon as it may arise, to address such concerns in a timely and appropriate manner. Each Participant understands that because mediation is not always an easy process, he or she will make his and her best efforts to discuss the consideration of withdrawing from the process in the presence of the other Participant and the Mediator, in attempt to make the most informed decision possible.

FAIRNESS

Although each Participant may have conflicting interests and would be adversaries if the issues were presented to a court, the goal in mediation is to jointly problem solve towards finding a fair and equitable solution for all interested Participants.

COMMUNICATION GUIDELINES

The most productive atmosphere for mediation is created when each person shows respect for the opinions and attitudes of the other even where there is disagreement. Difficult conversation can be improved if one speaks for himself or herself and refrains from telling the other what he or she needs, wants or thinks.

SHARING OF INFORMATION

The Participants recognize that in order to reach a satisfactory decision, and towards the goal of reaching informed decisions, each Participants needs to be able to talk in a free, open and honest atmosphere. To help create this atmosphere, the Participants agree to exchange all information and documentation available relating to the subject of this mediation and that such information shall be confidential, as provided below. The parties agree to complete financial disclosure statements including but not limited to a listing of all retirement accounts and other tangible and intangible assets, all forms of income, and copies of current (and prior) tax returns, and any other requested or relevant financial documents. If either Participant has any reason to doubt the honesty, accuracy or completeness of the other's disclosed relevant information, it is agreed to inform the Mediator as soon as such concern arises.

CONFIDENTIALITY

The voluntary nature of mediation relies on the development of trust from increasing openness and risk taking. As a result, everyone involved in mediation, all information shared, and the mediation process itself, needs the protection offered by complete confidentiality to all outside parties and proceedings, unless verbal consent is given by all Participants. This confidentiality provision shall apply to any attorneys participating in the process or any additional neutral professional.

It is agreed that all communications, including but not limited to oral, written, and digital communications, between the Participants (their attorneys, if any) and the Mediator about the dispute come within the rules of evidence, which exclude from court or any other proceeding any disclosures made with a view towards settlement. However, when credible information concerning child abuse or neglect or serious threatened harm to anyone comes to the attention of the Mediator, she may not adhere to confidentiality restrictions.

Since the law is still developing as to the extent a Mediator is protected by the laws of confidentiality, by signing this Agreement to Mediate, you agree that you will not call the Mediator as a witness to testify in any court or in any other proceeding regarding any aspect of the mediation. The parties shall not require the production in court or in any other proceeding any records or documents, including digital documents or recordings made by the Mediator. The parties understand that the mediator will discard all mediation notes subsequent to the mediation and all supporting records after 60 days, unless requested otherwise by the Participants prior to that time. If either Participant decides to subpoena the Mediator or her records, the Mediator shall have the right to quash the subpoena. That participant agrees herein to reimburse the Mediator for whatever expenses she incurred in such action (including attorney fees) plus the hourly rate charged by the mediator for her time taken up by this matter, including any time to appear or prepare for such appearance. The confidentiality of this process shall be deemed a condition that we are relying upon to work together.

Further, if the Participants and the Mediator are engaged in an online mediation, they expressly agree that their online mediation shall be also fully private. It is agreed that the Participants and the Mediator will do their best to ensure that other "third" parties are not able to see nor hear nor otherwise experience the Participants' private and confidential mediation discussions. Further the Mediator and the Participants agree that neither they nor anyone under their control or influence shall in any way record, photograph, scan or otherwise share any aspect of the Participants' online mediation discussions or materials with anyone outside of the Participants and Mediator. If the Participants request a departure from this provision, the request must be made via email in advance and agreed upon by all Participants and the Mediator via email prior to start of the mediation session.

PRESERVING THE STATUS QUO

While mediation is ongoing, and except in the ordinary course of business or usual household practice, the Participants agree not to (1) buy, sell, transfer, conceal or dispose of any property that may be the subject of this mediation, (2) make any changes in insurance(s) or (3) make any significant changes in the status quo, including, but not limited to incurring additional debt, without first discussing the issues in mediation so that both Participants can have input into how any such changes would be made.

The Participants understand that they cannot in good faith work both cooperatively and litigiously at the same time and therefore agree to refrain from preemptive maneuvers and adversarial legal proceedings (except in the case of an emergency), while actively engaged in the mediation process.)

FEES

Fees for mediation services by Alla Roytberg are [redacted] per hour and prorated for parts of an hour. Fees for mediation services by Lara Traum are [redacted] and prorated for parts of an hour. For all time on this matter other than face-to-face meetings, including online video meetings, the regular hourly fee of the Mediator selected shall apply, including but not limited to correspondence including letters, e-mails, and telephone calls (other than for scheduling appointments), drafting or reviewing parties' documents, and consulting with advisory counsel or other involved professionals. Unless otherwise agreed, fees for face-to-face meetings shall be paid prior to the start each session.

An initial retainer of [redacted] ([redacted] if paid by credit card) is required at the time of commencement of the first mediation session, to cover time spent by the Mediator between sessions. The initial retainer will be deposited into this firm's IOLA account located at Chase bank, Forest Hills and drawn on to cover time billed between sessions if it is paid by a wire or check and will be deposited into this firm's business operating account located at Chase bank, Forest Hills, if it is paid by credit card or Zelle. The balance of the retainer, if any, will be returned to the parties at the conclusion of the case. On the other hand, if it is depleted, the parties agree to maintain a minimum balance of at least $1,500 on retainer at all times, while the case is pending.

Cooperation with this policy greatly reduces our billing costs and enables us to provide more cost-effective services for our clients. Time shall be billed based on the standard increment of every 6 minutes (being every 1/10 of an hour). The Mediator shall have the right to charge for appointments not cancelled within 48 hours prior to a scheduled appointment. Postage, photocopying, and a $25 fee for "bounced" checks shall also be charged.

Where applicable, the fee for drafting the Agreement, if any, shall be between $1,250-$2,000, depending on its comprehensiveness and complexity. A deposit of $1,250 is required for the Mediator to begin drafting the Agreement and the completed document will not be released until the final balance is made in full. The drafting fee shall include up to one half-an-hour of time spent for additional revisions of the Agreement and/or telephone conversations with either party or with their advisors to finalize the Agreement. Any time beyond the first half-an-hour will be charged at the same hourly rate as the mediation.

Unless otherwise agreed in mediation, it is agreed between the parties that these fees shall be split equally between them. The Participants understand that these fees are not contingent upon the "success" of the mediation. In the event that either or both Participants should fail to pay any and all fees as defined in this Agreement, the participants shall be jointly and severally liable for the Mediator's fees and expense. Further, each Participant shall be held responsible for any and all costs incurred by the Mediator in the collection of such fees.

MEDIATION NOT BINDING

None of the agreements made in mediation are binding until a formal agreement is signed with proper legal formalities. Even if the Participants agree to something in one meeting, all agreements are regarded as tentative to allow for the opportunity to consider carefully and to obtain separate legal advice about the meaning and effect of the agreement. If a Participant changes his or her mind about an agreement made in one meeting after he or she leaves and reconsiders it, this is acceptable and is not regarded as a broken "promise." Careful thought is needed before any agreement is finalized. The Participants understand that it is the responsibility of each, not of the Mediator, to see to it that the other Participant carries out the terms and conditions of the Agreement and or Judgment.

SAFETY

Each Participant agrees that if there has been any violence or abuse in their relationship that may limit his or her ability to effectively participate in mediation or raise any safety concerns, that Participant will report this to Mediator. Regarding safety issues, Participants may inform the Mediator either directly during a mediation session, or confidentially in a private session or by telephone or email. If this issue arises, we will then discuss whether mediation can proceed and develop an appropriate plan of action. Participants also agree to notify their respective attorneys of any concerns they may have in this regard. **The online video/chat mediation model that allows for synchronous and asynchronous mediation process where Participants are not required to be physically present in the same room or location is particularly well suited for high conflict Participants or those who may have moderate safety concerns.**

INDEPENDENT COUNSEL AND ADVISORS

The Participants understand that the Mediator does not represent either or both of them. During the mediation, the Participants are each encouraged to consult with or be represented by an independent attorney at any time, certainly before any agreement is signed. Such representation serves to ensure a better understanding of the legal issues, as well as each Participant's legal rights and responsibilities. At the request of either Participant, the Mediator can be available to speak with the attorneys. If interested, the Mediator will provide Participants with a list of attorneys who are familiar with mediation and who can serve as independent counsel while still supporting the mediation process. Attorneys serving in this process are best used not as advocates for particular positions, but as a resource of legal information and settlement alternatives to enable Participants to represent themselves. The Participants understand that the Mediator cannot take responsibility for the level of review and/or involvement that each may choose for his or her respective attorney.

Other advisors, such as accountants or appraisers, may also be valuable during mediation and the Mediator will recommend this when it seems appropriate. The information obtained from such persons shall be gathered in a manner mutually agreed on by the Participants. The Participants will make the actual selection of advisors and payment for their services. Unless otherwise agreed in writing, any jointly retained neutral which may be brought into the mediation process shall be bound to the confidentiality provisions herein.

You acknowledge that you were informed that in the interests of efficiency it is this Law Firm's practice to communicate with you and others by email and other electronic means (including electronic billing), and that this Law Firm and /or third parties involved in your case may utilize cloud technology to store data relevant to your case and you understand that these communications may not be private and Cloud technology data may not always be secure. By signing this retainer you agree that this Law Firm can communicate with you via email and transfer relevant information to you and others involved in your case via electronic /online means. You confirm that your email addresses for communication purposes are _____________ and _____________.

This AGREEMENT TO MEDIATE is signed by the Participants and the Mediator and acknowledges the agreement to participate in the mediation on the basis of the Mediation Process Summary outlined herein, which we have read and understand and discussed generally with the mediator and the other party.

DATED: __________

______________________ ______________________

PARTICIPANT PARTICIPANT

____

MEDIATOR

APPENDIX M

Sample Divorce Mediation Agenda

Sample Divorce Mediation Agenda

Two types of issues are the subject of agreements in mediation and collaborative divorce: ***how*** the process of mediation/collaborative divorce and party interaction will work until an agreement is reached and ***what*** the points of the settlement will be. Here is a typical agenda outline (with sub-issues for each agenda topic) of the more than 250 possible issues of a divorce and how they can be handled:

1. Mediation process
   - *Lawyers and Other Divorce Professionals:* Which professionals will participate? What roles they will play? How will they be paid?
   - *Meeting protocol:* How often will parties meet? For how long, and when? Where will the meetings take place?
2. Personal conduct of the parties outside sessions
   - *Telephone calls between parties:* What are the ground rules as to time, length, and subject; the return-call policy; access during travel; and phones for children?
   - *Privacy of residences:* Does a party have a key or the right to enter the residence of the other? Are there areas of residence that are off-limits? Do both parties have the right to the home office, garage workshop, or other areas of the family residence?
3. Separation of the parties
   - *Physical separation:* What are the date and manner of physical separation from the joint residence? How will the children be told and be involved? How will parties handle dating and overnights with new romantic partners?
   - *Separation of finances:* How will income be allocated and deposited? Who pays for expenses and credit card bills? Who has rights to new business contracts and opportunities?

4. Temporary parenting issues
   - *Decision making:* How will parenting decisions be made? What is the balance between privacy and protection of children (for example, may children engage in sky diving, have tattoos, or smoke cigarettes or be subjected to parental second-hand smoke)?
   - *Time sharing:* How will parenting be handled during the regular school schedule, vacations, and special days such as grandparents' birthdays? How can schedules and plans be easily modified in the future?
5. Temporary financial issues
   - *Child and spousal support:* What is the amount and method of payment for expenses such as child care, sports or music lessons, or purchase of clothes? How will the marital standard of living and amount of available income be determined?
   - *Valuing and management of joint assets:* Who operates the family business or arranges for a real estate broker to sell the residence? How will appraisals and accountings be conducted?
6. Permanent property division
   - *Dividing assets and debts:* How will information and financial disclosures with final values and determine equalization and terms (if any) be handled?;
   - *Long-term deferred assets:* When and how will retirement plans and investments will be handled?
7. Other financial issues
   - How will taxes, medical and life insurance, payment of college expenses, trust arrangements for the children, and other issues be handled?
8. Permanent child and spousal support
   - *Income and need:* Will passive income from investment properties and marital lifestyle be used to determine final support amounts?
   - *Conditions for modification and termination:* How will cohabitation with new romantic partners, changes of income, and other factors influence agreed-on arrangements?;
9. Determination of the permanent parenting plan
   - *Revisit temporary plan:* How are the temporary arrangements working for the children? How will temporary agreements be confirmed? How will parents handle issues that were deferred during determination of the temporary plan?

10. Future dispute resolution process

   - *Future meetings:* Will parents arrange for regularly scheduled parenting meetings? How will parties collaboratively reevaluate changing income and needs?
   - *Anticipate future disagreements:* Will there be agreements for notice of disputes, mandatory mediation sessions, and possible use of parenting evaluations as buffers future against court litigation?

11. Draft settlement agreement and other documents

   - *Drafting process:* Who will draft the settlement agreement, and when? What other court, real estate, and business documents need to be drafted, and by whom? How will technical problems such as qualified domestic relations orders for retirement plans be handled?

12. *Review and signing process:* Who will be involved, and when will the ceremony for signing and closure take place? Will there be a formal closure process?

APPENDIX N

Sample Client Handout: My Role as Your Consulting Lawyer in Mediation

MY ROLE AS YOUR CONSULTING LAWYER DURING MEDIATION

As your consulting lawyer, I am committed to offering you all the professional obligations of competence and loyalty that you would have in any other lawyer engagement. In concrete terms, this means that I have a duty to pursue your objectives, protect you from financial harm and legal exposure, inform you of your legal rights, produce competent work, keep all attorney-client communications confidential, avoid conflicts of interest, and insure that my fees are understood and are fair.

Although my approach may differ from the traditional lawyer model with which you are familiar, I am still your lawyer. I pledge to give you the advice and professional support as lawyer while at the same time give you the benefit from my "meditative" non-adversarial approach values and perspective. I am constantly walking the tightrope between conciliatory facilitator with your spouse and your advocate.

My Different Roles as Your Collaborative Lawyer

Representative: I am your agent and I will convey your needs and concerns to the mediator, other party, and professionals.

Advocate: I will "advocate" for your interests throughout the mediation process.

Ally: I am your ally in helping you navigate through the mediation process.

Adapted from Forrest S. Mosten, *Collaborative Divorce Handbook*, Wiley (2009).

Coach: As you will often be talking for yourself in mediation sessions and with your spouse, I will coach you with legal, parenting, and financial issues, to help your communication, and to address your emotional needs.

What Do I Do as Your Consulting Lawyer Does During the Process

Educator: My job is to teach you about the various issues to be covered and the key stages of the mediation process. I will often assign you homework such as asking you to contact the children's school for vacation dates, finish your budget, or contact life insurance companies for insurability and rates. As the process develops, I will explain and prepare you for each stage. For example, prior to the first mediation session, I will go over the possible agenda, review the Mediator's Contract Agreement, and help you be ready for unexpected twists and turns.

Manager of the Process: I will work with you and the mediator in scheduling meetings, making sure legal and tax deadlines are met, and work out assignments for fact gathering and drafting. If outside experts are needed, I might raise the need for the expert, help find the expert, and coach you to arrange for the engagement. In essence, I will make sure that the train runs on time and gets to the station. I will also help choreograph communication and negotiation moves for you to be used with the other party and the mediator.

Counselor at Law: I will listen to your concerns and help frame the decisions that you need to make. Such decisions may be about particular issues (how spring break should be divided, who lives in the residence) or about the mediation process (how often should we meet, who should be at the next mediation session). I will present objective criteria (legal principles, financial viability, effect on the parenting relationship) and

Client Initial ___

options for you to make sound decisions. Once decisions are reached, I will help carry out the plan and monitor the situation to see if decisions need to be revisited or revised.

Fact Gatherer: With over 250 issues in a comprehensive divorce, I will make sure that you have sufficient information to make informed decisions. This information comes in many forms: legal and financial documents, emails, websites, conversations with experts and salespeople, and just looking around. For example, to determine where you might live after moving out of the house, someone will need to find out availability and pricing of appropriate apartments and houses for rent. It is my job to determine with you and the mediator what information is needed, how it will be obtained, how it will be analyzed, and how it is to be utilized in decision making. I will also work with you to prepare financial disclosures and review the disclosures from the other party.

Legal Researcher: I am responsible for making sure you have up-to-date legal information from which to evaluate decisions and plan proposals. I will also use relevant statutes, cases, and reports for you to provide to the mediator to help the other party gain reality in assessing possible bargaining range. I will be candid about the strengths and weaknesses of legal positions. However, I will never take advantage of possible ignorance of your spouse or attorney or the mediator in any way, including in the use of legal authority.

Negotiator and Negotiation Coach: Since you and I will work as a team, we will discuss and resolve issues, both small and large. If you choose, I can be your agent in negotiations with the other party's attorney and the mediator. I will also prepare you to present your own proposals both in mediation sessions when I am not present. I may even have simulated role playing practice sessions with you in which I could play the other

Client Initial ___

party and give you a rehearsal. Or you might play the role of your spouse so you can feel what it is like to have her perspective that might alter or refine your negotiation strategy.

Drafter/Ghost Writer: It will be my responsibility to review summary letters, interim or partial agreements, the full settlement agreement and/or court judgment/decree, other court documents, real estate, business, and other documents that may be required. If the mediator does not have the competence/expertise to draft a particular document or it is agreed that the lawyers should do so, it may be necessary to have me or the other lawyer or expert do that work. In addition to drafting documents, I can be "on-call" for you to review and edit letters, emails, and other documents that you might wish to send to your spouse or third person. If there is such as a qualified retirement plan that will be divided, I will want a highly technical document such as a Qualified Domestic Relations Order to be drafted by an outside expert rather than by either lawyer.

Preventive Legal Health Provider: Divorce can be one of life's most upsetting events. During the negotiation of the settlement agreement and afterward, my role may shift from dispute resolution to conflict prevention. In this preventive function, I can help you in several ways. I may recommend an expert to draft wills, trusts, durable powers of attorney, or living wills, recommend and draft future dispute resolution clauses, calendar and monitor future events provided in the agreement (e.g., buy-out of house, change of school in the 7th grade), or arrange for parenting or support update meetings.

There may be other roles that I can play based on our discussion or tasks that you will do yourself rather than have me do. The basis of our relationship is up-to-date communication and I shall be available to address your questions and concerns.

Client Initial ___

APPENDIX O

Sample Agreement for Attorney Disqualification in Mediation

Attorney Disqualification Agreement for Parties in Mediation

Wife and Husband are participants in mediation with Forrest S. Mosten, Mediator.

The parties agree that the engagement of consulting attorneys by each party will facilitate the mediation process by providing legal advice and support to each party.

The parties further agree that the below disqualification of attorneys upon any termination of mediation will permit the attorneys to support the parties' commitment to resolve all matters within the safe confidential container of mediation without threats of court action or court action itself.

Both parties agree that should mediation terminate and the attorneys are disqualified, there will be additional expense and time necessary to engage substitute legal counsel.

The parties agree that all communications by either the party or the mediator with their respective attorney swill remain confidential. The mediator may speak with the either or both attorneys outside the presence of the parties

The parties shall mutually agree whether the mediator shall send summary agreements directly to the attorneys.

If either party wants his/her attorney to attend a mediation session, this may occur without the agreement of the other party. However, the party intending to have his/her lawyer attend a mediation session must give at least 3 days notice to the other party and to the mediator so that the other party may bring her/his lawyer.

If a set time for a mediation is not convenient for either lawyer, it is agreed that the date of the mediation will be changed to accommodate both parties and both lawyers.

____________ has been retained by Wife to advise her during the course of this mediation and ____________ has been retained by Husband to advise him during the course of this mediation. Each attorney named above has agreed to be bound by the terms of this agreement. Should the mediation terminate due to request for termination by either party or the mediator, each attorney named above, and any attorney in association with such attorney, shall immediately withdraw and terminate legal services and is forever disqualified from appearing as an attorney of record in contested matters for either party named above in this proceeding or in any other family law or civil matter involving both parties. An attorney shall be deemed "in association" if, at any time during the pendency of these proceedings or future family law proceedings between these parties, such attorney is the employer or employee of, or co-employee with, or shares a relationship of partnership or independent contractor status with any attorney named above.

Client Initial ___
Client Initial ___

APPENDIX P

Sample Dispute Resolution Protocol and Mediation Clause

Mediation Clause

This clause may be used in any family law agreement or court order. As in any clause, this model provides a structure from which innovative modifications may be made.

In *Mediation: Law Policy and Practice*, Nancy Rogers and Craig McEwen cite a Connecticut statute dealing with enforcement of a physician's mediation clause: "In order to merit enforcement, the clause must be clear enough for persons with a sixth grade level of education to understand and on a form no longer than one page in length."

Is there a different standard in family law in which the clause is a product of a negotiated agreement, and would this model mediation clause be enforceable under the Connecticut standard?

Mediation Clause (Short)

Prior to filing any court action (absent emergency), the parties agree to participate in meaningful mediation with a mediator mutually selected or appointed by the court. The parties shall equally pay for the costs of mediation.

Mediation Clause (Long)

Absent emergency (which shall be narrowly construed by the court), neither party shall be permitted to file in superior court for any type of relief without filing a written stipulation of the parties' mutually requesting relief or without demonstrating to the court that the following have preceded the court filing:

1. Written notice to the other party detailing the following:

A. The specific relief requested and the facts supporting the requested relief. Such notice is encouraged (but not required) to include a statement indicating why the children and/or the parties would benefit from the relief requested or would be harmed if such relief is not be granted.
B. The names, addresses, and telephones numbers of three mediators acceptable to the requesting party who have been contacted by the requesting party and have available dates within 30 days of the notice.
C. The date and times of least one four-hour time block for each mediator.

2. A declaration under penalty of perjury that the requesting party has meaningfully participated in good faith in mediation for a minimum of four hours with the other party or that the other party has refused to participate meaningfully in mediation for a minimum of four hours.

If the matter is not resolved after four hours of mediation, the parties are encouraged to continue to mediate until final resolution.

All costs for mediation shall be advanced equally by the parties in a manner reasonably requested by the mediator. The final allocation of these costs may be an issue in mediation or determined by the court.

APPENDIX Q

Personal Legal Wellness Checkup and Protocol

Take the legal checkup yourself to monitor your own legal health. Does it stimulate any thinking or concerns about decisions or actions you wish to consider in your own life? How can you use it with your own clients in its present or modified form? Can you see ways of using it as a marketing tool to attract new clients or generate additional revenue for your law office?

Short Form Checklist:

Have You Made Plans For Your Estate? Yes/No

a. Do You Have a Will?
b. If Yes, has it been reviewed/revised within the past 3 years?
c. If No, are there reasons you have not yet sought one?
d. Are there any Estate Planning changes which should be considered?
e. Have you reviewed beneficiary designations on all documents that require one within the past 3 years? Bank Accounts? Life Insurance Policies? Retirement Plans? Other?
f. Have you executed a health proxy for yourself? Your spouse? Your parent(s)? Your emancipated child(ren)?
g. Have you executed a power of attorney for yourself? Your spouse? Your parent(s)? Your emancipated child(ren)?

Have You/Your Family Members Discussed/Agreed Upon Your or Your Family Members' Long Term Care and Retirement Plans? Yes/No

Have You Formalized Your Relationship Status? Yes/No

h. Are you currently married/separated/divorced?
i. Do you have a prenuptial, post-nuptial or other marital agreement? When was it last reviewed? Are terms still relevant or have there been changes?

j. Do you have a separation/divorce agreement/decree? When was it last reviewed? Are terms still relevant or have there been changes?

Do You Own/Rent Residential or Commercial Real Estate or a Cooperative Apartment? Yes/No

k. Do you have a mortgage and have you evaluated refinancing options within the past 3 years?

l. Have you sought a current valuation of your property?

m. Do you have difficulty paying monthly mortgage bills and carrying charges?

n. Did you speak with your CPA regarding maximizing tax deductions?

o. Do you need to review/renegotiate your residential/commercial lease?

Does Your Parentage Arrangement Protect Your Interests? Yes/No

p. Are you biologically related to all children that you parent? If not, might you need a second parent adoption?

q. Do you have access to all medical and education records pertaining to your child(ren)?

r. Are you free to travel and/or move with your children?

s. Are you taking care of grandchildren/Have access to them? Are there any legal issues?

Do You Currently Have Financial/ Liability Exposures? Yes/No

t. Is your contract of employment, partnership agreement, et al. current and adequate?

u. Are you in your own business? Are you considering starting a business alone or with a partner/family member? Do you have necessary startup corporate documents? A shareholder/partnership agreement? Does it provide for what happens if you and your partner cannot agree? If one of you becomes disabled or passes away?

v. Do you have life insurance?

w. Do you have vehicle insurance?

x. Do you have a disability?

y. Do you have any other insurance? Umbrella Insurance? Homeowners' Insurance? Renters' Insurance?

z. Have you reviewed your insurance policies within the past 3 years?

Are You Fiscally Organized? Yes/No

aa. Do you have a listing of all your assets and liabilities?

ab. Do you have a written and current listing of all important future dates associated with your finances, such as expiration, option, maturity, and due dates?

ac. Do you have a file, stored in a secure and fireproof location, containing all important documents? (wills, contracts, marriage/divorce papers, deeds, et al.?)

ad. Do you have an inventory of all your physical possessions, sufficient to support a claim in the event of loss?

Can Any Other Claims Be Asserted against You? Yes/No

Are any of the foregoing questions relevant to your spouse, minor child, or other dependent?

CLIENT LEGAL CHECK-UP

All of our lawyers and support staff are dedicated to not only solving your immediate legal problems but also insuring your on-going legal health and wellness. Like a legal thermometer, this check-up helps us assess your current legal health so that we can work as a team to prevent or minimize legal troubles in your life. Please take a few minutes to complete this confidential check-up.

Date: ______________________________

Name: ______________________________

Do you have a will which has been revised within the past three years?	Yes ❑ No ❑
Do you currently have any concerns about your job or business?	Yes ❑ No ❑
Do you have adequate life insurance protection?	Yes ❑ No ❑
Do you have adequate medical insurance?	Yes ❑ No ❑
Do you presently have a written and current listing of all important future dates concerning your legal and financial matters?	Yes ❑ No ❑
Do you have a file, stored in a secure and fireproof location, containing all important documents (wills, titles, securities, contracts, marriage, divorce papers, deeds, pension plans, profit sharing plans, etc.)?	Yes ❑ No ❑
Within the last three years have you reviewed the beneficiary designations on insurance policies, pension plans, bank accounts and other important documents?	Yes ❑ No ❑
Do you have a complete and current personal financial statement which lists in detail all of your personal assets and liabilities?	Yes ❑ No ❑
Do you currently have a monthly budget which details your current income and all expenses?	Yes ❑ No ❑
Do you have any concerns about your debts?	Yes ❑ No ❑
Do you have a complete and current inventory of all your physical possessions sufficient to support a claim in the event of a loss?	Yes ❑ No ❑
Do you have concerns about the academic, emotional, or social development of your child(ren)?	Yes ❑ No ❑
Are there currently extraordinary emotional pressures and stresses on your life?	Yes ❑ No ❑
If you and your spouse have been separated for less than two years, is the current support and economic arrangement between the two of you satisfactory?	Yes ❑ No ❑
If you and your spouse have been separated for more than two years, has the support and economic arrangement been reviewed in the last two years?	Yes ❑ No ❑

After reviewing these questions, are there any matters or issues which you believe should be updated, reconsidered or brought to the attention of your attorney? Please explain below. Yes ❑ No ❑

Have any of these questions caused you to consider taking some action or making some further review? Please explain below. Yes ❑ No ❑

Is there any other legal, financial, or personal concern which you believe should be brought to the attention of your attorney? Please explain below. Yes ❑ No ❑

On the lines below, please expand on any of your answers which you believe would give your attorney a better picture of your current legal health.

____

____

____

____

____

____

____

____

____

ATTORNEY NOTES:

Sample Personal Legal Checkup Protocol

Developed Jointly by the National Center for Preventive Law and the American Association of Retired Persons (AARP) for Model Program in Pennsylvania (Reprinted with Permission)

Every client and any type of contact provides an opportunity for the mediation- and prevention-friendly lawyers to educate and probe for asymptotic legal disease. Once diagnosed, it is the client's responsibility to decide whether to take action and, if so, whether professional help is needed.

The legal checkup provides an illustration of diagnostic tools that are available to the family lawyer to prevent future conflict and maximize legal health.

General Steps Individuals Can Take to Help Keep Their Legal Health in Order

When making agreements or transactions, or when dealing with important documents:

- Read documents carefully before signing.
- Ask for an explanation of anything you do not understand before signing.
- Consider writing the explanation you receive on the document you are signing.
- Keep copies of anything you sign.
- Put any agreement you consider important in writing.
- Use certified mail when sending important documents to verify transmittal.
- Keep documents, like wills, up to date by reviewing them after major events like births, death, marriage, or divorce.
- Keep notes of conversations you have that you consider to be important, especially if the conversation concerns money or property.

Keep the following documents for at least six years:

- Agreements, loan papers, and similar documents
- Bank statements and canceled checks
- Copies of income tax returns
- Real estate bills
- Child-care payments

Consider keeping the following documents in a safe deposit box for safekeeping (someone else should be made aware of the safe deposit box so that it can be accessed if you are somehow incapacitated):

- Adoption papers
- Automobile ownership certificate (pink slip)
- Birth certificate
- Marriage license
- Will
- Deed to your home and title insurance policy for your home
- Life insurance policies

- Stock certificates and bonds
- Passport
- A current list of personal property, including descriptions of major items along with identification numbers, purchase receipts for the items, and photographs of the items. This may help verify your loss to the police and your insurance company in case of theft or fire.

Keep your canceled checks or get and keep receipts when paying cash for the following:

- Mortgage or rent payment
- Insurance payments
- Automobile payments
- Credit card payments
- Consumer loan payments

General Steps

Consider making a chart of significant dates and keeping it in a handy place where you can refer to it as a reminder of when you need to take action. You may wish to include the following, and any additional dates of personal significance that you wish to remember:

EVENT	TRIGGER DATE
Federal income tax return and payment	
Estimated tax and payment	
Pennsylvania income tax return and payment	
Estimated tax and payment	
Auto insurance premium due	
Auto insurance policy expiration date	
Auto loan maturity date	
Auto loan monthly payment due	
Home insurance premium due	
Home insurance expiration date	
Life insurance premium due	
Life insurance option date	
Lease or rental agreement termination date	
Mortgage payment due date	
Real estate tax due	
Rent payment due date	
Automobile registration expiration date	
Drivers license expiration date	

EVENT	TRIGGER DATE
Passport expiration date	
Convertible securities—conversion date	
Bank loan maturity date	
Bank loan monthly payment due	
Credit union loan maturity date	
Credit union loan payment due	

Checklists

We're Getting Married

We must arrange for a:

- ❑ blood test
- ❑ marriage license

If one of us makes a last name change, we should notify:

- ❑ credit card companies
- ❑ charge accounts
- ❑ banks and other financial institutions
- ❑ other organizations where we have investments
- ❑ insurance companies
- ❑ Social Security Administration (need to get new Social Security card)
- ❑ employers
- ❑ Pennsylvania Department of Transportation (need to change name on drivers license & automobile registration)

We should review the beneficiaries listed in our:

- ❑ wills
- ❑ life insurance policies
- ❑ bank accounts
- ❑ annuities
- ❑ pension plans
- ❑ testamentary or living trusts

We should review the funds and possessions that will be considered to be our:

- ❑ joint property (things we own together)
- ❑ separate property (things we own apart from one another)

We should determine the best way (separately or together) to:
- ❑ sign income tax returns (for tax savings)
- ❑ sign leases (in terms of liability)
- ❑ own property (real and personal)

I'm Buying a Home

I may need to budget these costs:
- ❑ appraisal
- ❑ inspection
- ❑ down payment
- ❑ monthly mortgage payments
- ❑ escrow servicc
- ❑ loan application fee
- ❑ title insurance
- ❑ mortgage insurance
- ❑ monthly utility bills
- ❑ property taxes
- ❑ maintenance costs
- ❑ "fixer-upper" improvements
- ❑ insurance costs
- ❑ homeowner assoc. fees (in some cases)
- ❑ possible assessments (e.g., streetlights, sewers)

I should consider these inspections:
- ❑ general structural inspection
- ❑ pest control (termites and dry rot)
- ❑ asbestos
- ❑ soil stability (of, for example, hillside property)
- ❑ radon gas

My offer on the house should cover all important terms:
- ❑ complete description of the property (full street address and legal description, if available)
- ❑ description of anything else included in the sale (appliances, etc.)
- ❑ exact purchase price
- ❑ purchase price broken down into deposit, down payment, amount of loan
- ❑ my rights if inspections uncover a problem
- ❑ whether my deposit will be returned if I cancel

I can shop for a loan at:
- ❑ banks
- ❑ savings and loan associations
- ❑ insurance companies
- ❑ credit unions
- ❑ mortgage brokers
- ❑ mortgage bankers

Among other things, my loan may:
- ❑ have a fixed or adjustable interest rate
- ❑ be seller financed
- ❑ be assumed (taken over from seller)
- ❑ be due in full if I sell the house

I should consider the advantages/disadvantages of a:
- ❑ standard down payment
- ❑ larger down payment and smaller monthly payments

My taxes and heirs are affected by whether I own the house:
- ❑ by myself
- ❑ as tenants by the entirety with my spouse
- ❑ as a joint tenant with one or more people
- ❑ as a tenant-in-common with one or more people

If I fail to pay the mortgage, the lender can foreclose and:
- ❑ must notify me that my property will be sold
- ❑ must give me a chance to make the missed payments
- ❑ collect late fees and costs of foreclosure from me

APPENDIX R

Recommended Statutory Forms for Financial Disclosure (New York)

SUPREME COURT OF THE STATE OF NEW YORK
COUNTY OF
--X

Plaintiff,

- against -

Defendant.
--X

STATEMENT OF NET WORTH DATED:

Index No.

Date Action Commenced:

Complete all items, marking "NONE", "INAPPLICABLE" and "UNKNOWN", if appropriate

STATE OF NEW YORK)
)ss.:
COUNTY OF ________)

______________________, the Plaintiff/Defendant herein, being duly sworn, deposes and says that, **subject to the penalties of perjury**, the following is an accurate statement as of , [redacted], of my net worth (assets of whatsoever kind and nature and wherever situated minus liabilities), **statement of income from all sources** and statement of assets transferred of whatsoever kind and nature and wherever situated and statement of expenses:

I. FAMILY DATA

	(a)	Plaintiff's date of birth:	
	(b)	Defendant's date of birth:	
	(c)	Date married:	
	(d)	Names and dates of birth of Child(ren) of the marriage:	
	(e)	Minor child(ren) of prior marriage:	
	(f)	Custody of child(ren) of prior marriage:	
	(g)	Plaintiff's present address:	
		Defendant's present address:	
	(h)	Occupation/Employer of Plaintiff:	
		Occupation/Employer of Defendant:	

[UCS Rev. 6/2016]

II. **<u>EXPENSES</u>**: **(List your current expenses** on a monthly basis. If there has been any change in these expenses during the recent past please indicate). Items included under "other" should be listed separately with separate dollar amounts.)

(a)		**Housing: Monthly**	
	1.	Mortgage/Co-op Loan	
	2.	Home Equity Line of Credit/Second Mortgage	
	3.	Real Estate Taxes **(if not included in mortgage payment)**	
	4.	Homeowners/Renter's Insurance	
	5.	Homeowner's Association/Maintenance charges/Condominium Charges	
	6.	Rent	
	7.	Other	
		TOTAL: HOUSING	
(b)		**Utilities: Monthly**	
	1.	Fuel Oil/Gas	
	2.	Electric	
	3.	Telephone (land line)	
	4.	Mobile Phone	
	5.	Cable/Satellite TV	
	6.	Internet	
	7.	Alarm	
	8.	Water	
	9.	Other	
		TOTAL: UTILITIES	

(c)		**Food: Monthly**	
	1.	Groceries	
	2.	Dining Out/Take Out	
	3.	Other	
		TOTAL: FOOD	
(d)		**Clothing: Monthly**	
	1.	Yourself	
	2.	Child(ren)	
	3.	Dry Cleaning	
	4.	Other	
		TOTAL: CLOTHING	
(e)		**Insurance: Monthly**	
	1.	Life	
	2.	Fire, theft and liability and personal articles policy	
	3.	Automotive	
	4.	Umbrella Policy	
	5.	Medical Plan	
		5A. Medical Plan for yourself (Including name of carrier and name of insured)	
		5B. Medical Plan for children (Including name of carrier and name of insured)	
	6.	Dental Plan	
	7.	Optical Plan	
	8.	Disability	

[UCS Rev. 6/2016]

	9.	Worker's Compensation	
	10.	Long Term Care Insurance	
	11.	Other	
		TOTAL: INSURANCE	
(f)		**Unreimbursed Medical: Monthly**	
	1.	Medical	
	2.	Dental	
	3.	Optical	
	4.	Pharmaceutical	
	5.	Surgical, Nursing, Hospital	
	6.	Psychotherapy	
	7.	Other	
		TOTAL: UNREIMBURSED MEDICAL	
(g)		**Household Maintenance: Monthly**	
	1.	Repairs/Maintenance	
	2.	Gardening/landscaping	
	3.	Sanitation/carting	
	4.	Snow Removal	
	5.	Extermination	
	6.	Other	
		TOTAL: HOUSEHOLD MAINTENANCE	
(h)		**Household Help: Monthly**	
	1.	Domestic (housekeeper, etc.)	
	2.	Nanny/Au Pair/Child Care	
	3.	Babysitter	
	4.	Other	
		TOTAL: HOUSEHOLD HELP	

[UCS Rev. 6/2016]

(i)		**Automobile: Monthly** (List a date for each car separately)	
		Year:______ Make:________ Personal:_____ Business:________	
	1.	Lease or Loan Payments (**indicate lease term)**	
	2.	Gas and Oil	
	3.	Repairs	
	4.	Car Wash	
	5.	Parking and tolls	
	6.	Other	
		TOTAL: AUTOMOTIVE	
(j)		**Education Costs: Monthly**	
	1.	Nursery and Pre-school	
	2.	Primary and Secondary	
	3.	College	
	4.	Post-Graduate	
	5.	Religious Instruction	
	6.	School Transportation	
	7.	School Supplies/Books	
	8.	School Lunches	
	9.	Tutoring	
	10.	School Events	
	11.	Child(ren)'s extra-curricular and educational enrichment activities (Dance, Music, Sports, etc.)	
	12.	Other	
		TOTAL: EDUCATION	
(k)		**Recreational: Monthly**	
	1.	Vacations	
	2.	Movies, Theatre, Ballet, Etc.	

[UCS Rev. 6/2016]

	3.	Music (Digital or Physical Media)	
	4.	Recreation Clubs and Memberships	
	5.	Activities for yourself	
	6.	Health Club	
	7.	Summer Camp	
	8.	Birthday party costs for your child(ren)	
	9.	Other	
		TOTAL: RECREATIONAL	
(l)		**Income Taxes: Monthly**	
	1.	Federal	
	2.	State	
	3.	City	
	4.	Social Security and Medicare	
	5.	Number of dependents claimed in prior tax year	
	6.	**List any refund received by you for prior tax year**	
		TOTAL: INCOME TAXES	
(m)		**Miscellaneous: Monthly**	
	1.	Beauty parlor/barber/Spa	
	2.	Toiletries/Non-Prescription Drugs	
	3.	Books, magazines, newspapers	
	4.	Gifts to others	
	5.	Charitable contributions	
	6.	Religious organizations dues	
	7.	Union and organization dues	
	8.	Commutation expenses	
	9.	Veterinarian/pet expenses	

[UCS Rev. 6/2016]

	10.	Child support payments (for Child(ren) of a prior marriage or relationship pursuant to court order or agreement)	
	11.	Alimony and maintenance payments (prior marriage pursuant to court order or agreement)	
	12.	Loan payments	
	13.	Unreimbursed business expenses	
	14.	Safe Deposit Box rental fee	
		TOTAL: MISCELLANEOUS	
(n)		**Other: Monthly**	
	1.		
	2.		
	3.		
		TOTAL: OTHER	
		TOTAL: MONTHLY EXPENSES	

[UCS Rev. 6/2016]

III.		**GROSS INCOME INFORMATION:**	
	(a)	Gross (total) income - as should have been or should be reported in the most recent Federal income tax return. (State whether your income has changed during the year preceding date of this affidavit. If so, please explain.) **Attach most recent W-2, 1099s, K1s and income tax returns.** **List any amount deducted from gross income for retirement benefits or tax deferred savings.**	
	(b)	To the extent not already included in gross income in (a) above:	
		1. Investment income, including interest and dividend income, reduced by sums expended in connection with such investment	
		2. Worker's compensation **(indicate percentage of amount due to lost wages)**	
		3. Disability benefits **(indicate percentage of amount due to lost wages)**	
		4. Unemployment insurance benefits	
		5. Social Security benefits	
		6. Supplemental Security Income	
		7. Public assistance	
		8. Food stamps	
		9. Veterans benefits	
		10. Pensions and retirement benefits	
		11. Fellowships and stipends	
		12. Annuity payments	
	(c)	If any child or other member of your household is employed, set forth name and that person's annual income:	
	(d)	List any maintenance and/or child support you are receiving pursuant to court order or agreement	
	(e)	Other:	

[UCS Rev. 6/2016]

IV. <u>**ASSETS**</u> *(If any asset is held jointly with spouse or another, so state, and set forth your respective shares. Attach additional sheets, if needed)*

A.	1.	Cash Accounts:	
		Cash	
		1.1 a. Location	
		b. Source of Funds	
		c. Amount as of date of commencement	
		d. Current amount	
		TOTAL: CASH	
	2.	Checking Accounts:	
		2.1 a. Financial Institution	
		b. Account Number	
		c. Title holder	
		d. Date opened	
		e. Source of Funds	
		f. Balance as of date of commencement	
		g. Current balance	
		2.2 a. Financial Institution	
		b. Account Number	
		c. Title holder	
		d. Date opened	
		e. Source of Funds	
		f. Balance as of date of commencement	
		g. Current balance	
		TOTAL: Checking	

[UCS Rev. 6/2016]

	3.	Savings Account (including individual, joint, totten trust, certificates of deposit, treasury notes)	
		3.1 a. Financial Institution	
		b. Account Number	
		c. Title holder	
		d. Type of account	
		e. Date opened	
		f. Source of Funds	
		g. Balance as of date of commencement	
		h. Current balance	
		3.2 a. Financial Institution	
		b. Account Number	
		c. Title holder	
		d. Type of account	
		e. Date opened	
		f. Source of Funds	
		g. Balance as of date of commencement	
		h. Current balance	
		TOTAL: Savings	
		TOTAL: Accounts	$
B.	4.	Real Estate (Including real property, leaseholds, life estates, etc. at market value – do not deduct any mortgage)	
		4.1 a. Description	
		b. Title owner	
		c. Date of acquisition	
		d. Original price	

[UCS Rev. 6/2016]

		e. Source of funds to acquire	
		f. Amount of mortgage or lien unpaid	
		g. Estimate current fair market value	
		4.2 a. Description	
		b. Title owner	
		c. Date of acquisition	
		d. Original price	
		e. Source of funds to acquire	
		f. Amount of mortgage or lien unpaid	
		g. Estimate current fair market value	
		TOTAL: Real Estate	
C.	5.	Retirement Accounts (e.g. IRAs, 401(k)s, 403(b)s, pension, profit sharing plans, deferred compensation plans, etc.)	
		5.1 a. Description	
		b. Location of assets	
		c. Title Owner	
		d. Date of acquisition	
		e. Source of funds	
		f. Amount of unpaid liens	
		g. Value as of date of commencement	
		h. Current value	
		5.2 a. Description	
		b. Location of assets	
		c. Title Owner	
		d. Date of acquisition	
		e. Source of funds	

		f. Amount of unpaid liens	
		g. Value as of date of commencement	
		h. Current value	
		TOTAL: Retirement Accounts	
D.	6.	Vehicles (Auto, Boat, Truck, Plane, Camper, Motorcycles, etc.)	
		6.1 a. Description	
		b. Title owner	
		c. Date of acquisition	
		d. Original price	
		e. Source of funds to acquire	
		f. Amount of lien unpaid	
		g. Current fair market value	
		h. Value as of date of commencement	
		6.2 a. Description	
		b. Title owner	
		c. Date of acquisition	
		d. Original price	
		e. Source of funds to acquire	
		f. Amount of lien unpaid	
		g. Current fair market value	
		h. Value as of date of commencement	
		TOTAL: Value of Vehicles	$
E.	7.	Jewelry, art, antiques, household furnishings, precious objects, gold and precious metals (only if valued at more than $500)	
		7.1 a. Description	
		b. Title Owner	

[UCS Rev. 6/2016]

		c. Location	
		d. Original price or value	
		e. Source of funds to acquire	
		f. Amount of lien unpaid	
		g. Value as of date of commencement	
		h. Estimate Current Value	
		i. Value as of date of commencement	
		7.2 a. Description	
		b. Title Owner	
		c. Location	
		d. Original price or value	
		e. Source of funds to acquire	
		f. Amount of lien unpaid	
		g. Value as of date of commencement	
		h. Estimate Current Value	
		i. Value as of date of commencement	
		TOTAL:	$
		IF YOU HAVE NO OTHER ASSETS OR BUSINESS INTERESTS, GO TO THE LIABILITIES SECTION ON PAGE 16	
F.	8.	Interest in any Business	
		8.1 a. Name and Address of Business	
		b. Type of Business (corporate, partnership, sole proprietorship or other)	
		c. Your percentage of interest	
		d. Date of acquisition	
		e. Original price or value	

		f. Source of funds to acquire	
		g. Net worth of business and date of such valuation	
		h. Other relevant information	
		TOTAL: Value of Business Interest	
G.	9.	Cash Surrender Value of Life Insurance	
		9.1 a. Insurer's name and address	
		b. Name of insured	
		c. Policy number	
		d. Face amount of policy	
		e. Policy owner	
		f. Date of acquisition	
		g. Source of funds	
		h. Cash surrender value as of date of commencement	
		i. Current cash surrender value	
		9.2 a. Insurer's name and address	
		b. Name of insured	
		c. Policy number	
		d. Face amount of policy	
		e. Policy owner	
		f. Date of acquisition	
		g. Source of funds	
		h. Cash surrender value as of date of commencement	
		i. Current cash surrender value	

[UCS Rev. 6/2016]

H.	10.	Investment Accounts/Securities/Stock Options/Commodities/Broker Margin Accounts	
		10.1 a. Description	
		b. Title holder	
		c. Location	
		d. Date of acquisition	
		e. Source of funds	
		f. Value as of date of commencement	
		g. Current value	
		10.2 a. Description	
		b. Title holder	
		c. Location	
		d. Date of acquisition	
		e. Source of funds	
		f. Value as of date of commencement	
		g. Current Value	
		TOTAL: Investment Accounts/Securities/Stock Options/Commodities/Broker Margin Accounts	
		TOTAL Value of Securities	$
I.	11.	Loans to Others and Accounts Receivable	
		11.1 a. Debtor's Name and Address	
		b. Original amount of loan or debt	
		c. Source of funds from which loan made or origin of debt	
		d. Date payment(s) due	
		e. Amount due as of date of commencement	
		f. Current amount due	
		TOTAL: Loans to Others and Accounts Receivable	

[UCS Rev. 6/2016]

J.	12.	Contingent Interests (stock options, interests subject to life estates, prospective inheritances)	
		12.1 a. Description	
		b. Location	
		c. Date of vesting	
		d. Title owner	
		e. Date of acquisition	
		f. Original price or value	
		g. Source of acquisition to acquire	
		h. Method of valuation	
		i. Value as of date of commencement	
		j. Current value	$
		TOTAL: Contingent Interests	$
K.	13.	Other Assets (e.g., tax shelter investments, collections, judgments, causes of action, patents, trademarks, copyrights, and any other asset not hereinabove itemized)	
		13.1 a. Description	
		b. Title owner	
		c. Location	
		d. Original Price or value	
		e. Source of funds to acquire	
		f. Amount of lien unpaid	
		g. Value as of date of commencement	
		h. Current value	
		TOTAL: Other Assets	$
		TOTAL ASSETS:	$

[UCS Rev. 6/2016]

V.		**LIABILITIES**	
A.	1.	Accounts Payable	
		1.1 a. Name and address of creditor	
		b. Debtor	
		c. Amount of original debt	
		d. Date of incurring debt	
		e. Purpose	
		f. Monthly or other periodic payment	
		g. Amount of debt as of date of commencement	
		h. Amount of current debt	
		1.2 a. Name and address of creditor	
		b. Debtor	
		c. Amount of original debt	
		d. Date of incurring debt	
		e. Purpose	
		f. Monthly or other periodic payment	
		g. Amount of debt as of date of commencement	
		h. Amount of current debt	
		TOTAL: Accounts Payable	$
B.		Credit Card Debt	
	2.	2.1 a. Debtor	
		b. Amount of original debt	
		c. Date of incurring debt	
		d. Purpose	
		e. Monthly or other periodic payment	
		f. Amount of debt as of date of commencement	
		g. Amount of current debt	

[UCS Rev. 6/2016]

		2.2 a. Debtor	
		b. Amount of original debt	
		c. Date of incurring debt	
		d. Purpose	
		e. Monthly or other periodic payment	
		f. Amount of debt as of date of commencement	$
		g. Amount of current debt	$
		TOTAL: Credit Card Debt	$
C.	3.	Mortgages Payable on Real Estate	
		3.1 a. Name and address of mortgagee	
		b. Address of property mortgaged	
		c. Mortgagor(s)	
		d. Original debt	
		e. Date of incurring debt	
		f. Monthly or other periodic payment	
		g. Maturity date	
		h. Amount of debt as of date of commencement	
		i. Amount of current debt	
		3.2 a. Name and address of mortgagee	
		b. Address of property mortgaged	
		c. Mortgagor(s)	
		d. Original debt	
		e. Date of incurring debt	
		f. Monthly or other periodic payment	
		g. Maturity date	

[UCS Rev. 6/2016]

		h. Amount of debt as of date of commencement	
		i. Amount of current debt	
		TOTAL: Mortgages Payable	
D.	4.	Home Equity and Other Lines of Credit	
		4.1 a. Name and address of mortgagee	
		b. Address of property mortgaged	
		c. Mortgagor(s)	
		d. Original debt	
		e. Date of incurring debt	
		f. Monthly or other periodic payment	
		g. Maturity date	
		h. Amount of current debt	
		i. Current equity	
E.	6.	Notes Payable	
		6.1 a. Name and address of noteholder	
		b. Debtor	
		c. Amount of original debt	
		d. Date of incurring debt	
		e. Purpose	
		f. Monthly or other periodic payment	
		g. Amount of debt as of date of commencement	
		h. Amount of current debt	
		TOTAL: Notes Payable	$
F.	7.	Brokers Margin Accounts	
		7.1 a. Name and address of broker	
		b. Amount of original debt	
		c. Date of incurring debt	

[UCS Rev. 6/2016]

		d. Purpose	
		e. Monthly or other periodic payment	
		f. Amount of debt as of date of commencement	
		g. Amount of current debt	
		TOTAL: Broker's Margin Accounts	
G.	8.	Taxes Payable	
		8.1 a. Description of Tax	
		b. Amount of Tax	
		c. Date Due	
		TOTAL: Taxes Payable	$
H.	9.	Loans on Life Insurance Policies	
		9.1 a. Name and address of insurer	
		b. Amount of loan	
		c. Date incurred	
		d. Purpose	
		e. Name of Borrower	
		f. Monthly or other periodic payment	
		g. Amount of debt as of date of commencement	
		h. Amount of current debt	
		TOTAL: Loans on Life Insurance	
I.	10.	Installment accounts payable (security agreements, chattel mortgages)	
		10.1 a. Name and address of creditor	
		b. Debtor	
		c. Amount of original debt	
		d. Date of incurring debt	
		e. Purpose	

		f. Monthly or other periodic payment	
		g. Amount of debt as of date of commencement	
		h. Amount of current debt	
		TOTAL: Installment Accounts	$
J.	11.	Other Liabilities	
		11.1 a. Description	
		b. Name and address of creditor	
		c. Debtor	
		d. Original amount of debt	
		e. Date incurred	
		f. Purpose	
		g. Monthly or other periodic payment	
		h. Amount of debt as of date of commencement	
		i. Amount of current debt	
		11.2 a. Description	
		b. Name and address of creditor	
		c. Debtor	
		d. Original amount of debt	
		e. Date incurred	
		f. Purpose	
		g. Monthly or other periodic payment	
		h. Amount of debt as of date of commencement	
		i. Amount of current debt	
		TOTAL: Other Liabilities	$
		TOTAL LIABILITIES	$

[UCS Rev. 6/2016]

VI. ASSETS TRANSFERRED

List all assets transferred in any manner during the preceding three years, or length of the marriage, whichever is shorter. Note: Transfers in the routine course of business which resulted in an exchange of assets of substantially equivalent value need not be specifically disclosed where such assets are otherwise identified in the Statement of Net Worth.

Description of Property	To Whom Transferred and Relationship to Transferee	Date of Transfer	Value

VII. LEGAL & EXPERT FEES

Please state the amount you have paid to all lawyers and experts retained in connection with your marital dissolution, including name of professional, amounts and dates paid, and source of funds. Attach retainer agreement for your present attorney.

____

VIII. OTHER DATA CONCERNING THE FINANCIAL CIRCUMSTANCES OF THE PARTIES THAT SHOULD BE BROUGHT TO THE ATTENTION OF THE COURT ARE:

____

The foregoing statements and a rider consisting of_____ page(s) annexed hereto and made a part hereof, have been carefully read by the undersigned who states that they are true and correct and states same, under oath, subject to the penalties of perjury.

____

Sworn to before me this
day of____________, 2015

This is the_______ Statement of Net Worth
I have filed in this proceeding.

____
Notary Public

Attorney Certification:

____

REQUIRED ATTACHMENTS:

Retainer Agreement

Most recent W-2, 1009s, K1s and Income Tax Returns

[UCS Rev. 6/2016]

APPENDIX S

Required Statutory Forms for Financial Disclosure (California)

FL-140

ATTORNEY OR PARTY WITHOUT ATTORNEY *(Name, State Bar number, and address)*:	
2: FILING ATTORNEY'S NAME 75: SBN 4: NAME OF LAW FIRM FILING ACTION 5: STREET ADDRESS OF FIRM FILING ACTION 6: CITY STATE AND ZIP CODE OF FIRM TELEPHONE NO.: 3: FIRM PHONE # FAX NO.: 76: FIRM FAX # E-MAIL ADDRESS: 169: E-MAIL ADDRESS ATTORNEY FOR *(Name)*: 7: ATTORNEY FOR NAME	
SUPERIOR COURT OF CALIFORNIA, COUNTY OF 101: COUNTY FILED STREET ADDRESS: 9: STREET ADDRESS OF COURT MAILING ADDRESS: 10: POST OFFICE ADDRESS OF COURT CITY AND ZIP CODE: 11: CITY STATE AND ZIP OF COURT BRANCH NAME: 12: BRANCH OF COURT	
PETITIONER: 13: PLAINTIFF/PETITIONER LINE ONE RESPONDENT: 15: DEFENDANT/RESPONDENT LINE ONE OTHER PARENT/PARTY: 21: OTHER PARENT	
DECLARATION OF DISCLOSURE ☐ Petitioner's ☐ Preliminary ☐ Respondent's ☐ Final	CASE NUMBER: 17: CASE NUMBER

DO NOT FILE DECLARATIONS OF DISCLOSURE OR FINANCIAL ATTACHMENTS WITH THE COURT

In a dissolution, legal separation, or nullity action, both a preliminary and a final declaration of disclosure must be served on the other party with certain exceptions. Neither disclosure is filed with the court. Instead, a declaration stating that service of disclosure documents was completed or waived must be filed with the court (see form FL-141).

- *In summary dissolution cases, each spouse or domestic partner must exchange preliminary disclosures as described in* Summary Dissolution Information *(form FL-810). Final disclosures are not required (see Family Code section 2109).*
- *In a default judgment case that is not a stipulated judgment or a judgment based on a marital settlement agreement, only the petitioner is required to complete and serve a preliminary declaration of disclosure. A final disclosure is not required of either party (see Family Code section 2110).*
- *Service of preliminary declarations of disclosure may not be waived by an agreement between the parties.*
- *Parties who agree to waive final declarations of disclosure must file their written agreement with the court (see form FL-144).*

The petitioner must serve a preliminary declaration of disclosure at the same time as the Petition or within 60 days of filing the Petition. The respondent must serve a preliminary declaration of disclosure at the same time as the Response or within 60 days of filing the Response. The time periods may be extended by written agreement of the parties or by court order (see Family Code section 2104(f)).

Attached are the following:

1. ☐ A completed *Schedule of Assets and Debts* (form FL-142) or ☐ A *Property Declaration* (form FL-160) for *(specify)*:
   ☐ Community and Quasi-Community Property ☐ Separate Property.
2. ☐ A completed *Income and Expense Declaration* (form FL-150).
3. ☐ All tax returns filed by the party in the two years before the date that the party served the disclosure documents.
4. ☐ A statement of all material facts and information regarding valuation of all assets that are community property or in which the community has an interest *(not a form)*.
5. ☐ A statement of all material facts and information regarding obligations for which the community is liable *(not a form)*.
6. ☐ An accurate and complete written disclosure of any investment opportunity, business opportunity, or other income-producing opportunity presented since the date of separation that results from any investment, significant business, or other income-producing opportunity from the date of marriage to the date of separation *(not a form)*.

I declare under penalty of perjury under the laws of the State of California that the foregoing is true and correct.

Date:

____________________ ▶ ____________________

(TYPE OR PRINT NAME) SIGNATURE

1: SAMPLE CLIENT

FL-141

ATTORNEY OR PARTY WITHOUT ATTORNEY (Name, State Bar number, and address): 2: FILING ATTORNEY'S NAME 75: SBN 4: NAME OF LAW FIRM FILING ACTION 5: STREET ADDRESS OF FIRM FILING ACTION 6: CITY STATE AND ZIP CODE OF FIRM	
TELEPHONE NO.: 3: FIRM PHONE # FAX NO.: 76: FIRM FAX # E-MAIL ADDRESS: 169: E-MAIL ADDRESS ATTORNEY FOR (Name): 7: ATTORNEY FOR NAME	
SUPERIOR COURT OF CALIFORNIA, COUNTY OF 101: COUNTY FILED STREET ADDRESS: 9: STREET ADDRESS OF COURT MAILING ADDRESS: 10: POST OFFICE ADDRESS OF COURT CITY AND ZIP CODE: 11: CITY STATE AND ZIP OF COURT BRANCH NAME: 12: BRANCH OF COURT	
PETITIONER: 13: PLAINTIFF/PETITIONER LINE ONE RESPONDENT: 15: DEFENDANT/RESPONDENT LINE ONE OTHER PARENT/PARTY: 21: OTHER PARENT	
DECLARATION REGARDING SERVICE OF DECLARATION OF DISCLOSURE AND INCOME AND EXPENSE DECLARATION ☐ Petitioner's ☐ Preliminary ☐ Respondent's ☐ Final	CASE NUMBER: 17: CASE NUMBER

1. I am the ☐ attorney for ☐ petitioner ☐ respondent in this matter.

2. ☐ Petitioner's ☐ Respondent's *Preliminary Declaration of Disclosure* (form FL-140), current* *Income and Expense Declaration* (form FL-150), completed *Schedule of Assets and Debts* (form FL-142) or *Community and Separate Property Declarations* (form FL-160) with appropriate attachments, all tax returns filed by the party in the two years before service of the preliminary disclosures, and all other required information under Family Code section 2104 were served on:
☐ the other party ☐ the other party's attorney by ☐ personal service ☐ mail
☐ Other *(specify):*
on *(date):*

3. ☐ Petitioner's ☐ Respondent's *Final Declaration of Disclosure* (form FL-140), current* *Income and Expense Declaration* (form FL-150), completed *Schedule of Assets and Debts* (form FL-142) or *Community or Separate Property Declarations* (form FL-160) with attachments, and the material facts and information required by Family Code section 2105 were served on:
☐ the other party ☐ other party's attorney by ☐ personal service ☐ mail
☐ Other *(specify):*
on *(date):*

4. ☐ Service of ☐ Petitioner's ☐ Respondent's ☐ preliminary ☐ final declaration of disclosure
☐ current income and expense declaration has been waived as follows:
   a. ☐ The parties agreed to waive final declaration of disclosure requirements under Family Code section 2105(d.) (Form FL-144 may be used for this purpose.) The waiver ☐ was filed on *(date):*
   ☐ is being filed at the same time as this form.
   b. ☐ The party has failed to comply with disclosure requirements, and the court has granted the request for voluntary waiver of receipt under Family Code section 2107 on *(date):*
   c. ☐ This is a default proceeding that does not include a stipulated judgment or settlement agreement. Petitioner waives final disclosure requirements under Family Code section 2110.

**Current* is defined as completed within the past three months providing no facts have changed. (Cal. Rules of Court, rule 5.260.)

I declare under penalty of perjury under the laws of the State of California that the foregoing is true and correct.

Date:

_______________________________ ▶ _______________________________
(TYPE OR PRINT NAME) SIGNATURE

NOTE: File this document with the court. Do not file a copy of the Preliminary or Final Declaration of Disclosure or any attachments to either declaration of disclosure with this document.

Form Adopted for Mandatory Use
Judicial Council of California
FL-141 [Rev. July 1, 2013]

DECLARATION REGARDING SERVICE OF DECLARATION OF DISCLOSURE AND INCOME AND EXPENSE DECLARATION
(Family Law)

Family Code, §§ 2102, 2104, 2105, 2106, 2112
www.courts.ca.gov

1: SAMPLE CLIENT

THIS FORM SHOULD NOT BE FILED WITH THE COURT FL-142

ATTORNEY OR PARTY WITHOUT ATTORNEY *(Name and Address):* 2: FILING ATTORNEY'S NAME 4: NAME OF LAW FIRM FILING ACTION 5: STREET ADDRESS OF FIRM FILING ACTION 6: CITY STATE AND ZIP CODE OF FIRM ATTORNEY FOR *(Name):* 7: ATTORNEY FOR NAME	TELEPHONE NO.: 3: FIRM PHONE #
SUPERIOR COURT OF CALIFORNIA, COUNTY OF 101: COUNTY FILED	
PETITIONER: 13: PLAINTIFF/PETITIONER LINE ONE RESPONDENT: 15: DEFENDANT/RESPONDENT LINE ONE	
SCHEDULE OF ASSETS AND DEBTS ☐ Petitioner's ☐ Respondent's	CASE NUMBER: 17: CASE NUMBER

- INSTRUCTIONS -

List all your known community and separate assets or debts. Include assets even if they are in the possession of another person, including your spouse. If you contend an asset or debt is separate, put P (for Petitioner) or R (for Respondent) in the first column (separate property) to indicate to whom you contend it belongs.

All values should be as of the date of signing the declaration unless you specify a different valuation date with the description. For additional space, use a continuation sheet numbered to show which item is being continued.

ITEM NO.	ASSETS DESCRIPTION	SEP. PROP	DATE ACQUIRED	CURRENT GROSS FAIR MARKET VALUE	AMOUNT OF MONEY OWED OR ENCUMBRANCE
1.	REAL ESTATE *(Give street addresses and attach copies of deeds with legal descriptions and latest lender's statement.)*			$	$
2.	HOUSEHOLD FURNITURE, FURNISHINGS, APPLIANCES *(Identify.)*				
3.	JEWELRY, ANTIQUES, ART, COIN COLLECTIONS, etc. *(Identify.)*				

Form Approved for Optional Use
Judicial Council of California
FL-142 [Rev. January 1, 2005]

SCHEDULE OF ASSETS AND DEBTS
(Family Law)

Code of Civil Procedure, §§ 2030(c), 2033.5
www.courtinfo.ca.gov

1: SAMPLE CLIENT

ITEM NO. ASSETS DESCRIPTION	SEP. PROP	DATE ACQUIRED	CURRENT GROSS FAIR MARKET VALUE	AMOUNT OF MONEY OWED OR ENCUMBRANCE
4. VEHICLES, BOATS, TRAILERS *(Describe and attach copy of title document.)*			$	$
5. SAVINGS ACCOUNTS *(Account name, account number, bank, and branch. Attach copy of latest statement.)*				
6. CHECKING ACCOUNTS *(Account name and number, bank, and branch. Attach copy of latest statement.)*				
7. CREDIT UNION, OTHER DEPOSIT ACCOUNTS *(Account name and number, bank, and branch. Attach copy of latest statement.)*				
8. CASH *(Give location.)*				
9. TAX REFUND				
10. LIFE INSURANCE WITH CASH SURRENDER OR LOAN VALUE *(Attach copy of declaration page for each policy.)*				

ITEM NO.	ASSETS DESCRIPTION	SEP. PROP	DATE ACQUIRED	CURRENT GROSS FAIR MARKET VALUE	AMOUNT OF MONEY OWED OR ENCUMBRANCE
				$	$
11.	STOCKS, BONDS, SECURED NOTES, MUTUAL FUNDS *(Give certificate number and attach copy of the certificate or copy of latest statement.)*				
12.	RETIREMENT AND PENSIONS *(Attach copy of latest summary plan documents and latest benefit statement.)*				
13.	PROFIT-SHARING, ANNUITIES, IRAS, DEFERRED COMPENSATION *(Attach copy of latest statement.)*				
14.	ACCOUNTS RECEIVABLE AND UNSECURED NOTES *(Attach copy of each.)*				
15.	PARTNERSHIPS AND OTHER BUSINESS INTERESTS *(Attach copy of most current K-1 form and Schedule C.)*				
16.	OTHER ASSETS				
17.	TOTAL ASSETS FROM CONTINUATION SHEET				
18.	TOTAL ASSETS			$ 0	$ 0

ITEM NO.	DEBTS-SHOW TO WHOM OWED	SEP. PROP	TOTAL OWING	DATE INCURRED
			$	
19.	STUDENT LOANS *(Give details.)*			
20.	TAXES *(Give details.)*			
21.	SUPPORT ARREARAGES *(Attach copies of orders and statements.)*			
22.	LOANS - UNSECURED *(Give bank name and loan number and attach copy of latest statement.)*			
23.	CREDIT CARDS *(Give creditor's name and address and the account number. Attach copy of latest statement.)*			
24.	OTHER DEBTS *(Specify.)*:			
25.	TOTAL DEBTS FROM CONTINUATION SHEET			
26.	TOTAL DEBTS		$ 0	

27. ☐ *(Specify number)*: ______ pages are attached as continuation sheets.

I declare under penalty of perjury under the laws of the State of California that the foregoing is true and correct.

Date:

______________________________ ▶ ______________________________

(TYPE OR PRINT NAME) (SIGNATURE OF DECLARANT)

1: SAMPLE CLIENT

FL-150

ATTORNEY OR PARTY WITHOUT ATTORNEY *(Name, State Bar number, and address)*:	FOR COURT USE ONLY
2: FILING ATTORNEY'S NAME 75: SBN 4: NAME OF LAW FIRM FILING ACTION 5: STREET ADDRESS OF FIRM FILING ACTION 6: CITY STATE AND ZIP CODE OF FIRM TELEPHONE NO.: 3: FIRM PHONE # 76: FIRM FAX # E-MAIL ADDRESS *(Optional)*: 169: E-MAIL ADDRESS ATTORNEY FOR *(Name)*: 7: ATTORNEY FOR NAME	
SUPERIOR COURT OF CALIFORNIA, COUNTY OF 101: COUNTY FILED STREET ADDRESS: 9: STREET ADDRESS OF COURT MAILING ADDRESS: 10: POST OFFICE ADDRESS OF COURT CITY AND ZIP CODE: 11: CITY STATE AND ZIP OF COURT BRANCH NAME: 12: BRANCH OF COURT	
PETITIONER/PLAINTIFF: 13: PLAINTIFF/PETITIONER LINE ONE RESPONDENT/DEFENDANT: 15: DEFENDANT/RESPONDENT LINE ONE OTHER PARENT/CLAIMANT: 21: OTHER PARENT	
INCOME AND EXPENSE DECLARATION	CASE NUMBER: 17: CASE NUMBER

1. **Employment** *(Give information on your current job or, if you're unemployed, your most recent job.)*

Attach copies of your pay stubs for last two months (black out social security numbers).

a. Employer:
b. Employer's address: 30: OUR CLIENT'S BUSINESS ADDRESS
c. Employer's phone number: 32: OUR CLIENT'S BUSINESS
d. Occupation: 33: OUR CLIENT'S OCCUPATION
e. Date job started:
f. If unemployed, date job ended:
g. I work about hours per week.
h. I get paid $ gross (before taxes) ☐ per month ☐ per week ☐ per hour.

(If you have more than one job, attach an 8 1/2-by-11-inch sheet of paper and list the same information as above for your other jobs. Write "Question 1 - Other Jobs" at the top.)

2. **Age and education**
   a. My age is *(specify)*: 23:
   b. I have completed high school or the equivalent: ☐ Yes ☐ No If no, highest grade completed *(specify)*:
   c. Number of years of college completed *(specify)*: ☐ Degree(s) obtained *(specify)*:
   d. Number of years of graduate school completed *(specify)*: ☐ Degree(s) obtained *(specify)*:
   e. I have: ☐ professional/occupational license(s) *(specify)*:
      ☐ vocational training *(specify)*:
3. **Tax information**
   a. ☐ I last filed taxes for tax year *(specify year)*:
   b. My tax filing status is ☐ single ☐ head of household ☐ married, filing separately
      ☐ married, filing jointly with *(specify name)*:
   c. I file state tax returns in ☐ California ☐ other *(specify state)*:
   d. I claim the following number of exemptions (including myself) on my taxes *(specify)*:
4. **Other party's income.** I estimate the gross monthly income (before taxes) of the other party in this case at *(specify)*: $
   This estimate is based on *(explain)*:

(If you need more space to answer any questions on this form, attach an 8 1/2-by-11-inch sheet of paper and write the question number before your answer.) Number of pages attached: ______

I declare under penalty of perjury under the laws of the State of California that the information contained on all pages of this form and any attachments is true and correct.

Date:

______________________ ▶ ______________________
(TYPE OR PRINT NAME) (SIGNATURE OF DECLARANT)

Form Adopted for Mandatory Use
Judicial Council of California
FL-150 [Rev. January 1, 2007]

Martin Dean's ESSENTIAL FORMS™

INCOME AND EXPENSE DECLARATION

Family Code, §§ 2030-2032, 2100-2113, 3552, 3620-3634, 4050-4076, 4300-4339
www.courtinfo.ca.gov

1: SAMPLE CLIENT

FL-150

PETITIONER/PLAINTIFF: 13: PLAINTIFF/PETITIONER LINE ONE	CASE NUMBER:
RESPONDENT/DEFENDANT: 15: DEFENDANT/RESPONDENT LINE ONE	17: CASE NUMBER
OTHER PARENT/CLAIMANT: 21: OTHER PARENT	

Attach copies of your pay stubs for the last two months and proof of any other income. Take a copy of your latest federal tax return to the court hearing. ***(Black out your social security number on the pay stub and tax return.)***

	Last month	Average monthly
5. **Income** *(For average monthly, add up all the income you received in each category in the last 12 months and divide the total by 12.)*		
a. Salary or wages (gross, before taxes)	$	
b. Overtime (gross, before taxes)	$	
c. Commissions or bonuses	$	
d. Public assistance (for example: TANF, SSI, GA/GR) ☐ currently receiving	$	
e. Spousal support ☐ from this marriage ☐ from a different marriage	$	
f. Partner support ☐ from this domestic partnership ☐ from a different domestic partnership	$	
g. Pension/retirement fund payments	$	
h. Social security retirement (not SSI)	$	
i. Disability: ☐ Social security (not SSI) ☐ State disability (SDI) ☐ Private insurance.	$	
j. Unemployment compensation	$	
k. Workers' compensation	$	
l. Other (military BAQ, royalty payments, etc.) *(specify)*:	$	
6. **Investment income** *(Attach a schedule showing gross receipts less cash expenses for each piece of property.)*		
a. Dividends/interest	$	
b. Rental property income	$	
c. Trust income	$	
d. Other *(specify)*:	$	
7. **Income from self-employment, after business expenses for all businesses**	$	

I am the ☐ owner/sole proprietor ☐ business partner ☐ other *(specify)*:

Number of years in this business *(specify)*:

Name of business *(specify)*:

Type of business *(specify)*:

Attach a profit and loss statement for the last two years or a Schedule C from your last federal tax return. Black out your social security number. If you have more than one business, provide the information above for each of your businesses.

8. ☐ **Additional income.** I received one-time money (lottery winnings, inheritance, etc.) in the last 12 months *(specify source and amount)*:

9. ☐ **Change in income.** My financial situation has changed significantly over the last 12 months because *(specify)*:

10. **Deductions**	Last month
a. Required union dues	$
b. Required retirement payments (not social security, FICA, 401(k), or IRA)	$
c. Medical, hospital, dental, and other health insurance premiums *(total monthly amount)*	$
d. Child support that I pay for children from other relationships	$
e. Spousal support that I pay by court order from a different marriage	$
f. Partner support that I pay by court order from a different domestic partnership	$
g. Necessary job-related expenses not reimbursed by my employer *(attach explanation labeled "Question 10g")*	$

11. **Assets**	Total
a. Cash and checking accounts, savings, credit union, money market, and other deposit accounts	$
b. Stocks, bonds, and other assets I could easily sell	$
c. All other property, ☐ real and ☐ personal *(estimate fair market value minus the debts you owe)*	$

FL-150

PETITIONER/PLAINTIFF: 13: PLAINTIFF/PETITIONER LINE ONE RESPONDENT/DEFENDANT: 15: DEFENDANT/RESPONDENT LINE ONE OTHER PARENT/CLAIMANT: 21: OTHER PARENT	CASE NUMBER: 17: CASE NUMBER

12. **The following people live with me:**

Name	Age	How the person is related to me? *(ex: son)*	That person's gross monthly income	Pays some of the household expenses?
a.				☐ Yes ☐ No
b.				☐ Yes ☐ No
c.				☐ Yes ☐ No
d.				☐ Yes ☐ No
e.				☐ Yes ☐ No

13. **Average monthly expenses** ☐ Estimated expenses ☐ Actual expenses ☐ Proposed needs

a. Home:
   (1) ☐ Rent or ☐ mortgage $
   If mortgage:
   (a) average principal: $
   (b) average interest: $
   (2) Real property taxes $
   (3) Homeowner's or renter's insurance (if not included above) $
   (4) Maintenance and repair $

b. Health-care costs not paid by insurance $

c. Child care $

d. Groceries and household supplies $

e. Eating out $

f. Utilities (gas, electric, water, trash) $

g. Telephone, cell phone, and e-mail $

h. Laundry and cleaning $

i. Clothes $

j. Education $

k. Entertainment, gifts, and vacation $

l. Auto expenses and transportation (insurance, gas, repairs, bus, etc.) $

m. Insurance (life, accident, etc.; do not include auto, home, or health insurance) $

n. Savings and investments $

o. Charitable contributions $

p. Monthly payments listed in item 14 *(itemize below in 14 and insert total here)* $ 0

q. Other *(specify)* : $

r. TOTAL EXPENSES (a-q) *(do not add in the amounts in a(1)(a) and (b))* $ 0

s. **Amount of expenses paid by others** $

14. **Installment payments and debts not listed above**

Paid to	For	Amount	Balance	Date of last payment
		$	$	
		$	$	
		$	$	
		$	$	
		$	$	
		$	$	

15. **Attorney fees** *(This is required if either party is requesting attorney fees.)*:
   a. To date, I have paid my attorney this amount for fees and costs *(specify)* : $
   b. The source of this money was *(specify)* :
   c. I still owe the following fees and costs to my attorney *(specify total owed)* : $
   d. My attorney's hourly rate is *(specify)* : $

I confirm this fee arrangement.

Date:

2: FILING ATTORNEY'S NAME ▶ ____________________
(TYPE OR PRINT NAME OF ATTORNEY) (SIGNATURE OF ATTORNEY)

1: SAMPLE CLIENT

FL-150

PETITIONER/PLAINTIFF: 13: PLAINTIFF/PETITIONER LINE ONE RESPONDENT/DEFENDANT: 15: DEFENDANT/RESPONDENT LINE ONE OTHER PARENT/CLAIMANT: 21: OTHER PARENT	CASE NUMBER: 17: CASE NUMBER

CHILD SUPPORT INFORMATION
(NOTE: Fill out this page only if your case involves child support.)

16. **Number of children**
   a. I have *(specify number)*: children under the age of 18 with the other parent in this case.
   b. The children spend percent of their time with me and percent of their time with the other parent.
   (If you're not sure about percentage or it has not been agreed on, please describe your parenting schedule here.)

17. **Children's health-care expenses**
   a. ☐ I do ☐ I do not have health insurance available to me for the children through my job.
   b. Name of insurance company:
   c. Address of insurance company:

   d. The monthly cost for the **children's** health insurance is or would be *(specify)*: $
   (Do not include the amount your employer pays.)

18. **Additional expenses for the children in this case** — Amount per month
   a. Child care so I can work or get job training .... $
   b. Children's health care not covered by insurance .... $
   c. Travel expenses for visitation .... $
   d. Children's educational or other special needs *(specify below)*: .... $

19. **Special hardships.** I ask the court to consider the following special financial circumstances *(attach documentation of any item listed here, including court orders)*: — Amount per month — For how many months?
   a. Extraordinary health expenses not included in 18b .... $ ________ ________
   b. Major losses not covered by insurance (examples: fire, theft, other insured loss) .... $ ________ ________
   c. (1) Expenses for my minor children who are from other relationships and are living with me .... $ ________ ________
   (2) Names and ages of those children *(specify)*:

   (3) Child support I receive for those children .... $
   The expenses listed in a, b and c create an extreme financial hardship because *(explain)*:

20. **Other information I want the court to know concerning support in my case** *(specify)*:

APPENDIX T

Court Endorsement of ADR (San Mateo County)

ATTORNEY OR PARTY WITHOUT ATTORNEY (Name and Address) TELEPHONE NO.: ATTORNEY FOR (Name):	FOR COURT USE ONLY
SUPERIOR COURT OF CALIFORNIA, COUNTY OF SAN MATEO STREET ADDRESS: MAILING ADDRESS: CITY AND ZIP CODE: BRANCH NAME:	
PLAINTIFF/PETITIONER: **DEFENDANT/RESPONDENT:**	**CASE NUMBER:**

The San Mateo County Superior Court recommends Alternative Dispute Resolution options in lieu of formal court litigation.

"Alternative" or "Appropriate" Dispute Resolution (ADR) is a general term for methods of resolving a dispute without going through the formal court process. ADR can save you time, money, and increase your overall satisfaction with the outcome of your case.

ADR can be used at any point in your case to resolve disputes regarding property division, child support, spousal support, paternity, child custody, parenting plans, and many other family law issues.

Did you know that the vast majority of cases filed in court (95-98%) do not go to trial? Most cases are settled or decided in some other way. But in many cases, the settlement comes only after considerable resources have been expended. This is why the San Mateo County Superior Court supports the use of dispute resolution alternatives at the earliest possible time. Local Rule 5.5(A) states:

> California Rules of Court and the Family Law Act strongly encourage alternative dispute resolution (ADR) of family matters. The Family Law Department recognizes that formal litigation of legal claims and disputes is expensive and time consuming. The goals of this Court are: to reduce hostilities between the parties; facilitate the early resolution of issues; and provide parties with an opportunity to maximize their satisfaction with the resolution of their case. It is therefore the policy of this Court to promote and encourage the parties to settle their disputes by the use of appropriate dispute resolution options which include mediation, arbitration, collaborative practice, court supervised settlement conferences and/or judicial case management.

The court strongly encourages the use of ADR but does not favor any particular form of ADR, endorse any particular attorney, nor guarantee the outcome in any particular case.

Instructions: All parties and counsel shall read the Notice, sign on page three, and have this Notice served on the other party with any Petition or Response under the Family Law Act, Uniform Parentage Act, Order to Show Cause, Response to Order to Show Cause, Notice of Motion, Response to Notice of Motion, or any other family law pleading which will result in a court hearing or trial. A proof of service shall be filed with the Court. ***(Local Rule 5.5)(B)***

PLAINTIFF/PETITIONER: DEFENDANT/RESPONDENT:	CASE NUMBER:

DESCRIPTION OF SERVICES AND COST:

The Court manages a panel of attorneys with special training in mediation and arbitration and a commitment to finding alternatives to formal litigation. The attorneys who serve on the ADR panel have agreed to offer participants a 90-minute session for $100 ($50 per party). Additional sessions are available at the attorney's market rate. For more information call the ADR office at: (650) 261-5076 or (650) 261-5075, or visit the website at: www.sanmateocourt.org/court_divisions/adr/family_law/.

- **Mediation**

  Mediation through the ADR program is voluntary. A neutral attorney called a "mediator" meets with parties and/or their attorneys to assist them in reaching an agreement. The mediator facilitates communication between the participants, clarifies issues, explores each party's needs and interests, and helps the participants to consider options for settlement.

  The parties may resolve a single issue or the entire case. The agreements reached in mediation are not limited by the results available under the law so mediated solutions can more easily accommodate the circumstances of individual cases. An agreement reached in mediation is binding once it is turned into a court order and signed by the Judge. You cannot be forced to accept a decision in mediation and participating in mediation does not impact your right to a court hearing. If an agreement is not reached you may continue through the court system.

  Mediation is private and confidential. The sessions are conducted in the mediator's office. Anything spoken or written during mediation by any of the participants is confidential and may not be disclosed to the Court or any other person without the consent of the participants.

- **Arbitration**

  Arbitration is private and less formal than a court trial. In arbitration a neutral attorney called the "arbitrator" makes a decision based on the information presented by both sides. The arbitrator then prepares a written decision and sends it to both parties and the Court. This court's ADR program offers binding arbitration with a neutral serving as a temporary judge. "Binding" means there is no right to appeal and you will accept the arbitrator's decision as final.

- **Collaborative Law**

  In the collaborative law process, you and the other party each have a private attorney and make a commitment to resolve your disputes without going to court. Similar to mediation, collaborative law operates in the spirit of honesty and cooperation. In the collaborative process, both parties together with professionals (attorneys, mental health and financial experts) work as a team to resolve disputes respectfully with an emphasis on financial responsibility and cooperative co-parenting. Collaborative Practice San Mateo County is a private organization of professionals specially trained in collaborative practice. For more information, fees, or for a list of professionals, please see their web site at: http://www.collaborative-law.com/ or call (650) 590-2228.

Instructions: All parties and counsel shall read the Notice, sign on page three, and have this Notice served on the other party with any Petition or Response under the Family Law Act, Uniform Parentage Act, Order to Show Cause, Response to Order to Show Cause, Notice of Motion, Response to Notice of Motion, or any other family law pleading which will result in a court hearing or trial. A proof of service shall be filed with the Court. *(Local Rule 5.5)(B)*

PLAINTIFF/PETITIONER:	CASE NUMBER:
DEFENDANT/RESPONDENT:	

FAMILY COURT SERVICES MEDIATION:

The Court encourages the use of the ADR options described above to resolve custody and parenting plan disputes. However, if you do not reach an agreement on these issues, California law requires you to meet with Family Court Services (FCS) before submitting these issues to a Judge. FCS will first attempt to settle the issues through mediation, however, if no agreement is reached then the FCS counselor will prepare a written recommendation to the Court based upon the best interests of the child(ren). FCS mediation is not confidential and does not address your property or financial disputes. There is no fee for mediation with FCS.

DOMESTIC VIOLENCE AND ADR:

ADR is most effective when parties are able to communicate and solve problems without fear or intimidation. For this reason when there is a history of domestic violence in a relationship, ADR may not be appropriate.

The undersigned certifies that s/he has read this Notice in compliance with San Mateo County Local Rule 5.5.

Date: Date:

Signature of Petitioner Signature or Respondent

Attorney certification of compliance with San Mateo County Local Rule 5.5:

Date: Date:

Signature of Attorney for Petitioner Signature of Attorney for Respondent

Instructions: All parties and counsel shall read the Notice, sign on page three, and have this Notice served on the other party with any Petition or Response under the Family Law Act, Uniform Parentage Act, Order to Show Cause, Response to Order to Show Cause, Notice of Motion, Response to Notice of Motion, or any other family law pleading which will result in a court hearing or trial. A proof of service shall be filed with the Court. *(Local Rule 5.5)(B)*

APPENDIX U

Letter from Presiding Judge of Family Law Division Endorsing Mediation (English and Spanish)

The Los Angeles Superior Court has long distributed letters to family law litigants identifying self-help resources and encouraging consideration of non-litigation dispute resolution processes.

In 2017, the Los Angeles Superior Court updated its form letter to account for the advent of unbundled legal services. This updated letter (provided in both English and Spanish) identifies self-help resources, encourages consideration of various non-litigation dispute resolution processes, *and* specifically identifies limited scope/unbundled representation as an available option. In this letter, the court's former Supervising Judge of Family Law, Thomas Trent Lewis, credits Woody Mosten for playing an instrumental role in helping the court draft this update. This letter, bearing the signature of the local family court's supervising judge, is a testament to strong judicial support for limited scope representation and how attorneys and courts can work together to improve access to justice.

These letters are updated from time to time and can be useful to show your clients as a way of confirming judicial imprimatur and support for mediation. The protocols and guidance in different jurisdictions may vary. See whether such a letter or statement is available in your court. If available, review the letter with your client and invite a discussion about why and how mediation, unbundled services, Collaborative Law and other non-litigation options may be appropriate for your client and your client's family."

The Superior Court
STANLEY MOSK COURTHOUSE
FAMILY LAW DIVISION
111 NORTH HILL STREET
LOS ANGELES, CALIFORNIA 90012
CHAMBERS OF
THOMAS T. LEWIS
SUPERVISING JUDGE-FAMILY LAW

TELEPHONE
(213) 633-0252

Dear Parties:

I would like you to know that our court wants to help you and your family. I understand that you may be going through a confusing and difficult time and we have a number of resources to help you. The Court's website (www.LACourt.org) contains information that may help you understand the court process. Additionally, the Court has an easy-to-use web portal that allows parties needing language assistance in Family Law cases to request an interpreter free of charge in advance of their court hearing. The interpreter request form is available in English as well as in several other languages. While the court will make every effort to locate an interpreter for the date and time of the hearing, it cannot guarantee that one will be available. You may access the interpreter request portal by visiting the court's website at www.lacourt.org and clicking on the Language Access Services icon.

You may have a dispute with your spouse or the other party in the case regarding where your children will live, what support will be provided or how you will divide your property. You have the right to have a court hearing and have a judicial officer decide these matters for you. If you feel threatened by or fearful of your spouse or other party in this matter, there are ways to bring these concerns into court and get the protections allowed by law.

However, going to court is not the only way to resolve family law disputes. Many families find methods to agree to their own solutions. Some other ways include having attorneys and both spouses meet together to negotiate before going to court; having a neutral mediator help both sides negotiate a solution. You and spouse can work with a mediator without attorneys or have a lawyer come with you. Or you can use collaborative law in which the lawyers may work with financial and mental health professionals to use a team approach to help your family settle out of court. If you come to court, the court may be able to refer you to an expert attorney mediator volunteer.

Using a family law attorney can be very important to you. If you cannot afford a deposit (retainer) and are prepared to do some of the legal work yourself, many private attorneys and non-profit organizations offer unbundled legal services, also called Limited Scope Representation. If you cannot afford an attorney at all and you need to do all of the work yourself to complete your case, you can get guidance and information about workshops and assistance available at self-help centers in courthouses by visiting the court's website at www.lacourt.org and clicking on the Self-Help tab.

Using these and other tools to answer the questions you have and find solutions that both sides agree to may be better for several reasons: 1) You will directly participate in finding solutions; 2) You may be able to resolve your dispute sooner; 3) It may be much less expensive; 4) You may end the process with a better relationship with the other party; 5) You will likely find it less stressful than court and your children may feel less stress.

You can speak with your attorney, if you have one, about all of these methods of resolving your case. Some lawyers may offer you a free or low cost consultation to help you decide what process is best for you and your family.

I recommend that you focus on what is most important; moving to the next phase of your life. Many people spend time, effort and money attempting to obtain satisfaction by dragging out the dispute with the other party, but this does not guarantee either party will be fully satisfied with the outcome and may result in a way that does not benefit either of you.

If you have children, you must be particularly careful in choosing how to proceed. Everything you can do to avoid unnecessarily involving them in the dispute or engaging in conflict concerning them will benefit them and you. A successful agreement does not need to be perfect. For the mediation of disputes regarding your child(ren) and how they will spend time with each parent after divorce, the court offers a free mediation service through Family Court Services. To make an appointment via the internet, go to www.lacourt.org (click on Family and the On Line Services) or call (213) 830-0835.

Please save this letter and use it as a guide to the various alternatives available to you.

Sincerely,

Thomas Trent Lewis, Supervising Judge
Family Law Division

The Superior Court
STANLEY MOSK COURTHOUSE
FAMILY LAW DIVISION
111 NORTH HILL STREET
LOS ANGELES, CALIFORNIA 90012
CHAMBERS OF
THOMAS T. LEWIS
SUPERVISING JUDGE-FAMILY LAW

TELEPHONE
(213) 633-0252

Estimadas partes:

Quiero que sepa que la corte quiere ayudar a ustedes y a su familia. Comprendo que este puede ser un momento confuso y difícil, y contamos con recursos para ayudarlo. El sitio web de la corte (www.LACourt.org) tiene información que puede ayudarle a comprender el proceso de la corte. Además, la corte tiene un portal web fácil de usar si necesita ayuda con el idioma. En los casos de derecho familiar puede solicitar un intérprete sin cargo antes de su audiencia en la corte. Puede conseguir el formulario para solicitar un intérprete en inglés y varios idiomas más. Si bien la corte hará el mayor esfuerzo posible para ubicar a un intérprete para la fecha y hora de su audiencia, no garantizamos que haya uno disponible. Puede acceder al portal para solicitar intérprete en el sitio web de la corte www.lacourt.org haciendo clic en el icono *Language Access Services* (Servicios de idioma).

Es posible que tenga una disputa con su cónyuge, o con la otra parte del caso, sobre dónde van a vivir su hijos, el monto de manutención o cómo se van a repartir sus bienes. Usted tiene el derecho a pedir una audiencia en la corte para que un funcionario judicial decida estos temas. Si uno de ustedes se siente amenazado o tiene miedo de su cónyuge o la otra parte en el caso, hay maneras de informarle a la corte y obtener las protecciones permitidas por ley.

No obstante, la corte no es la única manera de resolver disputas de derecho familiar. Muchas familias encuentran maneras de ponerse de acuerdo por sí mismas. Por ejemplo, los abogados de las partes y ambos cónyuges pueden reunirse para negociar antes de ir a la corte, o pueden pedirle a un mediador neutral que les ayude a encontrar una solución. Usted y su cónyuge pueden trabajar con un mediador con o sin la participación de sus abogados. También pueden usar métodos de derecho colaborativo, donde los abogados se reúnen con profesionales de finanzas y de salud mental para tratar de llegar a un acuerdo en equipo fuera de la corte. Si acude a la corte, trataremos de remitirlo con un abogado con experiencia en mediación dispuesto a trabajar en forma voluntaria.

Un abogado de derecho familiar puede ser un recurso muy importante. Si no puede pagar el depósito (anticipo de honorarios) y está dispuesto a hacer algo del trabajo legal por su propia cuenta, muchos abogados privados y organizaciones sin fines de lucro ofrecen servicios "a la carta", también llamados de representación de alcance limitado. Si no tiene dinero para pagar un abogado y necesita hacer el trabajo legal por su propia cuenta para completar el caso, puede obtener guía e información sobre talleres y otro tipo de ayuda en los centros de ayuda de las cortes. Visite el sitio web en www.lacourt.org y haga clic en la ficha *Self-Help* (Autoayuda).

Usar estas y otras herramientas para aclarar dudas y encontrar soluciones que ambos puedan aceptar puede ser mejor por varias razones: 1) Participará en forma directa para encontrar las soluciones; 2) Podrá resolver su disputa más rápido; 3) Puede ser mucho más económico; 4) Puede terminar el caso manteniendo una mejor relación con la otra parte; 5) Es probable que el proceso sea menos estresante que ir a la corte y sus hijos también pueden sentir menos estrés.

Si tiene abogado, puede hablar con él sobre estos métodos de resolver su caso. Algunos abogados le pueden ofrecer una consulta gratis o de bajo costo para ayudarle a decidir el proceso que más le conviene a usted y su familia.

Le recomiendo que se enfoque en lo más importante: avanzar a la próxima fase de su vida. Mucha gente invierte tiempo, esfuerzo y dinero para tratar de obtener satisfacción prolongando la disputa con la otra parte, pero esto no garantiza que ninguna de las partes se sienta completamente satisfecha con el resultado, y puede terminar no beneficiando a nadie.

Si tiene hijos, tiene que tener mucho cuidado al decidir cómo proceder. Todo lo que haga para evitar que sus hijos se involucren en la disputa o el conflicto que les atañe será beneficioso no solo para ellos sino también para usted. Un acuerdo exitoso no tiene que ser perfecto. La corte ofrece un servicio de mediación sin cargo, a través de los Servicios de la Corte de Familia, para resolver disputas sobre sus hijos y cómo repartir el tiempo entre ambos padres después del divorcio. Si quiere hacer una cita en línea, visite www.lacourt.org (haga clic en *Family* [Familia] y después en *On Line Services* [Servicios en línea]). O llame al (213) 830-0835.

Guarde esta carta y úsela como guía sobre las diversas alternativas a su alcance.

Atentamente,

Thomas Trent Lewis, Juez Supervisor
División de Derecho Familiar

APPENDIX V

Hon. Lawrence Marks NYSUCS Press Release

PRESS RELEASE

New York State
Unified Court System

Hon. Lawrence K. Marks
Chief Administrative Judge

Contact:
Lucian Chalfen,
Public Information Director
Arlene Hackel, Deputy Director
(212) 428-2500

www.nycourts.gov/press

Date: May 14, 2019

Court System to Implement Presumptive, Early Alternative Dispute Resolution for Civil Cases

New York–In a transformational move to advance the delivery and quality of civil justice in New York as part of the Chief Judge's Excellence Initiative, Chief Judge Janet DiFiore and Chief Administrative Judge Lawrence K. Marks today announced a systemwide initiative in which, aside from appropriate exceptions, parties in civil cases will be referred to mediation or some other form of alternative dispute resolution (ADR) as the first step in the case proceeding in court. Dubbed "presumptive ADR," this model builds on prior successes of ADR in New York State and in other jurisdictions by referring cases routinely to mediation and other forms of ADR earlier in the life of a contested matter.

A broad range of civil cases, from personal injury and matrimonial cases to estate matters and commercial disputes, will, at the onset of the case, be directed to ADR–which comprises a variety of resolution approaches–with a focus on court-sponsored mediation. In mediation, a neutral facilitator works to foster negotiation and help narrow the issues, with a view toward settlement. ADR, especially mediation, helps the parties to understand each other's positions and interests, and consider options apart from conventional litigation to resolve their dispute, typically leading to more satisfying outcomes.

The large-scale initiative announced today, spurred by the recommendations of the Advisory Committee on ADR appointed last year by Chief Judge DiFiore, will build on the success of the courts' existing network of ADR programs. The court system, supported by its ADR Office, collaborates with trial courts, law schools and non-profit community dispute resolution centers around the State to offer parties access to free or reduced-fee ADR services in a variety of disputes, also assisting courts in maintaining rosters of ADR practitioners, among other responsibilities.

While the courts' ADR programs have grown in recent years, with thousands of New Yorkers benefiting from these services annually, court-sponsored mediation remains underutilized. Currently, most mediation referral relies on the parties to opt in to mediation or on individual judges to refer parties to mediation in individual cases. Transitioning to an early and presumptive ADR model–and expanding the scope of ADR to include the broadest possible range of civil case types–will play a significant role in decreasing costs to the parties and the judiciary and improving case outcomes as well as reducing case delays.

To accomplish this systemwide undertaking, Deputy Chief Administrative Judges George Silver and Michael Coccoma and their staffs, in collaboration with the statewide ADR coordinator, will work closely with Administrative Judges and trial court judges–and in consultation with local bar associations and other stakeholders–to expand the number and scope of court-sponsored ADR programs in their respective jurisdictions, taking steps to educate all participants in the constructive use of ADR.

The court system will issue uniform rules to authorize, endorse and provide a framework for courts to introduce and expand court-sponsored mediation programs, particularly early mediation via automatic presumptive referrals in identified types of civil disputes, subject to appropriate opt-out limitations.

The Administrative Judges will formulate plans tailored to local conditions and circumstances. The plans will take the fullest advantage of a wide range of existing resources, including volunteer mediators and neutrals on court rosters, judges, non-judicial staff, judicial hearing officers and community dispute resolution centers.

Implementation and rollout of this statewide program will begin in September, with local protocols, guidelines and best practices to be developed in each jurisdiction to facilitate the process. Additionally, comprehensive data will be collected to help evaluate the progress of court-sponsored ADR programs and allow for changes to improve the performance of programs going forward.

"Making ADR services widely available in civil courts throughout the State–and facilitating the use of such services as early as possible in the case–are major steps toward a more efficient, affordable and meaningful civil justice process. I commend the ADR Advisory Committee, led by John Kiernan, whose expertise and thoughtful study provided a foundation for this large-scale effort, as we strive to make ADR an integral part of our court culture," said Chief Judge DiFiore.

"Court-sponsored ADR has a proven record of success, with high settlement rates and strong user satisfaction among litigants and lawyers. We are eager to move ahead as we bring ADR into the mainstream, offering a far broader range of options to conventional litigation in our ongoing efforts to streamline the case management process and better serve the justice needs of New Yorkers," said Chief Administrative Judge Marks.

"This initiative reflects the strong evidence that court-sponsored automatic presumptive referral of disputes to early mediation often leads to upfront settlements, or to significant narrowing of disputes that foster future resolutions. Expanded early mediation will advance core goals of the Chief Judge's Excellence Initiative, promoting faster and less expensive outcomes, increasing parties' involvement in resolving their disputes and enhancing the administration of justice," said Mr. Kiernan, a partner at Debevoise & Plimpton.

A copy of the ADR committee's interim report is attached.

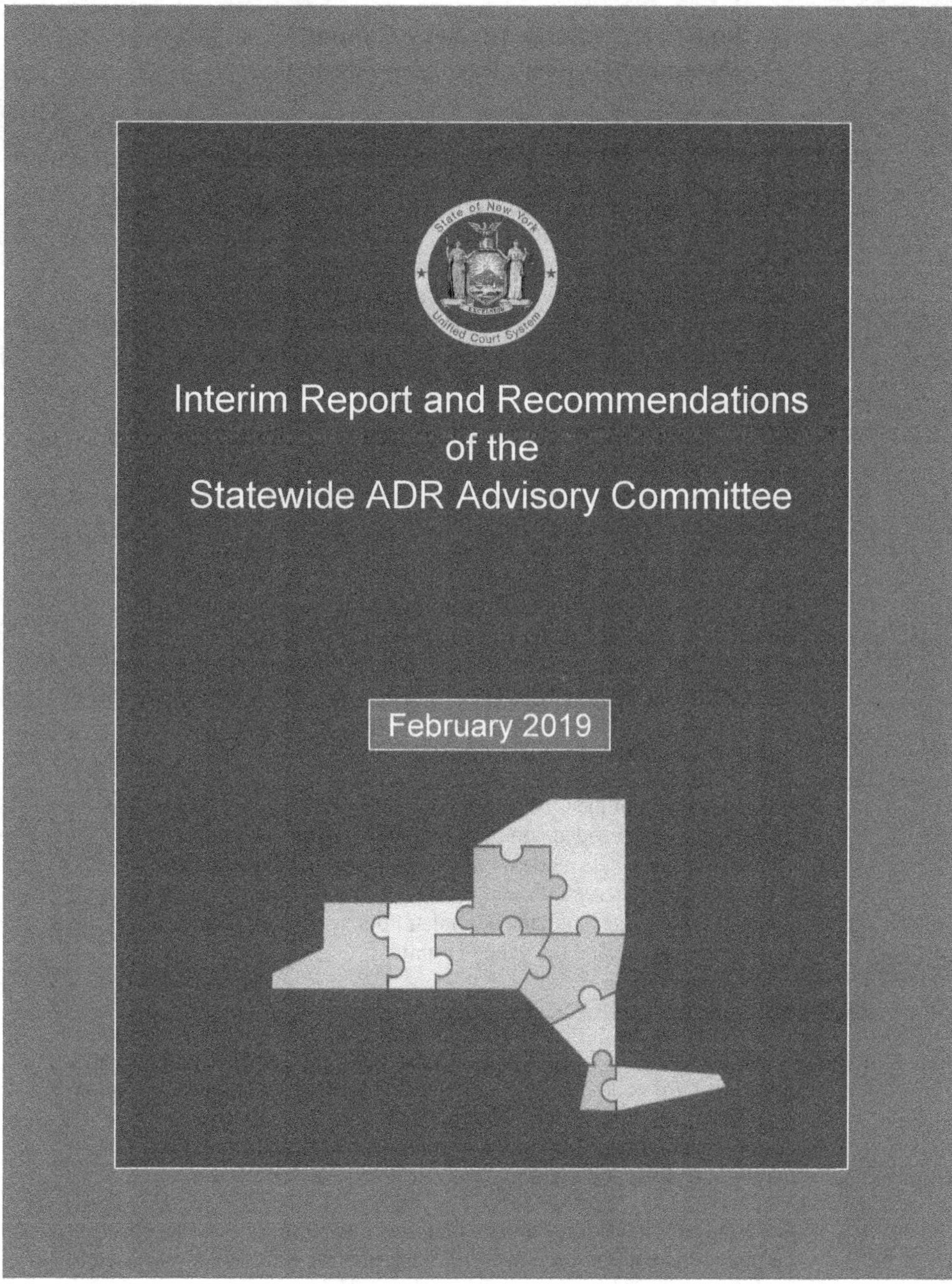

Interim Report and Recommendations
of the
Statewide ADR Advisory Committee

February 2019

Chief Judge's ADR Advisory Committee's Summary Interim Recommendations

1. **Significantly expand statewide infrastructures for developing and supporting court-sponsored ADR (and particularly court-sponsored mediation)**

   a. Expand the effectiveness and reach of the statewide Office of the ADR Coordinator by directing the District Administrative Judges for each Judicial District to appoint a dedicated local ADR Coordinator, and by funding positions, if necessary, for dedicated court staff to administer local ADR programs. Authorize each District Administrative Judge to appoint additional local Coordinators as necessary in individual counties and courts.

   b. Form a Statewide Judicial Leadership Team for ADR overseen by the Chief Administrative Judge to foster coordination of efforts, exchanges of information and experiences and expansion of court-sponsored ADR programs.

   c. Ask the District Administrative Judge and the ADR Coordinator(s) for each Judicial District – in consultation with the Statewide Judicial Leadership Team and the Office of the ADR Coordinator – to develop and present a plan for implementing expanded court-sponsored mediation programs (including study of existing programs, broadening of successful ones, development of new programs and tracking of program performance) in that Judicial District.

   d. Expand staffing of the Office of the ADR Coordinator to a degree that enables it to play needed coordinating, support, training, and communication roles, recognizing that as programs expand, there will be a greater need for increased training and education about court-sponsored mediation for judges, judicial administrators, court staff, advocates, parties, mediators, and the general public.

2. **Promulgate statewide uniform court rules**

   a. Issue statewide Uniform OCA Rules that authorize, endorse and provide a framework for courts to introduce and expand court-sponsored mediation programs – particularly including mediation early in disputes accomplished through automatic presumptive referrals (subject to appropriate opt-out limitations) of identified types of disputes.

   b. Generate templates of local rules that illustrate permitted options for particular mediation programs consistent with the framework presented by the Uniform Rules, and compile and make readily available a library of already adopted local rules, protocols, guidelines and best practices for existing programs to serve as resources for local programs implementing new programs.

3. **Increase court connections with and expand funding for Community Dispute Resolution Centers (CDRCs), as a significant component of scaling up existing court-connected programs**

   a. Make use of this already existing court-sponsored, statewide, high quality network of mediation providers and educators, which has infrastructure in place and is well situated to scale up quickly and effectively, take on increased referrals and train new mediators.

4. **Take steps to support, encourage, and educate about court-sponsored mediation**

   a. Use the ADR Advisory Committee, the Office of the ADR Coordinator, the Statewide Judicial Leadership Team and the ADR Coordinators in individual judicial districts to educate and encourage participants in the dispute resolution process in the effective use of court-sponsored mediation.

   b. Promulgate rules that require attorneys to become familiar with mediation and other processes, to discuss with clients both mediation and other potential alternatives to conventional litigation and to discuss ADR options with opposing counsel in good faith.

   c. Improve existing websites, court notices and other communications about the availability of court-sponsored mediation or other alternatives to conventional litigation.

   d. Expand trainings and communications with court personnel about administering court-sponsored mediation programs and serving as mediators.

   e. Expand trainings and communications with, and recruitment of, private mediators, to promote establishment of quality court-sponsored panels of approved mediators who will provide at least some mediation services without charge.

   f. Amend CLE rules to provide pro bono credit for periods when attorneys serve on court-approved mediator panels or provide other court-sponsored ADR services without charge.

g. Engage with and reach out to the legal community and law students concerning early mediation and other forms of ADR.

5. **Develop mechanisms for effective monitoring and evaluation of individual programs**

a. Establish mechanisms to identify and understand particular successes or shortcomings in existing programs and to identify best candidates for replication or expansion.

b. Engage the Statewide Divisions of Technology/Court Research to work with the ADR Coordinator's Office to develop data collection and analysis tools that track, by Judicial District and by individual program, referrals to mediation, opt-outs and matters actually mediated, settlements in the mediation (or sooner thereafter than if there had been no mediation), other mediation-related outcomes (such as opportunities for accelerated adjudication or other ADR processes), and litigant satisfaction with the experience.

c. Develop mechanisms for evaluating, monitoring and ensuring the quality of mediation services being performed by court personnel and members of court-approved panels.

The ADR Advisory Committee February 12, 2019

Interim Report and Recommendations of Chief Judge's ADR Advisory Committee

February 12, 2019

I. Introduction and Summary of Interim Recommendations

A. ADR and the Chief Judge's Excellence Initiative

The ADR Advisory Committee submits this interim report to offer initial recommendations in support of expanding and facilitating New York courts' use of court-sponsored alternative methods of dispute resolution, and particularly court-sponsored presumptive mediation. The Committee believes this proposed expansion will foster faster and less expensive resolutions of disputes, offer parties valuable alternative approaches to resolving their disputes, and advance the administration of justice.

Chief Judge Janet DiFiore formed the ADR Advisory Committee in early 2018 as an important component of her Excellence Initiative, encouraging it to work with the Office of the ADR Coordinator in boldly developing alternatives to conventional litigation that will promote greater efficiency and improve the dispute resolution process. The Committee strongly supports Chief Judge DiFiore's vision. That vision implicates not only thoughtful continued experimentation but also focused efforts to move ADR programs from the experimentation phase to a scaled-up statewide implementation phase.

Court-sponsored ADR should be a significant component of the judiciary's approach to resolving disputes. The cost of litigating to a final judgment often represents such a high percentage of the amount in controversy that the parties find litigating to a final judicial decision is unaffordable. In addition, settlements reached only after parties have litigated for extended periods beg the question whether effective earlier discussions could have yielded a less expensive resolution. Alternatives to conventional litigation undeniably help parties resolve their disputes more quickly and less expensively.

New York and other courts have long administered or sponsored efforts to promote more streamlined achievement of final decisions or negotiated settlements, including: (1) a wide variety of court conferencing processes led by judges or court personnel; (2) referrals of disputes to dedicated court staff neutrals; (3) organization of "settlement days" in which courts try to resolve large numbers of disputes involving the same defendant in a focused negotiation effort; (4) mediations; (5) arbitrations; (6) neutral evaluations; (7) summary mini-trials; and (8) accelerated fast-track litigations. The ADR Advisory Committee is considering all of these ADR mechanisms. This interim report, though, focuses on recommendations regarding court-sponsored mediation – the use of a neutral facilitator to foster negotiation, usually involving the parties as well as their counsel, with a view to settling the dispute, significantly narrowing the issues to be adjudicated, or at least helping the parties to understand each other's positions and interests and to consider ways of narrowing or resolving their dispute apart from conventional litigation.

B. Court-Sponsored Mediation

New York's judicial leaders have long supported mediation as a valuable dispute resolution mechanism. Following 1981 initiatives led by Chief Judge Cooke, Community Dispute Resolution Centers throughout the state have been mediating thousands of court-referred disputes to resolution annually for almost 40 years and provide a ready and established venue and infrastructure for mediating additional disputes. A Task Force on ADR established by Chief Judge Kaye strongly endorsed increased court-sponsored mediation in 1996, which led to the formation of the Statewide

Office of the ADR Coordinator and the introduction of numerous new ADR programs. Chief Judge Lippman also broadly supported experimentation with multiple forms of court-sponsored mediation and other alternatives to conventional litigation. Notwithstanding these laudable efforts, mediation remains underutilized. Chief Judge DiFiore has expressed strong support for significant expansion of ADR to embrace a much larger percentage of cases, in particular through expansion of early and presumptive mediation models.

Experience in New York and elsewhere indicates that well-managed court-sponsored mediation programs achieve high settlement rates, and can particularly advance efficient dispute resolution when the mediation takes place very shortly after the litigation has commenced. High quality mediation can dramatically reduce the time and cost of dispute resolution to both the parties and the judicial system compared to conventional litigation. Mediation also enhances parties' sense of personal agency and self-determination in pursuing a resolution, improves parties' communications with each other and understanding of each other's positions, permits consideration of important personal dynamics apart from the dispute's legal merits, provides opportunities for understanding alternative outcomes, encourages effective approaches to litigating efficiently or achieving workable and mutually acceptable resolutions, and fosters parties' sense that they have achieved procedural justice.

Courts tend to achieve these results most broadly and effectively when they implement programs for automatic presumptive referral to mediation, preferably as early as possible in a dispute, of all or nearly all cases of particular types. Although referrals to mediation often involve overcoming cultural and institutional resistance, the high settlement rates and participant satisfaction achieved from court referrals to early, presumptive mediation in this way suggest significant and growing public desire and appreciation for this streamlined dispute resolution.

The ADR Advisory Committee has been supporting and monitoring development of court-sponsored mediation programs in a variety of contexts, including disputes in family and matrimonial courts, surrogates courts, commercial and civil courts, and specialty courts that adjudicate matters involving essentials of life. This Interim Report presents a brief summary of Committee views and proposals developed to date, identifying some areas of near-consensus regarding court-sponsored mediation and some proposed courses of action going forward. Further recommendations will be incorporated into a final report at a later date.

These preliminary proposals advocate significantly increased use of high quality court-sponsored mediation programs in the New York State judicial system. These proposals are intended to help foster courts' development of mediation programs that give courts and parties opportunities to gain experience with this form of ADR, and that carry the potential to be scaled more broadly when they demonstrate capacity to promote substantial early settlement rates and high levels of participant satisfaction.

C. Summary of Proposals

We recommend the following steps by the Office of Court Administration and the court system generally:

1. Significantly expand statewide infrastructures for developing and supporting court-sponsored ADR, including by (a) directing District Administrative Judges in each Judicial District to designate a dedicated ADR Coordinator, or, in some districts, multiple local ADR Coordinators, to work with the Office of the Statewide ADR Coordinator (which may in certain circumstances involve establishing and funding new positions), (b) forming a Statewide Judicial Leadership Team for ADR, (c) asking the local Judicial District ADR Coordinators – in consultation with their counterparts in other Judicial Districts, the Judicial Leadership Team and the Office of the ADR Coordinator – to develop and present a plan for implementing expanded high-quality mediation programs in their Judicial Districts, and (d) increasing court connections to and financial support for CDRCs.
2. Promulgate statewide Uniform Court Rules that expressly endorse and provide a framework for courts to introduce court-sponsored mediation – particularly early in disputes, through automatic presumptive referrals of identified types of disputes that generally seem like promising candidates – and generate templates of local rules that illustrate permitted options for particular mediation programs consistent with the statewide framework.
3. Take steps to educate, support, and encourage participants in the dispute resolution process – judges, court administrators and staff, advocates, parties, and neutrals – in the constructive use of mediation, and provide for

sufficient staffing in the Office of the ADR Coordinator to facilitate significant communications and education about mediation.

4. Develop mechanisms (using the OCA's Divisions of Technology and Court Research) for effective monitoring and evaluation of individual programs, to identify and understand particular successes or shortcomings, and to identify best candidates for replication or expansion.

II. The Current State of Court-Sponsored Mediation in New York

Early court-sponsored mediation has become a routine and widely appreciated feature of judicial approaches to dispute resolution in the federal and state court systems. It is being successfully used to resolve many kinds of disputes, including high volume, low value cases; high value cases; cases in which the parties have continuing relationships; and complex cases in which the parties expect to have no future dealings. New York courts have been experimenting with court-sponsored mediation for decades, and the scope and scale of the progress has recently been expanding significantly. The rate of roll-out of new programs has increased so substantially in New York as to provide a basis for envisioning future large-scale early mediation in a significant percentage of disputes. Despite this promising expansion of programs, though, mediation continues to be underused.

Currently, most mediation referral relies on parties to mediate voluntarily or individual judges to exercise their discretion to refer parties to mediation in individual cases. By explicitly changing the default to a more automatic or presumptive form of referral to mediation, and by designating and supporting dedicated court staff to be responsible for the development and implementation of local mediation programs in consultation with the Statewide ADR Office, courts and court administrators could refer significantly more cases to mediation, increasing efficiency and procedural justice in line with the Excellence Initiative.

New York's largest-scale mediation program by far is its statewide network of CDRCs, which are operating and conducting mediations that result in the resolution of disputes in all 62 New York counties. CDRCs handled 31,000 disputes in 2017 (about half referred to them by courts), and achieved a 74% settlement rate in an average of 25 days from first contact to case closure, using 1,100 staff and volunteer mediators, on a budget of $5.9 million from the State and an approximately equal amount from other sources (an extremely low all-in cost of about $188 in state funds per case handled, and about $286 in state funds per case serviced by an ADR process).

Another notable large-scale ADR program operates in the New York City Small Claims Court, where parties, upon attending court, are asked to choose between same-day binding arbitration before volunteer arbitrators, same-day mediation by volunteer mediators or adjudication by a judge at some future date. Parties frequently choose one of the first two options, resulting in about 12,000 arbitrations to a final decision and thousands of successful mediations out of a total of 28,000 resolutions in 2017.

Other smaller but impressive programs are in effect throughout the State. For example:

- About 1,100 disputes are arbitrated or mediated each year in the Attorney-Client Fee Dispute Resolution Program.

- In the 8th Judicial District, the Martin P. Violante ADR Program has referred a broad range of disputes to early mediation by trained court staff, while also developing a panel of court-approved volunteer mediators who are available to permit expansion of the mediation program going forward.

- Nassau County mediated over 750 commercial, civil and matrimonial disputes through in-house and volunteer private mediators in 2017.

- Appellate Division courts for three of the four Judicial Departments mediate hundreds of cases annually at the appellate level using staff mediators and volunteers.

- Administrative judges in New York City have organized collections of mass settlement days with insurance carriers, achieving high settlement rates. They also conduct extensive in-court settlement conferences and refer parties to trained, experienced, and trusted court staff neutrals, who achieve impressive success rates.

- New York City Family Court's custody and visitation mediation program increased the number of cases mediated by 25%, and has focused on early on-site referrals to mediation. In the 7th JD, a Family Court mediation initiative has also significantly reduced court appearances for parties with parenting disputes, by referring them at the earliest opportunity to free community mediation services. These mediations typically yield 92% participant satisfaction rates and 74% resolution rates. The Family Court in the 6th JD implemented this model recently with great enthusiasm and efficiency.

- The Mediation Non-Jury (Med-NJ) Program in New York Country Supreme court, which makes use of an experienced court attorney and law school externs, has been expanded to mediate both pre-note and post-note cases, ending 2018 with a 70% success rate.

Other programs are in the early but promising stages of development:

- After unimpressive results in a 2014-15 experiment with mandatory early mediation of every fifth matter, randomly selected, in the New York County Commercial Division (where the jurisdictional minimum amount in controversy is $500,000), a more recent and ongoing New York County experiment with early automatic mediation of the same types of commercial cases involving amounts in controversy below the Commercial Division's $500,000 threshold reported a 2017 settlement rate of about 60% – results that appear to justify continuing this program and replicating it in Commercial Division courts that have significantly lower jurisdictional thresholds. This early referral to mediation model may benefit litigants and courts in other case types and for lower dollar cases types throughout the State.

- In Surrogates Court, where disputes often feature human dynamics not tied to the legal issues, a Manhattan program that offers mediation through CDRC staff and volunteers and through a bar-led group of private mediators has had success, and Westchester recently started a new early mediation program using an all-volunteer combination of experienced mediators and experienced trust and estates lawyers.

- Courts in Brooklyn and Suffolk have begun implementation of programs for early presumptive mediation of matrimonial disputes, and a pilot will begin in Rochester later this year.

The proliferation of new programs suggests a significant growth dynamic. But most of the new and even the fairly established programs remain small in relative terms. Automatic presumptive referral to mediation (with appropriate opt-out arrangements) of substantial categories of disputes, and establishment of pools of available trained court personnel or private panels of trained mediators, will ultimately be essential to achieving large-scale high-quality mediation presence in the state's judicial system.

Outside of New York, numerous states are similarly expanding their ADR programs. These expansions appear to be based on consistent experience of high settlement rates, including particularly for mediations early in disputes, that save significant party and court resources and apparently satisfy important public appetites for faster and less expensive resolutions (and for dispute resolution processes having different dynamics from conventional litigation). Some court systems require referral of all disputes of certain enumerated types to up-front mediations. Some provide for mediations by court staff, while others develop panels or rosters of approved mediators for parties to select or courts to assign in individual cases. Some provide for the first few hours of mediation without charge, and require virtually all parties to participate in these expense-free sessions (while permitting the parties to choose whether to keep mediating and compensate the mediator once the uncharged component is finished). These other court systems provide a wide variety of options for New York courts to consider and to determine what works best in each venue.

Nearly all jurisdictions administering court-sponsored mediation programs report general enthusiasm for the benefits of mediation processes, while recognizing that mediation does not always result in rapid settlements and acknowledging the challenges of achieving sufficient scale to affect court dockets and dispute resolution processes generally (although Florida and New Jersey, and parts of Texas, appear to have achieved that degree of scale).

III. Recommendations

A. Expansion of the Statewide Infrastructure for Developing and Implementing the Roll-Out of Increased Court-Sponsored Mediation

The Office of the Statewide ADR Coordinator is extraordinarily engaged in efforts to develop, expand and improve court-sponsored mediation and other forms of ADR around New York. Many programs are in advanced stages of development or in operation. As local courts look to develop ADR programs, the statewide office needs well-informed and engaged local coordinators to help implement and optimize the quality of specific programs. Further, local courts need at least one point-person in their courthouses charged with developing new and expanded programs and coordinating with and learning from a statewide network of ADR facilitators.

The ADR Advisory Committee recommends a significant expansion in statewide organizational infrastructure for the development of increased court-sponsored mediation. That expansion should start with the designation of a local ADR Coordinator by District Administrative Judges (DAJs) in each of the Judicial Districts. The DAJs and ADR Coordinator should be charged with inventorying and understanding ADR programs already in place, developing a plan for the roll-out and administration of new and expanded court-sponsored mediation programs within their Judicial District, working with local courts to facilitate implementation of that plan, and overseeing and participating in convenings of judges and administrators to share experiences and learn from each other's efforts. The DAJs should also be authorized and encouraged to appoint local court coordinators to oversee programs in individual counties (or smaller judicial units), and in individual courts.

To the extent ADR Coordinators are appointed for multiple courts in particular substantive disciplines – family, matrimonial, surrogates, commercial, small claims, civil or others – the Statewide Office should coordinate those specialized groups for interaction and sharing of best practices and ideas for rollouts and expansions of mediation programs in the particular contexts of their dockets, the nature of their disputes, and their individual administrative challenges.

The Chief Administrative Judge should also form a Statewide Judicial Leadership Team for ADR to provide organization in development, expansion and evaluation of court-sponsored mediation, in coordination with the DAJs and ADR Coordinators in each Judicial District and the Statewide Office of the ADR Coordinator. A Judicial Leadership Team could be particularly effective at fostering communication, emphasizing judicial support for expansion of ADR, setting priorities, identifying programs that seem like particularly appropriate candidates for expansion or replication, considering the budgetary implications of various forms of efforts to increase the scale of court-sponsored mediation, and coordinating the roll-out of expanded mediation programs around the State. If this group is formed, it should meet periodically with the Chief Administrative Judge to discuss new programs and evaluate progress.

Staffing at the Statewide Office of the ADR Coordinator – which is already highly stretched in engagement with courts around the state that are seeking to learn about, develop or enhance mediation programs – should be expanded as needed to permit coordination and oversight of local efforts and handling of the contemplated expansion. That expansion also should be sufficient to permit an allocation of substantial resources to effective communication and education about mediation, recognizing that judges, advocates and the public generally have limited experience with mediation and will need further information and encouragement for mediation programs to flourish. In addition, resources should be allocated as needed to ensure full language access for program participants.

These recommendations are presented with recognition that they contemplate some reallocation of already tightly stretched judiciary resources toward the proposed expansion. Effective roll-out of broadly expanded mediation programs should ultimately result in reduction of administrative burdens on courts, though, to a degree that the extra expenditures for developing these programs should ultimately pay for themselves. These resource allocations will also fulfill an important public need. Once such resources and infrastructure are in place, the Committee will work with the Statewide Office of the ADR Coordinator and the judiciary to study and coordinate an effective roll-out of new and expanded programs.

B. Statewide Uniform Court Rules and Local Templates

The ADR Advisory Committee recommends that the Office of Court Administration promulgate statewide Uniform Court Rules offering a formal endorsement of court-sponsored mediation and a framework to which individual local programs can refer. While individual districts and particular courts have adopted rules, protocols and best practices for local programs, the Committee believes that promulgation of Uniform Rules would advance important goals of confirming courts' authority to develop and operate mediation programs, and of providing a general roadmap to individual courts of how to initiate and manage court-sponsored mediation programs in their jurisdictions. New York's only current statewide rules regarding court-sponsored mediation are the provisions in Part 146 of the Rules of the Chief Administrative Judge identifying required training and experience for court-approved mediators, and Rules 3 and 10 of the Commercial Division (Section 202.70, Rules of the Commercial Division of the Supreme Court), authorizing judges to refer parties to an uncompensated mediator and requiring that counsel certify that they have discussed the availability of ADR options with their client.

The ADR Advisory Committee also believes that local courts would benefit from the availability of templates identifying options for potential approaches to court-sponsored mediations in their particular jurisdictions. These options, designed to fall within the framework of the statewide rules, would enable individual courts to experiment with different approaches to managing a court-sponsored mediation program. This identification of different options would reflect the current consensus that particularly at this developmental stage of thinking about effective mediation practices in New York, a "one size fits all" set of rules might not sufficiently permit courts to adapt and customize their programs to take account of relevant distinctive characteristics of their dockets, administrative staffs and legal communities. Existing sets of rules for programs already in place should be combined with these templates to generate a library of rules that courts can review in considering how to organize their own programs.

Promulgation of statewide rules and templates for local application of those rules would also help communicate to courts throughout the State the conviction that conventional litigation (and the use of extensive court resources to resolve litigations) should generally be viewed and treated as a backstop for circumstances where disputing parties have first exhausted efforts to resolve their disputes through negotiation or mediation. This shift in sensibilities could significantly enhance the process of resolving disputes and the administration of justice generally in New York State.

The Committee is aiming to present a set of proposed statewide Uniform Rules to the Office of Court Administration in the first quarter of 2019, following review by the Committee and by the statewide Office of the ADR Coordinator.

1. Uniform Rules

The Uniform Rules that the ADR Advisory Committee will propose for the OCA's consideration will address the following points, among others:

i. Courts are empowered to order parties to any dispute to participate in a mediation of that dispute (as distinct from case conferencing or other activities that can also sometimes lead parties to settlement). Recognizing the ultimately voluntary nature of any effort to reach a settlement, courts may permit parties to avoid or halt mediation processes under prescribed circumstances. Courts may also identify categories of disputes that will not be subject to mediation except as requested by all parties or under other special circumstances. Courts are authorized to direct parties to comply with local court rules regarding mediation, to ensure that mediation sessions are attended by the parties (or, in the case of an institutional party, someone with authority to settle for that party) as well as by their counsel, and to follow such procedures with regard to pre-mediation statements and exchanges of documents or information as the court or the local rules may direct, recognizing that such procedures may not be necessary in all programs. Those local rules may provide that failures to abide by mediation obligations (including failures to attend, to prepare or to bring representatives with settlement authority) may be treated as a violation of a court order.

ii. While courts can direct that any individual case be referred to mediation, courts can also direct, and are encouraged to experiment with directing, that all cases of certain categories be presumptively referred automatically to mediation. The categories of cases to be uniformly referred to mediation can include all cases featuring prescribed kinds of claims, arising under prescribed laws, or involving prescribed amounts in controversy. These categories can be selected based on courts' priority preferences, empirical records indicating that particular types of disputes are especially well-suited for mediation, or intuitions or experimental desires to gain knowledge about how well mediation works in previously untested types of disputes.

iii. Similarly, while courts are empowered to direct disputes to mediation at any time, courts are particularly encouraged to refer parties to mediation as early as practicable in disputes. Although many parties and advocates have assumed that mediation is most promising when disputes have ripened through motions and discovery, experimental programs have repeatedly yielded high settlement rates for disputes submitted to mediation early, and the goal of reducing avoidable litigation costs is often best served by early mediation. Litigations tend to take on their own momentum, leading to delays in serious engagement over settlement. Early mediation can sometimes forestall that delay at significant savings to the parties and to judicial resources.

iv. The mediators for court-sponsored mediation programs can be (1) specially trained court personnel, (2) private mediators approved by the court for membership in a panel, or (3) professional mediators who are affiliated with CDRCs or other court-approved dispute resolution organizations. In addition, parties are always free to choose private mediators not members of a court-approved panel. Courts can experiment with using mediators of any or all of these types.

a. If the mediators are court personnel, they must undergo training as mediators consistent with the requirements of Part 146, specifically communicate to the parties that they are acting as mediators, and observe the customary mediator requirements of strictly maintaining the confidentiality of all communications made during the mediation, playing no role in any decision regarding the dispute and having no communication with the judge charged with adjudicating the dispute regarding the mediation (apart from reporting whether the dispute settled or, depending on local rules, whether any party failed to abide by the court's mediation order).

b. If courts wish to refer disputes to a mediator who is a member of a court-approved panel, the courts may establish their own rules for selection of members of the panel, provided that all approved members must satisfy the requirements of Part 146. Courts may approve rosters of mediators who are volunteers or mediators who are compensated. If the mediators are compensated, they should nevertheless agree to provide some hours of preparation and mediation without charge, and/or should agree to handle some portion of their assigned mediations without charge, as prescribed by court rule. Amendment of current CLE rules to provide for pro bono credit to attorneys who serve on court-appointed mediator panels for periods when they provide mediation services without charge would provide appropriate extra incentives and rewards for this unpaid service.

c. Courts can also refer parties to mediation through the CDRC offices in their county or through other court-approved mediation organizations, subject to court rules or to CDRC rules and practices.

v. Parties can choose to mediate their disputes with a mutually agreed-upon private mediator at any time. Courts may also see value in providing parties they refer to mediation with an opportunity to respond to the referral by agreeing to use a private mediator of their mutual choosing, or by selecting their preferred mediator from a court-approved panel.

vi. Mediations should take place under guidelines for mediator conduct akin to the Model Standards of Conduct for Mediators approved by the American Arbitration Association, the American Bar Association and the Association for Conflict Resolution, the Standards for Conduct by Mediators promulgated by the New York County Commercial Division, or the Standards of Conduct for New York State Community Dispute Resolution Center Mediators. Mediators should also be governed by ethical rules established on a statewide basis and subject to an appropriate grievance procedure for parties wishing to present complaints about instances of assertedly improper mediator conduct.

vii. Assignment of a dispute to court-sponsored mediation should result in temporary suspension of courts' Standards and Goals time count – for example, for the shorter of 60 days or the time until the mediation is suspended or completed. This should prevent the undesirable result of courts avoiding potentially constructive mediations for the purpose of maximizing adherence to Standards and Goals timetables. Courts may also stay discovery or other litigation processes for some period to permit mediation, and may condition continuation of any such stay on receiving reports on whether the mediation appears to be making progress.

viii. Entry into mediation should not operate as a deterrent to consideration of other forms of streamlined dispute resolution, including court conferences, neutral evaluation, arbitration, requests that the court conduct a summary jury trial of discrete pivotal issues, or requests for fast-tracked litigation. These and other forms of ADR can all readily be subjects for discussion in mediation.

ix. Courts can determine by local rule, or may leave to mediators, such matters for management of mediations as the nature and scale of pre-mediation written statements, if any, to be provided to mediators in advance by the parties, and the timing deadlines for selection of mediators and commencement of mediation sessions.

x. The mediation process should be governed by principles of confidentiality, with the aim of ensuring that the mediation is kept entirely separate from the adjudicative process and that parties not suffer prejudice for engaging in candid communications during the mediation. Exceptions may apply to this principle of complete confidentiality for the purpose of permitting disclosures mandated by law (such as allegations or evidence of child abuse as defined in the Family Court Act, § 1012(e) and (f) and Social Services Law § 412, that may be subject to mandatory disclosure under Social Services Law § 413). Exceptions may also apply for the purposes of judicial administration (such as reports about refusals to abide by courts' mediation orders, if the applicable rules call for such reports, or for the limited purpose of compiling information about how mediation processes are working for presentation to administrative personnel). Confidentiality obligations may also be governed by provisions of the enabling statute for CDRCs, Judiciary Law § 849. A statewide rule defining the confidentiality parameters for court-sponsored mediation is desirable for the purpose of guiding individual courts in adhering to the principles of confidentiality while accommodating the exceptions.

xi. Court-appointed mediators should be protected by immunity and indemnification rules for actions in their capacity as mediators to the full extent permitted by law.

xii. Mediation programs should provide for interpreters as needed to ensure that language differences do not preclude a party from participating effectively in the mediation, and should provide for satisfaction of plain language targets in all public communications.

C. Local Templates and Libraries of Existing Local Rules

Mediation programs already in place in various New York courts apply a wide range of rules, protocols and practices that are broadly consistent with the framework that the proposed Uniform Rules are intended to provide, but with significant local variations customized to reflect such factors as the preferences of the judges overseeing the programs, the availability of court personnel able and willing to act as mediators or to help administer programs, the availability of knowledgeable and experienced private mediators to join court-approved panels, local court dynamics affecting voluntarism, budgets, and connections already forged between the court and local CDRC offices.

Judges who have expressed enthusiasm about the concept of mediation programs in their courts consistently ask how to go about establishing such programs. A template of possible local rules, identifying a range of permissible variations falling within the broad scope of the proposed Uniform Court Rules, should be helpful to courts in deciding how to structure their individual programs. A readily accessible library of the rules under which current mediation programs are being operated should also provide significant assistance to courts trying to introduce their own programs. Experience with different forms of local rules may lead over time to consensus views about which approaches work best, which ones have sufficiently general application to warrant their inclusion in Uniform Rules, and which ones best promote scalability to more universally applicable mediation programs.

Beyond access to templates and libraries of local rules, courts structuring and administering new mediation programs could benefit from access to existing or potential protocols, guidelines for program development, compilations of best practices and related support materials. These could include protocols on exchanges in advance of mediation sessions of basic documents or information independently of conventional discovery (which exist, for example, for certain kinds of disputes subject to automatic presumptive mediation in the federal court for the Southern District of New York). Some of these protocols have already been collected within the statewide Office of the ADR Coordinator. They should be made broadly available as exemplars to courts that would benefit from piggy-backing on others' organizational thinking.

D. Supporting and Expanding CDRCs

CDRCs' infrastructure – including mediation facilities, trained and certified mediators (many of whom currently are not fully utilized), and established relationships with local communities and organizations and court personnel who refer matters to them – is already in place throughout New York, with capacity in many individual offices to handle more mediations than they are currently handling.

The budget for CDRCs was cut substantially in the painful budgetary belt-tightening period associated with the financial crisis. CDRCs are likely to be central contributors to any effort to achieve substantial expansion of court-sponsored mediation and other forms of ADR in New York. Their extraordinary record of proven efficiency in achieving early settlements and reducing burdens on courts, their existing infrastructure, and their established reputation for effective and informed responsiveness to their communities present compelling reasons for increasing funding and other support for them and treating them as an important component of efforts to foster ADR throughout New York.

CDRCs' current structure and model would not readily absorb all new court referrals to mediation. For example, several CDRC offices are directed primarily to mediations that do not contemplate a need for the mediator to be a lawyer, but some disputes may require legal resolutions or otherwise call for mediation by lawyers with the training obligations spelled out in Part 146. But CDRCs can and should play an important role in the expansion of court-sponsored mediation throughout the state (as Part 146 also contemplates) and can serve as a model for how to expand many court-sponsored mediation programs in the future.

E. Support for Education and Encouragement of Participants About Mediation

Although many courts and participants in disputes have expressed enthusiasm for expanded experimentation with mediation, many judges, advocates and parties remain generally inexperienced with alternatives to conventional litigation and wary of these unfamiliar mechanisms for dispute resolution. Other states that have developed broad programs for court-sponsored mediation have reported that experience with early mediation consistently leads to increased enthusiasm for it among participants. But until mediation has become significantly more familiar and more widely embraced, education and encouragement will likely be important components of the development and expansion of court-sponsored mediation.

1. *Attorney communications with clients and adversaries.* The OCA should promulgate rules that require attorneys to educate clients about ADR options to conventional litigation, including early mediation. These rules could be akin to Rule 10 of the Commercial Division Rules, which requires counsel to certify at the initial conference and each subsequent conference that counsel has discussed with the client whether the client may be interested in mediation. The rules could also include development of a plain language statement about ADR alternatives that counsel would be required to provide to each client in a potential or actual dispute, either in the engagement letter or in a separate communication. The rules could further require opposing counsel to discuss ADR options in good faith with each other before the first conference in any dispute. Such rules would be expected to increase the frequency of parties' and their counsels' active engagement in thinking about how to resolve their disputes more efficiently and less expensively and about whether an early negotiated resolution is potentially achievable through mediation or otherwise.
2. *Judicial communications to the parties.* Courts should improve existing communications to counsel and parties about the availability of court-sponsored mediation or other alternatives to conventional litigation. These improvements could include active management of central and local court websites to explain, in plain language, types of available ADR, the potential benefits of mediation and other forms of ADR, available

mechanisms for pursuing mediation (including free and low-cost options, and including information about language access), the credentials and hourly cost of members of panels of available private neutrals, and how the mediation or other ADR process can be expected to work. Information about mediation options should also be available in the courthouse, for both unrepresented and represented litigants – including in petition rooms, Help Centers, help lines, clerks' offices, and on posters and brochures wherever information is made available to parties.

3. *Trainings and communications with court personnel.* Court clerks and other internal personnel regularly engage in a variety of efforts to help parties settle their disputes. Those efforts prominently include case conferences encouraging identification of common ground or efforts to achieve settlements. Some courts have designated court attorneys or other personnel to focus exclusively on mediation and other efforts to achieve settlements, and other courts have expressed interest in having personnel obtain training in mediation. Particularly because mediation carries characteristics of confidentiality, neutrality, engagement of clients as well as counsel, and other points of potentially significant differentiation from other forms of settlement efforts, court personnel who act as mediators should receive training in mediation techniques that is distinct from their prior work on settlement or case conferencing, as well as training in describing the mediation process to participants so that everyone

understands how it will work. Administrators also have shown a desire for training on how to establish and administer mediation programs in their courts. These forms of training have begun to take place. Increased training in these areas will be necessary in any courts that feature mediation by court personnel as part of their court-sponsored mediation programs.

4. *Trainings and communications with private mediators.* The success of mediation programs that draw on court-approved panels of private mediators who can be chosen by the parties or appointed by the court depends substantially on the quality and engagement of the mediators. Significant training programs for mediators already exist, but an effective panel-based program will require energetic and constructive communication with local and specialty legal communities about how to obtain admission onto the panel and why becoming a panel mediator (which should carry some component of voluntarism but also should provide some measure of increased professional stature for panel members) is a good step to take. Development and nurturing of effective and well-deployed panels of court-approved mediators will also require (i) thoughtful processes for the selection of members of the panel, (ii) communications with panelists that keep them engaged and enthusiastic about participating, (iii) communications with potential users about the mediators' qualifications and billing rates, (iv) engagement of

judges in understanding that the mediators to whom they are referring their matters can be trusted to make constructive contributions to dispute resolution, (v) establishment and monitoring of court appointments of mediators to ensure effective protocols for distribution of these appointments among volunteers, (vi) attention to pursuing diversity and inclusiveness in selection of the mediator panel and assignment of mediators, and (vii) communication to the Statewide ADR Coordinator's Office about results, in ways that can be used to improve processes and evaluate what works particularly well or less well.

5. *Communication with law students and with the legal community.* Many law schools have introduced thinking about methods of dispute resolution other than conventional litigation into their curriculum. Nevertheless, most law students graduate without substantial grounding in mediation and other forms of ADR. The courts, the Office of the Statewide Coordinator and the ADR Advisory Committee should play constructive roles in supporting the expansion of legal education about different ways of resolving disputes. Similarly, many members of the legal community generally remain inexperienced in and unaware of the benefits of early mediation and other forms of ADR directed to faster and less expensive resolution of disputes. Those same groups should devote resources to speaking at public events, writing and otherwise supporting openness to new efforts in this area.

F. Support for Monitoring and Evaluation of Programs

Information about the impressive settlement rates achieved through early automatic mediation programs has tended largely to be anecdotal, although the limited instances of compiling records of outcomes have tended strongly to reinforce the anecdotal impressions.[1] At this stage of thinking about significant expansion of court-sponsored mediation programs, given the limited quantity of reliable data about outcomes and the unfamiliar and unproved character of mediation in the public consciousness, it seems essential to devote some resources to collecting and organizing data about how (and how well) court-sponsored mediation programs work.

The Committee recommends that OCA's Statewide Divisions of Technology and Court Research be asked to work with the ADR Coordinator's Office to develop data collection and analysis tools that track, by Judicial District and by individual program, referrals to mediation, opt-outs and matters actually mediated, settlements in the

---

1 *See, e.g.*, Rebecca Price, U.S. District Ct.: S.D.N.Y., Mediation Program Annual Report, January 1, 2016 – December 31, 2016 6-7, 9 (Dec. 5, 2017), http://nysd.uscourts.gov/docs/mediation/Annual_Reports/2016/Annual%20Report.2016.Final%20Draft.pdf [https://perma.cc/24KV-578U]; Alternative Dispute Resolution Plan, U.S. District Ct.: W.D.N.Y. (May 11, 2018), www.nywd.uscourts.gov/sites/nywd/files/ADR%20Committee%20--%20Amended%20ADR%20Plan%20Effective%20Date%205-11-2018%20.pdf [https://perma.cc/T5VD-YEA4]; Alternative Dispute Resolution Report, July 1, 2015-June30, 2016, U.S. District Ct.: E.D.N.Y., https://img.nyed.uscourts.gov/files/local_rules/2015-2016mediationreport.pdf [https://perma.cc/N9Q3-7M7H]; Dispute Resolution Procedures, U.S. District Ct.: E.D.N.Y., https://img.nyed.uscourts.gov/files/forms/DisputeResolutionProcedures.pdf [https://perma.cc/QJ7X-5AJW] (last visited Sept. 8, 2018); *Mandatory Mediation Program Statistics*, U.S. District Ct.: N.D.N.Y., www.nynd.uscourts.gov/mandatory-mediation-program-statistics [https://perma.cc/384C-6267] (last visited Sept. 8, 2018); *see also* Hon. Robert M. Levy, *ADR in Federal Court: The View from Brooklyn*, 26 Just. Sys. J. 343 (2005) ("[R]eporting that of cases sent to non-binding arbitration in 2004, 74% settled before arbitration hearings and almost exactly half of the remainder that were arbitrated were resolved without the need for further court proceedings."); Gilbert J. Ginsburg, *The Case for a Mediation Program in the Federal Circuit*, 50 Am. U. L. Rev. 1379, 1383 (2001) (as of 2001, the Senior Staff Counsel for the Second Circuit estimated that 45-50% of the cases referred to the Second Circuit's CAMP mediation program–the first of its kind among federal courts of appeal–settled each year).

mediation (or sooner thereafter than if there had been no mediation), other mediation-related outcomes (such as opportunities for accelerated adjudication or other ADR processes), and participants' satisfaction with the experience. The Divisions of Technology and Court Research should also be consulted about ways technology can be used to facilitate effective early referrals to mediation, about whether it is feasible and desirable to integrate mediation processes into the Uniform Case Management System and other court databases, and about website and other communications relating to court-sponsored mediation programs.

IV. Conclusion

Some court systems are plainly aiming at the goal of treating mediation as a default up-front process to be presumptively pursued at the outset of nearly all disputes (apart from ones considered poor candidates for mediation for highly specific reasons). Those courts, the parties who appear before them, and advocates who practice in them widely regard early mediation as generally constructive and frequently capable of accomplishing an earlier and less expensive resolution that satisfies a significant public appetite – one often not fully appreciated by the parties before they are directed to mediation - while freeing up resources for adjudication of disputes that parties resolve to litigate to a decision.

The current environment presents an important opportunity to focus on scaling up mediation processes to a point that establishes mediation as the first step in nearly all disputes. Such scaling up would of course likely require a substantial expansion of resources and expenditure of money. But significant expansion along the lines proposed in these interim recommendations, which should help indicate how much and in what ways court-sponsored mediation should be expanded further, should be achievable through relatively modest additional expenditures coupled with redirection of existing priorities and energies and calls upon high quality lawyers to become members of court-approved panels (and to provide at least some of their mediation services without charge). As the value of mediation becomes more widely recognized and mediation programs demonstrate their capacity to reduce burdens on court dockets, serious consideration of significantly increased funding for broadly applied automatic presumptive mediation programs will be increasingly warranted.

The ADR Advisory Committee February 12, 2019

John Kiernan, Chair
Simeon H. Baum
Sasha A. Carbone
Alexandra Carter
Hon. Anthony Cannataro
Hon. Michael Coccoma
Hon. Andrew A. Crecca
Antoinette Delruelle
Hon. Paula Feroleto
Lisa Florio
Elayne Greenberg
Adriene Holder
Elena Karabatos
Michele Kern-Rappy
Daniel F. Kolb
Tashi Lhewa
Lela Porter Love
Hon. Rita Mella
Hon. Edwina Mendelson

Charles J. Moxley, Jr.
Melissa H. Nickson
Rebecca Price
Sarah Rudgers-Tysz
Hon. Brandon Sall
Paul Sarkozi
Hon. Carol Sherman
Hon. Saliann Scarpulla
Hon. Jeffrey S. Sunshine
Daniel M. Weitz
Lisa Courtney, Advisor
Brooke J. Willig, Counsel
Ming Ming Yang, Counsel

APPENDIX W

Making Your Office a Classroom for Client Education

Give yourself a mediation-friendly office quiz:	Yes	No
1. Does my waiting room have educational materials for clients?	___	___
2. Does my website have educational materials and resources for clients?	___	___
3. Does my Zoom waiting room provide clients with resources to peruse while they are waiting? ____	___	___
4. Do I have a dedicated space for a client library?	___	___
5. Do I have activities and books for children if clients need to bring them to wait in the waiting room? ______	___	___
6. Have I prepared written instructions and checklists to help clients?		
7. Do I have a staff training program geared to educate and assist clients in mediation?		
8. Do clients mediation in person have easy access to water, refreshments, the restroom, and the door?		
9. Will my clients feel welcomed and that their comfort and empowerment is the #1 priority of my practice? ___		

Establish a Client Library in Your Office

If informed client consent is the bedrock of mediation, clients must have access to sufficient information and materials.

Try walking in your client's shoes. How does it feel to be in your office? What tools, resources, and space are available to your clients to help them improve their experience as a client?

A client library can be the client's home and learning center within your office.

The concept of a client library is a collection of consumer-friendly books, video DVDs, audio tapes, brochures, or other client resources. The client library's materials should be easy to read and to access. Ideally, the client library should have chairs and tables (or even just a writing ledge) so that clients can comfortably do their own work there rather than in your office or in the public waiting room.

You might provide computers so clients can draft their own letters, court documents, or their opening statement for a mediation. In child support matters, clients can run the numbers using a guideline child support program in order to educate themselves and realistically prepare for an upcoming negotiation or mediation session. Cutting-edge client libraries also provide internet access so that your clients can access helpful programs such as www.uptoparents.org or www.ourfamilywizard.com .

When clients aren't visiting, the client library can serve as a breakout room for caucuses or an extra consultation room or inspirational setting for your mediation intern. Even if you do not have an extra office or fancy computer gadgets, you can still set up a client library in your waiting room. All you need to get started are a few books, a couple of videos, a DVD player and a monitor. Earphones are a nice added feature if the video is in the waiting room.

The very existence of the client library symbolizes that clients rank very high in the priorities of your office and that you highly value client empowerment. The client library demonstrates to clients that you are willing to devote expensive office space and purchase significant books and DVDs to provide for their education. If you were shopping for a family lawyer, would you choose one who has a client library or one who has no place to sit and no resources to use?

The client library also serves as another waiting room—a learning room. New clients get a sense of the firm and necessary information on their presenting problem. Just by leafing through books on your shelf, returning clients deepen their understanding and perspectives—and may uncover unmet needs and concerns that you can address.

It costs so much in hard dollars to acquire new clients that being able to serve their needs beyond the presenting problem helps amortize the high marketing and management costs to operate your practice. Your current client base is your highest profit center; tools such as the client library that help you maximize your current client base cannot be overvalued.

Another use of the client library is to serve as a child-care center. It is ideally better for your clients with dependent children to make arrangements for them outside the office. But we don't live in an ideal world, and sometimes due to cost or logistics, the kids come along in tow. If you have age-appropriate videotapes, books, toys, and games in your client libraries, pop them in. Most kids can be happily amused while their parent(s) do their business with you.

Show Videos to Clients

Sometimes, parties may watch a video together and are able to work out a full settlement on their own before the session ever starts.

Lending Books to Clients

There are two basic ways that your clients can use the client library: self-selected or prescribed by you. Once parked in the client library, many clients browse and self-select material that they want to use. The library's collection can be in a notebook or accessible by computer. At our office, most clients use the library without much staff help at all. That's the point. You should have clear written or video client instructions so that you do not need to spend additional monies in staff time to explain the library to clients.

Mosten Mediation Centers doesn't lend books to clients—they must be read on premises. In nine years of operation, we have never had a book or video stolen. But mediators such as Academy of Family Mediators President Nina Meirding, who do lend books from their client libraries, report about a 100% return rate as well.

The client library can also be a preventive classroom. Before every mediation, each client can be given a conflict-wellness checkup. The checkup is a thermometer for legal health and the client library is a perfect place for your clients to self-administer the written checkup questionnaire or read material on preventing future disputes in their lives. Maryland Legal Services Corporation is developing a legal checkup for the web and I already have one on my website (http://www.MostenMediation.com). As these technological developments increase, your clients will be able to improve their legal health from their seats in your client library or from home.

APPENDIX X

Books and Articles

This book is the foundation and beginning of your reading and training as a peacemaking family lawyer. You need to study and learn much more.

The following resource section is not a bibliography as found in scholarly articles and books. Since you are using this book to improve your practice, we have chosen not to flood you with most of the 2500 titles on conflict resolution currently in print. Rather, we have limited the reading list to key categories:

- Representing Clients in Mediation Mediator Concepts and Strategies Mediation Confidentiality Negotiation Concepts and Strategies Limited Scope Representation Collaborative Law
- Preventive Law Peacemaking
- Expanding Your Practice with a Client-Centered Consumer Approach Divorce Books for Clients
- Divorce Books for Children

REPRESENTING CLIENTS IN MEDIATION

Abramson, Harold, *Mediation Representation: Advocating as a Problem Solver in Any Country or Culture*, 2nd Edition (2010).
Galton, Eric R., *Representing Clients in Mediation* (1994).
Golann, Dwight, *Sharing a Mediator's Powers, Effective Advocacy in Settlement* (2014).

MEDIATOR CONCEPTS AND STRATEGIES

ABA Section on Dispute Resolution, Guidance for Online Dispute Resolution 2022.
Deutsch, Morton and Peter Coleman, *The Handbook of Conflict Resolution: Theory and Practice* (3rd ed.) (2014).
Folberg, Jay, Ann Milne, and Salem, Peter (eds.). *Divorce and Family Mediation: Models, Techniques, and Applications* (2004).
Frenkel, Douglas N. and Stark, James H., *The Practice of Mediation, A Video Integrated Text,* 3rd Edition (2018).
David A. Hoffman, *Mediation, Multiple Minds, and Managing the Negotiation Within,* 16 Harvard Negotiation Law Rev. 297 (2011).

David A. Hoffman, *The Self-Led Mediator: Using IFS in Dispute Resolution* (video prepared for IFS Institute Conference (Oct. 2022)), https://drive.google.com/file/d/1WDryewWgVYKlgVvz8n69WHcx7lfCdVeN/view.

Galton, Eric and Love, Lela, *Stories Mediators Tell: World Edition* (2017).

Guthrie, Susan, Online Mediation Guidelines and Ground Rules, Mosten Guthrie Training Academy, 2022.

Haynes, John M., *The Fundamentals of Family Mediation*. Albany, N.Y.: State University of New York Press (1994).

Kolb, Deborah M. *When Talk Works: Profiles of Mediators*. San Francisco: Jossey-Bass (2001).

Lang, Michael and Taylor, Allison, *The Making of a Mediator* (2000).

Saposnek, D., *Mediating Child Custody Disputes*. (Rev. ed.). San Francisco: Jossey-Bass (1998).

Moore, Christopher, *The Mediation Process: Practical Strategies for Resolving Conflict*. (4th Ed.) (2014).

Mosten, Forrest, *Mediator Career Guide,* Wiley (2001).

Mosten, Forrest and Potter Scully, Elizabeth (Hon). *Complete Guide to Mediation,* 2nd Edition, ABA (2015).

MEDIATION CONFIDENTIALITY

Cassel v. Superior Court (Wasserman, et al.) (2011) 51 Cal. 4th 113.

Coben, James, Hamline Mediation Case Law Project: Examining Lessons from Failed Mediations, http://www.hamline.edu/law/dri/mediation-case-law-project/. See also James Coben and Peter N. Thompson, *Disputing Irony: A Systematic Look at Litigation About Mediation* (2006) 11 HARV. NEG. L. REV. 43.

Waldman, Ellen, *Mediation Ethics* (2011).

NEGOTIATION CONCEPTS AND STRATEGIES

Chialdini, Robert B., *Influence: The Psychology of Persuasion*, Rev. (2021).

Coleman, Peter T., *The Five Percent Solution: Finding Solutions for Seemingly Impossible Conflicts* (2011).

Eddy, William A., *High Conflict People in Legal Disputes* (2006).

Fisher, Roger and Ury, William and Patton, Bruce, *Getting to Yes: Negotiating Agreement without Giving In*, 3rd Edition (2011).

Folberg, Jay and Golann, Dwight, *Lawyer Negotiation: Theory, Practice, and Law 4th Edition* (2022).

Korobkin, Russell, *Negotiation Theory and Strategy* (2002).

Krivis, Jeffrey, *Improvisational Negotiation* (2006).

Lande, John, *Lawyering with Early Planned Negotiation*, 2nd Edition (2015).

Lewicki, R. J., Barry, B., and Saunders, D. M., *Essentials of Negotiation* (7th ed.) New York: McGraw-Hill/Irwin, 2021.

Mayer, Bernard, *The Dynamics of Conflict Resolution*, 2nd Edition (2012).

Mnookin, Robert H et al., *Beyond Winning: Negotiating to Create Value in Deals and Disputes* (2004).
Mnookin, Robert H., *Bargaining with the Devil* (2011).
Riskin, Leonard, *Managing Conflict Mindfully: Don't Believe Everything You Think* (West Academic, 2023).

LIMITED SCOPE REPRESENTATION

Beck, Connie, Sales, Bruce, and Hahn, Richard K., *Self-Representation in Divorce Cases* (1993).
Bergman, P. and Berman-Barrett, S.J., *Represent Yourself in Court: How to Prepare and Try a Winning Case*. Berkeley: Nolo Press (1993).
Kimbro, Stephanie L., *Limited Scope Legal Services: Unbundling and the Self-Help Client* (2012).
Macfarlane, J., *Identifying and Meeting the Needs of Self-Represented Litigants* (May 2013).
Mosten, Forrest S. and Scully, Elizabeth, *Unbundled Legal Services: A Family Lawyer's Guide* (2017).
Rhode, Deborah L., *Access to Justice* (2005).
Talia, Sue M. *Unbundling Your Divorce: How to Find a Lawyer to Help You Help Yourself.* (Rev. Ed.) Nexus Publishing Company, 2006.

COLLABORATIVE LAW

Cameron, Susan, *Deepening the Dialogue* (2004).
Mosten, Forrest S., *Collaborative Divorce Handbook* (2009).
Mosten, Forrest S., The Lawyer as Preventive and Collaborative Peacemaker, in Herrera, Innovations in the Practice of Law, ABA (2014).
Tesler, Pauline H. and Thompson, Peggy, *Collaborative Divorce* (2007).
Mosten, Forrest S. and Cordover, Adam, *Building a Successful Collaborative Family Law Practice*, ABA (2018).
Smith, Nancy. *Untangling Your Marriage: A Guide to Collaborative Divorce* (2022).
Webb, Stuart and Ousky, Ron, *The Collaborative Way to Divorce* (2007).

PREVENTIVE LAW

Barton, Thomas D., *Preventive Law and Problem Solving: Lawyering for the Future* (2009).
Brown, Louis M., *Manual for Periodic Legal Checkup* (1983).
Brown, Louis M., *Lawyering through Life: The Origin of Preventive Law* (1986).
Israel, Laurie, http: www.MaritalMediation.com.
Mosten, Forrest and Traum, Lara. *The Lawyer's Role in Legal and Conflict Prevention, Family Court Review* (2017).
Rosenbloom, S. M., and Nesburn, J., *Isn't It Unromantic: Collaboratively Negotiating Pre and Post Nuptial Agreements*, 10(1) COLLABORATIVE REVIEW 18–19 (2008).

PEACEMAKING

Bowling, Daniel and Hoffman, David, *Bringing Peace into the Room* (2003).
Burnett, Nan Waller, *Calm in the Face of the Storm* (2007).
Daicoff, Susan, *Law as a Healing Profession: The "Comprehensive Law Movement*, 6 PEPP. DISP. RESOL. L.J. 1, 50–51 (2006).
Gopin, Mark, *Healing the Heart of Conflict: 8 Crucial Steps to Making Peace with Yourself and Others* (2004).
Galton, Eric R., *Ripples from Peace Lake: Essays for Mediators and Peacemakers* (2004).
Hoffman, David. Lawyers as Peacemakers, Really?, Ted Talk (2016).
LeBaron, Michelle, *Bridging Troubled Waters: Conflict Resolution from the Heart* (2002).
Lederach, John Paul, *The Little Book of Conflict Transformation* (2003).
Mosten, Forrest S., *Lawyer as Peacemaker: Building a Successful Law Practice Without Ever Going to Court*, 43 FAM. LAW Q. (Fall 2009).
Nolan-Haley, Jacqueline, *Finding Interior Peace in the Ordinary Practice of Law: Wisdom from the Spiritual Tradition of St. Teresa of Avila*, 44 J. CATHOLIC LEGAL STUD. 29, 39 (2007).
Noll, Douglas. *Peacemaking: Practicing at the Intersection of Law and Human Confl*ict (2003).
Schirch, Lisa, *The Little Book of Strategic Peacebuilding: A Vision and Framework for Peace with Justice (Justice and Peacebuilding)* (2005)
Wright, Kim J. *Lawyers as Peacemakers: Practicing Holistic, Problem-Solving Law* (2010).

EXPANDING YOUR PRACTICE WITH A CLIENT-CENTERED CONSUMER APPROACH

Binder, David A. and Bergman, Paul, et al., *Lawyers As Counselors: A Client-Centered Approach* (2nd Ed.) (2004).
Foonberg, J., *How to Start and Build a Law Practice*. (5th ed.) (2004).
Herrera, Luz, *Reinventing the Practice of Law* (2014).
Lovenheim. Peter, *Becoming a Mediator: An Insider's Guide to Exploring Careers in Mediation* (2002).
Mather, L., McEwen, C.A. & Maiman, R.J., *Divorce Lawyers at Work: Varieties of Professionalism in Practice* (2001).
McFarlane, Julie, *The New Lawyer: How Settlement Is Transforming the Practice of Law* (2008).
Mosten, Forrest S., *Mediation Career Guide: A Strategic Approach to Building a Successful Practice* (2001).
Sarat, A., and Felstiner, W., *Divorce Lawyers and Their Clients* (1995).

DIVORCE BOOKS FOR CLIENTS

Ahrons, Constance R., *We're Still Family: What Grown Children Have to Say About Their Parents' Divorce* (2005).

Diamond, Louise. *The Peace Book: 108 Simple Ways to Create a More Peaceful World* (2001).

Hartley, Gabrielle. *Better Apart: The Radically Positive Way to Separate* (2021).

LaViolette, Alyce D. and Barnett, Olga W., *It Could Happen to Anyone: Why Battered Women Stay,* 4th Edition (2014).

McGhee, Christina. *Parenting Apart: How Separated and Divorced Parents Can Raise Happy and Secure Kids* (2010).

McGhee, Christina and Bruno, Ellen. *SPLIT Guide for Parents and Professionals* (2016).

Newman, Jacqueline, *The New Rules of Divorce: Twelve Secrets to Protecting Your Wealth, Health, and Happiness* (2020).

Ross, Julie A. and Corcoran, Judy. *Joint Custody with a Jerk: Raising a Child with an Uncooperative Ex* (2011).

Thomas, Katherine Woodward, *Conscious Uncoupling: 5 Steps to Living Happily Even After* (2016).

DIVORCE BOOKS FOR CHILDREN

Brown, Laurene Kransy and Brown, Marc, *Dinosaur's Divorce: A Guide for Changing Families* (1986).

Drescher, Joan, *My Mother's Getting Married* (1989).

Moore-Mallinos, Jennifer, *When My Parents Forgot How to Be Friends* (2005).

Ricci, Isolina, *Mom's House, Dad's House for Kids* (2006).

Chung, A.S., *A Brand New Day: A Banana Split Story* (2014).

Roberts, Jillian, and Revel, Cindy, *Why Do Families Change?: Our First Talk About Separation and Divorce* (2020).

Schmitz, Tamara, *Standing on My Own Two Feet: A Child's Affirmation of Love in the Midst of Divorce* (2008).

Stead, Rebecca, *The List of Things that Will Not Change* (2020).

Glossary

Active listening: The process of picking up another's message and sending it back in a reflective statement that mirrors what you have heard. Active listening responses can mirror both content and feelings. Active listening is important not only to show that you hear and understand another, but also to motivate that other person's full expression. [Binder, Bergman, Tremblay, & Weinstein, Lawyers as Counselors, a Client-Centered Approach (4th ed. 2019)]

Agenda setting: The process of working with clients to determine which issues must be addressed as well as the order (priority) in which these issues will be discussed. The order and manner in which issues are discussed is an important tool used by the mediator to minimize dispute and bring about settlement.

Alternative dispute resolution (ADR), aka appropriate dispute resolution (ADR) or consensual dispute resolution (CDR): Traditionally viewed as dispute resolution processes used as alternatives to litigation. ADR, which includes negotiation, mediation, arbitration, and various hybrid forms, focuses on new and creative methods used to resolve disputes. Today, ADR is institutionalized and incorporated into a variety of court processes.

Arbitration: A dispute resolution procedure that involves the submission of proof and arguments to a third-party neutral (selected by the parties) who has the power to issue a decision, which can be binding or nonbinding. Generally, arbitration hearings are more informal than court hearings, and the rules of evidence are not strictly applied. [Stephen Goldberg, Frank E.A. Sander & Nancy Rogers, Dispute Resolution: Negotiation, Mediation and Other Processes 199–200 (1992)]

Bargaining range: A field of options, any one of which disputants would prefer to the resulting consequences of terminating negotiations. In the best possible scenario, the parties will have overlapping bargaining ranges so that there are mutually satisfactory solutions or divisions of resources. [Christopher Moore, The Mediation Process: Practical Strategies for Resolving Conflict (4th ed. 2014)]

Best alternative to negotiated agreement (BATNA), aka best alternative to mediated agreement (BATMA): The notion that parties should know the likely results that will occur if they do reach agreement in the negotiations. One who is unaware of the results that may be obtained if negotiations are unsuccessful runs the risk of entering into an unsatisfactory agreement or rejecting a satisfactory agreement. In addition, parties should know as much as possible about the other party's BATNA. [Roger Fisher, William Ury & Bruce Patton, Getting to Yes (3rd ed. 2011)]. May also consider Worst Alternative to a Negotiated Agreement (WATNA) and Most Likely Alternative to a Negotiated Agreement (MLATNA)

Brainstorming: The process by which ideas are rapidly generated by an individual or a group. Brainstorming is often useful because it separates the generation process from evaluation procedures, so that there are multiple options to consider. [Christopher Moore, The Mediation Process: Practical Strategies for Resolving Conflict (4th ed. 2014)]

Breakout rooms: Rooms within a mediation suite or online setting that are used during mediation for caucuses between parties and the mediator and for discussions between clients and their lawyers. Breakout rooms can also provide a place for parties to wait when other discussions and caucuses are taking place. This function is particularly important in the family law context because estranged spouses are often uncomfortable waiting in the same room due to present or past conflict.

Caucus, aka private time: Part of the mediation session in which the mediator meets confidentially and individually with each party, lawyer, aligned expert, or a combination of the parties. To allow parties to be more candid and explore various ideas that they are not comfortable sharing with the other party, caucuses can be a very important tool for mediators. In addition, caucuses provide a good opportunity for the mediator to do reality testing with the parties. It should be noted that many mediators choose to eschew the use of caucuses as one or both parties may question the neutrality of the mediator if the parties do not meet jointly.

Client coach, aka divorce coach, life coach, conflict coach, negotiation coach, limited scope or unbundled professional: As part of a client's preparation for negotiations, a lawyer or other professional can teach the client some of the essentials of negotiation theory and give supervised individual training to the client in preparation for the mediation session. In addition, the lawyer can help the client assess the strengths and weaknesses of various proposals and help the client develop not only initial proposals but also backup proposals based on anticipated responses. Coaching can be a separate field from representation or serving as an independent expert for which helping parties negotiate successfully is key.

Co-mediation: Mediation is frequently conducted by interdisciplinary teams, often consisting of therapists along with lawyers. Co-mediation can be effective as a result of the diversity of mediation teams (such as gender, expertise, style). The teams can work together at all times or meet with couples (or individual spouses in caucus) separately.

Comprehensive mediation: Mediation model in which a mediator works with couples on all issues involved in a family dispute. Issues related to child custody, economic distribution, child support, and alimony are addressed alongside the couple's emotional and conduct issues.

Conciliation: Traditionally used interchangeably with *mediation*, the term usually denotes a process that strives to minimize unnecessary conflict and build a positive psychological relationship between parties. Conciliation is the psychological component of mediation in which the third party attempts to create an atmosphere of trust and cooperation that is conducive to negotiation. [Christopher Moore, The Mediation

Process: Practical Strategies for Resolving Conflict (4th ed. 2014); also Stephen B. Goldberg, Jeanne M. Brett & Beatrice Brenneur, How Mediation Works: Theory, Research, and Practice (2017)]

Confidential mini-evaluation (CME): A nonbinding expert's opinion used to defuse custody conflicts when mediation does not resolve the dispute. The CME gives the parties the input of an experienced custody evaluator without the cost, delay, adversarial posturing, and virtually binding decisions of a court-appointed evaluator being imposed on the family and being part of the permanent court record. [Forrest S. Mosten, *Confidential Mini Child-Custody Evaluations: Another ADR Option*, 45 Fam. L. Q. 1 (2011); Forrest S. Mosten, *Confidential Mini Child Custody Evaluations*, 30 Fam. Conciliation & Cts. Rev. (1992)]

Confidentiality: In most jurisdictions, negotiations concerning a disputed legal claim are not admissible in evidence to prove the claim or its amount (see Federal Rules of Evidence 408 or comparable state rules). The rule results in exclusion of evidence in most, but not all, circumstances. Courts have found several types of evidence outside the purview of the rule (e.g., information that is also requested through the discovery process and negotiations not involving legal claims). [Stephen B. Goldberg, Jeanne M. Brett & Beatrice Brenneur, How Mediation Works: Theory, Research, and Practice (2017)]

Conjoint sessions (*see also Co-mediation*): Mediation sessions involving mediation teams that work together throughout the entire session, including intake, joint sessions, and caucuses. During conjoint sessions, mediation teams, often consisting of lawyers and therapists, do not necessarily retain their separate professional roles.

Consensus building: A mediative process, often used with large groups, involving multiple conflicts. Consensus building often takes place over an extended period of time and is conducive to large public policy disputes, such as disputes involving environmental issues. [Kimberlee K. Kovach, Mediation: Principles and Practice (3rd ed. 2004)]

Countertransference: Countertransference involves not only the professional's distorted perceptions of the client but also distorted expectations of his or her services and the outcome of those services. [Rhonda Feinberg & James Tom Greene, *Transference and Countertransference Issues in Professional Relationships*, 28 Fam. L. Q. 111 (Spring 1995)]

Dispute resolution manager: Role played by mediator that includes educating the client about dispute resolution options both inside the courthouse and in the private sector, helping the client select the appropriate options, and effectively representing the client within that process to obtain settlement.

Early neutral evaluation (ENE): A process, designed by federal district courts in northern California, that encourages parties to identify the real areas of agreement and dispute and helps them develop an approach to discovery that focuses promptly on central issues and discloses key evidence. The goal of ENE is to provide parties with an early opportunity to try to negotiate a settlement. [Joshua D. Rosenberg & H. Jay Folberg, *Symposium on Civil Justice Reform: Alternative Dispute Resolution: An Empirical Analysis*, 46 Stan. L. Rev. 1487 (1994); Jordan Leigh Santeramo, *Early*

Neutral Evaluation in Divorce Cases, 42 Fam. Ct. Rev. 2 (2004); Joanne J. Paetsch & John-Paul E. Boyd, QC, *An International Review of Early Neutral Evaluation Programs and Their Use in Family Law Disputes in Alberta*, Canadian Rsch Inst. L. & Fam. (2016)]

Flip chart, aka Google Jamboard: A large, prominently displayed pad of paper used by the mediator and parties. Flip charts are often used by parties in presenting proposals or discussing issues within a proposal. Unlike information written on a white board, information on a flip chart or electronic Jamboard can be preserved. In addition, various pages of the flip chart can be posted around a mediation room to serve as a review of previous discussions and/or settlement progress that has been made.

Framing: The manner in which a conflict situation, issue, or interest is conceptualized or defined. Individuals generally frame situations according to history and direct experience (subjective reality). [Barbara Gray, Mediation as Framing and Framing within Mediation (2017)]

Impartiality: The obligation of a mediator to maintain a posture toward parties free from bias or favoritism toward one or some parties in either word or action. Impartiality implies a commitment to aid *all parties* in reaching a mutually satisfactory agreement. [Christopher Moore, Center for Dispute Resolution Code of Professional Conduct (1982); Rachael Field & Jonathan Crowe, Mediation Ethics: From Theory to Practice (2020)]

Impasse: In mediation, parties often reach a point where they are stuck on particular issues. Often a declaration of a bottom line by the parties does not mean they are unwilling to move; instead, it is a bargaining strategy. An important skill for mediators involves effectively dealing with situations where an impasse is evident. [Kimberlee K. Kovach, Mediation: Principles and Practice 128–29 (1994)]

Interest-based bargaining: Negotiation style focusing on the interests of the parties. Focusing on interests may uncover the existence of mutual or complementary interests that will make agreement possible. Negotiators can seek integrative solutions that meet as many of the needs of both parties as possible. [Roger Fisher & William Ury, Getting to Yes (3rd ed. 2011)]

Intervention: Words or actions of the mediator that enter into the family system for the purpose of altering the power and dynamics by influencing beliefs or behaviors of individual parties, by providing knowledge or information, or by using a more effective negotiation process and thereby helping participants settle contested issues. [Christopher Moore, The Mediation Process: Practical Strategies for Resolving Conflict (4th ed. 2014)]

Judicial case management: Process in which parties voluntarily give a judge discretion to determine interim orders and amount and order of discovery and to hold settlement conferences. The judge is available to the parties by phone, zoom, or in person so that emergency court hearings are rarely needed. Parties waive not only their rights to appeal and other judicial review but also their rights to sue their family lawyers who have consented to the use of the process.

Mandatory mediation: Most jurisdictions have court-annexed mediation programs that often require participation by litigants. Mediations often take place in the courthouse or in mediation centers and may be conducted by court staff mediators, private mediators, or pro bono volunteer lawyers. Although child custody and visitation are the issues most often mandated by court-annexed mediation, some court systems provide for mediation of financial issues as well.

Mandatory settlement conference (MSC): Court procedure that encourages the parties to attempt to settle their case before trial with judicial supervision. Generally held within 30 to 60 days of trial dates, MSCs occur at a point when parties are expected to have completed trial preparation.

Med-arb: Process in which a neutral functions first as a mediator, helping the parties to arrive at a mutually acceptable consensual outcome. If mediation fails, the same neutral then serves as an arbitrator, issuing a final and binding decision. [Stephen Goldberg, Frank E.A. Sander & Nancy Rogers, Dispute Resolution: Negotiation, Mediation, and Other Processes 226 (1992); Megan Elizabeth Telford, Med-Arb: A Viable Dispute Resolution Alternative (2000)]

Mediation: A process by which a third-party neutral facilitates parties in resolving a dispute. The role of the mediator is to facilitate communications between the parties, assist them in focusing on the real issues of the dispute, and generate options for settlement. The goal of mediation is that the parties themselves arrive at a mutually acceptable resolution of the dispute. [Kimberlee K. Kovach, Mediation: Principles and Practice 17 (1994)] The Model Standards of Practice for Family and Divorce Mediation defines mediation as follows: "family and divorce mediation is a process in which a mediator, an impartial third party, facilitates the resolution of family disputes by promoting the participants' voluntary agreement."

Mediation briefs: Written for the purpose of educating and persuading the other spouse about a party's interests and goals. Briefs must be researched and drafted carefully to be used as a tool of persuasion. Some parties, lawyers, and mediators prefer confidential briefs that are only submitted to the mediator. Hybrid processes are sometimes used in which a nonconfidential brief containing facts and legal authority are shared with the other party and only settlement proposals are submitted to the mediator.

Multisession mediation, aka sequential mediation sessions: Mediation model in which participants work out a schedule of mediation sessions ranging from one-half hour to four hours in length. The goal for each session is to accomplish as much as possible with the understanding that the parties will continue meeting until all of the issues have been resolved.

One-issue mediation: Issues often arise in mediation that require experts from another field. These experts are brought in to mediate a single issue. For example, a real estate broker can be brought in to help the parties determine the fair market value of a house.

Positional bargaining: Negotiation style based on a perception that contested resources are limited and a distributive solution, one that allocates shares of gains and losses to each party, is viewed as the only solution. [Chris Voss, Never Split the Difference: Negotiating as If Your Life Depended On It (2017)].

Power imbalance: In many instances, an imbalance of power between the parties might bring about an unfair result. Because mediation lacks many of the formalities and safeguards of adjudication, there is a concern that, as a result of gender, cultural, language, education, or class differences of participants, certain parties may have unfair advantages in the mediation process. In light of the mediator's role as a neutral, the extent to which mediators should address these power imbalances is unclear.

Preliminary joint session, aka preliminary planning session: The most common format of mediation involves the parties initially meeting jointly with the mediator. The rationale behind preliminary joint sessions is to make both parties feel part of the process, to create or reinforce trust in the mediator that there will be no secret or hidden agendas, and to show the parties that they can negotiate directly with one another.

Preventive mediation: The use of mediation in preventing future conflict. It can be used in the divorce context to educate both parties (and their lawyers) as to how to avoid future problems, not just with each other, after the judgment is entered. Preventive mediation can be especially useful in sparing family members (especially children) future conflict and pain if either spouse breaks up with a new romantic partner. [Mosten, Mediation Career Guide]

Reality testing: The role of the mediator in working with the parties to assess the realistic possibility of attaining what they are hoping for. Because reality testing often involves issues that are sensitive or personal to the parties, the mediator should do reality testing in private caucuses. [Kimberlee K. Kovach, Mediation: Principles and Practice 166–68 (1994); Christopher Moore, The Mediation Process: Practical Strategies for Resolving Conflict (4th ed. 2014); also Stephen B. Goldberg, Jeanne M. Brett & Beatrice Brenneur, How Mediation Works: Theory, Research, and Practice (2017)]

Reframing (*see Framing*)

Settlement weeks: A court system's attempt to maximize judicial and volunteer lawyer resources to resolve outstanding cases through mediation and other settlement procedures.

Simulated coaching, aka role playing: As part of preparing clients for mediation, a lawyer can help clients by practicing several scenarios of issues likely to be raised in mediation. As a result of these simulations, the client receives an orientation about possibilities and an early reality check. In addition, simulations increase the client's comfort level in the actual mediation.

Single-session mediation: Mediation model in which parties, counsel, and mediator attempt to reach agreement in a single session. As a result of impasse or other issues that block progress, single-session mediations often must adjourn with an agreed-upon set date to continue the mediation.

Summary letter of mediation sessions, aka mediator notes, progress notes, minutes: Correspondence initiated by the mediator to parties, counsel, and other authorized persons (e.g., accountants, therapists) to set forth agreements made, areas of disagreement, agendas, assignments of parties, and observations of the mediator to facilitate the process. [Mosten & Scully, Complete Guide to Mediation (2nd ed. 2015)]

Transference (*see Countertransference*)

Transformative mediation: A view of mediation that emphasizes its capacity to transform the character of both individual disputants and society as a whole. Because of its informality and consensus-based framework, mediation can allow parties to define problems and goals in their own terms; consequently, the important role of these problems and goals in the parties' lives is validated. Rather than placing an emphasis only on reaching agreement, transformative mediation focuses on (1) empowerment, by instilling the parties with a greater sense of self-respect, self-reliance, and self-confidence, and (2) recognition, by engendering acknowledgment and concern for others as human beings. [Robert Baruch Bush & Joseph Folger, The Promise of Mediation (2004)]

Trust building: Mediators strive to build trust between parties to reinforce beliefs that commitments and agreements will be carried out. Mediators can make specific interventions that will build trust between the parties and change their perceptions. These techniques include creating situations in which parties must perform joint tasks, vocally identifying commonalities, and facilitating a discussion of their perceptions of one another. [Roger Fisher, International Mediation: A Working Guide (1978)]

Unbundling, aka discrete task or limited scope representation: Unbundling offers clients a middle ground between dispensing with lawyers altogether and signing on for full-service representation. In unbundling, the client determines which services will be performed by the client and the extent and depth to which the lawyer will perform the services engaged. [Mosten and Scully, Unbundling Legal Services (ABA 2017)]

Index